KNOWING GOD

This book is dedicated to my wife and partner, Maggie Mansueto, with whom I spent four hours debating epistemology on our first date, who reintroduced me to Thomism and to the debates which this book is intended to resolve, and who, by challenging me to grow each and every day in justice and the other virtues, helps me ever so gradually to attain the connaturality with God which makes true knowledge possible.

Knowing God

Restoring Reason in an Age of Doubt

Anthony E. Mansueto Jr,
Institute for Philosophy and Social Progress, USA

ASHGATE

Published by
Ashgate Publishing Limited
Gower House
Croft Road
Aldershot
Hants GU11 3HR
England

Ashgate Publishing Company
101 Cherry Street
Burlington, VT 05401-4405 USA

Ashgate website: http://www.ashgate.com

British Library Cataloguing in Publication Data
Mansueto, Anthony E.
    Knowing God : restoring reason in an age of doubt
    1. Reason 2. God – Knowableness
    I. Title
    128.3'3

Library of Congress Cataloging-in-Publication Data
Mansueto, Anthony E.
    Knowing God : restoring reason in an age of doubt / Anthony E. Mansueto.
        p. cm.
    Includes bibliographical references.
    ISBN 0-7546-0853-0 (alk. paper)
    1. Knowledge, Theory of (Religion) 2. God—Knowableness. I. Title.

    BT50 .M265 2002
    212'.6—dc21

                                                                2002016328

ISBN 0 7546 0853 0

Typeset in Times by J. L. & G. A. Wheatley Design, Aldershot and printed in Great Britain by MPG Books Ltd, Bodmin, Cornwall.

Contents

Acknowledgements

This work was made possible by the many, many people who have challenged me to grow in justice and the other virtues, and who have shared their wisdom with me in debate and discussion, especially:

- those who participated in the Italians in Chicago Project in 1979–80,
- those who helped me grow in the struggle for justice and the search for truth during my two periods of service in Dallas, Texas, especially the people of the Catedral Santuario de Guadalupe, and Blessed Sacrament, St Cecilia, Our Lady of Lourdes, Our Lady of Perpetual Help, and St Michael's parishes, the members of the Center for Human Rights, the members of Mexican-American Democrats, and above all Josephine Torres, Tony Hinajosa and Paul Kerr,
- the students in my classes at the Carlow College, the University of Pittsburgh, Robert Morris College, the Community College of Allegheny County, the University of Dallas, the College of Santa Fe and Santa Fe Community College, Harper College, Loretto Academy, the *Universidad Autónoma de Ciudad Juárez*, the University of St Mary of the Lake, St Joseph Seminary, Dallas County Community Colleges, and the University of New Mexico – Gallup,
- my colleagues in search for wisdom and social justice, especially Ernesto Cardenal, Francois Houtart, Errol Harris, Rosemary Ruether, Samir Amin, James Daly, Boris Goubman and Colin Harper,
- the individuals mentioned in the Introduction, whose struggles provided the immediate impetus for this book,
- Marcia Kannry, whose challenge to my Christianity helped me sort out just what is and is not useful in the Catholic tradition, and
- my wife and partner, Maggie, who is as responsible as anyone else for my thinking about the problem of knowledge.

Finally, I would like to extend special thanks to Francis Cardinal George, Archbishop of Chicago, for his generous (if indirect and unintended) financial support of this project.

Introduction

Statement of the Problem

This book began with two conversations which took place more than fifteen years ago. The first was with a young Marxist economics professor teaching for the first time at an elite university in the American Midwest. She found herself confronted with a group of students who shared nothing of her concern for the impact of economic structures on human development. What was worse, she felt utterly unable to argue for her position. 'Knowledge, after all, is just a matter of perspective. If the social sciences have taught us nothing else, it is that knowledge is just a matter of perspective. Who am I to say that my perspective is better than theirs?' She soon found herself working for the Federal Reserve Bank and drifting away from any attempt to defend rationally her commitment to social justice. The second conversation was with a pastor of a Catholic parish in the Chicago metropolitan area. We were discussing the challenge of ministry to teens and young adults, who generally leave the Church after confirmation and return, if at all, only when they have children themselves. 'I have to say I don't like working with them. I feel inadequate. They are constantly asking questions I can't answer – questions like "Does God exist?" or "Is the universe ultimately meaningful?" Hell, those are questions which simply can't be answered rationally. Either you have faith or you don't.'

These were strange positions, I thought, for representatives of traditions historically committed to the power of reason to resolve the most pressing questions of human life, but not at all surprising given the intellectual tenor of our times. The truth is that we have become unsure of what we know, of what we even *can* know, and as a result have become incapable of resolving fundamental questions of meaning and value. If knowledge is just a matter of perspective – or, as my friend's neoliberal students would have had it, simply a matter of organizing experience in a way which has survival value – then there is no way for us to determine whether or not the universe ultimately has meaning, whether or not God exists, and whether or not there are transcendental principles of value in relation to which we ought to order our lives and structure our societies. And appeals to faith (I suppose the secular Marxist equivalent would be 'class stand') really aren't enough. On the one hand, they invite either a liberal laziness which never engages others in dialogue around fundamental questions and thus does nothing for their development, or else an authoritarian dogmatism before which submission or ideological warfare are the only options. And, as we will see, belief grounded in faith alone leaves unanswered important questions about the ultimate meaningfulness of the universe, creating a chasm between our love of God and our love of creation, thus promoting an otherworldly spirituality which is vulnerable to the charge that it is merely a neurosis or an opiate.

None of this is taking place in a social vacuum. On the contrary, radical scepticism, especially scepticism about the ability of reason to address fundamental questions of meaning and value, serves very definite social interests. Without rationally grounded principles of value we have no basis on which to challenge the market allocation of resources. The carefully cultivated doubt or 'critical rationality' which has become synonymous with intellectual maturity in our culture ultimately shows itself to be little more than an alibi for consumerism. For those who are dedicated to justice there can be no more important task than that of addressing the prevailing scepticism of our time. We need to address the question of human knowledge comprehensively – show what and how we know, and how we rise from the senses and from the more rudimentary forms of intellectual knowledge to knowledge of God and thus address fundamental questions of meaning and value.

We have two principal adversaries in this struggle: subjective idealism and postmodernist perspectivalism. By subjective idealism we mean any doctrine which regards all knowledge as radically immanent – as something which takes place internally to, rather than transcending, human subjectivity or human consciousness. This includes radical empiricism (Berkeley 1710; Hume 1777), positivism (Mach [1905] 1914; Avenarius 1888–90) and their contemporary expression, information theoretical neoliberalism, or what I have called *infokatallaxis* (Barrow and Tipler 1986; Hayek 1988; Tipler 1994), as well as logical positivism and analytic philosophy (Ayer 1935), and critical idealism (Kant [1781] 1969). Our principal argument with most of these philosophers will have to do with their scepticism regarding sensation, which they for the most part believe is unable to give us accurate information regarding the world around us, and thus hardly constitutes an adequate basis for abstraction and a dialectical ascent to first principles. We will see that most philosophy of this sort is more or less directly supportive of the market order. If reason cannot address questions of value then there is no basis on which to question the market allocation of resources.

By postmodernist perspectivalism, we mean those doctrines which regard knowledge as largely a function of social location and claims about truth and value as instruments in an ultimately unresolvable struggle for power. Nietzsche (Nietzsche [1889] 1968) is, of course, the foundational figure here. Derrida (Derrida [1967] 1978) is the most important contemporary representative of the trend, but softer versions of it are widespread where the social sciences wield significant influence. Here the problem is not so much with sensation but with the intellect and the way ideas are shaped by and serve to reinforce or challenge social structures. Postmodernists often take up a posture of radical opposition to the existing order, but (like my friend) they are forced to admit that their own ideas are also just a reflection of certain social interests and end up delegitimating the entire critical enterprise.

In so far as it is our aim to lay the epistemological groundwork for a proof not only of the existence of God, but also of the ultimate meaning of the universe, we will also need to answer those doctrines which largely accept subjective idealist or perspectivalist strictures on the senses and on discursive reason, but which attempt to save meaning by 'getting around' these limitations. This includes those doctrines which make knowledge of God, usually qualified as preconceptual and nonthematic, a 'condition for any possible knowledge': transcendental theism of both the process (Hartshorne 1967; Gamwell 1990) and 'Thomistic' (Rahner [1957] 1968) varieties, and those doctrines which argue that human beings can achieve knowledge of God only on the basis of some sort of divine illumination or revelation.

Transcendental theism is essentially a form of subjective idealism which, however, recognizes knowledge of God to be essential if it is to adequately ground the relatively progressive form of liberalism which it wants to defend. It is a thoroughly bourgeois phenomenon. Objective idealism, on the other hand, reflects the outlook of various nonmarket elites which have, however, been drawn into the market system and even transformed into rentiers, and which at once suffer from the alienation that the marketplace engenders and want to act to stem the tide of social disintegration.

It might seem necessary to include dialectical materialism among the antimetaphysical doctrines which we must confront. It will become apparent, however, as we develop our argument, that (except where it loses confidence in the superior epistemological standpoint of the working classes and shades over into postmodernism) the dialectical materialist theory of knowledge is basically sound if rather rudimentary and undeveloped and allows room for claims about intelligible principles, including God. The dispute with dialectical materialism regarding the existence of God and the nature and role of religion will take place, rather, in the cosmological, metaphysical and ethical arenas.

Thesis

In answer to the trends identified above, and drawing on neuropsychology (Luria 1973; Sacks 1985; Damasio 1994), cognitive development theory (Luria [1974] 1976), and the sociology of knowledge (Durkheim [1911] 1965; Lukacs [1922] 1971, [1953] 1980; Fromm 1941, 1947), I advance a general theory of knowledge which is in broad continuity with Aristotle, the Jewish, Arab and Latin Commentators, and Aquinas – and, interestingly enough, with dialectical materialism. This theory claims that

1 sensation produces an image in the brain which records data about the organization of the universe, rather than merely organizing sensations in a way which has little or no relationship to the objective determinations of the things which give rise to them, and that
2 intelligence consists in the capacity – made possible by the complex physiology of the human nervous system, but activated only by participation in human society, which provides the basis in experience for complex ideas – to abstract the intelligible content of images, a content from which the ultimate meaningfulness of the universe and the existence of God could, at least in principle, be inferred.

Central to this theory is a return to two ideas from medieval Thomism: the idea of the 'Agent Intellect' and the idea of connatural knowledge. Together these ideas help us to transform the 'hermeneutic circle' in which the theory of knowledge has been caught at least since Kant, and which the sociology of knowledge has only tightened, into a dialectical spiral which permits an authentic ascent to Truth. The Agent Intellect in Aristotelian psychology (Aristotle, *De Anima* III) is the faculty which illuminates the images we garner from experience and reveals their intelligible content. Due both to ambiguities in Aristotle's thinking on the matter, and contemporary socio-religious interests, the Middle Ages witnessed a vigorous debate between those (including most of the Arab commentators) who saw the Agent Intellect as a single unified intelligence illuminating all of humanity, and those who, like Thomas, treated it as a faculty of the human person (von Steenberghen 1980). Connatural knowledge is knowledge we have preconceptually due to a similarity of nature with the object of knowledge (Aquinas, *De Veritate* 2:2, *Summa Theologiae* II-II Q 45 a2). I argue, against both Thomas and the Averroists, that the Agent Intellect is both individual and collective – that it is in fact nothing other than human society. By living in the way social structures of varying degrees of complexity require us to, and thus in a very real sense living these social structures, we gain a kind of preconceptual connatural knowledge of these structures which then illuminates the images we garner from experience, revealing their intelligible content. This 'social intellect' is of course internally differentiated across different social systems, and is internalized differently by each individual within each society, depending on social location, the specifics of family structure and socialization and so on.

This approach acknowledges the insight of thinkers since Kant into the ways in which the particularities of the human cognitive apparatus generally, and specific cultures in particular, limit human knowledge, so that only certain aspects of reality are revealed to knowers from a particular perspective. At the same time it shows that for all their specificity and limitation, both the human nervous system and human societies operating as cognitive organs do in fact produce real knowledge of their objects.

From this point I go on to defend the historic (Dominican) Thomistic theory of the three degrees of abstraction.[1] Totalization abstracts from the particular image to the logical whole in which it is included. This sort of abstraction is essentially a matter of classification. Formalization abstracts from the image to its structure. This is what we do when we write an equation for a parabola, or in general reduce an image to a mathematical formalism. Transcendental abstraction concludes from the definition of a thing (which may be more or less formal) to a judgement of Being or value. In this judgement we have a vision of Being as such, the Beautiful, the True, the Good, the One and so on. What my approach adds to the traditional Dominican presentations is an analysis of the social conditions for the development of each degree of abstraction – and thus of the intellect's ascent to God. In this sense the book is as much a sociology of knowledge as it is an epistemology in the traditional sense of the term.

It is on the basis of this sort of transcendental abstraction that we are able to rise to a doctrine of first principles. Here we find ourselves joining, at least briefly, the cosmological, metaphysical and ethical dimensions of the argument about ultimate meaning. Validation of transcendental abstraction makes it possible for us to cast a critical eye on 'science' which terminates in nothing more than a formal, mathematical description, and fails to produce (or even aspire to) a complete explanation of the universe. We will show briefly, in a way that points towards a subsequent work devoted specifically to this problem, that complete explanation is necessarily teleological in

---

[1] In this sense my book constitutes a vindication of the historic Dominican interpretation of Thomas represented by the commentators Cajetan and John of St Thomas and in the present period by Maritain and Garrigou-Lagrange (Maritain 1937, Garrigou-Lagrange 1938) against critics such as McCool (McCool 1977) who prefer the Jesuit 'transcendental' or Gilsonian 'historical' schools.

nature and that the evidence for such an explanation does in fact exist. This, in turn, makes possible a validation of the cosmological and teleological arguments for the existence of God. The strongly teleological understanding of the first principle which results from our approach, furthermore, makes possible an answer to dialectical materialist and postmodern/nihilist critiques of religion and 'ontotheology'. It also permits us to ground ethics in a way which at once provides objective principles of right, virtue and justice and respects the historical dynamism and diversity of human societies.

It would be possible to terminate our argument at this point, with a defence of philosophical knowledge of God. But having shown the existence of infinite, perfect, necessary Being, we cannot help but want to know more than finite reason alone can demonstrate. And it would be inconsistent to predicate any limitation of infinite Being. Our defence of philosophical knowledge of God is thus also an argument for the possibility, necessity and reasonableness of revelation. The question remains, however, just how revelation takes place. As it turns out our general theory of knowledge provides some useful indications. Just as participation in the complex structure of human society creates a preconceptual, connatural knowledge of the categories, structures and purposes which make up natural knowledge, so too participation in the infinite structure of the universe provides a basis for preconceptual connatural knowledge of the categories, structures and purposes which make up the body of knowledge which has traditionally been called revealed. Revelation is a kind of 'superabstraction' in which, however, the agent is no longer human society, but the transcendental intellect itself. From here we are able to treat such questions as faith, mysticism, prophecy, problems of interpretation, theological method and so on.

What this means is that our argument sketches out the whole process by which the human soul rises from sensation, through imagination and the various degrees of abstraction to a supernatural knowledge of God which does not negate, but rather completes human reason. We conclude with a systematic analysis of this ascent, intended both as a summary and as a guide for those who, doubting the ultimate meaningfulness of the universe but still hoping to overcome their doubt, want to climb upwards towards God.

Method

The method of our investigation is that of *dialectics*. Given the many different ways in which this term is used, perhaps we should pause to explain just what we mean by it. Dialectics is first and foremost the method of dialogue – of dialogue which interrogates existing scientific and philosophical trends regarding the principles behind and the implications (theoretical and practical) of their teaching. This process of dialogue identifies contradictions and helps point us towards a higher synthesis which is then similarly interrogated. The result is a progressively more adequate grasp of the principle which is sought, coupled with a recognition that the production of knowledge is always an ongoing dialogue in which even the best attempts can be improved.

Much is often made of the distinction between the logical (Platonic/Aristotelian) and the historical (Hegelian/Marxist) dialectics. We will address this question directly in a later chapter, but it may be useful to point out that, because of the central role played in our theory by the social intellect and by connatural knowledge grounded in practice, our approach is dialectical in both senses of the term. Indeed, the two senses become quite indistinguishable. Every struggle between scientific and philosophical doctrines is also always a struggle between the social classes or class fractions they represent and the social projects they help or hinder. As our argument develops it will become clear that this does not mean that scientific and philosophical debate is somehow reduced to the class struggle, but rather that the class struggle is, among other things, a struggle over the relative epistemological adequacy of various social locations.[2] In later volumes we will see that it is also a struggle over ontological and ethical superiority.

How does this work in practice, in the context of our argument? Our dialogue or dialectic begins at the level of the special sciences. Philosophy depends on the sciences in order to describe, analyse and explain the universe of which it seeks the first principle. This work is dependent on the results of the sciences in two ways. First, our core argument regarding the nature of human knowledge draws explicitly on research in neuropsychology, cognitive development and the sociology of knowledge (Luria 1973 and [1974] 1976; Sacks 1985; Damasio 1994; Piaget 1952, 1968; Kohlberg 1963, 1983; Durkheim [1911] 1965; Lukacs [1922] 1971, [1953] 1980; Fromm 1941, 1947). At the same time, our approach has been forged in part as a critique of the information-theoretical approach to human intelligence (Shannon and Weaver 1949; von Neumann 1966; Tipler 1994) and of postmodernist and deconstructionist sociology (Foucault [1966] 1970; Derrida [1967] 1978; Lyotard [1979] 1984). Second, in so far as we attempt to map out just what a rational ascent to God would involve, and thus broach cosmological questions, we engage the debate regarding the epistemic status of mathematical physics and its affiliated disciplines and thus look at some recent work in the physical, biological, and social sciences (Barrow and Tipler 1986; Bohm 1980; Lerner 1991; Prigogine 1979, 1988; Prigogine *et al.* 1977, 1984; Sheldrake 1981, 1989; Tipler 1994).

At the same time, even as philosophy depends on the special sciences, it draws out the limitations and internal contradictions which are present in even the best scientific explanations which are, by their very nature, partial and incomplete. Neuropsychology, cognitive development theory and the sociology of knowledge (even taken together) can never provide a complete theory of knowledge because they cannot, in the end, answer questions about the objects of knowledge – questions which are, in the final analysis, metaphysical. Physical cosmology and complex systems theory, similarly, even taken together, and even extended to provide an account of biological and social organization, cannot provide a complete explanation of the universe because they cannot answer questions about Being as such. Philosophy alone can draw out the metaphysical claims which are implicit in various scientific theories and test them for their internal consistency and their capacity to provide a complete explanation. In this sense philosophy is the governor of the sciences and the arbiter of scientific debate.

---

[2] This is, in fact, as true of the Platonic/Aristotelian dialectics, as it is of the Hegelian/Marxist. What, for example, is Plato's *Republic* if not simultaneously an argument about the nature and possibility of a certain kind of knowledge (knowledge of the Good) and an argument about the social location from which such knowledge is most accessible? For an argument that Plato's project should, in fact, be seen in the context of resistance to the emergence of a petty market economy, see Chapter 2.

Of particular importance in our own argument is the task of correcting facile, relativistic conclusions drawn from otherwise very useful neurophysiological and sociological approaches to the problem of knowledge. This depends on distinguishing the process of knowledge from its term or end, and showing how a finite, contingent, often distorted process can, nonetheless, be authentically ordered to an end which is infinite, necessary and perfect.

Of course there have been a number of very different attempts from opposing philosophical perspectives to address the questions posed in this study, and many, though not all, would claim a basis in the results of the special sciences. Our argument, therefore, is necessarily also a debate about the relative adequacy of various philosophical trends. In practice this means assessing the ability of these trends to account completely, consistently and economically for the emerging scientific picture of human cognition. Thus, we will lodge charges of incompleteness against radical empiricists who attempt to explain the persistence of certain ideas in terms of their survival value, but then leave that survival value unexplained. Rationalist and fideist doctrines, on the other hand, which attempt to ground the objectivity of sense experience by arguing that a perfect being would not equip us with senses which deceive us, will be charged with a lack of economy.

Thus far, therefore, our dialectics appears 'logical' rather than 'historical', and certainly cannot be charged with sociological reductionism. It remains, however, to explain how and why 'incorrect' (or relatively inadequate) as well as 'correct' (or relatively more adequate) ideas arise. And here the social-historical dimension which is built into our theory becomes central. Inadequate ideas can be shown to be the product of limitations in social location or social practice, which do not permit the development of certain cognitive capacities. And inadequate ideas, of course, lead to inadequate practice, holding back still further the full development of human capacities. Thus our claim that subjective idealism is a reflex of the market system, and more specifically expresses the position of the bourgeoisie within that system, while objective idealism reflects the position of rentierized nonmarket elites. Our own dialectical approach, on the other hand, reflects the position of the working classes (intelligentsia, proletariat, peasantry) in active resistance to the market system. Any implication of circularity is avoided. Claims about cognitive adequacy are grounded before any reference is made to the social basis or practical implications of ideas – albeit in a way which compels such reference at a later stage in the argument.

The reader should be aware that the 'order of discovery' or the 'order of the argument', is not everywhere identical with the order of presentation, which is systematic rather than dialectical. The various chapters of this book deal, in other words, with sensation, intellect, the various degrees of abstraction and revelation, rather than with various scientific or philosophical doctrines. I have chosen this method of presentation for two reasons. First, my critique of the various trends which I oppose is dependent on the establishment of my own position at each stage in the argument. Thus empiricism is largely answered in Chapter 1, which treats sensation, but Kant only partially so. My answer to Kant is completed in Chapter 2, and a more or less complete answer is also given to most variants of objective idealism. A thorough critique of rationalism and postmodernism, however, is not possible until Chapter 5, which treats formal abstraction. Second, this method of presentation seems to me to be more accessible, especially to readers who are not specialists, for whom a dialectical critique of one doctrine after another would have little appeal, but who may find in the present work an answer to at least some of their doubts about the ultimate meaningfulness of the universe. Thus, while the reader who approaches this book with a primarily practical interest may find him/herself drawn into what may seem like arcane scientific and philosophical debate, the path will always return to questions of practice – to the task of restoring humanity's ability to see the ultimate meaningfulness of the universe, so that it can contribute effectively to realizing that meaning and thus its own specific vocation as knower and lover of – and co-creator with – God.

Chapter 1

Sensation

Human knowledge begins with sensation. To the reader who is approaching this work without much formal background in philosophy – and especially recent philosophy – this claim may seem so obvious as to require no demonstration. After all, the ordinary, everyday knowledge that we use when we get up in the morning and get ready for work, navigate the highways or mass transit systems – and much of the scientific and technical knowledge we use when we get to work, as well – seems to be either directly sensory in character, or else to depend in a more or less straightforward way on the manipulation of sensory data into relatively simple ideas like 'coffee mug' or 'subway stop' – or more complex ideas such as 'integrated circuit' or 'tensile strength of steel'. It is not that these ideas are reducible to sensation – they clearly involve something more, which we will call 'abstraction', and which we will analyse in detail in the next five chapters – but they are certainly inconceivable without it.

Matters are not, however, quite so simple. Many people who would never think to question the role of sensation in their everyday ordinary common-sense knowledge, or even in the scientific or technical knowledge they use at work, would baulk at the idea that our knowledge of God and thus of the ultimate meaningfulness of the universe also begins with sensation – that this higher knowledge is fundamentally of a piece with all the rest of our knowledge, which it extends and completes by abstraction, but with which it does not constitute a radical breach. Knowledge of God is either excluded entirely, precisely because God is not a possible object of sensory experience or, it is argued, any possible knowledge of God must be of a radically different kind than the sort of knowledge which begins with sensation – the product of divine illumination, of a primitive revelation, or some sort of direct intuition.[1]

Most people who think this way don't imagine that they are followers of important philosophers like Berkeley, Hume, Descartes, Malebranche, Kant, Schelling or Husserl, but they are. People who are sceptical about the possibility of proving the existence of God usually point to the absence – indeed the impossibility – of empirical evidence.

---

[1] Intuition is a tricky term. Throughout this work it refers to a direct and unmediated perception of the object of knowledge. For the most part we use the term as a shorthand for intellectual intuition, that is, a direct perception of intelligible truths without mediation of the senses. Examples of intelligible realities include the definition of the term 'cat', the equation for a parabola, or the idea of Being itself, or the other concepts convertible with it: Beauty, Truth, Good, One, God and so on. If we arrive at this knowledge by means of some other knowledge then it is mediated and not intuitive. If this mediation involves the senses and the imagination we use the term 'abstraction' to denote the process by which the intelligible truth is extracted from the image. Intelligibles may also be arrived at by deduction from other intelligibles. Intuitive does not mean affective, and we thus distinguish between knowledge which the knower (incorrectly we will argue) believes to be direct and unmediated (intuitive) and a decision to believe on affective grounds without adequate justification. Kant uses the term somewhat differently, to refer to sensuous experience.

Not only can't we 'see' God; we can't detect Her[2] either, in the way we might detect a new 'elementary' particle predicted by quantum theory. But of course no sensible person would claim otherwise. A finite system could never tell (at least not in any finite period of time) whether or not an object it thought might be God was actually infinite and thus divine. When we say that knowledge of God is based in the senses, what we mean is that it can be inferred from data given to the senses, using arguments which depend heavily on such concepts as order and causality. Our ability to rely on such concepts, however, depends on the claim that, even if we need to use intellectual operations such as abstraction in order to extract them, structural and causal relationships are, in fact, given in sense data and are, therefore, a feature of the way the universe is organized and not simply of the way in which the human mind is structured. And this precisely is what people who deny our ability to infer the existence of God from sense data are actually denying. Radical empiricists such as Hume (Hume [1777] 1876) regard order and causality as nothing more than an impression arising from the constant conjunction of facts and events. Critical idealists such as Kant (Kant [1781] 1969) treat space and time, on which perceptions of structure depend, as 'forms of intuition' and causality as a 'category of the understanding'. Both are regarded as aspects of the way in which the mind organizes our experience, rather than as features of the universe itself. In either case we have no warrant for using perceptions of structure or causality to infer the existence of something which itself lies beyond any possible experience. This, in turn, renders impossible all of the a posteriori arguments for the existence of God – that is the cosmological argument, which begins with the fact that the universe exists, and the eutaxiological and teleological arguments, which begin with the fact that the universe, or at least certain systems within it, appear to be well ordered and even purposeful.

People who claim knowledge of God which is not grounded in sensation appear to be of a very different sort – ready and willing to abandon the world of 'sound common sense' and 'empirical verification' for difficult to demonstrate claims to 'nonthematic preapprehensions',[3] divine illumination, primitive revelation or direct artistic, religious or intellectual intuition of the divine – or else for a 'faith' (a willingness to believe) which is little concerned about its own reasonableness and deeply bound up with the movement of the appetites. But here, too, the starting point is a scepticism about the senses. Indeed, it is scepticism (or discursive reason which has its point of departure in the senses) which makes the turn to extra-rational forms of knowledge – and indeed to the idea of God – necessary in the first place.

There are, fundamentally, two variations on this theme. Subjective idealists, we have noted, make all knowledge radically immanent, internal to human consciousness. This would seem to make knowledge of God impossible, but this is not true for all subjective idealists. On the contrary, the founder of subjective idealism, George Berkeley (Berkeley 1710), saw himself as vindicating religion against the attacks of the materialists. Berkeley says that we know *nothing* except what we experience. But

---

[2] I use the term God combined with the feminine pronoun so as to convey the ungendered, or rather bigendered, character of the divine while avoiding the awkwardness of He/She constructions and the specifically neopagan associations of the pairing God/Goddess.

[3] This is Karl Rahner's term for the knowledge of God (understood as Being as Such) which is implicit in every judgement we make which something exists.

we don't actually experience anything *outside* the mind. While we are experiencing something it is inside the mind. This led him to the conclusion that 'to be is to be perceived'. But what does this do to things which are not currently perceived – to the famous tree which falls in the forest with no one to hear it? Berkeley must resort to the idea of an Ultimate Observer – God – who guarantees the possible objects of sensation by perceiving them when we are not. Variations on this theme have been developed in the present period by information theoretical 'physical idealists' such as Frank Tipler, who attempt to resolve the dilemmas of quantum cosmology by reference to an ultimate observer.[4]

In addition to Berkeleyan empiricism and its contemporary manifestations in physical idealism and information theory, there are a variety of other subjective idealist approaches to knowledge of God. 'Transcendental idealists' (Rahner [1957]1968; Hartshorne 1967; Gamwell 1990), make God a 'condition of any possible experience', generally by stressing the implication of Being as such in any judgement of existence. Certain thinkers in the phenomenological tradition argue that the structure of human consciousness itself, which is always intentional – always consciousness of something – grounds the objectivity of knowledge, and that among the objects intended are not only physical and biological systems, but persons, values and even God. Similar themes appear in much religious existentialism and intuitionism, which has little concern with rational demonstration and wanders dangerously close to self-conscious myth-making (Lukacs [1953]1980).

Objective idealists differ from their subjectivist cousins less in their outlook on sensation than in the rather stronger claims they make for the extrasensory, extra-rational knowledge we have in divine illumination, revelation or direct intuition. Where for subjective idealists knowledge of God is either impossible, or indirect and immanent in our own consciousness, for the objective idealist the human intellect comes into direct contact with God by extrasensory, extra-rational means. The whole turn to God, however, is rooted in the conviction that sensation, precisely because it is subjective and immanent and subject to constant flux as our body changes, is fundamentally unreliable. The roots of this tradition lie in the Pythagorean school and in the more mystical forms of Neoplatonism, but the first really rigorous formulation is that of Augustine. Augustine accepted much of the sceptical critique of the senses as unreliable and limited to things which are constantly subject to change and degradation. He pointed out, however, that this does not mean certainty is impossible. On the contrary, we can be certain that we exist, because to deny our own existence is internally contradictory (Augustine, *Civitas Dei* 11: 26). And, he argued, the fact that we have

---

[4] According to quantum theory, subatomic particles (and by implication the universe, which is composed of such particles) cannot be described in terms of their position and momentum, but only by a wave function which describes the relative probability of various 'quantum states'. According to one interpretation (the so-called 'Copenhagen interpretation') this wave function is 'collapsed' when an observation is made and a definite value given to position, momentum and so on. The alternate 'many worlds' theory suggests that the wave function never collapses and that *all* possible values are in fact realized, so that the universe branches out into an infinite number of worlds, each corresponding to a specific quantum state of each particle. Tipler synthesizes these two approaches, arguing that all possible values of the quantum wave function describing the universe as a whole exist mathematically, but that only those which permit observers exist physically (the Berkeleyan criterion) and that all those which permit observers evolve necessarily to an 'Omega point' which is, in effect, Berkeley's Ultimate Observer (Barrow and Tipler 1986; Tipler 1994).

ideas about eternal objects, be they mathematical objects or God Himself, is itself evidence that these objects exist (Augustine, *Contra Academicos* II: 5, *De libero arbitrio* II: 3–5). Later thinkers built on this foundation, claiming that not only our own existence, but also the existence of God is analytically self-evident.[5] On this basis, an attempt is then made to secure the basic reliability of the senses. A perfect being, after all, would never deceive us by creating us with senses which fail to give at least a roughly accurate picture of what is going on in the world. This is, broadly, the strategy of Anselm, Bonaventura and Descartes. In its most extreme form – the 'ontologism' of Malebranche, Gioberti and Rosmini – this approach leads to attempts to ground all knowledge in an immediate intuition of God, who is regarded as the 'first object of knowledge'.

As reason became increasingly associated with anticlerical and even atheistic polemics, many objective idealists turned to faculties other than reason to provide contact with the divine. Traditionalists like de Maistre and de Bonald opted instead for a 'primitive revelation' on which language and social order and everything else depend (McCool 1977). Objective idealism in the German tradition, such as that of Schelling (Schelling [1810]1994), makes a comparable staged retreat from the revolutionary implications of dialectical reason as developed by Hegel and the Hegelian left. For Schelling sensation and reason alike are impotent in the mind's ascent to God. We depend rather on a nonrational intuition which allows us to see as a unified and meaningful whole what the senses and reason fragment.

All of these idealist approaches to God, objective or subjective, take as their starting point something other than sensation. All do so because they – like those who reject the possibility of rising to knowledge of God at all – believe that sensation does not convey sufficient information about the world to permit inference to the first principle.

Ultimately, I would like to suggest, this kind of scepticism regarding the senses – whether it leads to atheism or to an attempt at some sort of a priori or nonrational knowledge of God – is not only unworkable but also unwarranted. My argument here is simple. Radical empiricism, and subjective, critical, transcendental and objective idealist doctrines which accept radical empiricist strictures about the limitations of sensation, cannot give an adequate explanation of either the fact that most of our ideas work reasonably well most of the time, or the fact that sometimes we make what we later recognize as fundamental errors. The effect of this scepticism regarding the senses is to undermine not only our ability to rise to knowledge of God, but also the whole foundation of both everyday pragmatic/common sense and of scientific knowledge, which are reduced to nothing more than ways of organizing experience.

Let us consider first the fact that most of our ideas work. This point is acknowledged by radical empiricists, especially those in the Humean tradition (Hume [1777]1886; Hayek 1988), who frame the problem in terms of survival value. These Humeans generally begin by granting that we can perceive 'facts' and 'events'. But since such things as 'structures' and 'causal relationships' are not direct observables, they deny their objectivity. All we are really seeing is a 'constant conjunction' of phenomena.

---

[5] An analytic argument is one which proceeds by picking apart (to analyse means to take apart) a premise and seeing what it implies. Something which is analytically self-evident is so because we can demonstrate it immediately by analysing relatively simple ideas which are themselves self-evident.

Some ways of organizing this experience are better than others only because they lead to practices which work. Ideas which work survive; those which don't die out. Survival value is not, however, the same thing as truth value. There is no claim, especially among contemporary Humeans such as Hayek, that ideas which work also correspond in some sense to the way in which the universe is organized. Science is reduced to little more than tried and true tradition and any attempt to rise above science to first principles is ruled out. What this approach fails to ask is *why* some ideas work (and thus have 'survival value') and others don't. It is an incomplete and thus an inadequate explanation.

Berkeley (Berkeley 1710) takes the additional step of claiming that what we know is not the object but only our experience. The image is not a means to knowledge but its term, the only thing really known. This leads him, as we noted above, to reject the idea of matter and to call on an Ultimate Observer to guarantee the existence of things when we are not observing them. What Berkeley cannot deal with, however, is the phenomenon of error. If all that we know are our experiences, then how is it that sometimes we discover that we are wrong, and wrong not just at the level of analysis or interpretation, but at the level of the image itself? If our images are utterly cut off from the objects of experience then it is hard to explain those difficult and painful experiences which seem to bring our images back into line with reality. And yet even my in-laws' dog seems to have learned that transparent doesn't mean permeable. We don't always 'see what we want to see', and when we do the illusion doesn't last for long. What this means is that our images convey information not only regarding the nature of the object, information from which universals can be abstracted, but also regarding its existence, its relative independence from us and its ability, under certain circumstances, to impose itself on us, and sometimes painfully so.

The same points can be made in a more dramatic way if we consider the problem of hallucination and other disorders in perception – such as *The Man Who Mistook His Wife for a Hat* (Sacks 1985). If we are to accept the sceptical critique of the senses, then we must dispense once and for all with any notion that the pink elephant which an old friend of mine saw in his living room after disregarding my cautions against ingesting LSD, really wasn't there. We must also dispense with language which treats the altered perception of people who are suffering from various brain lesions as 'disorders' or diseases, rather than simply new and interesting images which are on the same level as our own.

It is fortunate that scepticism about the senses turns out to be unwarranted, because attempts to get around the supposed unreliability of the senses by grounding sensory knowledge in a priori or extra-sensory, extra-rational knowledge of God, simply don't work. We will have occasion to analyse these approaches to God in greater detail in Chapter 2. Here we confine ourselves to showing that they fail to fully escape dependence on sensation. Consider the ontological argument, which attempts to show that the existence of God is analytically self-evident. The argument depends on the fundamental principles of formal logic, which are usually taken to be a priori. But is this really true? The real reason that we accept the principles of logic is that when we make abstractions from sensation, as we do, for example, in the sciences, and use the principles of logic to make inferences from those abstractions to other abstractions, the resulting predictions, when checked against new observations, generally work, and if they don't then it is because of an error either in the process of abstraction or in our logic. Far from being truly 'self-evident' in any sense an idealist would find meaningful, the rules of logic are in fact empirically testable a posteriori propositions. The Cartesian road around the supposed unreliability of sensation is thus closed.

Claims to divine illumination, revelation, or direct intuition of God also fail to escape fully dependence on the senses. A complete demonstration of this claim will have to await our discussion of revelation in a later chapter, where it will become apparent that revealed no less than natural knowledge depends on abstraction from sensation and thus always involves a turn to the image. For now it will suffice to point out that the actual illuminations, revelations, or intuitions which real historical religions claim always involve an imaginative layer, even if they also have very significant intellectual content. Philosophy, intellectually-oriented prophecy and theology are all dependent on religious images, the elements of which clearly originate in ordinary sensation, even if they are recast and recombined in a way which endows them with a higher meaning. The vision of the burning bush or pillar of cloud comes first; only later is it followed by a philosophical or theological reflection on the meaning of the divine name, יהוה. The same is true of mathematical objects, which play a significant role in Augustine's argument for divine illumination. We know triangles first of all not as eternal and immaterial objects seen in the mind of God, but rather as forms abstracted from images garnered by the senses. We know the triangular face of this particular pyramid first, and only later the notion of a triangle as such.

There is a further problem with doctrines which deny our ability to rise to knowledge of God by abstraction from the senses. This is a problem at which I have already hinted in the Introduction, but I am reluctant to press it at this point in the argument, because I will be able to show that it is a problem only much later, after our main points have been established. For now I can present it only as something which is 'at stake' in the argument. The issue concerns the relationship between knowledge and the appetites. It is fairly obvious, I would like to suggest, that we cannot love – or hate, or take joy or sorrow in, or hope for, or fear, or be angry at – something which we do not know. In this sense knowledge precedes the appetites. But if knowledge of God is possible only on the basis of something other than rational inference from sensory experience, then we cut a chasm between our ordinary sensual appetites and any possible love of God. Love of God is not just higher than love of objects we know through the senses: it is radically different. And this is, of course, precisely the position of the whole tradition, beginning with Augustine, and continuing right up through the party currently in power in the Vatican, which grounds knowledge of God in this way. A whole host of evils follows in train – hatred of matter, of women, of sensuality and ultimately of the whole universe. It is difficult to see how, from this point of view, 'natural' humanity, still submerged in sensation and the sensual appetites, is not radically depraved, or how such a 'natural' humanity would ascend even to civilized behaviour, without the benefit of divine intervention – which is, of course, precisely what the religious right argues. But clearly 'theism' of this kind has nothing to do with the ultimate meaningfulness of the universe. On the contrary, it is as Marx suggested, an opium for those who, living under conditions of brutal oppression, have lost faith in the world (Marx [1843]1978: 54). What he failed to add is that it is also a practical atheism – a conviction that the universe, if it is indeed the handiwork of some great power, is shoddy work indeed, showing nothing of divine majesty, and pointing not towards God but towards a cosmic tyrant, and a cosmic incompetent.[6]

And so, while the greater part of this book will discuss abstraction, and acts of faith and theological understanding, knowledge and wisdom which can be shown to be reasonable only on the basis of abstraction, I must begin with the senses. I must give an account of sensation which shows that the scepticism we have been analysing is not only unworkable, but also unwarranted. I must show that the senses give us a knowledge of the world which, while not sufficient by itself, at least for human beings, nonetheless contains within itself all that we need to permit the intellect, acting on images which arise from sensation, to climb through the successive degrees of abstraction to the first principle, God Herself, and thus provide us with both an adequate principle of explanation and an adequate object of devotion. I need to show that in seeing and hearing and touching and smelling and tasting, in forming images, in remembering and recalling and transforming them, and in that estimative judgement which always accompanies the passions, we are already beginning (though only beginning) to love God. This will, in turn, permit me to show that the desire which is awakened by the smell of garlic or the curve of a woman's body is already, incipiently, the love of God. And in this way believing in and hoping in and loving and serving both the universe and God, far from being ruled out by reason, or set against each other, will be shown to be reasonable and compatible in one single movement.

Having shown that our ascent to knowledge of God must begin with sensation, we need now to turn to an analysis of sensation itself, in order to identify clearly just what is required for sensation to be possible, and just what is involved in the act of sensation itself. We begin by recalling the first systematic account of the process of sensation, considered as the basis for abstraction: that found in Aristotle's *De Anima* and further elaborated by the great Arabic commentators, Ibn Sina and Ibn Rushd, as well as by Thomas Aquinas. It is the final, Thomistic form of the doctrine that we present here. We will see that this account accords remarkably well with the results of contemporary neuropsychology.

Within the Aristotelian tradition, sensation is an act of the soul, and must therefore be understood in the context of psychology. The 'soul' in this context means nothing more or less than the 'form of the body' – that is, that which makes the body what it is, and not something else. It is the 'first degree of actuality of the body'; without the soul the body would lapse into pure potentiality and cease to exist as body.

Aristotelians identify several different kinds of soul or degrees of animation, each of which is defined by certain definite capacities or potentials. The 'mineral soul' is simply the capacity of a body to retain its form. The 'vegetable soul', on the other hand, is the capacity for nutrition, growth and reproduction – it marks the threshold of life. Animals have the additional capacity for sensation, including both sense-perception

---

6 It should be noted that key points of Catholic teaching – and indeed some broader Christian claims as well – depend on something like my defence of sensation as the starting point for knowledge of God. I am thinking not just of the historic Catholic rejection of radical depravity, but also the affirmation of the goodness of creation and the rejection of any necessity in the fall. It is also difficult to see why one would bother with sacraments on the Augustinian view, or hope in the resurrection of the body, if knowledge of God has no basis in the senses.

and sensual appetite – and, in some cases, for locomotion. The rational soul, which humans possess, includes the intellect – the capacity for knowledge of universals – and the will, or intellectual appetite, which is the capacity to desire things known by the intellect.

Let us focus in some more depth on the sensory powers. Thomas Aquinas (*Summa Theologiae* I Q 78 a3, 4), following Aristotle, makes a useful distinction here between the external and the internal senses. By the external senses we mean the capacity to collect data from our environment through touch, taste, smell, hearing and sight. We humans are clearly not unique in possessing such senses; on the contrary they seem quite common among animals, many of which possess far keener sensory capacities than we do, and some of which may even possess senses which we lack – that is, the bat's capacity to use sonar to locate objects in its flight-path. By the internal senses we mean the capacity to internalize and organize experience, represent it to ourselves, and make pre-rational judgements on it. This means first of all the ability to organize the data we collect into recognizable images – what Aquinas called the *sensus communis* and what later Thomists (Rahner [1957] 1968) called 'sensory cognition'. This is the capacity which allows us, when observing a room, to see walls, chairs, desks, carpets and so on, and not just an undifferentiated feed of data regarding colour, light and shadow and so on. Clearly this is a capacity shared by at least many of the higher animals – otherwise the dog would always be walking into the wall, something which, to my knowledge, occurs regularly only on certain television sitcoms. It means, secondly, the ability to store these images in memory, recall them and even break them up into parts and recombine them, so that we can imagine things which we have never seen, and which presumably do not exist, such as unicorns and Romulans. The latter, creative form of imagination (which probably represents a 'return' to imagination on the basis of higher operations, including various degrees of abstraction) we cannot document for other animals, but the fact that Fido remembers us and appears to dream suggests that a rudimentary faculty of imagination is present. Finally, the internal senses involve what Aquinas called the estimative faculty. This is the ability to make judgements prior to any knowledge of intelligible universals. Thus Mr Kepler, my cat, knows when we are visiting my in-laws to come to me for food and affection, and to avoid my father-in-law, who does not share my fondness for small domesticated carnivores. This doesn't mean that he is capable of even a simple idea, such as 'likes me' and 'doesn't like me'. It simply means that he remembers and recalls images and associates them with pleasant and unpleasant experiences. We humans make similar estimative judgements when, regardless of our current speed, we slow down at the sight of a police car in our rear-view mirrors – a behaviour which can hardly be called rational, but which is deeply ingrained.

This last internal sense points to the important connection between the senses and the sensual appetites – our natural tendency to seek and enjoy goods and avoid and regret evils which we experience with the senses. Aquinas identifies two sensual appetites: the concupiscible and the irascible. The concupiscible appetite is the capacity to be drawn towards goods and away from evils perceived by the senses. The irascible appetite is the capacity to be drawn towards and away from goods and evils which are 'arduous' – that is difficult to obtain or avoid. Acts of these sensual appetites are called passions. Passions of the concupiscible appetite include desire and aversion, love and hate, joy and sadness. Passions of the irascible appetite include hope and despair, fear and daring and anger. These passions are not disconnected 'feelings' produced spontaneously by the organism for no reason at all, but rather natural reactions to goods or evils perceived by the senses. According to the Aristotelian and Thomistic tradition, therefore, both sensation and the sensory appetites are ordered to the good, at least in so far as that good is accessible to the senses (Aquinas, *Summa Theologiae* I Q 80, 81 and I-II Q 22–48; Daly 1984: 197–259).

What is interesting about this approach to the problem of sensation is that it turns out *both* to be strikingly compatible with the developing science of neuropsychology *and* to lay the groundwork for a strong doctrine of abstraction – one which will allow us to rise intellectually to the divine. The key here is the capacity of the organism to form internally an image (what Aquinas called the *phantasm*) of the objects of its experience. It is from this image that abstraction will take place.

Clearly the most elementary organisms do not have this capacity. We might instead speak of 'sensitivity', of a capacity to interact with the environment in a way which conserves the integrity of the organism and eventually permits its reproduction. All of the complex biochemical exchanges which are involved in nutrition, growth and reproduction thus involve sensitivity. A virus is able to 'recognize' a possible host cell, and thus 'knows' when to shed its protein covering and penetrate the cell and its nucleus. A cell is able to 'recognize' one molecule as glucose and thus as an energy source, or as a protein which it needs to maintain its organelles and thus as 'desirable', while another it recognizes as waste matter or a toxin, it expels or screens out. It appears that energy and chemical gradients can even serve as motive for a primitive sort of locomotion: an amoeba or paramecium moves across a glucose gradient towards regions with a higher concentration of this foodstuff, but away from high concentrations of sodium chloride. A plant turns towards the sun. Gradients of this sort also appear to play a role in morphogenesis – the mysterious process by which new organisms take shape. While the genome encodes vitally important information regarding the structure of the organism, this information appears to be exclusively molecular in character. It concerns the structure of protein chains, and tells us nothing about why, even though all the somatic cells of an organism contain essentially the same genetic information, some become eye cells and others become stomach cells. One explanation for this phenomenon is that the cells are responding to morphogenetic fields, and that these fields consist in, among other things, certain chemical gradients, so that a certain concentration of a certain chemical activates the portion of the genome which (in a way which under this theory is still unexplained) produces eye cells; a different concentration, perhaps of an entirely different chemical, activates the production of stomach cells (Prigogine and Stengers 1984).

It is no accident that in discussing sensitivity we have felt constrained both to use the word 'know' and to keep it in quotation marks. On the one hand there is an action of the organism which involves a (usually) correct response to real internal or external conditions. The organism is structured in such a way that it reacts in a certain way to certain circumstances. This means that, in a certain sense, it must be able to register those circumstances in a way that a rock dropped from a cliff does not. This 'registering' involves an internal modification of the structure of the organism which does not, however, make it something other than it was. The amoeba remains an amoeba, but undergoes complex biochemical changes which initiate movement towards the glucose. The plant remains a plant – and indeed a basil plant – but undergoes complex biochemical changes which induce it to grow towards the ever-waning autumn sun. These changes, furthermore, not only do not degrade the organism, but help it to maintain its integrity, and indeed to become more fully what it is. They are 'perfections',[7] they render the organism more fully 'made' or developed. The rock, on the other hand, is merely subjected to physical law without undergoing a structural transformation – until it gets to the bottom of the cliff and breaks into many tiny bits. 'Knowledge' therefore, in even its most primitive 'sensitive' form, involves a structural or formal change in the organism which perfects it and thus realizes its latent potential.

Even so, we must acknowledge that this sensitive knowledge involves knowing in only the most limited sense. The amoeba does not know the glucose molecule, or my basil plants the sun, in even the very limited sense that a fish or a lizard knows the difference between a rock and a plant which it uses for food, or between animals one of which is its predator and the other its prey. For this some higher order structures are required: specialized sensory organs together with a nervous system which can process the data collected by those organism into 'images' which can be stored, recalled, and to which the organism can react either instinctively or by learning or both – images which, incidentally, can also be transformed to create imaginary beings and which form the basis for abstraction in those organisms which have the higher faculties which make this possible.

In assessing just what is required in terms of specialized sense organs if images are to be formed, one must walk a fine line between anthropocentrism and a biological relativism which may not be warranted by the evidence. On the one hand, the very use of the word 'image' marks the degree to which we humans privilege sight. Aristotle and Thomas consider it to be the best and most excellent of the senses because it is somehow the most intellectual (Aristotle, *Physics* VIII: 7; Aquinas, *Summa Theologiae* I Q 78 a 4). Just as astronomy has played a critical role in the development of our ideas about God and God's relation to the universe, optics and the theory of vision have played a key role in sketching out the link between sensory and intellectual knowledge. Indeed, up through the seventeenth century astronomers were also often opticians. Clearly we want to be careful that we are not unduly privileging one particular route from sensation to abstraction. It is quite possible that the cetaceans (dolphins and whales) have, or are developing, an intellect which abstracts first and foremost from sound rather than sight. And clearly there is *also* this capacity among human beings: thus the link between music and mathematics. And there does not seem to be any reason to rule out the formation of images from which abstraction would be possible on the basis of the senses which have traditionally been regarded as more corporeal – smell and taste and touch. This may seem difficult to us simply because these senses are relatively undeveloped in humans. Mary Doria Russell, in her novel *The Sparrow* (Russell 1996), on the other hand, provides a vivid description of a clearly intelligent, vaguely canine species on one of the planets of the Alpha Centauri system for which smell rather than sight or hearing is the dominant sense, and which is actually able to abstract chemical structures from the things it smells! There seem, furthermore, to be certain concepts, especially those having to do with the appetites, which are abstracted primarily from experiences of the more corporeal senses. The idea of desire is thus

---

[7] The Latin *perfectum* originally meant 'complete' or 'fully made'.

abstracted primarily from feelings of hunger and sexual tension; that of joy from the experience of sexual climax. Perhaps, therefore, even as we 'see' God we will actually 'taste' salvation!

At the same time, it is interesting to note that Kosmos appears to share our bias towards sight. Eyes which are structurally very similar to our own appear to have evolved *independently* fully 40 times (Salvini-Plawen and Mayr 1977). This suggests that seeing is a powerful attractor, and while probably not the only route to intelligence it may be among the preferred routes at least under the kind of conditions which exist on our planet. Consider once again, for example, the role of astronomy in the development of philosophy and theology. On a planet with two suns, or a thick cloud cover, where the stars are not visible, astronomy could never develop and sight would lose much of its value as a bridge to the intellect. Other senses might move to the fore. But could touch or taste or smell or even hearing give us the same kind of window on the universe as a whole, and thus lead us to pose questions regarding the ground of its structure and existence, and thus rise to the idea of God? One craves the conversation of the dolphins to help us resolve this question and hopes some day to encounter an advanced canine-type species to help us discern whether or not there really is an 'odor of sanctity'.

Now, in addition to the 'external' specialized sensory organs, we need to have nervous systems which can process the data collected from the senses into what we are calling images. While the way in which this happens still remains largely mysterious, recent neuropsychological research in fact appears to be giving us far more than we actually need to refute those who are sceptical about the senses and to establish something like the historic Aristotelian and Thomistic doctrine of the image or phantasm. Signals from the sense organs are relayed along neural fibres to the early sensory cortices – those parts of the brain which seem to be largely responsible for sensation. There they form what Antonio Damasio calls 'topographical representations' (Damasio 1994: 98–9). Certain patterns of electrical activity in the brain appear to correspond to certain objects of experience. Experiments regarding sight in monkeys have even found that there is actually a resemblance between the pattern of, say, a grid which is shown to the monkey and the pattern in which the neurons fire (Damasio 1994: 104) – though how this would work with highly complex visual images, or with the other senses, is not clear. These images are then stored not, to be sure, in the form of topographical representations, but as what Damasio calls 'dispositional representations'. These dispositional representations are modifications of the brain structure which tell certain neurons to 'fire' under certain definite conditions. Some dispositional representations encode innate knowledge. These are stored in the hypothalamus, the brain stem and the limbic system and contain commands related to biological regulation. Those which interest us here, however, those encoding acquired knowledge or memories, are stored in the higher cortices.

When images are recalled, what happens is that these dispositional representations cause neurons to fire producing a rough facsimile of the original topographic representation. But this is not all that happens. All of our experiences are intimately bound up with feelings – what the Aristotelian tradition calls the passions. The same is true of all of our decision-making processes. Even the most rationalistic among us never really sit down and analyse options in an emotional vacuum. Indeed, were it not for the powerful emotions which accompany the sight of a large truck turning on to the highway just a few dozen feet ahead of us, while we are travelling at sixty miles per hour, we would not long survive to consider such matters as the nature of sensation. Damasio, following William James and others, points out that these passions always involve body states (Damasio 1994: 129). Try to imagine desire or anger without that quickening of the heart – somehow slightly different in the case of each passion. It is impossible. The implication is that our memories – our dispositional representations – store not only images but also body states, which are recalled along with the image, setting our hearts racing and our blood surging and, perhaps, engorging certain members and creating a complex affective or, to use a more Thomistic term, 'passional' context for our decision-making. It is this capacity not only to form and store and recall images, but to link them to body states or passionate responses to our perceptions and to store and recall those states and those links which constitute what Thomas called the 'estimative faculty'.

Contemporary neuropsychology, in other words, far from suggesting that the old Aristotelian and Thomistic understanding of sensation is outmoded is, in fact, developing an account which is remarkably similar. What happens in the act of sense-perception, as in the simpler act of sensitivity, is that the organism undergoes a structural modification – it takes on a new form, that of the object perceived. This modification does not degrade the organism but rather, because it is linked to body states or passions through complex dispositional representations, helps it to maintain its integrity and to realize its latent potential. The new form is a perfection, a second degree of actuality of the body which, in addition to its own form, can take on myriad others, though at the level of sensation these are still particular forms. The soul is not yet capable of becoming 'all things'. Similarly, it becomes ordered to its own good, which implies the Good in itself, yet cannot intend this higher end, but only serve it implicitly with the humble but beautiful service rendered by the animals simply by being what they are.

Having outlined our understanding of the act of sensation, we need now to see whether and to what extent our theory answers the sceptics who claim that the senses offer us little or no knowledge of the world – and certainly not the kind of knowledge which might permit us to abstract universals and eventually rise to the first principle. We should remind the reader at this point of the basic unity of sceptical criticism, whether it is coming from a rationalist or an empiricist direction – or, as in the case of Kant, from a perspective which integrates elements of both tendencies. The sceptics are united in their conviction that, at the very least, sensation fails to deliver much information regarding the real nature of things – their properties, structure, interrelationships and so on – and at the worst fails to offer real evidence that anything at all exists outside the human mind. Empiricism, rationalism and critical, transcendental and objective idealism are all simply solutions to the problem of knowledge in the wake of this critique. Empiricists attempt to salvage what little they can from the senses, even at the expense of a retreat into de facto solipsism. Rationalists attempt to dodge the senses entirely and seek to derive all logically possible knowledge from self-evident rational principles, ignoring the distinction between real and possible beings. Critical idealists seek validation for the principles of science and ethics ('transcendental' idealists would add theology as well) in the synthetic a priori – that is in the conditions of any possible experience. Objective idealists look to artistic, intellectual, or religious intuition – or, what amounts to the same thing, to divine illumination. But all are agreed, to put the problem in terms of a possible response to our theory, that the image or 'phantasm' produced by the mind in response to data received from the external senses (if indeed it is a response to the outside world at all), at best contains little or no information regarding universal properties, structures, relationships and so on and at worst may be nothing more than an hallucination.

Let us begin by granting the sceptic his due. It is clear that our sensory apparatus is selective in what data it collects and in just how it fashions that data into images. A dog experiences me differently than a monkey would – no colour, mostly smells. Human sensation, like that of all animals, privileges some data over others and thus gives an incomplete image of the object.

Second, while we have identified some evidence for the existence of a structural similarity between, for example, the images which we see and their topographical representation in the brain, it is not at all clear how this would hold for complex visual images, or 'images' derived from the other senses. And clearly images are not stored in the form of topographical representations. We have no reason to suppose that the relationship between image and object is either 'one to one' or 'onto'.[8]

Third, it is apparent that the universal is not given *directly* in sensation. This is apparent from cross-cultural studies which show that people in different cultures actually perceive things differently. It is well known, for example, that the Inuit have over 50 words for snow, and to all appearances actually *see* the stuff differently than do non-Inuits. Even two such closely related languages as English and French understand the distinction wood/forest very differently (Saussure [1915] 1973). But the pattern extends even to people occupying different social locations in the same culture. Aleksandr Luria, for example, conducting research in Uzbekistan in the late 1920s and early 1930s, found that peasants in remote villages which had not been touched by collectivization or formal education, failed to perceive a figure like the one below as a triangle, regarding it instead as a collection of stars.

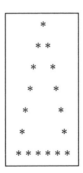

---

[8] Given a relation between two sets A and B a relation is 'one to one' if no two distinct elements in set A are mapped to the same element in set B. A relation is 'onto' if every point in set B is an image, under the relation, of a corresponding point in set A. These are very rudimentary degrees of similarity. Higher degrees of correspondence would involve similar topologies (shape), metrics (ways of defining distance) and so on. We are granting that we cannot demonstrate even the most rudimentary levels of similarity.

They also refused to place in the same broad category skeins of silk coloured in various shades of the same basic hue, often describing the colours in terms of something possessing nearly the same appearance, for example, 'spoiled silk' or 'liver' (Luria [1974] 1976: 24, 36). And what is true of basic physical properties such as shape and colour is going to be even more true of concepts which embody a definition in terms of specific difference (cat) or structure (parabola) or which presuppose a judgement of existence or value.

The truth is, however, that none of these concessions compromises realism. We do not need for the images on which our ideas are based to be complete, 'onto,' or even 'one to one' representations of the objects we perceive for them to contain useful information. But we do need for them to connect us to reality in some way. My male rabbit, U Nu, needed to be able to tell the difference between his mate Rashida in heat and a hungry neighbourhood cat. We have shown how this happens. The object, or rather light or sound waves produced or reflected by the object or chemicals emanating from it, modify the external sense organs, which in turn modify the nervous system (the Thomistic internal senses) in a way which is more or less specific to the object in question. The modifications include, furthermore, an association between 'Rashida's scent' and sexual pleasure and the smell of the neighbourhood cat and a racing heart – and perhaps the memory of a nasty confrontation. While the rabbit does not abstract from these images the concept of rabbit, cat, pleasure, danger, causation and so on, it should be apparent that the modification contains everything which will be necessary to permit such an abstraction. Ideas or, in the case of animals or humans operating at the level of pure sensation, images have survival value because as incomplete and limited as they may be, they involve a modification of the psyche by objects observed in a way which encodes information regarding not only facts and events, but also their internal structure and the relationships (for example, causal relationships) between them.

The theory which we are proposing, furthermore, not only explains more than our adversaries are able to, but does so in a way which stands up far better than they can to the criterion of Occam's Razor[9] – the principle of economy. This is especially true with regard to those who, having denied too much to the senses, attempt to shore up the objectivity of knowledge by appealing to the a priori knowledge of the structures of the human mind or, worse still of God. Is this not a case of 'multiplying beings unnecessarily', of positing the existence of structures or principles for which we have

---

[9] William of Occam, a fourteenth-century Franciscan nominalist, argued that when we must choose between two explanations for some phenomenon, both of which seem to work, we should, other things being equal, choose the simpler of the two: the one which makes fewer unproven assumptions and which therefore, as he put it, does not 'multiply beings unnecessarily', positing the existence of principles for which we have no direct evidence and in which we are tempted to believe only because of their usefulness in the context of an explanatory strategy. This principle is in itself quite sound and does not depend on Occam's larger philosophical system. There is, however, a danger that the principle will be implemented in a reductionist way, that is as a preference for explanation in terms of observable rather than inferred principles or in terms of lower-order (physical or biological) rather than higher-order (sociological or spiritual) causes, even when, in fact the higher-order principle permits the more economic observation. For this reason good scientists and philosophers always include in their tool kit not only 'Occam's Razor' but also 'Mansueto's Switchblade', which holds that the simplest explanation is not always an explanation in terms of observable rather than intelligible principles or lower-order rather than higher-order causes.

no direct evidence in order to explain something which can, in fact, be explained more completely and more simply with something like the theory we have advanced? Our subjective and objective idealist adversaries badly need a shave.

We are left, therefore, with the conclusion that the simplest way in which to explain our images, and their apparent effectiveness in helping us to grapple with the real world, is in terms of a real interaction between our bodies and the objects of experience, an interaction the nature of which Aristotle and Thomas sketched out long ago and which neuropsychology is finally beginning to describe in more detail. This interaction not only assures us that the world around us actually exists, but also produces in the image a detailed structure from which, when an intellect is present to the image, universals may be abstracted.

It remains, however, to explain just how it is that scepticism regarding the senses emerges in the first place, and just what effect it has on the development of human civilization. What we have to say on this matter will be more meaningful and more convincing after we have developed our argument regarding the intellect in subsequent chapters. But at least a few indications are in order at this point. Scepticism regarding the senses is as old as the market system. This is because in a market economy, the single most important characteristic of commodities – their price – is not something objective but is, rather, determined in part, at least, by the way in which people perceive them. Already in the Greek city states, which were characterized by a petty market or 'petty commodity' rather than a generalized market or 'generalized commodity' economy,[10] we see the emergence of radically relativistic doctrines, such as sophism, which denied that there is any such thing as the Beautiful, the True, the Good and the One. Indeed, as we will see in Chapter 2, the whole project of Socratic philosophy can be understood as an attempt to reground a doctrine of meaning and value in the light of sophistic and sceptical critiques (Mansueto 1995, 1998a).

In petty-market societies there remains a 'fixed-frame' of reference (the network of nonmarket relationships) against which exchange takes place. This is reflected in an enduring belief in the objectivity of sense-experience, the existence of a fixed space within which events take place over time and so on. It is merely judgements of value which are relegated to the realm of subjectivity.[11] In a generalized market society, on the other hand, the 'fixed frame' tends to disappear. As in the derivatives markets, everything is defined in terms of everything else – and thus nothing has a stable definition at all. The fixed frame of Newtonian physics gives way first to relativistic

---

[10] By a petty market or petty commodity economy we mean one in which production is increasingly for exchange, but labour power and capital have not yet been commodified. Production is carried out by village communities, individual peasants or artisans, or by large producers using nonmarket means of extracting surplus (rents, taxes, forced labour or slavery). As the development of the marketplace proceeds, first labour and then capital are transformed into commodities. The large-scale transformation of labour into a commodity began with the Industrial Revolution which involved, among other things, the proletarianization of peasants and artisans and continues in the present period as ever larger numbers of intellectuals are transformed into little more than skilled wage labour. The transformation of capital into a commodity is largely a phenomenon of the present period, as the perfection of capital markets and electronic information processing have made possible the constant reallocation of capital among different activities in the constant pursuit of an ever higher rate of return (Mandel 1968; Mansueto 1997a).

[11] A few of the more radical sophists, such as Gorgias, may have gone further, but their views were never widely held.

and eventually to quantum schemae in which even the underlying structure of space-time becomes a dependent variable – dependent, as we noted above, on an act of observation (Mansueto 1997a; Tipler 1994). It should thus come as no surprise to discover that scepticism regarding the senses begins to grow in the late Middle Ages with the resurgence of the market economy (the Augustinian reaction of the late thirteenth and fourteenth centuries), that it becomes a major philosophical force with the establishment of the first 'world market' under English hegemony in the eighteenth century (Berkeley, Hume), becomes effectively hegemonic with the advent of imperialism at the end of the nineteenth century, and returns, in our own time, with the 'completion' of the liberal project of establishing a unified world market within which nearly instantaneous transfers of capital are possible with relatively few barriers, legal or otherwise. The interludes between these periods were times during which major breakthroughs in the development of human civilization refocused attention on the real world, the alienating impact of market forces notwithstanding: the scientific revolution (seventeenth century), the Industrial Revolution (late eighteenth/early nineteenth century) and the rise of socialism (late nineteenth/mid-twentieth century).

The political valence of radical scepticism is no less clear. We have already noted that doctrines which are sceptical regarding the senses must *either* reject the possibility of proving the existence of God altogether, or opt for an a priori proof independent of sensation. But as we noted in the Introduction, without some absolute criterion, judgements of value – especially judgements regarding the allocation of resources – become very difficult. The market order is thus secure. If, on the other hand, we opt for a priori knowledge of God, we fall into the Augustinian trap. Love of God is pitted against love of the world. The drive to creativity, on the basis of which we would challenge the market order, turns out to be at best a distraction, and at worst an affront to an absolute cosmic sovereign. Capitalists might *also* be condemned, for example, for their selfishness and absorption in consumption, but this does nothing to provide a moral ground for the human civilizational project or for its protagonist, the working class.

In either case, therefore, scepticism regarding the senses is at once rooted in and serves to reinforce the market system. This is why Lenin devoted his only published philosophical work to this problem (Lenin [1908]1970) and why Lukacs (Lukacs [1953]1980) stresses the critical leading role of the subjective idealist theory of knowledge in the ideological resistance which the bourgeoisie mounted to socialism beginning in the late nineteenth century. Our own effort to reground the objectivity of sensation is thus a vitally important contribution to the task of rebuilding the ideological framework necessary for a credible critique of the market order.

This said, it should be clear that sensation by itself is an insufficient basis for a doctrine of meaning and value. For this abstraction is also necessary. It is to the nature of the act of abstraction that we now turn.

Chapter 2

Intellect

We have established that human knowledge begins with sensation, and specifically with the production of an image, a modification of the structure of the body and in particular of the nervous system, which encodes real information regarding the world around us. But clearly this is not all that is involved in human knowledge. There is something more. Unlike Mr Kepler (my cat, not his human namesake) I have the idea of a cat, of the elliptical orbit of the planets and even (and this is what will really interest us) the idea of Being itself – that is, of God – and the convertible ideas of the Beautiful, the True, the Good and the One. It is knowledge of intelligibles generally and of this latter class of intelligibles in particular – those we call the transcendentals – which makes possible the judgement that the universe is meaningful, that God exists, and thus grounds moral judgement. And it is, of course, knowledge of intelligibles which makes possible our appetite for them, which we call the will, and thus our love of God, and our hope that our service to the Good is not in vain. The question is how we rise from sensation to this higher kind of knowledge, which is intellectual rather than sensual, and ultimately to knowledge of God.

In order to answer this question in a way which will be satisfactory for our sceptical age, it will be necessary to do more than simply define a method, as Plato did in the *Republic*, or to describe the process by which the mind ascends to God, showing the logically necessary motion from lower to higher degrees of Spirit, as Hegel did in the *Phenomenology*. We shall certainly do both of these things, but we also need to show how this ascent is possible in the first place. We must analyse the act of the intellect in a convincing way which *begins* from its embeddedness in physiological (neurological) and social processes, and shows how, far from keeping the intellect earthbound and unable to mount to the Truth, these neurological and social processes in fact speed it quickly on its way. We must, in other words, broach the 'mind/body' and the 'mind/society' problems.

The emergence of the intellect from the matrix of the animal senses must be located first and foremost in the context of a comparative analysis of adaptive strategies. Even among the higher animals which have highly developed specialized sensory organs and which give evidence of the full range of 'internal senses' which we analysed in Chapter 1, there is quite a diversity of different adaptive strategies. Population biologists analyse adaptive strategies using something called the 'logistic equation':

$$dN/dt = rn(K - N) - mn$$

where N is the population, r the birth rate, m the death rate, and K the carrying capacity of the ecological niches which the species in question exploits. Given this equation, the Darwinian fitness of a species is given by:

$$f = K - m/r$$

A species can adapt, in other words, by increasing either its reproductive rate or the carrying capacity of its niche(s). Some species – most rodents and lagomorphs, for example – seem to have 'opted' evolutionarily for the first strategy, which is referred to as an 'r-strategy' because it is centred on increasing the reproductive rate. Species which have opted for an r-strategy generally mature quickly, have large numbers of offspring, and survive *in spite of* numerous casualties due to predation, disease and periodic depletion of the food supply due to overpopulation. Other species, such as most carnivores, have opted for a 'K-strategy', developing complex behaviours which allow them to exploit their niche more effectively. Generally speaking this involves hunting, either alone or in packs. The necessary skills require a long time to learn and it is the clumsy early efforts of young carnivores which we find so charming. Our favoured pets – dogs and cats – are simply neotenized carnivores, animals which have evolved to reach sexual maturity while conserving the juvenile care-seeking behaviour and play which make them so attractive to us (Budiansky 1992).

Clearly, however, opting evolutionarily for a K-strategy is not enough to set a species on the road towards intelligence, otherwise dogs and cats would have become our companions in conversation as well as in cuddling and mock battle. A generalist strategy as opposed to high-order specialization is also required. Carnivores have developed highly complex hunting behaviours which require a good long time to learn, but these behaviours are quite narrow in their range. Dogs and cats do not move back and forth between social pack hunting and individual stalking as the situation requires, much less mix periods of hunting with the gathering of protein-rich seeds and nuts. Humans, on the other hand, are defined among other things precisely by our ability to adapt our adaptive strategies to new situations. And when we look for other species which have opted for a generalist K-strategy we begin to find animals which are constantly startling us with their ability to at least appear 'human': raccoons, for example, with their larcenary antics – and, of course, many of our fellow primates.

It is not at all unlikely that when a species opts for a generalist K-strategy its new pattern of behaviours creates an evolutionary pull towards the development of physiological characteristics which support the emergence of the intellect.[1] Chief among these, of course, is a more complex nervous system. If sensation is centred in the 'early' or lower cortices, then the intellect seems to be centred in the higher,

---

[1] If the term 'evolutionary pull' seems teleological, that is precisely the intent. Evolutionary biology has, in recent years, placed increasing emphasis on the role of new behaviours in creating the context in which natural selection is played out. A group of animals moves into a new niche – generally through migration – for which it is pre-adapted, in the sense of possessing physiological characteristics which make it at least possible to exploit this niche. Genetic variation then produces new physiological characteristics, and those which make possible more effective exploitation of the niche are favoured by natural selection. While Neo-Darwinists such as Mayr (Mayr 1982) insist that this kind of explanation is not teleological, its structure is, in fact, classically Aristotelian. The phenomenon in question – selection for certain traits rather than others – is explained in terms of its final cause – perfection of the 'form' or new behaviour which has been acquired. It remains, of course, to explain more adequately the fact that so many highly adaptive genetic variations are produced in the first place. Several studies (Prigogine and Stengers 1977) have shown that these occur at a much higher rate than would be predicted by mere random variation, suggesting the impotence of Neo-Darwinism as an evolutionary theory.

'neocortex'. Thus John Allman has found that fruit-eating monkeys have a larger neocortex than leaf-eating monkeys, because they must remember where to find edible, as opposed to inedible or rotten fruit, and thus require a larger storage capacity (Allman *et al.* 1993a, b). Of particular importance in this regard are the frontal and prefrontal cortices, which, as Luria points out (Luria 1973: 187) are hardly apparent at all in lower animals, but become prominent among the primates and in humans occupy fully one quarter of the cerebral mass. This part of the brain, it appears, does not mature in humans until some time between the ages of 4 and 7.

This said, we should point out that the intellect is not a function of some specialized region or organ within the brain. On the contrary, it is becoming increasingly apparent that at the neurological level intelligence involves the development of complex *relationships* between various parts of the brain. The areas of the brain involved in a complex activity such as reading, furthermore, are not static, but change as the activity is learned. Initially this requires recognition of the graphic form of each letter; later a more complex and subtle process of pattern recognition develops which is not so dependent on the recognition of visual images. Different areas of the brain are, accordingly, involved. These networks of relationships can, in the case of lesions or other damage to the brain, sometimes be relocated from one area to another. Thus a lesion of a particular part of the brain in childhood will actually prevent the development of those higher functions which are dependent on it. A lesion in the visual cortex will inhibit development of complex visual thinking. If the lesion develops later in life, on the other hand, these higher functions will be undisturbed, and only the basic processing of visual information will be affected (Luria 1973: 30–4). Indeed, what makes the tissue of the higher cortices, and especially the prefrontal cortex, unique by comparison with the rest of the brain is its initial lack of organization and the fact that a far higher percentage of their mass is made up of dendrites and glia, which serve to connect neurons, rather than of core neurons as such. This is, furthermore, a tendency which increases as one moves up the evolutionary ladder. The ratio of the mass of extracellular grey matter (dendrites and glia) to the mass of the bodies of 'Betz cells' is 52:1 in lower monkeys, 113:1 in higher monkeys and 233:1 in humans (Luria 1973: 82).

We should also point out that the development of intellect is associated not only with the emergence of new kinds of tissue, but also with the enlargement of older areas, and their linking to the emergent structures of the neocortex. Allman's research points out that longevity in primates is connected not only with a larger neocortex, but also with an enlarged hypothalamus, an archaic area of the brain devoted to biological regulation. This is the same subcortical area which we identified in Chapter 1 as intimately involved in producing the body states we associate with the passions.

In addition to development of new neurological equipment, there are other physiological modifications which can affect the development of intelligence. Once again these features affect the ability of the animal in question to increase the carrying capacity of its ecological niche, and to do so in a highly flexible, generalist fashion. Of particular importance in this regard is the opposable thumb and the highly dexterous human hand which it makes possible. The fangs and claws of carnivores are adapted for certain specific kinds of hunting, just as the snout of a hog is adapted for rooting around. The human hand, coupled with the advanced sensorimotor capacities which the human brain makes possible, allows the creation of complex tools which can be used to hunt, to gather, to store food, to cultivate plants or husband animals and so on (Engels [1880] 1940). This is not to suggest that intelligence is, by its nature, technological. On the contrary, we have reason to believe that certain other higher animals – the cetaceans or certain birds, for example – may possess an entirely non-technological intellect. But clearly the physiology of an animal affects the kind of intellect which it can develop. While we would not be too surprised to find something like music or poetry among the dolphins, or science and philosophy among the whales, we do not expect to find secret underground cities stockpiled with sophisticated tools.

Let us pause at this point and ask how much of the intellect we are able to explain on the basis of this neuropsychological approach – and what kind of intellect is possible if we restrict the intellect to the operation of the brain. Intelligence, given what we have said so far, is going to consist largely in the development of a complex system of interconnections, made possible by the development of the higher neocortex, between the images produced and stored in the lower sensory cortices. Ideas, in other words, are simply associations between images. If we add to this network of neural relationships complex interconnections with the hypothalamus and other subcortical regions responsible for biological regulation, we get an approximate definition of the 'will' and its relationship to the passions. If passions arise because of dispositional representations which associate sensory images with body states, the will exists because of dispositional representations which associate *relationships between images* with body states. Thus, the *passion* of maternal love might consist in a link between the image of a newborn baby and a body state which predisposes us to care-taking behaviour. Love understood as an act of the will would link the same body state with a complex of relationships between images which includes images of babies (perhaps with bloated stomachs and large searching eyes), aid workers distributing grain and ourselves writing cheques.

There is an entire philosophical school which restricts the intellect to the kind of operations which we have been describing. I am referring to the radical empiricists, especially Berkeley and Hume and their positivistic and information-theoretical successors. Frank Tipler's statement of the radical empiricist position (Tipler 1994: 20–44) brings out nicely the full implications of this way of understanding the intellect. Tipler argues that organization is essentially information content. Life is information which is conserved by natural selection. By this definition an automobile is every bit as much a life as a mushroom or a pygmy marmoset. It is simply a sort of parasite which depends on us for its reproduction. We differ from the automobile only in our greater complexity. Like the automobile we are a finite state machine. Unlike the automobile, we are capable of being in some 10^{1045} states and can undergo some $4 * 10^{53}$ changes of state per minute.

It is this complexity which make intelligence possible. Intelligence is simply a particularly sophisticated form of information storage and processing. By 'storage' Tipler means recording a symbol; by 'processing' he means mapping one symbol to another. 'Meaning' is simply the way in which these symbols are related to the environment. Thus, in an oil refinery control system, '5546' might mean 'open valve 46'.

Tipler's agenda here is to demonstrate both the possibility and imminent probability of artificial intelligence. He regards as intelligent any information-processing system which can pass the 'Turing Test'. According to Alan Turing and most information theorists who follow him on this question, a system is intelligent if its information-processing behaviour is indistinguishable from that of a human being. Now the behaviour of a system is determined by its capacity. The human mind can store up to about 10^{17} bits of information and process at a rate of roughly 10 teraflops – that is, 10 trillion floating point operations per second. It follows from this that it will not be difficult to create an intelligent machine. Many current machines already store more information than the human brain. Speed, however, remains an issue. Most PCs do a few megaflops. The Thinking Machines CM-5 can do 100 gigaflops. Tipler expects machines to reach the level of 100 teraflops, ten times the speed of the human brain, within the next decade.

It should be apparent, however, that Tipler's theory also formalizes at least certain aspects of the neurophysiological account of the way the brain functions. Sensation stores images, 'intellect' simply maps images to other images or to actions. It is, in other words, quite possible to conceive of the brain as an information-processing machine.

There are, however, real dangers and limitations here. First, we should note that Tipler does not really theorize adequately what we have called the passional context of thought and action, which turns out to involve a complex nexus of relationships linking dispositional representations in the neocortex and cortex to others in the hypothalamus which code for body states and impel us towards action. Is a machine recognizing that it is low on electricity and needs to recharge really the same thing as a human being sensing hunger, the need to defecate, or sexual desire? This is not clear and at the very least needs further demonstration.

Second, and more important, it is one thing to say that even our most complex ideas and appetites can be broken down into relationships between images stored in and processed by the nervous system. It is quite another thing to say that our ideas can be adequately explained in these terms, or that they are 'nothing more than' mappings between images. A turtle swimming ashore to lay eggs (Mayr 1988) is certainly a chemical system and both her motion and whatever cognitive processes are involved in her motion clearly involve many complex chemical reactions. But the chemistry doesn't explain why she comes ashore or why, in general, the eggs are laid on land rather than at sea. The same is true of intellect. Thinking the idea of God may involve relating myriad bits of data (or images) to each other and, at the physiological level, the establishment of complex neural networks, but that is not *why* some people have the idea of God. It is only *how*. Indeed, we shall see that it is only a *part* of how. In both cases there is a higher level of organization at issue, the emergence and operation of which cannot be explained adequately in terms of the lower levels.

Reductionism is not, however, the only danger facing the theory of knowledge. As we have noted, there are philosophical trends which see intellectual knowledge as utterly distinct from what we know through sensation. We have already encountered some of these doctrines in Chapter 1, which we grouped together under the title of 'objective idealism', and where we focused on their underlying scepticism regarding the senses. We need now to assess in greater depth the account given in these doctrines of the act of the intellect itself. Broadly speaking there are six variants of this approach, which Thomas had already identified and criticized in the thirteenth century (Aquinas, *Summa Theologiae* I, Q 84):

1   The human intellect knows through its own essence.
2   The human intellect knows through innate species or ideas.
3   The human intellect knows by being informed by various separate species.
4   The human intellect knows by deduction from analytically self-evident first principles.
5   The human intellect knows by divine illumination.
6   The human intellect knows by artistic, religious or intellectual intuition.

The first three variants have relatively little contemporary influence and we will consider them only very briefly. The first variant derives originally from certain pre-Socratic philosophers who held that forms exist in the same way in the knower and the known. Thus Empedocles says that the universe consists of the four elements, fire, air, water and earth, and two principles of motion. The soul is able to understand the universe because, as part of it, it too is composed of these principles, which it can discover by self-analysis. Aristotle demonstrated that this doesn't make sense: knowing these principles does not explain how we know bone, flesh and so on, much less how we know things which are not included in our essence. It is, furthermore, on this basis, impossible to explain why stones or plants would not understand at least some things through their own essences. Later, more sophisticated versions of the thesis argued that the soul contained the form of all things immaterially – that to be human meant to be all things. This, however, would involve an identification between the human and divine which, quite apart from theological considerations, is highly problematic. We do not experience ourselves as possessing naturally the essence and thus the powers of everything in the universe (Aquinas, *Summa Theologiae* I, Q 84, a2).

The second and third alternatives derive from a misreading of Plato. The notion that the intellect knows through innate species or ideas was advanced by Plato in certain dialogues and was elaborated by some of the more gnostic of the Neoplatonists. The notion here is that the human intellect is a sort of divine spark which naturally knows all things. It has somehow become trapped in matter, leading it to become clouded and to forget the divine knowledge which it possesses. Thomas makes short work of this thesis (Aquinas, *Summa Theologiae* I, Q 84, a3). First of all, he points out, we do not forget those things which we know naturally, such as the self-evident first principles of explanation: for example, that the whole is greater than the part. Second, someone who is blind from birth lacks any concept of colour – something which suggests that the idea is not innate, but rather abstracted from the data of the senses.

The third variant involves the so-called doctrine of the Forms, according to which the intellect knows by direct, intuitive contact with the intelligible forms of things, which, according to this reading of Plato, exist independent of both matter and the mind of God. This theory has insuperable metaphysical problems, because it is difficult to see how forms or ideas can exist separately from *both* mind and matter. It also fails to meet the test of economy. We are explaining something complex in terms of something even more complex, which is hardly satisfying, and we are 'multiplying beings unnecessarily'. We have no evidence for or reason to believe in the existence of these independent Forms except as a way of explaining the act of the intellect – something which is done more simply using other strategies.

We say that these are misreadings of Plato because they take ideas put forward in one or more dialogues and rip them out of context in order to make them the basis of a fully elaborated theory of knowledge – something which Plato lacked. Indeed, Plato is best understood not as a systematic thinker with a clear teaching or doctrine on every point, but rather as a philosopher deeply concerned to solve a problem. He wanted to reground ethics, by showing that there is a Good as such. This involved demonstrating our ability to rise above images and to advance to knowledge of universals – something he does very effectively in the *Republic*. The notion that we know by innate species or by the influence of independent Forms were merely ways Plato used to illustrate just how the act of the intellect might take place. But he never seems to have settled on a single theory, or even to have advanced real arguments.

Rather more important are the theories which understand the act of the intellect in terms of rational analysis of self-evident principles, divine illumination, or artistic, religious, or intellectual intuition. These theories all have a common lineage. They derive from the Augustinian critique of scepticism. In the ancient world, as in our own time, there was profound scepticism regarding the possibility of knowledge, whether based on the senses or on the intellect. This is not surprising, given the disintegration of the social fabric under the pressure of developing market relations. People experience a market society as either a system of quantities (prices) or else as a system of atoms (individuals) which are only externally related to each other. This experience provides their model for understanding the universe as a whole: thus the two hegemonic ideologies of highly marketized societies – rationalism and empiricism. Knowledge is a result either of the logical manipulation of ultimately mathematizable formalisms or of the action of 'atoms' (however understood) on the sense organs. As we have seen, however, it is very difficult to theorize knowledge on a radically empiricist basis. Empiricism always begins with the common-sense assumption that sensation alone conveys knowledge of the principal characteristics of the things we experience, but on analysis discovers that much of what we think we sense we are actually abstracting or inferring from abstraction – including, ultimately, the idea that what we experience actually corresponds to something outside the mind. The result is an obsession with the notion that the senses are deceiving us.

We have already, of course, taken the first steps towards addressing this sort of scepticism, by laying the groundwork at the level of sensation for a doctrine of abstraction. There has, however, historically been another approach to the problem, which we must assess before we can move on to our own. This is the approach pioneered by Augustine and elaborated in somewhat different ways by the later Augustinians, and by rationalists, ontologists and objective idealists. The argument is simple: 'I know for certain that I exist and know and love. About such truths I fear no arguments from the Academy's sceptics. "What if you are deceived?" they protest. If I am deceived I exist! For one who does not exist cannot be deceived' (Augustine, *The City of God* 11: 26).

This is, of course, nothing other than the *cogito* which Descartes did not so much discover as restate in a slightly more rigorous way. Our own existence is analytically self-evident, because in order to deny it we must first exist.

Clearly the point is well taken. And it is understandable why this would be such a tempting point of departure for philosophy. If one can begin with an analytically self-evident starting point and derive all knowledge from that starting point, one need not deal with the messy business of the senses or show how, if at all, it is possible to derive knowledge of the universal from the sensible particular. But matters are not so simple. The *cogito* may be a secure starting point, but its security is that of a prison. It provides no obvious exit to knowledge of things outside ourselves.

There are, broadly speaking, two ways out of this prison. The first is through analytic reason itself. This is, of course, the great ideal of mathematics – to derive from one single analytically self-evident truth all logically possible truths. It is also the path on which all of the historic rationalist philosophers – Descartes, Leibniz and Spinoza – first set out. What one discovers, however, on a careful reading of their work, is that none really persevered. Leibniz was quite clear from the very beginning that it is only for God that all truths are (analytic) truths of reason; we depend for knowledge of particulars on our senses, however flawed they may be. Descartes appears to adhere more strictly to the rationalist programme, but in fact opts out early, attempting an analytic proof of the existence of God, a version of Anselm's ontological proof, to supplement an Augustinian proof based on divine illumination, but then grounds the objectivity of our knowledge of things in the outside world in God rather than directly in analytic reason. Spinoza, on the other hand, attempted to follow the mathematical model rigorously. This, at least, is the impression which Spinoza attempts to give us. He begins with a number of definitions and axioms and – skipping over the *cogito* entirely – proceeds through analysis of the idea of substance (something which can be conceived in and through itself, independently of any other conception) to a proof of the existence of God and of the identity between God and the universe. All particular systems are simply modifications of God; thought and extension those two of the infinite divine attributes of which we are able to conceive (Spinoza [1675] 1955). The difficulty, of course, is that Spinoza, unlike the Augustinians, has not really answered the sceptics. How do we know that 'substance' exists at all? The analytic argument presented in Proposition VII of Part One of *Ethics* – that existence belongs to the notion of substance – simply begs the question. What Spinoza actually proves here is that if anything exists at all, something exists necessarily – and is, therefore, divine. He has not, however, shown that anything exists. Spinoza's real answer to the question comes only in Part Two, Proposition XVIII, where he acknowledges that *we* know that something exists because our bodies are modified in certain ways by other bodies. Our knowledge of the universe, in other words, derives from sensation of finite particulars, from which we *infer* the existence of God. Spinoza, in other words, is not really a rationalist, but rather an Aristotelian who is writing in an atmosphere powerfully influenced by rationalism and the mathematical ideal, something which leads to certain powerful insights – the radical interconnectedness of all things – and also (we will argue) to certain errors – the rejection of teleology. The same can be said for the many philosophically inclined physicists in our own period, such as Albert Einstein and Benjamin Gal-Or, who find in Spinoza's doctrine an attractive way to draw out the philosophical implications of the mathematical model of the universe derived from Einstein's theory of general relativity. Here too, the turn to sense data in order to demonstrate that the universe thus described actually exists is unavoidable. Analysis gives us only knowledge of possible beings; it is by comparison with the data of the senses that we know that the possible actually exists.

It is, perhaps, poetic (or should we say mathematical) justice that the definitive defeat of the *via mathematica* should have come at the hands of a mathematician. I am referring here to Gödel's Theorem, which states that it is impossible to construct a formal system sufficiently complex to contain the rules of arithmetic, and which is also complete and consistent. It is, in other words, necessary, either to make unproven assumptions or to run into internal contradictions (Korner 1968: 91ff). And if one cannot construct a system containing even the rudimentary truths of arithmetic, then it is hardly possible to construct a system containing all logically possible knowledge.

The second route out of the prison house of the *cogito* is to claim that the intellect is illuminated from the outside by an intellectual light in which it can directly perceive the essence of things in themselves. In order to ground the objectivity of this knowledge it is generally claimed that the illuminating light is divine. This is the approach which was taken by Augustine himself (Augustine, *Contra Academicos* II: 5; *De libero arbitrio* II: 3–5), by Bonaventura (Bonaventura, *Quaestiones disputate de Scientia Christi* Q 1, a1), and by a whole cluster of doctrines which emerged after the seventeenth century, the most important of which are ontologism, traditionalism and the strain of objective idealism which owes its origins to Schelling. It is also the approach implicit in much Reformed theology. It is neither possible nor necessary to consider these doctrines, and the not insignificant differences among them, in detail here. The basic thrust of the argument is simple. We have in our minds the idea of God – that is, of Being, which is infinite, perfect, necessary and so on. Clearly this idea does not arise directly from the rational self-knowledge we have in the *cogito* or from whatever vague knowledge we may derive from the senses, since in both cases the knowledge in question is of a finite system. But the idea must come from somewhere, indeed it must come from something capable of producing the idea of infinite, perfect, necessary Being. But only such Being itself could explain the presence of this idea. Thus we have an immediate rational intuition of God. This knowledge of God then guarantees the objectivity of our knowledge of finite systems, which are either seen in the mind of God, or for those more concerned to safeguard divine transcendence, such as Augustine himself, in a divine light which bathes the intellect, revealing the intelligible properties of things just as natural light reveals their sensible properties. Indeed, the fact that we know anything changeless and eternal, such as the Pythagorean theorem or other mathematical formalizations, was for Augustine evidence of an eternal light which made such knowledge possible, and thus evidence for the existence of God.

This approach is highly unsatisfactory. It is, first of all, at least open to question whether everyone has in their minds from the very beginning the idea of infinite, perfect and necessary Being. There are certainly many – namely most atheists – who would claim to have this idea only mediately, through the claims of others. And even if we were to dismiss this claim as an act of sinful pride (a move for which, at least at this point in the argument, there is precious little basis), there remains the fact that many societies, while certainly possessing a profound sense of the sacred, have nothing like the idea of infinite, perfect, necessary Being. Australian totems, or even the deities of most communitarian, archaic and tributary societies just don't fit the bill. At this point our Augustinian adversaries will once again press the charge that the absence of this idea is a mark of our fallenness, a fallenness which is shared by all humanity. But this charge presupposes not only the existence of God but an entire theological system the reasonableness of which has not yet been demonstrated. In other words, it begs the question. It is more straightforward to simply allow that the idea of God, understood as infinite, necessary, perfect Being, develops only under certain social conditions. The presence or absence of the necessary social conditions may well have something to do with phenomena which may *later on* be interpreted as fallenness, redemption and so on. But this is very different from simply assuming the whole theological apparatus necessary for this interpretation from the very beginning.

It should, furthermore, be pointed out that many of us who do have the idea of infinite, necessary and perfect Being do not experience this idea as the product of direct intuition. Indeed, for most of us it is neither direct nor intuitive, but is intimately bound up with our experience of the universe as a radically interconnected, structured system ordered to an end. The idea of God is something we abstract from this experience in a more or less formal way. Our knowledge of God is, furthermore, entirely unlike our knowledge of mathematicals, of which we have a true intuition. When I know the equation for a parabola, I can see it clearly and completely in my mind and comprehend in that equation everything which is contained or implied in it. This is the sort of knowledge which Thomas ascribed to the angels and to God, and to humanity at the moment of the Beatific Vision. Our knowledge of God, on the other hand, especially our natural knowledge of God, is lacking in this sort of clarity and distinctness. We see 'as in a mirror darkly'. While the idea of God is certainly useful for explaining the existence and organization of the universe, we cannot derive from our idea of God other truths, such as Fermat's Last Theorem or the colour of the woodwork in our neighbour's den. Indeed, it would not be too much to say that the Augustinian solution to the problem of intellectual knowledge fails utterly to distinguish between reason and revelation, or even between reason and the Beatific Vision, much less to distinguish the various grades of intellectual knowledge, natural and supernatural. It leads inevitably either to fideism, which ascribes all knowledge to revelation of one kind or another,[2] or else to an intellectual overreaching which, in claiming as intuitive our limited and impoverished knowledge of God, ultimately deprives us of the true intuition of the divine which we have fully only in beatitude, and which we taste in this life only in the prophetic-mystical union which derives from connaturality with God in the supernaturally just act (Maritain 1937).

The finite intellect, then, knows only by turning to something outside itself. And this something cannot be God who, as we have suggested, we know only mediately, by inference from particulars. It must, therefore, be the data of the senses or, as we specified in Chapter 1, the image or 'phantasm' produced by the brain in response to stimuli received from the external sense organs. The action of the intellect on the data of the

---

[2] Thus the radical Reformed doctrine of Dooyeweerd who argued that even our knowledge of mathematicals depends on faith in Jesus Christ.

senses can, however, be conceived not only as abstraction (the option for which we will argue) but also as a sort of unification under the forms of intuition and the categories of the understanding. This is, of course, the doctrine of Kant, who we have already encountered in our discussion of sensation. We need now to assess Kant's account of the action of the intellect itself, and see whether or not this action is best understood as unification.

In order to do this we need to understand a little better just what motivated Kant. He recognized that both empiricism and rationalism had run into dead ends. Rationalism had proven itself incapable of escaping the prison house of the *cogito* (at least on an authentically rationalist basis), while empiricism had 'demonstrated' (his main point of reference in this regard being Hume) that very little is actually given in sensation. The effect was to call into question the foundations of science, of ethics and of religion. It was these foundations which he wanted to secure as best as possible, given the limits on human cognition which the rationalists and empiricists had already discovered. While we have already undermined the motive for Kant's analysis, by showing that radical empiricist scepticism regarding the senses is unwarranted, we must still evaluate his claims regarding the act of the intellect, which is logically if not historically separable from his views on sensation.

Kant begins by making a distinction between two types of judgements: analytic and synthetic. In analytic propositions the predicate is already contained in the subject; analysis merely draws it out.

All triangles have three sides.

Synthetic propositions, on the other hand, join ideas which were previously separate.

The chair is red.

Prior to Kant, it was taken for granted that analytic arguments are a priori, and that synthetic arguments are a posteriori. The judgement that all triangles have three sides requires no observation; we conclude directly from the definition. The judgement that the chair is red, on the other hand, is possible only after we have observed the chair and determined its colour. What Kant proposes is that there is another sort of synthetic argument, the synthetic a priori, which provides the solution to his problem. Synthetic a priori judgements join two ideas prior to any observation, by showing that they are the condition of any possible experience. Kant claims that we make this kind of judgement all the time in mathematics. The idea of '7' is not, he claims, contained in the ideas of '3' and '4', nor is the idea 'shortest distance between two points' (which is quantitative) contained in the idea 'straight line' (which is qualitative). The same is true of physics. The conservation of matter for example involves not an analysis but rather a synthesis of ideas. But in none of these cases are the judgements based on observation. We make the judgement prior to any observation whatsoever.

What Kant concludes from this is that knowledge is not so much a matter of conforming our minds to objects as it is of conforming objects to our minds. He did not mean by this that the object is created by the mind, and therefore exists only within it, but rather that we know the object only as it is structured for us by the operation of the intellect. What the mind does is to take the manifold data of experience and impose on it a unified structure which makes thought possible. The forms of intuition, space and time, structure our actual sensory experience; the categories of the understanding – quantity, quality, relation and mode – structure the way we relate experiences to each other and form them into a unified whole.

What this does for Kant is to establish a firm foundation for mathematics and science. Universal and necessary knowledge is possible in these disciplines because everyone organizes and unifies the given data of the senses in the same way. The same is not, however, true for metaphysics. Because the intellect unifies rather than abstracting, we cannot conclude to anything supersensible. Concepts such as the self, the cosmos and God, which Kant calls the transcendental ideas, reflect nothing more than the drive of the intellect to unify our experience perfectly. These ideas do not, however, correspond to any possible object of experience and we thus have no basis on which to claim that they correspond to anything outside the mind. Indeed, when we try to treat the transcendental ideas as if they were objects of experience, reason runs into contradictions or antinomies from which it cannot extricate itself. Thus the interminable debates regarding freedom and necessity, the finitude or infinity of the universe and its infinite divisibility or reducibility to simple parts (atoms), and the existence or non-existence of God.

It is on this basis that Kant rejects the historic arguments for the existence of God. The ontological proof he rejects out of hand. Being, he points out, is not a real predicate which can be deduced by analysis of some other predicate, such as 'than which nothing greater can be thought' or 'perfect'. We know something actually exists only by observation. But he goes on to reject the cosmological and teleological arguments as well. The cosmological argument, he points out, turns on extending the category of causality, by which the understanding orders sensible experience, to the supersensible realm – a move he claims is illegitimate. Similarly, the teleological argument argues from the presence of cosmic order to the notion of an orderer who is, however, beyond any possible experience.

Unable to conclude to a first principle, Kant had to seek some other way in which to ground ethical judgements. Here, too, Kant turned to a priori reason. Like science, ethics is grounded in the a priori structure of human reason. Just as the mind unifies experience under certain definite categories and forms of intuition, so it seeks to unify our action under a single, internally consistent and universal principle, the categorical imperative: 'Act only on that maxim whereby you can at the same time will that it should become a universal law.' From here, Kant goes on to argue that in order to follow this principle through consistently, we must assume (though we cannot prove) freedom of the will, immortality and the existence of God.

There are a number of difficulties with Kant's approach. The most fundamental of these we have already identified in Chapter 1. If space, time, quantity, quality, relation and mode are structures imposed on experience by the mind, rather than characteristics of objects given in experience and abstracted by the intellect, then it is difficult to understand why these forms and categories have such powerful survival value. Put slightly differently, this is fundamentally the Hegelian critique of Kant (Harris 1991, 1992). Our ideas are, after all, a part of the world – one might even say that they are the world's own consciousness of itself. That these ideas structure our experience and forge out of disparate sensations a unified totality does not mean that the unity and structure is something imposed. It might equally be something discovered – or, to use

Hegelian language, something implicit which has been made explicit and brought to conscious certainty of itself. Indeed, this is both the simpler and more powerful explanation. It is simpler because it does not require us to postulate a unifying drive in the mind, complete with forms and categories. It is more powerful because it explains why these forms and categories have survival value: they reflect (albeit perhaps selectively and imperfectly) the way the universe is actually structured. Or, if we do think of the action of the mind as a unifying drive, then this drive itself is not simply postulated, but itself explained as part of a larger tendency of matter towards form, a drive which takes a new and important step in the transition from diffused and disorganized sensory experience to organized categorical thought (Harris 1991, 1992).

Kant's strategy for regrounding science, ethics and religion, finally, leaves him vulnerable to criticism from cultural relativists. Kant claims that the forms of the intuition and the categories of the understanding are universal structures of the human mind. But is it really true that all human beings order the data of the senses in the same way? This seems increasingly difficult to maintain given the growing evidence that diverse languages and cultures embody fundamentally different concepts of space, time, quantity, quality, relation and mode. This criticism might seem to compromise even further the realism we are attempting to defend, but we will see that it is in fact quite possible to reconcile a moderate sociological relativism with an underlying philosophical realism strong enough to ground science, metaphysics and ethics. For Kant, on the other hand, who grounds science and ethics in the universal structure of human reason, any concession to relativism spells disaster.

In the final analysis, Kant can be understood as a response to the realization that we have no immediate intuition of intelligibles – that we cannot see 'turtle' the way we see a turtle, and that we cannot see God in any meaningful sense at all. This is of course the very point we made in our critique of rationalism and objective idealism. The absence or darkness of vision, however, is not absence of knowledge. The human mind is limited and must make do with concepts which are not in any sense an intellectual vision. These concepts do, however, nonetheless provide the basis on which we can advance to an authentic knowledge of God – and also demonstrate the possibility and reasonableness of a revelation which begins to close the gap between our desire to see and the dark and indirect knowledge we have through the medium of the concept.

We are now in a position to advance the principal thesis of this work: that the intellect knows intelligibles by an act of abstraction from the images formed by the brain in response to the data of the external senses, and that this act of abstraction depends on a preconceptual connaturality with the object known which derives not principally from our biological, but rather from our social nature. It is, in other words, participation in definite social structures which provides the basis for our capacity to abstract intelligibles from images and eventually to rise to the first principle. This epistemological thesis is closely related to an historical thesis which will be developed in greater detail elsewhere, but which must be stated and explained if the relationship between our position and that of others is to be clear: that there is a single unified dialectical tradition which has its roots in the work of Socrates, Plato and Aristotle, which is carried forward by the medieval commentators (Islamic, Jewish and Latin), and which persists in the historical dialectics of Hegel, Marx and their interpreters. What the diverse thinkers of this tradition share at the epistemological level is, first of all, a common project – grounding knowledge of a transcendental principal of value which can provide a criterion by which to criticize the market order – and a common understanding of the act of the intellect, even if this commonality is often covered over by differences in terminology, polemics against the idealist or materialist excesses of others in the tradition and so on. For all of the principal thinkers in this tradition the intellect rises from sensation, through various degrees of abstraction, to knowledge of the first principle through a process which involves both the working out of an internal logic and engagement in increasingly complex social practice. What separates the older 'logical' dialectics of Socrates, Plato and Aristotle from the historical dialectic of Hegel, Marx and Engels is simply the realization of historical progress as a constitutive dimension of social practice.

Both our principal, epistemological thesis, and our secondary historical thesis are best explained by presenting the development of dialectical epistemology historically and the best place to start is with Plato's *Republic*. A correct understanding of Plato is impossible apart from the Athenian context. What makes Greece so unique is that it was the planet's first market society. Long on the periphery of the great empires of the Mediterranean basin, Greece benefited from the emergence of new agricultural technologies centred on the cultivation of grapes and olives. The result was the development of a vigorous commercial economy centred on production for export. Gradually Greece and its colonies replaced the tributary empires as the 'centre' of the Mediterranean system. The marketization of Greek society was accompanied by internal differentiation. Nouveaux riches elements challenged traditional dynasts while many of the peasants fell into debt peonage. But then something interesting happened. A series of rebellions in the fifth and sixth centuries halted this process, and imposed a kind of compromise. The reforms of Solon and Pericles guaranteed the land rights of the peasantry, providing credits and other protection against debt peonage and permitted them to participate in the political arena. But these reforms also left intact the landholdings of the ruling classes, who were forced to turn to chattel slaves to work their large estates (Anderson 1974: 29–32, 38).

This combination of a formally democratic political arena and fundamental class conflicts imposed on the ruling classes the task of securing the consent of a majority which did not share their interests: thus the function of the *rhetor*, whose job it was to sway the masses in the public assembly. The sophists, of course, were first and foremost teachers of rhetoric, who trained rich young men in the arts of persuasion, so that they could ably serve their families' interests in the public arena. Trained by the sophists, these *rhetors* could 'make the worse appear the better cause', so that in a few short years people began to doubt that there really was any such thing as the Beautiful, the True or the Good. Where in the tributary state there was still one common end, even if it was deformed and turned to the interests of a single warlord, here the state became simply an instrument of purely private ends. The polity itself lost all integrity.

The Socratic dialectic is first and foremost an attempt to rectify this situation, by showing that there is, in fact, something Good in itself which can serve as a criterion of judgement – a standard by which it is possible to find the money-makers wanting and argue for an alternative allocation of resources. This is the programme which is set out so powerfully in the *Republic* and to which, despite their many differences, both Plato and Aristotle and the whole body of their successors adhered. Plato argues that those who rule the city, the guardians, must be knowers of the Good – and that they can become knowers of the Good only through a long process of theoretical and practical education. This education begins with gymnastics and music (which for the Greeks included all those activities over which the Muses presided, roughly corresponding to what the Middle Ages would call the liberal arts).[3] This training, which the guardians share with their military auxiliaries, lasts until the age of about 15–18; after which there is a period of military training. After this those selected as guardians proceed to the study of more advanced mathematics, and then, after the age of 30, to the study of the higher or dialectical logic which leads to knowledge of the Good. Only after a long period of political service in subordinate posts between the ages of 35 and 50, however, will they be called to membership in the high council which devotes itself at once to philosophical reflection and to governing the city (Plato, *Republic* 376e–412b, 521c–541b).

This means that the dialectic by which we rise to first principles is both theoretical and practical. It begins with a solid grounding in the arts, especially the arts of argument. We must master the process of drawing out the implications and internal contradictions of our own ideas and those of others, and driving towards a higher synthesis. This, in turn, prepares us to engage the people regarding their interests and projects, drawing out their latent potential, wrestling with difficult social contradictions, and gradually leading the *polis*, as we ourselves are led, to seek a higher good.

Already with Plato, therefore, the ascent to first principles has a definite social basis. For Plato, no less than for Hegel and Marx, theory and practice are intimately bound up together. If Plato seems to restrict access to knowledge of the Good to a few – if he speaks of a city governed by philosophers rather than a city of philosophers – it is because given the level of technological development achieved by Hellenic society, it was still necessary for the vast majority to be engaged full time in food production. Athens could never have supported the whole population in the pursuit of the course of studies which Plato recommends. It is only now, with the technological progress of the past two centuries, that we can begin to think about a philosophical democracy, and even so it remains a long way off. In the meantime Marx's position is not really so different from Plato's. 'Philosophy is the head of the revolution; the proletariat is its heart' (Marx [1843] 1978: 65).

The difficulty is that Plato's account of the dialectical method is simply that: it is a method or a discipline, not an account of the act of knowledge, which alone can really show how knowledge of intelligibles is possible. As we noted earlier, Plato himself

---

[3] The Latin '*ars*' and the English 'art' translate the Greek *techne*, or excellence in making things. Where the instrumental arts make tools and the fine arts create beauty, the liberal arts are concerned with making arguments. Thus the *trivium*: grammar, rhetoric and logic, which teach us to make arguments using natural languages, and the *quadrivium*: arithmetic, geometry, harmonics and astronomy, which teach us to make arguments using mathematics. Properly speaking these are the lower liberal arts. The higher liberal arts include training in the specific forms of argumentation used in the various special sciences and the higher or dialectical logic which, we will see, allows us to rise to the first principle. These arts set us free because they permit us to make and evaluate arguments and thus participate in political life and approach questions of ultimate meaning and value with the capacity to make independent judgements.

seemed less than certain with respect to this latter question, sometimes speaking as if the knowledge of intelligibles was a matter of *anamnesis* – the recovery of memories lost with birth and obscured by the constant changes of material existence. At other times he speaks as if the mind is illuminated by the Forms or by the Good. The *Republic*, however, seems to lean very strongly towards the notion that we ascend to knowledge of intelligibles beginning with the images which we garner from experience, and gradually, by means of the dialectic, teasing loose the intelligible principles which are present therein. This, at least, is the impression given by the Allegory of the Cave and the Divided Line. Even here, however, Plato gives no real account of what is involved in those operations.

The first systematic attempt to provide such an account was made by Aristotle, and further elaborated by the medieval commentators. According to Aristotle (Aristotle, *De Anima* III) and his interpreters a natural faculty called the Agent Intellect abstracts from the image produced by the *sensus communis* (common sense) the intelligible essence of the system in question. Another natural faculty, the Passive or Potential Intellect then takes on the form of the thing known – what Thomas calls the 'impressed species', thereby 'becoming' it 'intentionally'. Thus informed the potential intellect expresses itself in the 'mental word' of the concept, or the direct universal. Examples of such direct universals, at varying degrees of abstraction, would include 'cat', 'a circle, that is, a curve of the form $x^2 + y^2 = r^2$', or 'good'. The abstracted form, existing as it does in the mind rather than in the thing itself, is only a possible essence. But because it is identical in form with the concrete singular from which it was abstracted, the existence as well as the essence of the thing is carried over into the concept, something which is affirmed in the 'second mental word' of the judgement.

Knowledge thus becomes a way of transcending human finitude and ultimately of rising to the first principle, to God. Thus Aristotle writes in *De Anima* that 'the soul is, in a sense, all things' (Aristotle, *De Anima* III: 8, 431b: 20). Aquinas goes even further.

> There are two ways in which a thing can be found perfect. In the first, according to its own being, in what is proper to it according to its own rightful species. But because the specific being of one thing is distinct from the specific being of another thing, the result is that in every created thing the perfection which it possesses lacks absolute perfection in the degree to which equal perfections are possessed by all other species, in such a way that the perfection of anything considered in itself alone is imperfect, as being only part of the total perfection of the universe, which is born from the union of all these particular perfections gathered together into it.

> And therefore, in order that there may be a remedy for this imperfection, another mode of perfection is found in created things, according as the perfection which is the property of a thing is itself found in another thing. Such is the perfection of knowing in so far as it is such, for in the degree to which it knows, the known in a certain way exists in it . . . And according to this mode of perfection it is possible that the perfection of the entire universe may exist in a single and particular thing. (Aquinas, *De Veritate* 2: 2)

The power of this way of understanding knowledge should be apparent. For Aristotle and the commentators knowledge is a means of 'connaturality' and exit from our finitude. It is a way of sharing in the perfection of all things. As we ourselves expand through knowledge so too does our love, for loving the object of our knowledge is really just an extension of our own self-love. We naturally take an active interest in the well-being and development of everything, because that well-being and development is really and truly our own. And if we should be able to rise to knowledge of God then, to the extent of our knowledge, we also become God, and share in God's creative activity.

But before we can address the question of God – or even, for that matter, assess the adequacy of this theory of knowledge as an account of what happens in pre-scientific and scientific knowledge, we must confront a major ambiguity in Aristotle's theory. Aristotle left the status of the Potential and Agent Intellects rather undefined. On the one hand, the intellect is a power of the soul, which is the form of the body, and would appear to be something individual. On the other hand, the intellect for Aristotle must be an immaterial principle. This is required if it is to be connatural with intelligible and therefore immaterial objects of knowledge. While material things are individuated by matter, so that there is, for example, more than one cat and more than one human, immaterial principles are individuated by their species. Having no matter, they cannot differ from each other in spatio-temporal place or extension, or in the degree to which or the accidentally different ways in which they realize their latent potential. Immaterial principles are fully and completely what they are, and can be individuated only by differences at this most essential level – that is, by species. There is, in other words, only one immaterial principle of each species. This would suggest that there is, in fact, only one actual or Agent Intellect for all of humanity (von Steenberghen 1980: 29–74).

The issue became hotly contested with the revival of Aristotelian ideas in the Islamic empire and later in medieval Europe. Ibn Sina (Avicenna) regarded intellection as a fundamentally divine activity and treated the Agent Intellect as the lowest of the intelligences which emanates from the unmoved mover. This Agent Intellect was responsible for creating the forms of all material objects and for 'informing' the individual 'potential intellects' of each individual with the essence of the objects it experienced. The result is what amounts to a theory of 'angelic' rather than divine illumination, cast in slightly different language, but sharing all of the problems of the former doctrine and perhaps a few more.

Later commentators, such as Ibn Rushd (Averroes) went further, arguing that not only the Agent but also the Passive Intellect is one – that we know universals not with individual minds but with a single collective mind which, in effect, does our thinking for us, using individual human animals essentially as data collectors. Here again the principal argument is that intellection, even the passive reception of forms, is a fundamentally immaterial activity. This is a point which is accepted implicitly even by opponents of monopsychism such as Thomas, who allow that the angels, which are wholly immaterial, nonetheless move from potency to act in knowing the universe through their own essence and through species infused by God – that is, by a sort of intellectual revelation. Because of the immateriality of the intellect there can be only one intellect for each species.

Ibn Rushd and his followers were fully aware, of course, that different people have different ideas. This does not present a problem for them. The single intellect is naturally ordered to individuals and, as it makes use of the differing images produced by the differing sensory experiences of those individuals, its activity in them is also different, producing the appearance of individuals doing their own thinking. Even so, monopsychism presented, and presents, very serious problems. While it is still possible to account for our experience of doing our own thinking, the explanation offered is very roundabout and hardly meets basic standards of economy. It also seems to compromise not only personal immortality, but also the integrity, freedom and responsibility of the human person. Immortality in the Aristotelian tradition is connected with immateriality. The intellect, as an immaterial power, is also immortal. But if there is only one intellect for all of humanity, then this immortality would not be personal in any meaningful sense. Similarly, personality itself, together with moral responsibility, is generally associated with the intellect. But if there is only one intellect for all of humanity, it is difficult to see how individual human beings could be held responsible for their actions which would seem, rather, to be acts of humanity as a whole determined by the particular sense data collected by the individual in question.

Still, the argument for the doctrine is very strong. As von Steenberghen points out, unless one is willing to depart from a strict Aristotelian metaphysics, which is otherwise so powerful, it is in fact quite unavoidable (von Steenberghen 1980: 33). There is no way for an immaterial principle to be generated in time and individuated by matter. Thomas's solution from this standpoint is also unsatisfactory. He takes as his starting point the psychology of the *De Anima*, which he deploys against both the monopsychists and the prevailing dualistic anthropology of the Augustinians, which distinguished in human beings two distinct substances, body and soul, which however intimately united in this life, are fundamentally distinct from each other (von Steenberghen 1980: 44–5). Human beings, Thomas argues, are one single substance composed of both form and matter, but the human soul is different from mineral, plant and animal souls in being an immaterial and subsisting form, which is therefore incorruptible and immortal. This soul is, furthermore, directly created by God at the end of the biological process which leads to the production of a new human individual (von Steenberghen 1980: 45–7). The problem with this approach is that the economy which is gained at the psychological level is lost – and then some – at the metaphysical level when Thomas posits the special creation of each individual human soul. This claim is, furthermore, entirely incompatible with his larger Aristotelian metaphysics, in which new individuals are always and only drawn from the potency of matter by the action of God as final cause. For this reason we must regard the problem as still unresolved.

If, perhaps, the reader is thinking that this is an odd medieval debate that has very little real import for our own understanding of the nature of knowledge, let us point out that it is largely convertible with contemporary debates regarding the relation between the brain, or the nervous system generally, and the intellect, a debate we already entered earlier in this chapter. It will be recalled that, on the one hand, human intellection as we experience it seems indissolubly tied to the brain and its capacity to produce images and relate them to each other. This would seem to argue for the individuality of the intellect, though not necessarily for the details of Thomas's theory. On the other hand, we have not been able to identify anything in the brain which accounts for the full range of processes we call intellectual. At best, neuropsychology allows us to theorize intellection as 'information processing', that is, a complex system of mappings between images or bits of data. This approach cannot account for the teleological ordering to an end which is constitutive of human intellection – and indeed even of animal sensation. Thus the enduring tendency to see intellect or mind as something immaterial. But here we run up against the powerful logic of Aristotle's metaphysics. How can something which is immaterial be differentiated from other immaterial things except by its essential nature? Thus the incoherence of dualist approaches which posit a mind separate from the brain and body, but somehow also individual and unique to a particular human organizm. One cannot help but wish that we could identify something which is somehow 'less material' than the brain, which could account for the intellect's ordering to an end, but not so 'wholly immaterial' that it was incapable of individuation apart from essential difference.

Among the medieval sources there is only one hint of such a conception, and it comes from someone who was a poet first, and a philosopher only second – but a political philosopher, and this is the key. I am referring to Dante Alighieri. Dante had been influenced by the Latin Averroists, and especially by Siger de Brabant. Even so, he rejected the unity of the intellect for all of the very good reasons we have cited above. Still it seemed to him that knowledge was not merely an affair of the individual, or even of the individual and God. Rather, the intellect develops in interaction with other human beings, and it takes humanity as a whole, collectively, to realize the full potential of the human intellect. Thus the importance of institutions, such as the university and the church which can promote the development of the human intellect, and thus the importance of the empire, which secures the public order necessary for the existence of such institutions, which centralizes and allocates the resources which they need to carry out their functions, and which leads humanity in the struggle for justice, which, as we shall see, is itself a way of knowing (Dante Alighieri, *De Monarchia*, Gilson 1968: 167).

Dante's solution to the debate around the Agent Intellect appears not to have been taken up by other medieval thinkers, and with the triumph of neo-Augustinian voluntarism and nominalism in the fourteenth century and the rise of rationalist and empiricist epistemologies after that the whole problematic of which it was a part was abandoned entirely. It is only in the nineteenth century that the idea that knowledge is a social act re-emerges and in fact becomes a central theme for philosophy and for the new discipline of sociology. The most important sources for this sort of reflection are Durkheim, Hegel and Marx.

Durkheim occupies a unique position in European intellectual history. He is, on the one hand, part of the great movement of secularization which swept France during the nineteenth century. As a Jew, Durkheim was intensely aware of the oppression his people had suffered at the hands of the Catholic Church and the Catholic State, and could not help but regard secularization as the precondition for liberation. Indeed, Durkheim's assignment, as the first Professor of Education at the University of Bordeaux, was to lay the theoretical foundations for a new secular educational system after the definitive victory of lay forces in 1870. At the same time Durkheim was intensely aware of the contradictions of liberal capitalist society and sought to combat the anomie and egoism – the sense of meaninglessness and social disintegration – which he had discovered in his study on *Suicide*, without yielding ground to the traditionalist forces which were still so powerful in French society. Among other things this involved him in an attempt to reground science, morality and religion in a way which transcended both the alienating individualism of the liberals and the authoritarianism of the traditionalists.

In approaching these tasks he drew on the resources of French traditionalism, as they had already been partially transformed by Comte and the positivists. Thinkers like de Maistre and de Bonald, the principal theoreticians of reaction in the wake of the French Revolution, had focused attention on the role of religion generally and ritual in particular, in constituting and maintaining the social order. As we have already noted they regarded the social order, including language and religion, as part of a primitive revelation which provided humanity with the tools it needed in order to think – and indeed survive. Comte and the other positivists had turned this theory on its head, arguing that society was not a divine creation, but rather that God was a social creation, and that it is human society itself which is the real object of worship, something which Comte attempted to make explicit with his system of socialatry.

Durkheim continues this line of development, but gives it a uniquely Jewish flavour, something which allows him to avoid both the authoritarianism of the traditionalists and the simple-minded anticlericalism of the positivists. And he does so with the clear intention of providing a solution to the epistemological, metaphysical and ethical quandaries which were facing his generation. Indeed, it is impossible to read the last paragraph of *Elementary Forms of Religious Life* without thinking that he was at least approaching a solution similar to our own, and may even have been aware of the debate around the Agent Intellect.

> Up to the present, thinkers were placed before this double alternative: either explain the superior and specific faculties of men by connecting them to the inferior forms of his being, the reason to the senses, or the mind to matter, which is equivalent to denying their uniqueness; or else attach them to some super-experimental reality which was postulated, but whose existence could be established by no observation. What put them in this difficulty was the fact that the individual passed as being the *finis naturae* – the ultimate creation of nature; it seemed that there was nothing beyond him or at least nothing that science could touch. But from the moment when it is recognized that above the individual there is society, and that this is not a nominal being created by reason, but a system of active forces, a new manner of explaining men becomes possible. To conserve his distinctive traits it is no longer necessary to put them outside experience. At least, before going to this last extremity, it would be well to see if that which surpasses the individual, though it is within him, does not come from this super-individual reality which we experience in society. (Durkheim [1911] 1965: 496)

Thus, in his *Elementary Forms of Religious Life* (Durkheim [1911] 1965), Durkheim demonstrates that the structure of human communities provides a kind of model for structuring human experience of the universe as a whole. Participation in even the simplest society provides the basis in experience for the idea of whole and part, relationship and a rudimentary idea of the connectedness of things. Participation in a tribe, with an intricate kinship system, provides a basis for the development of more complex schemes of classification and thus a rudimentary sense of structure. At the same time, it is the sense of being part of something larger than ourselves, an experience which we have immediately only in human society, which provides the basis for religious belief and practice. On the one hand Durkheim agrees with the positivists that religion is a social product. On the other hand, he seems to suggest that far from holding back the development of human capacities, religion is constitutive of society, morality and science.

This is neither a positivist reductionism nor a traditionalist doctrine of primitive revelation. Rather, it is the old Jewish doctrine of *da'ath elohim* – a knowledge of God which is grounded first and foremost in fulfilment of the law, that is, in ethical conduct. This is apparent in Durkheim's account of ritual. Ritual, for Durkheim, is not the original but rather the crystallized and routinized form of collective effervescence. The original moments of collective effervescence are moments of great revolutionary upheaval.

> In such moments of collective ferment are born the great ideals upon which civilizations rest. These periods of creation or renewal occur when men for various reasons are led into a closer relationship with each other, when reunions and assemblies are most frequent, relationships better maintained and the exchange of ideas most active. Such was the great crisis of Christendom . . . in the twelfth and thirteenth centuries. Such were the Reformation and the Renaissance, the revolutionary epoch and the Socialist upheavals of the nineteenth century. At such moments this higher form of life is lived with such intensity and exclusiveness that it monopolizes all minds to the more or less complete exclusion of egoism and the commonplace. At such times the ideal tends to become one with the real, and men have the impression that the time is close when the ideal will in fact be realized and the Kingdom of God established on earth. (Durkheim in Bellah 1973: 1)

Durkheim hoped fervently for the renewal of such collective effervescence in his own time, and had little doubt concerning its probable source.

> Who does not feel . . . that in the depths of society an intense life is developing . . . We aspire to a higher justice which no existing formulas express . . . One may even go further and say with some precision in what region of society these new forces are forming: it is in the popular classes. (Durkheim in Bellah 1973: xlvii)

The implication here is that through the collective effervescence generated by revolutionary practice – by seeking a higher justice – we actually discover new principles, both of explanation and of action. It is these principles which, in turn, ground a new and more complex social order. Durkheim does, to be sure, remain a bit ambiguous on this latter point, stopping short of a well-defined epistemological and metaphysical realism. He seems particularly reluctant to take the step of explicitly acknowledging any principle higher than human society. But this is where the logic of his argument points. And we may cross into that promised land even if he – like Moses – chooses to remain on the far side of the Jordan.

Within the dialectical tradition itself reflection on the nexus between theory and practice becomes central beginning with Hegel, whose *Phenomenology* (Hegel [1807] 1967) presents the development of consciousness towards Absolute Knowledge as a real historical process in which labour, politics, art, religion and philosophy all play a constitutive role. Hegel is quite clear that the Idea can become conscious of itself in Art, Religion and Philosophy only when mediated through the Ethical Life of the Family, Civil Society and the State. We even see in Hegel an understanding of the centrality of the class struggle – something which comes through in the 'master-slave dialectic'. Far from being a one-sided idealist, Hegel's claim is that living in increasingly complex ways involves thinking in increasingly complex ways, so that over the course of history we become capable of understanding the Idea, or organizing principle of the universe, in an ever more adequate manner.

This new focus on the historical development of the intellect informs an otherwise essentially Aristotelian theory of knowledge. In order to understand Hegel's epistemology – as opposed to his original insights into the social character of cognition – it is necessary to turn from the *Phenomenology* to the *Encyclopaedia* (Hegel [1830] 1971), and specifically to the Third Part, the *Philosophy of Spirit*. Here Hegel begins with what amounts to an account of the biological basis of consciousness – what he calls Anthropology – and summarizes the account which he gave in the *Phenomenology* of its historical development. Only then does he turn, in a subsection which he calls Psychology, to an account of the actual act of knowledge. And this account is solidly Aristotelian, even if it differs in certain points from Thomas and is enriched by Hegel's historical insight.

Hegel is quite clear that knowledge begins with sensation of an immediate, material object (Hegel, *Encyclopaedia* para. 445–7). It proceeds through what he calls 'attention' which recognizes the object as something distinct from but related to it (para. 448), to 'intuition' or a mental vision of the object (para. 448). The intuition is then internalized by the mind in an image, which can be stored in memory and reproduced in imagination (para. 450–64). From this image the understanding (*Verstand*) produces a universal (species, genus) which can then be related to other universals in various laws (para. 465–7). The universal is referred back to the concrete individual in the judgement (para. 467), advancing finally to reason (*Vernunft*) which knows itself to be identical to the object (para. 467–8).

Now clearly one could identify certain differences between this account of the act of knowledge and that of Aristotle or Thomas. While it is not always clear what Hegel means by the term, the notion of an intuition of the concrete singular *may* suggest something more characteristic of Scotus than of Thomas. Hegel stresses even more than Thomas that the lower sensory powers are subsumed under the higher intellectual powers when these are present, so that his understanding of the image and the imagination, for example is more clearly intellectualized. Even so, it must be remembered that for Thomas as well sensory cognition in humans is 'formed' by the intellect. Hegel must stop to make it clear that the active role of what he calls intuition (and what Thomas would have called the common sense) in shaping the image does not mean that the form it receives (spatial, temporal) is purely subjective, as Kant claimed, but rather what he calls an 'honouring' of the form given to the object by the Infinite Mind – that is, God, quite independent of individual consciousness. At the same time the broad outlines of Hegel's theory track those of Aristotle and Aquinas, and set him off clearly from any of the principal alternatives.

Even the single claim which sets Hegel apart sharply from Aristotle and Aquinas – the claim that we can actually *comprehend* the absolute idea or the divine essence – in fact arises from premises shared by Hegel with his Aristotelian predecessors. This is the notion of connaturality – that the knower potentially, and in the act of knowledge actually, becomes connatural with the object. We must not become confused by differences in language. Between the Aristotelian claim that the Idea of the Good awakens in matter a latent potential for form which perfects itself in the intellect and the will, leading to the emergence of a human society organized and directed by knowledge of the Good, and the Hegelian claim that the Idea externalizes itself in

Nature and gradually becomes conscious of itself in Spirit (human society) as human beings develop an increasingly adequate understanding of the Idea there is (once we are clear that matter is just the potential for organization, and not in any sense a thing) simply a difference without a real distinction. Both accounts, as we have seen, stress the role of ethical conduct in intellectual development, and thus the absolutely central role of human society in mediating the production of knowledge. Where Hegel differs *really* is only in his claim that over the course of human history we become sufficiently complex to share fully and actually, rather than only partially and incompletely, in the divine essence both in theory and practice.

It must be recognized here that Hegel is at once achieving a profound insight and at the same time making a grave error. The insight is that as human society becomes more complex, so too does our capacity to know, because (to revert to our way of describing the act of knowledge) the forms which illuminate the images we garner from sense experience have also become more complex. Furthermore, this growing complexity is tantamount to deeper connaturality with God. He even comes close to specifying for us the nature of this growth in connaturality. As the master/slave dialectic demonstrates, it is the servant and not the master, the worker and not the consumer, who has a basis in experience for grasping the organizing principle which brings the universe into being, because it is they who participate in the creative activity of the universe and thus share its creative nature. Marx, of course, allows us to deepen this insight enormously, without some of the undesirable metaphysical baggage – though also, unfortunately, without the explicit recognition that he has discovered the profound depths of human connaturality with God.

It is one thing, however, to say that we share *in* the divine essence, and that, for example, the greater productive capacity of human societies in the wake of the Industrial Revolution somehow increases this share; it is quite another to say that we actually *share* the same essence – that we are simply God becoming conscious of himself. Contemporary Hegelians such as Errol Harris recognize this difference and make far more modest claims for human cognition (Harris 1991, 1992). And there is, indeed, evidence in Hegel for this interpretation. The Idea in the *Logic* is, after all, the Idea of the Good, which acts always and only as final cause. Once we take this into account, the resulting system looks far more Aristotelian.

Dialectical materialism builds on Hegel's insights, even if it sometimes also gives it a reductive turn. Hegel's account of the historical development of human knowledge is set in the context of a larger metaphysics and cosmology in which nature and history themselves represent the self-realization of the Idea, so that his focus on the rootedness of knowledge in social practice is often lost. Marx, on the other hand, makes it clear that 'it is not the consciousness of men which determines their existence but, on the contrary, it is their social existence which determines their consciousness' (Marx [1859] 1966: 217). Marx further specifies that social existence is first of all productive existence.

> In the social production of their means of existence men enter into definite, necessary relations which are independent of their will, productive relationships which correspond to a definite stage of development of their material productive forces. The aggregate of these productive relationships constitutes . . . the real basis on which a juridical and political superstructure

arises and to which definite forms of social consciousness correspond. (Marx [1859] 1966: 217)

And it is not new ideas which catalyse social revolutions, but rather blockages in the process of technological development.

> At a certain stage of their development the material productive forces come into contradiction with the existing productive relationships, or what is but a legal expression for these, the property relationships within which they had moved before. From forms of development of the productive forces these relationships are transformed into their fetters. Then an epoch of social revolution opens. (Marx [1859] 1966: 218)

These insights permitted later dialectical materialists to analyse in depth the impact of both forces and relations of production on the human intellect. It is worth citing here not only critical studies, such as Lenin's investigation of the social basis and political valence of positivism (Lenin [1908] 1970) and Lukacs's social history of irrationalism (Lukacs [1953] 1980), but also a number of studies which analyse the social conditions for epistemological progress. Bogdanov (Bogdanov [1928] 1980), for example, pointed out the role of the village community, in which each individual has a definite function in the context of a complex division of labour directed towards a common end, for the emergence of the idea of organization, and of the universe as an organized, meaningful system. Working from a very different perspective, Lukacs (Lukacs [1922] 1971) made a convincing case that, in so far as the proletariat embodies without modification the universal human nature – which is to labour or create – its standpoint is in fact the standpoint of totality. Perhaps most important, however, is the work of Soviet psychologist Aleksandr Luria (Luria [1974] 1976), who worked in Uzbekistan in the late 1920s and early 1930s, during the period of forced collectivization. He compared cognitive development across many dimensions (perception, generalization, inference, problem solving and so on) among both traditional villagers and people who were participating in collective farms or receiving rudimentary formal education. The results were startling. Traditional villagers simply didn't see particular shapes or colours as falling under larger categories, such as square or circle, blue or green. Each shape and colour was treated as unique, often compared to some specific sort of object which it closely resembled – a fruit for example. Indeed, the traditional villagers lacked any real concept of systematic classification at all. Given a series such as 'hatchet, log, saw, hammer', and asked to identify which member of the series did not belong, they almost uniformly said that all were 'necessary', the log to work on and the other things to do the work. Formalization of problems in terms of a closed logical system was foreign to them. Collective farm workers and those receiving formal education, on the other hand, readily performed all these tasks much as a Moscow office worker or school teacher might.

As we saw with Hegel, the dialectical materialist account of the social determination of knowledge informs an essentially Aristotelian epistemology. Neither Marx nor Engels really address this question in any depth, except to affirm Hegel's dialectical penetration of the inner logic of things, and to reject what they saw as the idealist element in Hegel's account of how we arrive at this dialectical penetration, by which they mean the notion that our knowledge is the self-consciousness of the divine Idea. We have also noted that their failure to address this question led to no end of controversy within the dialectical materialist tradition. Some, such as Bogdanov, gravitated for a while to empiricism; others, such as Deborin and Lukacs, adopted an essentially Hegelian approach, treating dialectical knowledge as the self-consciousness not, however, of God, but rather of the working class, without addressing the question of how or in what sense such knowledge would be objective. Lenin, on the other hand, opted for what he called the 'reflection theory' or 'copy theory', hints of which are already present in Engels. According to this view knowledge takes place in two stages. Sensation involves 'the transformation of the energy of external excitation into a state of consciousness' (Lenin [1908] 1970: 39). In the second stage mental representations are transformed into abstractions. Regarding exactly how these two moves take place, dialectical materialism has been little interested; its main concern has been to establish the objectivity of sensation – that is, that even such qualities as colour, smell, taste and so on, are real qualities of the object perceived – and to argue for the ability of abstract ideas, including the ability to grasp the inner essence or organizing principle of material systems (Wetter 1958: 498–507). What we have here is simply a very schematic Aristotelianism – more a set of dogmatic safeguards against doctrines deemed to be erroneous than a fully developed theory. It is this approach which became dominant in the Soviet Union.

It remains to be demonstrated however, that in socializing and historicizing the Agent Intellect, we have not opened the floodgates for relativism and undermined the possibility of any authentic knowledge of intelligibles. If society *is* the Agent Intellect, aren't these 'intelligibles' merely social products, artefacts of the way particular societies organize themselves, useful, perhaps, for understanding the customs and mores of the societies in question but hardly a window on the organization of the universe, much less on God and the transcendental principles of value? Indeed, to claim universality for the ideas of a particular group is to generate a 'totalizing metanarrative' which covers totalitarian ambitions.

This objection, which has become commonplace among our postmodernists and 'deconstructionists' (Lyotard [1979] 1984) is really just a version of the one we have addressed twice above – once with respect to the senses and once with respect to the intellect in general. There can be no doubt that human societies, like the sensory systems of various animal species, are finite and can reveal only part of the systems which they perceive. There is, furthermore, no doubt that the part of reality which is revealed by these structures is selected by the needs of the social systems in question, just as animals develop those senses which serve their adaptive strategies.

Two points are, however, in order. First, Marx argues that some social locations are epistemologically privileged relative to others – that is, that certain social locations offer better insight into reality than other social locations. This principle, though never formally stated, is the basis of the whole discipline of ideological criticism which is so central to Communist theory and practice. Let us see how it is grounded.

Labour for Marx is central not because of some arbitrary option for the working classes but rather because it is for him, as for Engels, an expression (in fact the most advanced expression) of the evolution of matter from lower to higher degrees of organization – an evolution which Engels analyses in detail in his *Dialectics of Nature* (Engels [1880] 1940). The standpoint of labour is, therefore, the standpoint of the universe itself. While exploiting classes do, indeed, see aspects of reality, something which allows them to make their own distinctive historic contributions, workers grasp the organizing principle of reality as such. The struggle between social classes is, among other things, a struggle for epistemic primacy.

Further guarantees against relativism are provided by the test of practice. Ideas that work are ideas which have a basis in reality. Abstractions which help a society to survive and flourish must disclose something important about the way the universe really works, just as well-adapted sensory systems disclose something important about an animal's environment. Ideas and systems of ideas which lead to stagnation and decline are probably flawed in some way. And this is all we really need in order to show that abstractions are not *merely* social products which have no relationship whatsoever with the organization of the universe, but rather products of an interaction between human beings and the world which discloses real if limited truths, truths which can be tested in practice and then serve as the basis for further development.

This suggests that the truth of ideas can be judged by their political impact. Ideas which help to legitimate systems which hold back the development of human social capacities cannot be true. This is the basis of the whole enterprise of ideological criticism which is so central to the socialist movement. Validation of this latter claim will have to wait until we have analysed the nature of the higher, transcendental form of abstraction in Chapter 6. We will then show that the doctrine, which is essentially a claim that something which is evil cannot also be true, can be upheld on the basis of the convertibility of the transcendentals, specifically of the Good and the True.

But if dialectical materialism has avoided relativism, it has not always avoided reductionism. Partly this was because Marx's polemic against Hegelian 'idealism' tended to simplify the complex interaction of theory and practice. Production is, after all, an intellectual act, which depends on an understanding of physical, biological and social organization and which advances only as science advances. This much has been acknowledged by later dialectical materialists who treat science as itself a productive force.

More important, however, was the transformation of the critique of religious alienation into a critique of religion as such. Marx largely took over Feuerbach's critique of religion (Feuerbach [1841] 1957). Feuerbach regarded religion as a projection or alienation of our underlying human creativity. We deny that we are creative, powerful, wise and loving and ascribe these qualities to God instead. The result is passivity and social stagnation. Marx added that this alienation was itself a social product – the result of living in a society in which people experience their creative capacity as the property of others rather than themselves (Marx [1843] 1978, [1844] 1978, [1846] 1978). As Moses Hess (Avineri 1985) pointed out, this theory provides both an apt characterization of German Protestantism in the early nineteenth century and a good analysis of its social basis, but as a global theory of religion it leaves a great deal to be desired. Not all religions deny human creativity, power, wisdom, or goodness or pit these against divine transcendence in the manner of evangelical Christianity. More to the point, Marx's global rejection of religion both reflects and leads to profound inconsistencies. In criticizing bourgeois economics, for example, Marx does not conclude that the social location of the bourgeoisie causes them to imagine the marketplace in a world that does not have one, but only that it causes them to misunderstand it, or more precisely to fail to grasp the real laws which govern its operations. The same should be true of religious claims, which often, but need not always, reflect the deforming impact of alienated social relations.

We have already noted, furthermore, that Marx's claim for the epistemological superiority of the standpoint of the proletariat is grounded in the claim that as producers workers carry forward the general movement of matter towards ever higher degrees of organization which, from the standpoint of dialectical materialism, is the motive force behind the whole cosmo-historical evolutionary process. But if this evolutionary dynamic continues into infinity, it terminates (logically) in a system which realizes all logically possible forms of organization – that is, in God. To reject the idea of God is to say that this evolution is not infinite but, rather, gives way to entropy or some other disintegrating principle. This, of course, is precisely the position which Engels (however reluctantly) took in the *Dialectics of Nature* (Engels [1890] 1940). The result is to make the drive towards higher degrees of organization (and thus labour or creativity) into just one tendency in the universe, and ultimately the losing one. Apart from a doctrine of God which establishes creativity as a value, it is difficult to say why the standpoint of the creative class (labour) should somehow be more fundamental than that of the consuming class (capital). The proletariat loses the cosmological and ontological basis for its claim to epistemological superiority, and dialectical materialism is reduced to one class ideology among others. Reductionism, in other words, leads inevitably back to relativism.

Dialectical materialism, like Durkheimian sociology, seems reluctant to cross over into the promised land of a complete and consistent epistemological and metaphysical realism. But the steps that Durkheim and Marx failed to take we have shown to be both possible and necessary if we are to build on the strengths and resolve the contradictions of the epistemology bequeathed to us by Aristotle, Aquinas and the medieval commentators. And our solution begins with the insight, due above all to Durkheim and Marx, that the act of the human intellect, while it clearly involves the nervous system and perhaps the whole body also, in some way seems to involve the society as a whole, which alone provides to the nervous system of the individual, who is involved in the society, a direct, living, but not strictly sensory experience of the complex categorical systems, structural relationships and 'orderings to an end' which characterize intelligibles. These intelligible categories, structures and orderings to an end, existing actually in human society, illuminate the images we garner from sensory experience and allow us to discover in them their intelligible structure – or at least those dimensions of their intelligible structure which our social system is sufficiently complex to permit us to comprehend. Human society *is*, in other words, the Agent Intellect (at least for humanity), the faculty which enables us to abstract from sense-images the intelligible essence of things and thus to know what they are. The Aristotelian Potential Intellect, on the other hand, is located in the nervous system and specifically in the neural networks which link images to each other and to various body states.

How, exactly, should we characterize this 'not strictly sensory experience' of the intelligible organization of human society? Here we must have recourse to a concept which we have thus far only mentioned, but which will become increasingly central to our entire argument: the concept of connatural knowledge. It is, first of all, the connaturality between sensible objects and our external and internal sense organs – the fact that they are physical systems – which makes sensation possible in the first place. But there is more. According to Thomas, there are certain things which we know because they form a part of who and what we are. Thus a virtuous person judges rightly individual cases pertaining to a virtue because that virtue has become 'second nature' for her. This knowledge is immediate and nonconceptual; the judgement is made without reference to a mental word or definition. Similarly, the Australian aborigine of Durkheim's *Elementary Forms of Religious Life* knows additive classification[4] because her own identity as a member of a particular clan, phratry and tribe is defined by such a system. When she turns to the images garnered from sensory experience, therefore, she naturally applies such a classificatory system, even though if asked to define additive classification she would not understand what is being asked. In much the same way, someone who lives in a complex market society, in which relations between people can be represented using complex mathematical formalisms, knows those mathematical formalisms implicitly, and when he turns to the images garnered from the senses – or rather to categorical or taxonomic universals abstracted from those images – is able to discover therein similar formal relationships. Indeed, they can do this before they or anyone else have adequately formalized the mathematics involved. Calculus developed on the heels of Newtonian physics, not vice versa. And people who live in communities ordered to an intelligible end (villages or states which have a common conscious aim, for example) know implicitly the 'ordering to' which is constitutive of the transcendental properties of Being (the Beautiful, the True, the Good and the One) long before they have elaborated an adequate metaphysical theory. This is what we mean when we say that living in a certain kind of society provides a 'basis in experience' for the development of certain ideas.

This nonconceptual, experiential knowledge exists fully and actually only at the level of the social system itself. It becomes available to the individual only to the extent that the individual is socialized – that is, incorporated intellectually and morally into the system. This is why we say that the individual human intellect is merely potential and is actualized only in the context of human society. At the same time, we should note that the social intellect is not 'single' or 'separated' in the manner of the Agent Intellect of the Radical Aristotelians. As a separated substance, the Agent Intellect of Ibn Rushd and his followers was radically simple and uniform. It really was, in his eyes, one mind thinking for us. The differences between the ideas of one individual and the next could be explained only in terms of the differences between the sense-data they collected. And since the Averroist Potential Intellect is also one, there is no sense in which the individual human being is ever actualized intellectually, and thus no sense in which we transcend the condition of finite animal systems. The solution which we are suggesting, on the other hand, does not suffer from these difficulties.

---

[4] Classification systems may be either additive or multiplicative. Additive systems simply break larger taxa down into smaller components, creating the kind of classificatory tree used by taxonomists to classify living things. Thus Animals may be Arthropods, Molluscs, Chordates and so on. Chordates may be Fish, Amphibians, Reptiles, Birds or Mammals. Mammals may be Insectivorous, Rodents, Ungulates, Lagomorphs, Carnivores or Primates . . . In a multiplicative classification, on the other hand, there are two or more series of cross-cutting categories running along distinct dimensions: for example, red, blue, green and wood, metal, plastic. Classification, as we will see in Chapter 3 is, in fact, a kind of concrete mathematics which implies, though it has not yet attained, the formalism of abstract mathematics (Piaget 1952).

Human societies are complex, highly differentiated systems which integrate diverse and incommensurate structural elements, articulated across different regions of the social space. Even in highly marketized societies like our own, communitarian and tributary elements survive, and socialist tendencies are beginning to emerge. These diverse structural elements, furthermore, affect different groups of people in different degrees. Unlike the single, separated intellect of the Averroists, the social intellect is complex and diverse. It should also be noted that our approach avoids the metaphysical problems implicit in the doctrine of St Thomas. It will be recalled that this problem arose because of the apparent immateriality of the intellect – our inability to account adequately for the act of knowledge on the basis of physical or biological systems like the human nervous system, or what Aristotle and Thomas would have called the vegetative and animal souls. At the same time, asserting the immateriality of intellect seemed to imply necessarily that it is unique in its species, and also ungenerated and thus eternal. Thomas escaped this dilemma only with a highly unsatisfactory doctrine of the special creation of each human soul at the end of the biological process which produces a new human animal. This seems to multiply forms of causation unnecessarily. Our solution avoids these problems. When we say that intellection is immaterial what we are really saying is that it is 'formal', to use the Aristotelian-Thomistic term, or organized in a degree that cannot be accounted for by purely physical or biological processes. Thus our inability to account for the act of knowledge in purely neurophysiological terms. This does not mean, however, that the intellect is entirely immaterial. Indeed, if we understand the relation of matter to form as the relation of potency to act, then since only God is Pure Act, only God is purely immaterial. And since society is not purely immaterial, there is no reason why it cannot be individuated by matter (that is, by the potential to develop in different directions), with numerous different societies realizing their latent potential differently and numerous different individuals internalizing the 'form' of the society to a different degree and in a different way. Nor is there any reason why societies cannot be generated from matter like any other material form, through the univocal action of God as final cause, which awakens the potential for organization which is latent in all matter and cultivates it by the power of teleological attraction. The result is an account of causation which is at once perfectly materialistic, because organization emerges from matter as the realization of matter's own latent potential and not as an imposition from above, and perfectly spiritual, because it is God alone with her immeasurable Beauty, Truth, Goodness and Integrity which can account adequately for the motion of matter, which as pure potential really isn't anything, towards the perfection of form and the actuality of organization.[5]

It may be objected that the one thing our approach does not do – and which Thomas's does do – is to safeguard personal immortality. This is not really true. It is just that our theory requires a different approach to the problem. Remember, to begin with, that the soul is simply the form of the body. When the body dies, the form it would seem, disintegrates with it. Once, however, we establish the existence of God, it follows from the perfection of God that this form also exists intentionally and eternally in the mind of God. What God knows, furthermore, is not simply 'that we knew' but also our actual knowing, not simply 'that we willed' but also our actual willing. It follows

---

[5] This account of causation, which is at the heart of our cosmological and metaphysical theory, will be established briefly in a later chapter. A full account, however, will have to await a later work.

that the act of our knowing and willing is eternally present in the mind of God as an actual knowing and willing. This presence is, to be sure, different than anything we can imagine now, because it is immaterial. There is no further reception of new forms through sensation, no motion of the passions and our only experience of duration is the logical movement from one idea to the next. But it is a real knowing and willing, a consciousness if you will – indeed an eternal consciousness – of what we have become throughout the course of our lives. This is at least a reasonable argument for something like a natural personal immortality – and not too different in character from what Thomas had in mind.[6]

Once we have realized the social character of the Agent Intellect, the continuity between the ancient and the modern dialectic becomes easier to see. What is Hegel's *Phenomenology of Mind* if not an account of the development of the Agent Intellect through the complex struggles of human history until, at last, it reaches the point where it is able to comprehend the organizing principle of the universe itself – what Hegel calls Absolute Knowledge? What is Marx's doctrine that being determines consciousness except a recognition that connaturality is a condition for the possibility of knowledge? What is his claim – later restated with greater clarity by Lukacs – that the standpoint of the proletariat is the standpoint of totality, except a claim that one particular social class, because of its productive (that is, creative) character is more connatural with the self-organizing dynamic of the universe than the others? At the same time, situating Hegel, Marx and their interpreters in the context of the same tradition as Plato and Aristotle allows us both to validate the authentic insights which these thinkers achieved, and to locate the origin of the errors which led Hegel to claim for humanity a knowledge which can only be divine, and which led Marx and Engels to deny the existence of God altogether.

---

[6] More can be said on this point, but only after we have developed a more complete cosmology and metaphysics, something which will have to await other books. For now a few brief comments will have to suffice. It is important to remember that the human person cannot be identified with the matter which makes life possible, for we constantly exchange matter and energy with the environment and in this sense are by no means the same people we were even a few minutes ago. Nor can we lodge personal identity in the particular form or structure of either the body or the personality, since both of these also undergo constant change. Indeed, we cannot even ground identity in a particular unique purpose which the individual serves, since we are constantly growing and coming to understand our aim or purpose in new and more profound ways. And each of these particular aims or purposes is nothing more than a participation in Being as such, the Common End which moves all things. Rather, our identity is lodged in a particular trajectory, shaped by definite material conditions and physiological, psychological and social structures. What we are, each and every one of us, is a particular pathway towards God.

Now failure, decay and death are real, but success, which is success in Being, is conserved. This is true for individual pathways as for civilizations. Even after the death of the body, and indeed of the personality, the pathway along which that body and that personality travelled remains open, at least in so far as it was successful. And everything which *is* succeeds in some degree, and is thus conserved in some degree, and being conserved continues its movement towards God over an infinite period of time. Other bodies, other personalities will take up that pathway and follow it towards God. Or rather, God, who is the cause of all things, will draw new matter towards Herself along that pathway, along *our* pathway, giving us new life so that over an infinite period of time, we eventually realize our full potential. In this sense not only the universe as a whole but every system within it is ordered to God and ultimately realizes its end. It does so, however, by the free exercise of its own powers, without any other compulsion than the attractive power of God, and with the ever-present possibility of failure, death and disintegration.

The question remains, however, just how the alternative accounts of the intellect, which we have shown to be relatively less adequate than the theory of abstraction, might have arisen. Our epistemology gives us a potent tool for explaining alternative theories. For the purposes of this analysis, we need to divide these doctrines into four groups:

1   the empiricist variant of subjective idealism, which regards the act of the intellect as nothing more than a search for patterns in sense data or (in its contemporary information theoretical form) mappings between bits of information;
2   the rationalist variant of objective idealism, which understands the act of the intellect as exclusively an analysis of self-evident truths;
3   critical and subjective idealism which understand the act of the intellect to be immanent to the subject itself; and
4   the nonrationalist forms of objective idealism, which understand the act of the intellect in terms of illumination by or intuition of some superior (generally divine) principle.

We also need to account at least briefly for the social basis of the theory of abstraction and the larger dialectical tradition of which it forms a part, though we will return to this issue in greater depth in the next chapter.

Empiricism is straightforwardly a reflex of the market order. People who experience society as a system of only externally related individuals bouncing off of each other are apt to regard knowledge as, at least initially, the product of external interaction and thus of sensation. Higher order organizations in a market society, furthermore, tend to be fluid and cross-cutting and ordered to the limited purposes of individuals or groups of individuals. (This is by sharp contrast to the systematically hierarchized structures of archaic, tributary and socialist societies which are, furthermore, generally ordered to a single global end, be that the full development of human capacities or the luxury consumption of the ruling classes.) As a result, the intellect is seen simply as an instrument for making limited and relatively low order generalizations which link sense data in a way which has survival value or which serves some limited purpose. There is little sense that things have an underlying structure invisible to the senses or that they are ordered to an end.

Empiricism is the standpoint of the small capitalist or entrepreneur operating in a petty commodity, mercantile or competitive capitalist economy. As capitalism develops, however, the entrepreneur is either ruined or is gradually transformed into a manager or investor, whose concern is less and less with complex patterns of sense data and more and more with prices – first of all that of the factors of production and of the commodities he is trying to sell, and increasingly with such derivative prices as the rate of profit, the rate of interest and the prices of the various stocks and bonds in his portfolio. And a system of quantities (prices) is, at least in principle, susceptible to formalization. Soon people begin to think of the universe as a whole in much the same way. This leads to the emergence of mathematical physics, and gradually to the mathematization of all disciplines. Now mathematical formalisms, while they can arise from a process of fitting equations to data, can in principle at least also be derived logically from certain general premises. If these premises can be shown to be self-evident, then it is possible to construct a universal deductive science which comprehends the universe as a whole exclusively on the basis of an exercise of analytic reason. And this, of course is precisely the rationalist ideal.

We have already noted, in our analysis of the social basis of scepticism regarding the senses, how the gradual penetration of market relations into every sphere of life gradually undermines faith in the objectivity of sensation. The effect on reason's understanding of itself, and thus on the rationalist programme, is no less dramatic. In petty market societies where there remains a fixed frame of nonmarket relations against which exchange takes place, the existence of a fixed frame of space and time is also assumed. Indeed, in the early stages of commodification, where prices change very little and the idea of a natural price is thus commonplace, one even sees the notion (bizarre to us, but self-evident to the Pythagoreans) that every thing has its own 'number'. With the formation, globalization and (relative) perfection of markets in goods and services, labour and capital, this fixed frame gradually dissolves. Thus the emergence of relativistic and quantum physics and eventually of quantum cosmologies in which there are no fixed frames or independent variables. On the one hand this represents the triumph of mathematics, since in the newer theories less and less is given and more and more depends on the mathematical formalism. At the same time, mathematics itself faces a crisis as it attempts to ground itself in a purely analytic fashion – something which, as Gödel demonstrated, turns out to be quite impossible. At the philosophical level this is reflected in the turn of even the most determined rationalist philosophers to illumination (Descartes), sensation (Spinoza) or some combination thereof (Leibniz).

The impossibility of rationalism is nothing other than the impossibility of the marketplace – that is, its fundamental internal contradiction, which in turn requires the support of either a nonmarket periphery or a coercive state apparatus, or both. While it is only with Marx that these economic contradictions were understood scientifically (and then only in a preliminary and inadequate way), they already asserted themselves at the political and ideological levels by the end of the eighteenth century: politically in the form of internal contradictions within the 'third estate' which was then prosecuting the democratic revolution, and ideologically in the contradictions which Kant identified within and between rationalism and empiricism. Critical idealism is, above all, the philosophical embodiment of these contradictions, and the recognition of the impossibility of any resolution – within the framework of the market system. On the one hand Kant tries valiantly to salvage the gains of the scientific and democratic revolutions by supplying the 'metaphysical' foundations which rationalism and empiricism could not. On the other hand he can do so only in bourgeois terms – that is, only in terms of human subjectivity. The formalisms which govern the behaviour of the marketplace, after all, and of which the formalisms of mathematical physics are the ideological reflex, are formalisms which govern a fundamentally subjective quality – that is, price, which is not a quality of the object but something imposed on it by the operation of market forces. The commodity is the form in which the bourgeoisie intuits its object, price the category under which it comprehends them. This contradiction reappears at the ethical level as a contradiction between the 'formal' principles of right, which are essentially the bourgeois principles of property and contract, and the 'democratic' principles of morality, which require that each rational being be treated not as means, but only as an end – a norm from the standpoint of which the market system and all actors within it can only be condemned.

The bourgeoisie, of course, cannot afford to admit the existence of these contradictions, even in their sublimated, philosophical form. Thus the very real difference between Kant and nearly all of his 'Neo-Kantian' successors. Kant's insistence on the objectivity, as well as the inaccessibility, of the thing in itself marks the contradiction at the heart of bourgeois society. The later Neo-Kantian (and also neopositivist and phenomenological) tendency to abandon the thing in itself is first and foremost an attempt to dissolve this contradiction by denying the reality of the object behind the commodity, the value which underlies the price. As Lukacs points out (Lukacs [1953] 1980) this 'forgetting' of the thing in itself is accompanied, at the ethical level, by an abandonment of the Kantian insistence on treating all rational beings as ends in themselves in favour of an insistence on the 'uniqueness' of the individual, or any of a variety of other intentionally aristocratic ethical criteria. Where Kant must be regarded as an authentic democrat, albeit one who fails to transcend the constraints of bourgeois society, Neo-Kantian, neopositivist and phenomenological subjective idealism represents a more or less organic expression of the social reality of finance capital in its 'highest' stages of development.[7]

The various forms of objective idealism represent quite a different reality. On the one hand, they presuppose the emergence of a market system, at one or another degree of development. This is reflected at the epistemological level in both a scepticism regarding the senses, which we explained in Chapter 1, and the relatively privileged place granted to analytic reason, which we have seen is a reflex of the market system. At the ethical level the rootedness in a market reality is reflected in a more or less pessimistic reading of human nature, the first fully coherent statement of which is Augustine's. It is only in a society with a very significant market sector that people begin to experience themselves and others as fundamentally selfish and egoistic. But the objective idealist recognizes far more profoundly than the critical or subjective idealist the impossibility of the market order and of its ideological reflex, analytic reason. Thus the turn to illumination by, or intuition of, some higher, generally divine, principle. Sociologically this represents a turn to nonmarket institutions – Church, State, or some combination thereof to shore up the social order which the market destroys day by day.

---

[7] The social basis and political valence of the 'transcendental' variants of process philosophy (Hartshorne) and Thomism (Rahner, Lonergan) should be seen in this light. What these thinkers do is to recognize the fundamental necessity of an ontological ground to any coherent science, ethics or religion – and thus to the full development of human capacities. They argue further that, *contra* Kant, God is a condition for any possible experience, and not merely, as Kant claimed, a moral postulate. But they fail to transcend the realm of the subject which, for the reasons we have outlined above, is first and foremost the realm of the marketplace and the bourgeoisie. It is little wonder that at the political level the resulting theologies tended, on the one hand, to legitimate action to restrict and modify the operation of market forces in accord with general moral principles without, however, advocating a real break with the market order. For this reason it is legitimate to speak of 'liberal' Protestantism and 'liberal' Catholicism. For a contemporary work which reflects this problematic see Franklin Gamwell's *The Divine Good* (Gamwell 1990), which argues for the necessity of a divine τελος if ethics is to be properly grounded, but which refuses to define the Good in sufficiently substantive terms to permit, for example, rational decisions regarding resource allocation. Professor Gamwell's work on justice *Democracy on Purpose* (Gamwell 1999), similarly, defines the polity in terms of debate about the nature of the Good, a move which opens up the possibility of democratically-directed state intervention in the market, but which also makes agnosticism about fundamental questions of value the cornerstone of the political order, providing effective constitutional protection for bourgeois right.

Lukacs, whose principal point of reference is Schelling, regards objective idealism as an ideology of the Restoration, the period between 1815 and 1848 when the bourgeoisie, frightened by the radicalism of its proletarian allies in the democratic revolution, temporarily yielded politically to the feudal classes which it had just displaced in order to restore order. And in the specifically German situation there is, indeed, a case to be made for this analysis. A similar and perhaps even stronger argument can be made regarding French traditionalism. But his further conclusion that objective idealism always and everywhere represents a feudal ideology is unwarranted. First of all, the ideology arises only in the presence of a market sector and the contradictions which this produces.[8] In this sense its base is never in a purely nonmarket institution, but rather in a nonmarket institution which has undergone at least partial bourgeoisification. In the present period this usually means transformation into a rentier dependent on income from interest, dividends and so on. Second, the nonmarket institution to which the bourgeoisie turns is not always feudal in character. There is a strong case to be made that the Catholic Church, for example, integrates 'archaic' elements with feudal deformations – a claim the case for which we will make in detail in Chapter 3. Resources are extracted only partly by coercive means (rents, taxes, forced labour) and are used primarily to support activities which promote human development and only secondarily to support the luxury consumption of the hierarchy and to ideologically legitimate the feudal and/or upper-bourgeois strata from which much (but by no means all) of the hierarchy is drawn. Similarly, the state to which they turned might be democratic and even have significant socialist features, and contain social disintegration as much by investing in human development as by repressing social unrest. In some cases, there may even be a turn to the village community, as in the case of certain forms of populism. For this reason objective idealism must be regarded as an ideological strategy or even a cluster of similar strategies which can potentially serve to legitimate diverse regimes of social integration at the political-economic level.

Even within a single ideological lineage there may be fundamental differences in social basis and political valence. The arguably semi-feudal Schelling, for example, is an important ideological ancestor (via theologian Paul Tillich) of the North American sociologist Talcott Parsons. This is apparent in Parsons's notion that social order is determined in the final instance by the way in which a society perceives or (to use Schelling's term) intuits, ultimate reality. But Parsons can hardly be regarded as an apologist for feudalism or Restoration politics – on the contrary, he clearly represents an attempt to resolve the contradictions of capitalism by drawing on the moral authority of liberal Protestant churches and the regulatory authority of a state which has always been at least partially an instrument of Protestant reformism. This turn to Protestant congregations is even more apparent in Parsons's student Robert Bellah (Bellah *et al.* 1991). One might even regard certain forms of liberation theology as objective idealisms. This is especially true where political norms are sought on extra-rational

---

[8] Even Augustine, it must be remembered, wrote in the context of a market economy, albeit one which was disintegrating, and which had never advanced beyond the petty market stage. Augustinian objective idealism develops further in the medieval period, as one response to the reassertion of market forces which accompanied economic revival, and becomes dominant in the fourteenth century as contradictions begin to accumulate.

grounds in scripture and so on. What all variants of objective idealism share, however, is an attempt to ground knowledge (and thus love) in a direct illumination by, or intuition of, supersensibles, something which leads inevitably into the Augustinian trap which we noted in the previous chapter. Love of God and love of creation are pitted against each other, and it becomes very difficult to ground a doctrine of the ultimate meaningfulness of the universe or an ethics of social progress.[9]

Thus the importance of the theory of abstraction, and of the larger dialectical epistemology to which it is so central. There can, furthermore, be little doubt regarding the social basis of this theory. It lies in the working classes (peasant, artisan, proletarian, intelligentsia) which depend for their survival directly on labour which adds more to the universe than it takes away in consumption, and the very nature of which involves a practical engagement with the physical, biological and social universe. It is precisely this sort of interaction which at once teaches the basic reliability of the senses, and the need to transcend the purely sensible – to classify, to comprehend the underlying structure of things, and to reason regarding the ends to which they are ordered.

It is time now to begin to look at the process of abstraction and its fruits in more detail, in order to see how it permits us to make the ascent to the first principle, and thus solve the cosmological, ontological and ethical problems that we have identified.

---

[9] This (and not any putative feudal social basis) is why, however sharply objective idealists may criticize the market order, they always end up legitimating it indirectly. Consider, for example the political impact of the current papacy. John Paul II has been nothing if not a critic of the market order, and yet he allied himself with global finance capital against what ought to have been his allies in the Kremlin. And consider the fate of liberation theology, which has been largely unable to mount an intellectually coherent response to the Vatican's critique. The exception here is the more moderate Segundo, whose theological roots are in Jesuit transcendental Thomism rather than the Servite or Franciscan left-wing Augustinianism of the Boffs.

Chapter 3

The Degrees of Abstraction

The preceding chapters have laid the groundwork for a new theory of knowledge. We have shown that the image produced in the nervous system by data gathered by the external sense organs encodes real information regarding the world around us. We have also shown that we advance from this purely sensory knowledge of things through images to an intellectual knowledge of their being and essence by abstraction from these images. This act of abstraction is made possible, on the one hand, by the complex structure of the human nervous system and, on the other hand, by participation in increasingly complex forms of social organization. When we participate in a society we live its structure and thus become connatural with that structure. The result is a preconceptual connatural knowledge of the 'form' of the society, a knowledge which illuminates the images we garner from the senses and reveals similar structures therein.

This is, however, only the beginning of an adequate account of the act of knowledge. What we have called abstraction covers a broad range of different activities. Every time we recognize something as rock or water, grass or tree, dog or cat, we engage in a kind of abstraction. Unlike other animals, we know not just a distinction of images, but also a definition which allows us to recognize what these things are. Clearly, however, this kind of rudimentary, everyday abstraction is very different from the kind of abstraction employed by mathematicians when they derive the properties of Minkowski spaces and Hilbert spaces or by mathematical physicists when they use these mathematical objects to describe the physical organization of the universe. And both of these two types of abstraction are different from the activity of the philosopher when he or she demonstrates the existence of God or the convertibility of the Transcendentals. If these activities were not fundamentally different, then we would not have the experience of being better at one or two than at the others, nor would we encounter people who respond to higher mathematics or metaphysics with utter incomprehension. We need, therefore, to define clearly the various degrees of abstraction.

Our account of the process of abstraction tells us, furthermore, that in so far as abstraction depends on the social and not simply on the individual intellect, and in so far as different societies are structured in fundamentally different ways, the process of abstraction will vary considerably across different social formations. More complex social structures will support higher degrees of abstraction – though it is by no means clear that development of the capacity for abstraction progresses in a series of well-defined epigenetic stages for either the individual or for human civilization.

It is to the first question – that of defining the degrees of abstraction – that this chapter is devoted. This may seem simple enough. We have, after all, already distinguished between ordinary classification, mathematical formalization and the sort of abstraction philosophers use when they do metaphysics, and this seems like a sensible enough division if not, perhaps, the only possible one. It turns out, however, that the question of the degrees of abstraction – and the equivalent question in the historical branch of the dialectical tradition, that of the relationship between *Verstand* and *Vernunft*, Understanding and Reason – is a highly controverted one, and has grave political-theological implications. The issue, as it has been framed by contemporary Thomism, concerns not only the proper way of understanding the different degrees of abstraction, but also whether or not the act by which the philosopher rises to knowledge of Being in general, and thus to God, is properly characterized as abstraction at all. On the answer one gives to these questions depends the precise route of the mind's road to God. Does this road run through the physical, biological and social sciences and thus pass by way of a judgement on the ultimate meaningfulness of the universe? Or does it take a detour around this question, with the dangerous consequences we have already identified above? Once the mind rises to God, can it really say anything at all, or does it know God only in a manner which is so austere as to carry with it few if any consequences for ethics or the special sciences? Also hanging on this question is the very possibility of a science of human society which is at once practical and theoretical – one which might bequeath to ethics the tools necessary to pass judgement on the market system or other social structures.

The issues at stake in our assessment of the relation between the Aristotelian-Thomistic way of distinguishing the degrees of abstraction and the Hegelian-Marxist distinction between *Verstand* and *Vernunft* are no less serious. If, as is usually assumed, these two ways of distinguishing degrees of intellectual knowledge are either entirely incommensurate or perhaps even diametrically opposed then our claim about the unity of the dialectical tradition cannot stand. Cosmic teleology in the Aristotelian sense and the dialectical doctrine of cosmo-historical progress have nothing to do with each other. Atheism is, in fact, essential to Marxism and an inevitable consequence of moves already made of Hegel. And Thomistic natural law and the Marxist critique of capitalism rest on entirely different epistemological foundations. If, on the other hand, these two ways of distinguishing the degrees of intellectual knowledge can be shown to differ more in terminology than in substance, then we have cleared one more hurdle – and a major one – in our argument for the underlying unity of the dialectical tradition.

Once again, these issues will be clearest if we present them in historical context, beginning with the first attempt to distinguish degrees of knowledge, Plato's 'divided line', and continuing through the formulations of Aristotle, Thomas, the contemporary Neo-Thomist schools and modern historical dialectics.

We have already discussed briefly the historical context of Plato's project – a struggle against the sophism and scepticism generated by an emerging petty commodity economy. And we have already noted that Plato offered no clear and consistent theory regarding the act of the intellect. He does, however, have a fairly well-developed doctrine of the degrees of knowledge, of which he identifies four:

1 *eikasis* or imagination, which knows things simply in terms of their appearance as reflected in some other medium, as 'in water or in close-grained, polished surfaces',

2   *pistis* or trust, 'knowledge of the actual things of which the first [that is, the objects of *eikasis*] are likenesses', which advances from mere appearances to define things in terms of their visible properties,

3   *dianoia* or thought, in which 'the mind uses as images those actual things which themselves had images in the visible world . . . and is compelled to pursue its inquiry by starting from assumptions and travelling not up to a principle but down to a conclusion' so that the entire argument remains merely hypothetical and

4   *noesis* or intellection, which rather than reasoning from premise to conclusions advances from 'conclusions' to 'a principle which is not hypothetical . . . the first principle of all; and, having grasped this, may turn back and, holding on to the consequences which depend upon it, descend at last to a conclusion . . .' (Plato, *Republic* 509d–511b)

Now the first degree of knowledge is clearly not intellectual but rather sensory, and corresponds to what Thomas called imagination. But where Aristotle and Thomas will focus on the role of imagination as a foundation for higher degrees of knowledge, Plato focuses on its limitations. In spite of the narrowness with which Plato specifies the media of reflection in the divided line itself, it is clear from the larger context that he also has in mind here images which are reflected in the psyche, in what Aristotle would later call the internal senses: memories, imaginative reconstructions, poetic images and so on. The problem here is not that imagination takes nothing from the real world; on the contrary, we have already shown that for Plato as for Aristotle we rise from the sensible (including the imaginative) to the intelligible, and that the intelligible is already reflected in the sensible. Rather, Plato is concerned about the distortions which take place in the formation of images. Rather ironically, perhaps, he uses the visual image of a distorted reflection in water or a curved polished surface to suggest the ways in which images in our internal senses can become distorted. Confused memories of another's face, the sort of exaggeration which forms the basis of the storyteller's art, and prejudice based on limited experience or hearsay are all examples of the way in which images, even as they convey information about the real world, can also deceive us. But Plato's biggest concern here is the poetic presentation of the gods which, by depicting them as driven by lust, greed and boundless rage, turns people away from the True and the Good and undermines the development of virtue (Plato, *Republic* 595a–608b).

The second degree of knowledge presents more difficulties. Plato clearly regards *pistis* as purely sensory. He characterizes it as knowledge of 'visible things'. At the same time it is apparent that he intends by this degree of knowledge our everyday ordinary knowledge of what the things around us are, a knowledge which clearly involves the intellect as well as the senses. Visible things, after all, have names, at least for us humans, and names involve language and thus the intellect. Indeed this precisely is what makes human perception of, say, a cat, different from a feline's perception of another member of its species. Where the cat sees another cat by means of an image, we see a cat by means of an image and know that it is a cat by means of a universal – the word 'cat' – for which we have a definition the requirements of which the image we have of the cat seems to meet. It is probably best to regard Plato's *pistis* as a combination of sensation and intellect, which checks the remembered, recollected, or constructed image against new observation, with the sort of rudimentary classifying abstraction which we will eventually call totalization.

The third degree of knowledge Plato associates with mathematics, understood in the broad sense to include not only arithmetic and geometry, but also harmonics (music theory) and astronomy, which produce mathematical models of sensible reality. What is known here is a form, or what we would call a structure. This includes not only numbers and arithmetic operations upon and relationships between them, and geometric objects such as a circle or sphere, but also the forms of sensible things such as music or the motions of the heavenly bodies. For Plato the scope of applied mathematics was limited to astronomy and harmonics, but there is nothing in his definition which would prevent one from including under it the whole of mathematical physics, chemistry and biology and even attempts (mathematical or structuralist) to formalise social phenomena. Two points are in order here. First, we should note that whatever he may say elsewhere, Plato here treats mathematical objects as hypothetical – that is, as possible rather than actual beings, and in this sense is closer to Aristotle than to most so-called 'mathematical Platonism'. Second, while he regards the mathematical form as 'the actual thing which had an image in the visible world', his inclusion of astronomy and harmonics rules out any notion that mathematics is an a priori science. On the contrary, it can only arise as we penetrate behind the sensory image to the form or structure which underlies it. We will see that this makes the Platonic *dianoia* very close to the Thomistic formal abstraction.

The fourth or highest degree of knowledge, *noesis*, ascends to a principle which is not hypothetical, and from which all other principles can be derived logically. This means that the principle in question must be necessary – it must have its cause and thus its explanation in itself. There can be nothing which, strictly speaking, is excluded from it. As such it is infinite and perfect. Elsewhere in the dialogue Plato specifies this principle as the Good from which 'the objects of knowledge derive not only the power of being known, but their very being and reality' (Plato, *Republic* 509c). The implication (and here the Plato of the *Republic* differs sharply from the Plato of the *Timaeus*) is that the causal principle underlying reality is fundamentally teleological in character.

We should note that Plato seems to include under this fourth degree of knowledge not only the ascent to the first principle – what we might call metaphysics – but also an attempt to explain the universe in terms of that principle. It is interesting in this regard that Plato sometimes uses *episteme* (translated 'knowledge' or 'science') to name the fourth degree of knowledge. What he has in mind here is not unlike the Aristotelian ideal of a deductive science (Aristotle, *Ethics*; McKeon 1973) or the Hegelian 'philosophical science' which has transcended the hypothetical character of the special sciences, which take their data as given, and grasped their inner logic and thus their necessity (Hegel, *Encyclopaedia* paras 1–8). For Plato – as for Aristotle, when he was at his best, and for the Hegelian-Marxist tradition – science is quite impossible apart from knowledge of the first principle and the fundamentally teleological reasoning which this involves. This will be important when we address later the role of the highest degree of knowledge in the special sciences.

Aristotle largely took over Plato's analysis of the different degrees of knowledge and grafted it onto his own account of the act of knowledge centred on the process of abstraction. In Aristotle, however, even more than in Plato, analysis of the different degrees of knowledge is hidden in a discussion of the proper division of the sciences. And the criterion here is first of all the nature of the object, which is the final cause and thus the real principle of the science; only secondarily is it the precise nature of the abstraction involved in knowing that object, which is the formal cause of the science in question. Aristotle begins by distinguishing between theoretical, practical and poetic sciences. The theoretical sciences study things which have their principle of motion or stability in themselves – that is, natural phenomena. In order to understand Aristotle's meaning here we must keep in mind that 'motion' for him means not only local motion or change in place, but growth or development, decay or degeneration, or indeed alteration of any kind. That something does not change because it has already achieved, or possesses eternally, the perfection of form, does not for Aristotle make it any less natural or any less an object of the theoretical sciences. The practical sciences study those things that have their principle in the decision of an actor or doer: that is, actions, and the larger social reality to which actions give rise. The practical sciences thus include Ethics and Politics – though interestingly enough Aristotle often uses the term 'political science' to describe both. The poetic sciences or the arts study things which have their principle in the skill of a maker or artist (Aristotle, *Metaphysics* VI.1). This includes, for Aristotle, the products of the mechanical or instrumental arts (those producing useful things, such as metal working or the physician's art), the products of the fine arts (those which produce beautiful things, such as poetry or sculpture) and the products of what would eventually be called the liberal arts or the arts involved in making an argument: grammar, rhetoric and logic.

Our interest here is primarily in the theoretical sciences. These Aristotle further subdivides. Physics deals with being which is mobile and, therefore, by definition material (since motion for Aristotle is motion from potency to act and thus implies the potential for receiving form, which is matter). Physics thus includes not only the general science of motion (which he treats in the *Physics*), but also biology and psychology. Mathematics deals with objects which are eternal and immobile but (*contra* Plato) exist apart from matter only in the mind, as the result of a special sort of abstraction which considers them apart from matter. Mathematics for Aristotle as for Plato includes not only arithmetic and geometry, but also harmonics and astronomy. Where physics, for example, attempts to explain the motions of the heavenly bodies (with motion understood in the broad Aristotelian sense of change), astronomy attempts to formalize their local motion mathematically. Theology or first philosophy (which Aristotle treats in the *Metaphysics*), finally, deals with things which are eternal and immaterial by nature – for example, the first principle or unmoved mover (Aristotle, *Metaphysics* VI.1).

Each science represents a higher degree of abstraction from the images which we garner from the senses. Physics abstracts simply from individuating matter so that it can rise to laws which govern motion in general. Thus, for example, the physicist abstracts from the motion of this heavenly body and the motion of that heavenly body, to an explanation of why the heavenly bodies move in general. The biologist abstracts from the growth of this plant or the reproductive behaviour of that animal to an explanation of nutrition, growth, reproduction, sensation and locomotion in general. The psychologist abstracts from my passions or your act of abstraction to explain the passions and the act of the intellect in general.

Mathematics abstracts entirely from matter, without, however, arriving at a necessary and necessarily immaterial principle. Arithmetic, for example abstracts not only from these particular rabbits, but from the matter which makes them capable of nutrition, growth, reproduction, sensation and locomotion. It does not attempt to explain how they reproduce. Rather, it abstracts only their number, and abstracts from the fact that it is *their* number, and considers only operations on and relationships between the numbers thus abstracted. And even a mathematics applied to rabbits (what we would call mathematical biology or mathematical population biology) would seek only a formalism describing their rate of reproduction in terms of other quantities – that is, the so-called logistic equation which we encountered in the previous chapter. Geometry abstracts not only from the motions of this particular heavenly body, but also from the motion of the heavenly bodies in general. It does not attempt to explain their motion. Rather, it considers only the form of the mathematical object traced out by said motion, and its difference from and similarity to other forms. Even a mathematics applied to the heavenly bodies (astronomy) would seek only a formalism describing the motion, and not an explanation of it.

Aristotle seems quite clear on the difference between the objects of physics and mathematics, and is thus able to define with reasonable clarity just what sort of abstraction is involved in each. When he arrives at the task of defining what he calls, in various places, 'first philosophy', 'theology', or 'divine science', and what we (owing to the placement of his treatise on this subject *after* the *Physics*) have come to call 'metaphysics', he begins to run into difficulties. He is not even clear on the object of this science. He says that it deals with things which are 'immovable and independent' (Aristotle, *Metaphysics* VI.1), but also with 'anything in so far as' it 'represent(s) being' (Aristotle, *Metaphysics* XI.3, 4). His treatment of the method or mode of abstraction proper to metaphysics is even less clear.

> . . . mathematics begins its study by concentrating on some aspect of its proper subject matter, such as lines, angles, numbers or some other quantity, and examines not how they are, but what properties they have as continuous quantities in one or two or three dimensions. Now philosophy [that is, first philosophy or metaphysics] investigates these things, not in part, in so far as each of them has certain attributes, but asks how such beings exhibit the properties of anything as a being.
>
> Natural science proceeds much as mathematics does: for it, too, studies the attributes and principles of beings, in so far as they are moved, and not in so far as they are. But the first science [that is, first philosophy or metaphysics], we have said, deals with these subject matters in so far as they represent being, and not in any other respect. (Aristotle, *Metaphysics* XI.4)

What are we to make of this? As a result of the ambiguities we have just noted, Aristotle's *Metaphysics* has often been regarded as, on the one hand, a doctrine of the 'common being' which everything shares, and which treats such questions as substance, accident and so on as an auxiliary to the other sciences and, on the other hand, as an adjunct to the *Physics* which expands briefly on the doctrine of the first unmoved mover without ever really advancing to the concept of Being as such. Thus the claim, which we will see made by certain Neo-Thomists, especially those of the historical or Gilsonian school, that Thomas breaks fundamentally with Aristotle, and that the Thomistic doctrine of the act of existence, and the Thomistic mode of rising to God, thus have little or nothing to do with physics or an effort to explain the universe.

There is little doubt that, by comparison with that of Thomas, Aristotle's doctrine of Being is undeveloped and even deficient. But this does not by itself justify the Gilsonian verdict. Let us consider Aristotle's definitions in greater depth. For Aristotle change is fundamentally a movement towards the perfection of form, and only secondarily degradation or neutral alteration. For something to be 'immovable' means that it is perfect: that it has in itself all possible perfections and cannot lose them. For something to be 'independent' means that it has its principle in itself. Now the principle of a thing is what makes it actual rather than merely potential, and thus the principle of its being. For Aristotle, this is its form and the end or τελος to which that form is ordered. What is 'immovable and independent' is thus qualitatively infinite, possessing all possible perfections, and necessary, since there can be nothing outside of it on which it could be dependent. It is God or Being as such, which draws all things from matter to form, potency to act by the attractive power of its Beauty, Truth, Goodness and Integrity. It is just that Aristotle never drew out all of these links clearly, with the result that the teleological attractive power of the first unmoved mover is not recognized as the power of Being itself, opening the way for the Gilsonian misunderstanding of the act of existence.

The same point can be made by looking at Aristotle's actual, as opposed to his stated method. Aristotle begins in the *Physics* by seeking the principles or causes of motion (*Physics* II.3), an inquiry which terminates in the recognition of a first unmoved mover (*Physics* VIII, *Metaphysics* XII.6). He then goes on to show that this first unmoved mover is infinite, necessary, perfect and thus divine (*Metaphysics* XII.7). Metaphysics is indeed an extension of physics, which is already teleological. The difference is that where physics uses the τελος to complete its explanation of particular forms of motion, metaphysics focuses on the τελος itself and tries to understand just how it brings things into being in the first place. That Aristotle never drew out all of the conclusions of his insight does not invalidate it; it simply means that certain ambiguities remained – and still remain – to be sorted out. Above all he never makes it clear whether the conclusion to the first unmoved mover is best understood as a new and higher degree of abstraction, distinct from those employed by physics and mathematics or if, rather, it is simply an inference or judgement on the basis of abstractions made by physics.

It is this Aristotelian schema which constitutes the basis for the historic Thomistic understanding of the degrees of abstraction, and (as was the case with the question of the Agent Intellect) it is ambiguities in the Aristotelian account which set up later controversies. Thomas himself left us no mature, magisterial treatment of the question. The text in which he treats it in the greatest detail is a youthful (1255–59) commentary on Boethius's *De Trinitate* (Aquinas, *In Boethius De Trinitate* Q 5, 6; Maritain 1937, Peifer 1964). There are substantive and terminological ambiguities even within this text. In the *Summa* (Aquinas, *Summa Theologiae* I Q 85 a 1) his treatment is less developed and he seems to leave behind certain distinctions which some scholars in the present period have thought important.

Thomas's earlier account of the degrees of abstraction tracks Aristotle's closely. Here he distinguishes clearly between three degrees of abstraction, *abstractio totius*, *abstractio formae* and *separatio*. *Abstractio totius* abstracts from individualizing matter, that is, it leaves behind Fido and Rover to rise to the notion of 'dog'. For Thomas as for Aristotle this sort of abstraction is especially characteristic of physics, but it is, of course, employed by all of the sciences. *Abstractio formae* abstracts from matter as such, in order to render the form fully intelligible. For Thomas as for Aristotle this is the sort of abstraction which is characteristic of mathematics. One leaves behind the orbits of the particular planets in order to rise to their intelligible form, which is that of an ellipse.

With the third degree of abstraction, however, Thomas makes a new departure, one which, depending on how one reads it, either extends and completes or breaks fundamentally with Aristotle. He makes a distinction between two ways of abstracting: by simple apprehension, as when we abstract the idea of 'dog' or 'ellipse' from the data of the senses, and by judging, as when we say 'Fido is a dog' or 'God exists'. It is this latter sort of abstraction, which he calls *separatio*, which is characteristic of first philosophy or metaphysics. Here the intellect 'separates' the act of existence from not only the matter but also the form, and judges that existence is possible apart from matter, and that there is indeed something which exists apart from matter, namely God or Being itself. After making this distinction Thomas ceases using the term abstraction to apply to metaphysics at all (Aquinas, *In Boethius De Trinitate*, Q 5).

The way Thomas frames the issue in his commentary *In Boethius De Trinitate* seems to suggest a sharp divergence between metaphysics on the one hand and physics and mathematics on the other hand. It would also seem to argue for a rather spare metaphysics, one in which we do not so much apprehend as infer the concept of Being as such, of which we have no intuition. And this is, indeed, the way the commentary has often been interpreted. Other texts, however, are more ambiguous. The account in the *Summa* is briefer, focusing on the distinction between abstraction through simple apprehension and abstraction through judgement or inference. To this extent it seems to point in the same direction as the earlier account and, if anything, to sharpen the distinction between the two forms of abstraction, and (were the first taken to apply to physics and mathematics, and the second to metaphysics) to sharpen even further the distinction between metaphysics and the other disciplines. But in the *Summa*, Thomas speaks of abstraction and separation as if they were interchangeable terms and applies them to physics, mathematics and metaphysics more or less interchangeably (Aquinas, *Summa Theologiae*, I Q 85 a 1). Here the impression is given that we abstract through both apprehension and judgement in all three disciplines. The result is nothing short of total confusion.

As the great Dominican commentators of the Baroque era, Cajetan and John Poinsot (also known as John of St Thomas) attempted to make sense out of this suggestive but confusing mass of texts, they turned to that most Thomistic of tools, the clarifying distinction. Before one can properly understand the distinction between *abstractio totius*, *abstractio formae* and *separatio*, they argue, it is necessary to grasp the prior distinction between two other concepts, *abstractio totalis* and *abstractio formalis*. The first abstracts a logical whole from the multitude of individual exemplars – that is, 'dog' from the multitude Fido, Fifi, Rover, Rufus, Bowser and so on, without however rising to an actual definition of the essence 'dog'. The second abstracts the intelligible nature or essence from the unintelligible matter. Total abstraction is characteristic of both ordinary and scientific thought; formal abstraction, on the other hand, is what sets scientific reasoning apart from ordinary, everyday thought. The three degrees of abstraction which Thomas identified in his commentary *In Boethius De Trinitate* (*abstractio totius*, *abstractio formae* and *separatio*), become the three degrees of *abstractio formalis*. *Abstractio totius* differs from *abstractio totalis* in that it arrives at the definition of a nature or essence rather than just a logical whole. The lower degree of abstraction, for example, might correctly categorize humans as featherless bipeds; the higher degree of abstraction recognizes that while this is one way of classifying us, it does not correctly define our essential nature. All three degrees of abstraction involve a real apprehension or intellectual visualization of the formal object of the science in question, culminating in what Maritain would later call the 'eidetic intuition of Being' which is constitutive of metaphysics (Cajetan, *In De Ente et Essentia*, *Prooemium*, Q 1, n 5, *De Nominium Analogia* 5; John of St Thomas, *Ars Logica* II, Q 27, a 1; Simmons 1952; Pugh 1997).

Other trends in twentieth-century Thomism, including the 'historical' school of Etienne Gilson and the 'transcendental' school of Rousselot, Marechal, Rahner and Lonergan, have dissented from this reading of Thomas in two ways. First of all, they regard the basic distinction between total and formal abstraction as un-Thomistic, and largely a creation of the seventeenth-century commentators. Second, they argue that *separatio* is not an apprehension of the 'form of Being' at all, but simply a negative judgement that being need not be material in character, without any element of intellectual intuition. This is closely connected with a substantive rejection of what these schools see as a tendency on the part of the Dominicans to regard being as fundamentally form or essence rather than as a pure act of existence – a doctrine of being which they regard as fundamental to Thomas's own metaphysics. The result, they argue, is a system which is more Aristotelian than authentically Thomistic.

These may, to the uninitiated reader, seem like rather minor issues – 'scholastic' in the very worst sense. But they have some important implications, directly for the way in which we rise to first principles and the way we characterize the first principle once we get there and, indirectly, therefore, for ethics and ultimately for politics. The two readings of Thomas also have implications for the way in which we situate him in the larger philosophical tradition. Let us look at each of these questions in turn.

If each degree of abstraction represents a distinct stage in the intellect's quest for a complete explanation, in which it achieves a progressively more adequate grasp of the organizing principle of its object, then the mind's road to God follows a winding upward path from ordinary abstraction through the special sciences, to first philosophy or metaphysics. This means that the claim that there *is* a first principle, and that this principle is infinite, perfect and necessary, is as much a statement about the organization of the universe as it is a statement about God. The claim that God exists is convertible with the statement that the universe is ultimately meaningful and ordered to a perfect end. If, on the other hand, the ascent to knowledge of Being takes the form of a negative judgement or 'separation' of the object's act of existence from its essence, then this in no sense requires an ascent through the special sciences, nor do the resulting arguments for the existence of God presuppose or imply that the universe is an organized, ultimately meaningful system, or even that what exists is something which can meaningfully be called a universe, but only that something is. Dominican Thomism situates metaphysics in the context of a larger quest for a complete explanation. Each degree of abstraction represents a step in this quest. The move to metaphysics comes only after physics has demonstrated the ultimate meaningfulness of the universe, or rather at the very point of this demonstration, when we ask what sort of principle it might be which could raise matter from potency to act, from nothingness to being, and thus give rise to the universe, and then begin to understand the transcendental properties of Being (Beauty, Truth, Goodness, Integrity) and their incredible creative power. The other schools render physics and thus the nature and ultimate meaningfulness of the universe largely irrelevant to metaphysics and theology, opening themselves up to all of the dangers we have already associated with this approach: otherworldliness and hatred of matter, life, humanity, labour, women and so on.

But this is not all. In conserving the connection between 'being' and 'form' characteristic of the larger Aristotelian tradition, Dominican Thomism keeps open the possibility of at least a dim intuition of *what* Being is. This is the significance of Maritain's doctrine of eidetic intuition. The content of this intuition will turn out to be nothing other than the transcendental properties of Being – Beautiful, True, Good and One – all of which are simply ways of characterizing a formative or organizing principle. Being is organization. To be is to be organized; Being as such is the organizing principle, the τελος which draws things out of the pure potency of matter and towards the perfection of form.[1] In this sense, the Dominican tradition also keeps open the link

---

[1] This is a point to which we will return in our chapter on transcendental abstraction but it merits at least some explanation here. By organization we mean a structure or form ordered to an end. To be is to be organized. In order to understand this we need simply to imagine something which is wholly lacking in organization. Such a thing would be formless and thus unimaginable. Or consider what happens when we degrade the organization of a living thing: it dies, or ceases to exist. It follows that the power of Being is the power to organize, and this belongs fundamentally to the end or *telos* to which things are ordered. Forms or structures arise to serve a purpose.

This link between being and organization is captured in the Thomistic doctrine of the convertibility of the transcendentals. Consider, for example, the nature of Beauty. By the Beauty of a system, we mean simply its level of organization, understood as the object of (sensory or intellectual) perception. The greater the diversity of the elements organized, and the more perfect the harmony in which they are united, the more beautiful the system. This is true throughout the natural world, from simple harmonies of the night sky, through the more complex forms of the crystalline structures and living organisms to the rich, lush diversity of complex ecosystems and human societies. And it is true as well of great works of art, which are nothing if not a complex manifold of relations harmoniously arranged. Beauty itself, as Albertus Magnus and Thomas Aquinas taught long ago, is the capacity to bring things into being, and is thus convertible with Being itself, or God.

The truth value of a statement, a concept, or theory, similarly, is its capacity to organize large quantities of qualitatively diverse, and therefore highly complex, experience. It is necessary in this connection to focus equal attention on the complexity of the experience organized and on the level of organization of the experience in question. Our experience is most highly organized when we identify highly compact 'organizing principles', knowledge of which permits us to derive logically all the rich particularity of the experience on which the principle was based. It is this organizing capacity of theories which leads us to speak analogously of their 'power'. The most powerful theories are those which comprehend the full range of experience in unique, compact statements which are themselves pregnant with rich experiential content.

The Good, similarly, is organization realized as something desirable, and thus as final cause. As final it is the object of our desire or appetite, whether sensual or intellectual, and as cause, it is the actual capacity to organize.

All of the transcendentals – Beauty, Truth and Goodness – are ultimately just aspects or modes of Being as such, or of organization. This is the significance of the fourth and last transcendental: the One. For what

between Thomas and the Platonic teaching which made the Good prior to existence. The focus on the pure act of existence characteristic of Gilson and the historical school, on the other hand, tends to make of Being an impenetrable mystery, thus weakening the explanatory power of first philosophy and creating a rupture between it and the special sciences, which no longer have any reason to look to it for direction. Similarly, by making philosophy itself terminate in mystery it undermines the distinction between natural and supernatural wisdom, and makes it difficult to specify in a way which preserves its radical reasonableness and intelligibility just what revelation contributes to human knowledge.

Differences at the level of metaphysics lead inevitably to differences at the level of ethics. Once we have grasped Being as organization, and the transcendentals as ways of understanding organization, the nature of the moral imperative becomes clear. We must promote the development of complex organization in the universe. Armed with the results of the special sciences (especially, but not only, psychology and sociology) we can then draw out specific conclusions regarding the nature of virtue and justice and just how to promote them which are both cosmologically and ontologically well-grounded and rich in specific detail. If, on the other hand, metaphysics is reduced to an austere discipline which achieves only an indirect and inferential knowledge of the first principle, the result will be an ethics which is correspondingly spare and formal.

Finally the Dominican reading of Thomas, precisely because it sees him as extending rather than breaking with Aristotle, situates him historically within the context of what we have been arguing is a unified dialectical tradition, focused on laying the epistemological, cosmological and ontological groundwork for ethics and characterized by a commitment to realism and cosmic teleology. Within this tradition Thomas does, indeed, add a great deal. His doctrine of Being, and of its convertibility with the transcendentals, marks a fundamental advance. But it is an advance within, not a break with, the dialectical tradition. Historical and transcendental Thomism, on the other hand, with their narrow focus on the act of existence, and the dynamic ordering of the intellect towards the Infinite Being, makes Thomism radically independent of any claims regarding cosmic teleology, and thus from the larger Aristotelian tradition through which Thomism is so intimately connected with historical dialectics of both the idealist and materialist forms. It is, of course, cosmic teleology which ultimately grounds any secure doctrine of historical progress, making it a real participation in the larger motion of matter towards the perfection of form, and thus a moral imperative as well as an empirical fact.

It should already be apparent that we prefer the Dominican approach to the problem of abstraction. This said, however, it must be pointed out that there are in fact difficulties shared by *all three* Thomist schools (Dominican, historical and transcendental), albeit in different degrees. All seem determined to reconcile Thomism with modern mathematical physics in a way which leaves unchallenged the scientific

---

is organization if not the capacity to make all one, not in the sense of negating difference, but in the sense of integrating infinite difference into a single, harmonious whole, so that each particular system draws its strength from the cosmos as a whole, while contributing with all its power to the organizing activity which brings the cosmos into being. In this sense, the One is the complex synergistic integrity of the universe (Mansueto 1997a).

status of this discipline. The historical and transcendental schools do this by rejecting Aristotelian and medieval physics entirely, as an overextension of the philosophical enterprise into realms for which it is unfit (Maurer 1963). It is for this reason that they seek a route to God which does not pass through the special sciences: mathematical physics cannot support the sort of cosmic teleology which makes such a route tenable. The Dominican tradition, on the other hand, attempts to save the scientific status of both Aristotelian and mathematical physics. This is the real import of the distinction between *abstractio totalis* and *abstractio formalis*. By characterizing *abstractio totius* as a type of formal, scientific abstraction which grasps the essential nature of things – and specifically of material, mobile being – the Dominicans make room for an Aristotelian physics or what Maritain calls a philosophy of nature. This discipline exists alongside of, and not in series with, the *abstractio formae* which is characteristic of mathematics and of mathematical physics.[2] In neither case is there a real recognition of the utter inability of mathematics or mathematical physics to realize the fundamental task of all science, which is to explain.[3] While the Dominican insistence on preserving an Aristotelian philosophy of nature alongside mathematical physics secures a place in which a doctrine of cosmic teleology can be developed, it also leaves open the possibility of two contradictory cosmologies which differ on questions of ultimate importance. How, for example, can the universe *both* be ultimately meaningful *and* terminate, as most mathematical physicists believe it must, in either a 'big crunch' or an infinite expansion which disperses matter and dissipates energy in such a way as to leave little of interest? The effect here is to retain, in the heart of Neo-Thomism, an alien element of cosmological pessimism – something which inclines this school in a rightward, Augustinian direction, with all the political-theological implications we have identified above in Chapter 2.

Characterizing the method of the natural sciences in terms of *abstractio totius*, furthermore, imposes severe limits on the scope and power of these sciences. On the one hand, it renders these sciences incapable of completing the ascent to the unmoved mover, and thus to knowledge of God. But there is more. Restricted to the *abstractio totius* they are also limited to grasping static essences, and miss the creative dynamism of matter in motion towards act, or what is the same thing, towards God. This is especially problematic when it comes to the human sciences, which are restricted only to analysis of human potential (the content of Aristotelian psychology) and cannot broach the human act which is reserved for the less certain practical sciences of Ethics and Politics. In point of fact, however, the human act (and the social context in which action takes place) are no less motion in the Aristotelian sense than the movement of the heavenly bodies or the growth of a plant. And this motion is no less subject to the attractive power of the unmoved mover or *telos* which draws all things to itself – and

---

[2] Strictly speaking mathematical physics is treated as a *scientia media* intermediate between mathematics and physics and using both the *abstractio totius* and the *abstractio formae*. But in so far as the idea of mathematical physics is the formalism, and not the physical concept, it is the *abstractio formae* which predominates.

[3] Mathematics can explain only in the very limited sense that *given* one formalism, certain other formalisms follow. The sum of the angles of a triangle equals 180° 'because' this follows from the definition of a triangle. No formalism, however, can ever explain why things are or why things are the way they are, except in so far as their being any other way would imply a logical contradiction.

thus no less an object of theoretical science than any of the other forms of matter in motion.

In order to rectify these problems we reject the distinction between *abstractio totalis* and *abstractio totius*. The lowest degree of abstraction we will call total abstraction or totalization and define as abstraction of a logical whole from its parts (abstraction from Mr Kepler Cat, Joe Muzzarelli Cat and Carmine Crocco Donatelli Cat to the category of 'cat' in general), without any reference to material or mobile being. Totalization is fundamentally an act of classification, and while it is a precondition for science, it is not restricted to the sciences nor is there any science which relies exclusively on it or is somehow particularly characterized by it.

Second, we reject the distinction between *abstractio formalis* and *abstractio formae*, together with the definition of *abstractio formae* in terms of the accidental form of quantity. Once we have dispensed with any attempt to save the scientific character of mathematical physics, or of some hypothetical physics which depends on the *abstractio totius* alone, the category of *abstractio formalis* loses its function. Defining *abstractio formae* in terms of quantity, furthermore, seems to us to miss what is really going on in the tremendous drive towards mathematical formalization of the sciences during the past several hundred years. We prefer, instead, to say that formal abstraction, as we will call it, is an attempt to grasp the structure of its object in a way which permits exhaustive knowledge of all its properties, and which is, therefore, equivalent to an intuition of the essence of the thing in question. This drive achieves its aim only in the case of mathematicals, which are purely possible beings, for reasons which we will examine shortly, but is also present in the kind of science which aims at grasping the underlying structure of things, either as its term (for example, mathematical physics and the chemistry and biology which depends upon it, but also structural linguistics, anthropology and psychology) or as a way of defining just what it is that is ordered to an end (for example, the dialectical materialist account of the structures of various economic systems). Here too, there is a drive towards mathematization, but it is never really fully complete because the objects are real rather than possible and thus cannot be defined as static structures, but rather as structures undergoing transformation under the attractive influence of the final cause.

Given what we have said above, it should be clear that we cannot regard any discipline which relies exclusively on formalization, or simply on formalization and totalization, as scientific. Neither explains. This does not require us to reject the achievements of mathematical physics and its daughter disciplines, or of the structural turn in the social sciences. It does, however, require that we recognize these disciplines as auxiliaries to science, rather than as science itself, which will require a fundamentally higher degree of abstraction in order to do its work. What formalization contributes is a rigorous description, coupled with a strict determination of the logical limits of possibility – and nothing more.

Third, in view of what is known at the highest degree of abstraction we propose to refer to it as 'transcendental abstraction' rather than as 'separation'. This is not to negate the role of the judgement of existence, but rather to shift the focus from the act of existence to its principle, which is the transcendental principle (Beauty, Truth, Good, One) to which it is ordered and from which it derives. This move makes it clear that a grasp of final cause is ultimately an act of transcendental rather than total abstraction, which is reduced to a mere classifying dynamic. This means that in so far as judgements regarding purpose or end are an integral part of ordinary everyday reasoning and are essential, furthermore, for development of a complete scientific explanation, the highest degree of abstraction is not the exclusive prerogative of the metaphysician, but rather an integral part of the fabric of human thought in all its forms. At the same time, because of this, metaphysics or first philosophy, which has as its aim knowledge of the transcendentals – that is, of the end as such – becomes intensely relevant to all spheres of human life, as the authentic science of the first principles which govern not only explanation, but also action and therefore ethics. While we will see eventually that revelation provides to the intellect a light superior even to that provided by metaphysics, this will not so much displace metaphysics as enrich the content of the wisdom it is able to bring to bear.

Before we proceed to an analysis in depth of each degree of abstraction, we need to consider what at first appears to be an alternative and even opposed classification of the degrees of intellectual knowledge suggested by Kant and Hegel and, in somewhat different form, by dialectical materialism. This is the distinction between '*Verstand*' or Understanding and '*Vernunft*' or Reason. *Verstand* grasps merely the external relationships among phenomena, through the media of categories (logical wholes, mathematical formalisms) whereas *Vernunft* penetrates their inner essence and comprehends their organizing principle. For Kant, of course, such a grasp of the organizing principle is possible only for practical reason, which grasps the principles of our actions; for Hegel, who regards Spirit as the Idea become conscious of itself as it emerges from its self-externalization in nature, *Vernunft* is in fact the principle of the natural as well as the social worlds, both of which can be comprehended in their totality.

> Prior to Kant no distinction had been made between Understanding and Reason . . . for the latter, the object is determined in and for itself, is the identity of content and form, of universal and particular, whereas for the former, it falls apart into form and content, into universal and particular, and into an empty 'in-itself' to which the determinateness is added from the outside . . . (Hegel, *Encyclopaedia* para. 467 *Zusatz*)

Hegel gives as an example of *Verstand* Kepler's laws of planetary motion. The existence of the planets, their nature as planets and their motion are all given; there is no necessary relationship between these givens and the laws of motion themselves. This does not mean that Kepler's laws are without value. 'Understanding . . . is a necessary moment of rational thinking' (Hegel, *Encyclopaedia* para. 467 *Zusatz*). Before we can advance to *Vernunft* we must first 'separate the essential from the contingent' (that is, the general or universal from the particular) and advance to a rigorous definition. Kepler's discovery thus merits 'eternal fame' (Hegel, *Encyclopaedia (Outline)* para. 212). But the categories in terms of which the laws are framed can themselves be comprehended only by the higher faculty of *Vernunft* which, having grasped the Idea, can then return to derive from it 'the concepts of space and time, the moments whose relation is motion' (Hegel, *Encyclopaedia (Outline)* para. 212).

Dialectical materialism makes a similar distinction between modes of intellectual knowledge, though the terminology used is less regular and consistent. Marx, for example, distinguished between bourgeois political economy, which grasped only the external relations between commodities, and his own critique of political economy which penetrated to the inner essence of the commodity. Bourgeois political economy, with its mathematical formalisms for determining price and so on, is a 'necessary precondition for a genetic presentation' (Marx 1971: 500), but it leaves its categories themselves (commodity, money, capital, price, profit and so on) unexplained.

> Classical political economy seeks to reduce the fixed and mutually alien forms of wealth to their inner unity by means of analysis and to strip away the form in which they exist independently alongside one another . . . it is not interested in elaborating how the various forms came into being, but seeks to reduce them to their unity by means of analysis, because it starts with them as given premises. (Marx [1905–1910] 1969: 500)

This limitation he attributes to what he calls its 'analytic method' (Marx [1905–1910] 1969: 500). Bourgeois political economy takes its categories as given and then analyses their properties, reducing them ultimately to mathematical formalisms. The task of Marx's 'critique of political economy' is to look behind these categories to the principle which alone can explain them:

> Now, however, we have to perform a task never even attempted by bourgeois economics. That is, we have to show the origin of this money-form, we have to trace the development of the expression of value contained in the value-relation of commodities from its simplest, almost imperceptible outline to the dazzling money-form. When this has been done, the mystery of money will immediately disappear. (Marx *Capital*, [1867] 1976: 139).

Marx finds this principle in labour-power, which is the source of all value, and in terms of which alone the capitalist economy can be explained.

There is more at issue here, however, than simply penetrating beneath the phenomenon to the organizing principle. This organizing principle is, for both Hegel and Marx, a principle of motion or of development. Once one has grasped the inner logic of something, one has also grasped its internal contradictions and thus the conditions for its supersession by a still more complex form of organization. Thus in Hegel's 'critique of mechanics' a rational comprehension of space, time and motion is also, at the same time, a grasp of the rational necessity of the 'elementary particle', the existence of which is implied by these more abstract categories. And in Marx's critique of political economy, comprehending capitalism means comprehending the crisis tendencies which lead ultimately to its dissolution and supersession by a higher form of organization, that is, socialism. Where *Verstand* can only describe change, *Vernunft* comprehends it. Later dialectical materialism attempted to capture this difference by distinguishing between 'metaphysical' and 'dialectical' reasoning (Lenin [1916] 1976; Mao [1937a] 1971, [1963] 1971). The former regards the universe as a system of discrete, externally related things or essences; the latter regards it as an internally related system of relations, constantly undergoing transformation and development.

Philosophers working in what might be called the German tradition, by which we mean not only historic dialectics in its idealist and materialist forms, but also critical, transcendental and objective idealism (Kant, Fichte, Schelling), have tended to regard Aristotelian (and by extension Thomistic) philosophy as a philosophy of *Verstand*. And there does, indeed, appear to be prima facie evidence for such a judgement. Hegel, for example, identifies the legitimate activity of *Verstand* as an act of abstraction which separates the contingent from the essential (Hegel, *Encyclopaedia* para. 467 *Zusatz*) – just precisely the function which Aristotle assigns to the Agent Intellect. And certainly no philosopher working in the Aristotelian tradition would grant to the human intellect the capacity to comprehend with rational certainty, as the result of a deduction from logical first principles, the rational necessity of a mathematically formalized empirical generalization such as Kepler's laws of planetary motion – much less the Absolute Knowledge to which Hegel in certain places seems to pretend. The impression is reinforced by the fact that Kant and Hegel use for the lower form of intellectual knowledge the term *Verstand* which is generally used to translate the Greek *nous* and the Latin *intellectus*, while using *Vernunft* to translate the Greek *logismos* and the Latin *ratio*, which for the Aristotelian tradition represents a lower, discursive reasoning. Similarly, there appears at first glance to be little doubt that the Aristotelian tradition, especially as developed by the great Dominican commentators on Thomas, nearly as much as the Platonic tradition, stressed the existence of stable essences almost to the exclusion of fundamental innovation. Change was confined to the growth and development of the individual organism and the individual human soul – to the realization of a pre-existing form, not to the emergence of fundamentally new forms. The universe itself, on a large scale, was eternally changeless. Indeed, the impression that Aristotelian philosophy is confined to the understanding of external relations and static essences became so strong in the nineteenth century that many Catholic theologians began to abandon Thomas in favour of theologies (such as that of Drey) based on one or another version of the Germanic *Vernunft* – usually in its objective idealist form as a kind of religious intuition little distinguishable from faith, which they thought better accommodated the social-historical character of the Christian tradition (McCool 1977).

But let us look again, through the tangle of linguistic and terminological differences, to see if we can understand what is actually being said. We have already granted that no Aristotelian will allow to human reason the comprehension of the Absolute – that is, of the divine – as Hegel does. But apart from this, the common ground between the Aristotelian and historical-dialectical positions is, in fact, very significant. The way in which Hegel characterizes *Verstand* is actually very close to what we have called total and formal abstraction.

> . . . thought is (a) understanding, with its formal identity, working up the representations, that have been memorised, into species, genera, laws, forces and so on, in short into categories . . . (Hegel, *Encyclopaedia* para. 467 *Zusatz*)

The only real difference here is that Hegel includes as one degree of knowledge what Thomas distinguished into two. And the reason for this (rather uncharacteristic) failure to distinguish is simply his focus on what he sees as the more important distinction between *Verstand* and *Vernunft*.

> . . . thought is, (b) essentially an act of partition – judgment, which, however does not break up the concept again into the old antithesis of universality and being, but distinguishes on the lines supplied by the interconnections peculiar to the concept.

> . . . in the judgment it explains the individual to be a universal (species, genus). (Hegel, *Encyclopaedia* para. 467 *Zusatz*)

This is, of course, essentially the Thomistic 'second act of the intellect', in which the intellect turns to the image and affirms that the singular which it represents is in fact an example of the universal.

> ... In these forms the *content* appears as given: (c) but in inference (syllogism) it characterises a content from itself ...

> Only on the third stage of pure thinking is the Notion as such known. Therefore, this stage represents comprehension in the strict sense of the word. Here the universal is known as self-particularizing, and from that particularization gathers itself together into individuality; or what is the same thing, the particular loses its self-subsistence to become a moment of the Notion ... Here, therefore, the object is distinguished from thought only by having the form of being, of subsisting on its own account. (Hegel, *Encyclopaedia* para. 467 *Zusatz*)

This third stage Hegel specifies as that of *Vernunft*. What is at issue here is really nothing more or less than a passage from the Platonic *dianoia* to the Platonic *noesis* – or, what we have already shown to be essentially the same thing – an advance from formalization to an Aristotelian deductive science in which, the first principle having been comprehended, one can then descend deductively and systematically to the particulars. Hegel even characterizes the activity of Reason in distinctly Aristotelian fashion as a syllogism.

This latter point merits some focused attention. Much is often made of the distinction between Aristotelian 'formal logic' and Hegelian and Marxist 'dialectical logic'. The former addresses only questions of internal coherence; the latter claims to grasp the logic of Being itself, and thus to be an ontology as well as a logic (Harris 1987). Thus Aristotle treats the syllogism without respect to its content (Aristotle, *Prior Analytic*). Hegel, on the other hand, after analysing the various forms or figures of the syllogism (Hegel [1812] 1969: 599–704), goes on to suggest that the very structure of reason implies a content, a move which seems very un-Aristotelian. But let us look more closely. What is this content, this onto-logic which is as much a principle of explanation as the formal structure of the syllogism? The concept or organizing principle of things can, for Hegel, be understood only by recourse to explanations which are not merely mechanical or chemical, but also teleological (Hegel [1812] 1969: 705–54), and ultimately by reference to a principle which is living (Hegel [1812] 1969: 761–74) – that is, self-organizing. This self-organizing principle is the True and the Good (Hegel [1812] 1969: 774–824). Hegel even goes so far as to insist that this principle, which he calls the Absolute Idea, possesses the quality of personality (Hegel [1812] 1969: 825). This 'Absolute Idea' is nothing more or less than the Aristotelian First Unmoved Mover, unless it is also the personal divine creator of St Thomas. What has happened here, of course, is simply a fusion of logic and metaphysics; the content of each remains broadly Aristotelian.

If Hegelian *Vernunft* is simply a variant of Aristotelian-Thomistic transcendental abstraction which has, perhaps, made excessive claims for itself, then Marxist dialectical reason is simply this same transcendental abstraction unduly restricting the sphere of its own activity. The movement of the Marxist dialectic is the same as that of the Platonic, Aristotelian, Thomistic and Hegelian dialectics before it: from the data of the senses to the abstraction, and from the general law or formalism to the principle which can explain that law. From here it returns to the particulars, armed with the organizing principle, in order to explain them.

> Of course the method of presentation must differ in form from that of the enquiry. The latter has to appropriate the material in detail, to analyse its different forms of development, to trace out their inner connection. Only after this work is done, can the actual movement be adequately described. If this is done successfully, if the life of the subject-matter is ideally reflected as in a mirror, then it may appear as if we have before us a mere *a priori* construction. (Marx [1867] 1976: 28)

Thus Marx begins with the categories of bourgeois political economy (money, price . . .) and resolves them dialectically into the one principle in terms of which they can be explained: the principle of labour-power, which is the source of the value which *appears* in the marketplace under the guise of price. He then uses this principle to explain the phenomena of the marketplace: the extraction and accumulation of surplus value, its realization as profit, and the persistent tendency towards crisis which derives from the underlying contradiction between labour-power and the market system which organizes it. The science in *Capital* is an Aristotelian deductive science par excellence.

What Marx does not do is to rise all the way to a first principle which, being itself infinite, necessary and perfect, is self-explanatory and which can then be mobilized to explain everything else. We would not, of course, expect ascent to such a principle in *Capital* or any other work of the special sciences. But Marx does not merely restrict the scope of his inquiry; he actually denies the existence of such a divine first principle, as does Engels in a work – the *Dialectics of Nature* – the scope of which can hardly be called restricted. This is a fundamental question and would seem to compromise our claim that dialectical reason and transcendental abstraction are fundamentally the same.

When we look more closely, however, at just why dialectical materialism rejects the existence of God we find not an overreaching but rather an abbreviation of the dialectic. What Engels is attempting to do in the *Dialectics of Nature* is to demonstrate the universality of the laws of the dialectic, which amount to nothing more or less than the laws of the motion of matter from less complex to more complex forms of organization – or, to use Aristotelian language, from potency to act. One would think that this project would have pointed Engels towards an Aristotelian theism or pantheism, and in fact neither Engels nor his Soviet interpreters (Dahm 1988) were unaware of this affinity. But Engels's project founders on no less than the Second Law of Thermodynamics which, for him as for most of his contemporaries, appears to condemn the universe to a slow thermal death, and to predict a gradual degeneration and disintegration of intelligence, of life, indeed of all complex organization. Such a universe is clearly not ordered to an end, much less an end infinite, necessary and perfect and thus divine in character. Thus the 'scientific' atheism of the dialectical materialist tradition.

In this sense dialectical materialism fails in precisely the same way as the various Neo-Thomist schools: by conceding too much to bourgeois science. It is true that Engels (like the Dominican and unlike the historical and transcendental Thomists) argues for the necessity of a discipline *alongside* the special sciences which abstracts from them certain general principles regarding 'matter in motion'. But this leaves the sombre conclusions of bourgeois 'science' intact. What was needed, and still is needed, is a 'critique of mathematical physics' which parallels Marx's critique of political economy, and looks beyond the 'laws of motion of matter' (the level of *Verstand* or of formal abstraction) and comprehends the organizing principle which makes matter possible in the first place (the level of *Vernunft* or transcendental abstraction). As we noted above this does not mean abandoning the achievements of mathematical physics, but rather recognizing it (like bourgeois political economy) as a propaedeutic to science rather than as science itself.

The second dialectical materialist objection to Aristotle – that he is 'metaphysical' in the sense of favouring stable essences over cosmo-historical dynamism – is more easily answered. Aristotle's whole break with Plato can be understood as an attempt to grasp motion and development, and to do so in a materialistic way – as the result of immanent material processes rather than simply through the imposition of form on matter from the outside, which is the way Plato approached the problem in the *Timaeus*. Indeed, even the Unmoved Mover, while itself changeless because it is perfect, is first and foremost a principle of change. What is missing in the Aristotelian tradition up through the great Dominican and Jesuit commentators is a doctrine of historical transformation. But this is hardly surprising. Without great historical transformations to observe there can be no science of human history. The next best thing, however – the closest thing to a science of progressive change – would be biology. And many, even the majority of the great Aristotelians and Thomists, were trained as physicians and/or biologists, beginning with Aristotle himself, through the Arab commentators and Albertus Magnus, up to the great twentieth-century Thomists Maritain and Marechal. By the same token, dialectical materialism is seriously misunderstood if it is regarded as rejecting entirely the concept of stable essence (Meikle 1985). On the contrary, Marx's critique of political economy itself presupposes the notion that in spite of the empirical diversity of capitalist societies, there really is such a thing as the capitalist mode of production which is defined by definite laws of motion. It is simply that the resulting structure is regarded as unstable – as open rather than closed under transformations, to use the language favoured by the structuralists – and thus as issuing in the more complex, more highly integrated structure of socialism. In this sense, dialectical social science can be regarded as an extension of Aristotelian psychology in the light of the great historical transformations of the capitalist epoch, which provided for the first time the comparative historical basis necessary to make such a science possible. What dialectical materialism is not always fully aware of is that its argument against capitalism depends not simply on comprehending the essence or structure of capitalism and thus its internal contradictions, but on a more fundamental understanding of human nature as creative or productive – and as ordered to the Good. It is the inability of capitalist structures to realise the latent potential of human nature which makes them inadequate and thus unjust – a judgement which requires reference to a transcendental principle of value, which dialectical materialism lacks. If anything, dialectical materialism, especially in its more 'structuralist' forms, can be regarded as too focused on form or essence – as stopping short at the level of *Verstand* or formal abstraction – and of failing to advance to the first principle which alone can make its judgements absolutely valid.

What all this suggests is that historical dialectics does not actually propose a higher degree of intellectual knowledge than that proposed by the Aristotelian doctrine of abstraction. Rather, it enriches that doctrine with the fruits of a science of human history and human society, which was not possible in the time of Aristotle or Aquinas. With this gain come certain dangers. On the one hand, there is a tendency in idealist dialectics to see in the more profound vision of Being which the science of history makes possible a definitive and final penetration of the Absolute and the Infinite, which clearly it is not. The finite intellect can always and only have a partial (if also ever deepening) grasp of the Infinite. On the other hand, there is also a tendency, especially among more structurally-minded Marxists, to become transfixed by the powerful comprehension of essence which dialectics makes possible and to fail to ascend to judgement and to the principle of value (True, Good) which makes that judgement possible. Having, in a certain sense, 'completed' the scientific revolution by establishing the science of human society, Marx and Engels were reluctant to call on 'metaphysical' principles to question the conclusions of the results of earlier (physical, biological) stages in this revolution. Ultimately, this latter fault is what leads to the atheism in the materialist form of historical dialectics. This tendency is, we will see, a reflex of market forces which always favour the cultivation of formal over transcendental abstraction.

We should clarify finally why, given the above argument, and our larger commitment to the notion of a unified dialectical tradition, we opt for a terminology which calls the highest form of abstraction 'transcendental' rather than 'dialectical'. The latter terminology is after all the more common one among both dialectical materialists and such idealist dialecticians as Errol Harris, whose doctrine is in fact very close to our own. It might also seem that our terminology would be confusing in the contemporary setting, in which the term 'transcendental' is associated with Kantian rather than Aristotelian or Hegelian philosophy. Harris, for example, distinguishes between formal, transcendental and dialectical thinking, with formal thought corresponding roughly to what we mean by formal abstraction, transcendental thought to the Kantian search for the 'conditions for the possibility' of experience, judgement and so on, and dialectical thought corresponding to the logic of a system which grasps internal relations, structure and purpose, and thus advances to principles of value. There are three reasons for our decision. First of all, all of the various stages of cognition, including not only intellectual but also sensory cognition are integral to the dialectic understood in the original Platonic sense of the whole journey towards the first principle. We do not leave sensation, imagination, totalization or formalization behind once and for all; we simply subsume them under the higher abstraction which orders them to knowledge of the Beautiful, the True, the Good and the One. Second, we regard the Kantian transcendental thinking, which grasps the conditions for the possibility of experience, action, judgement and so on, as a kind of abbreviated form of our own transcendental abstraction – abbreviated because it stops short of the judgement of existence, and regards the transcendentals as simply regulative ideas rather than as real properties of Being, of which we enjoy an authentic eidetic intuition. Finally, we want our terminology to be as descriptive as possible, and the most adequate way to describe a form of abstraction is by what it abstracts: logical wholes, forms or structures, or the transcendentals.

Before analysing each degree of abstraction in more detail, we must stop to consider briefly, as we have in earlier chapters, the social basis and political valence of the various doctrines we have been considering. Specifically, we must elaborate and substantiate, but also qualify, the claim made at the end of Chapter 2, that what we have argued is a unified dialectical tradition reaching from Socrates through Marx, and his interpreters finds its social basis in the working classes. The qualification is this: that dialectics has historically been carried by a very specific 'working intelligentsia'[4] which has struggled with difficulty to establish its independence both from older clerical intelligentsias and from the rising bourgeoisie, but has often been allied in one way or another with both of these social forces as it has sought to advance its project under often difficult social conditions. These alliances have shaped and at times deformed the development of the dialectical tradition, and account for the errors which we have noted above.

Let us take first of all the alliance between the dialectical tradition and the Catholic Church, an alliance which has produced many different philosophical trends, the most important of which, however, is Thomism – including both the original 'Thomism' of Thomas himself and the later (Dominican, Jesuit and other) Neo-Thomisms. In order to understand the impact of alliance with the Church on the development of the dialectical tradition generally, and on Thomism in particular, it is necessary first to understand the social character of the Church itself. Dialectical materialist analyses have generally treated the Catholic Church in the Middle Ages as a feudal institution, and specifically as the ideological apparatus of the feudal nobility. And clearly there were significant feudal aspects to the Church's social basis and political valence. Itself a large landowner, the senior members of the Church's hierarchy were drawn from the nobility and often served it quite faithfully. At the same time, the Church always drew a significant part of its revenue from noncoercive contributions, and always used a significant part of that revenue in ways which helped to conserve the social fabric or to promote the development of human capacities. In this sense it retained significant archaic[5] features.

---

[4] By a 'working intelligentsia' we mean a group of intellectuals which gains its livelihood primarily from the exercise of its intellectual vocation, either by selling its services (in which case it is a petty bourgeois intelligentsia), or by selling its labour-power (in which case it is a proletarian intelligentsia). This is by distinction from the intellectuals of the exploiting classes who gain their livelihood from rents, taxes and forced labour, from intellectuals who gain their livelihood from some other activity (such as priestly intellectuals who support themselves by performing rituals) and from intellectuals who are supported by noncoercive donations and contributions (the intellectuals of communitarian and archaic societies as well as many monastic intellectuals).

[5] By 'archaic' we mean a system in which many villages are linked together so that surplus can be centralized to support a major ritual centre where higher level artistic, scientific and philosophical activity can take place. Some evidence exists that societies such as the Anasazi in the area which is now in the states of Arizona and New Mexico, as well as the original societies of the great river basins (Nile, Mesopotamia, Indus, Yellow) prior to the Aryan and other invasions, were 'archaic'. We thus use the term 'archaic' not in the colloquial sense of old and outdated but rather in the technical sense of 'ordered to an *arche* or principle'. Archaic social formations centralize surplus largely through public liturgies which make present to the people the organizing principle of the universe and thus cultivate a desire to contribute something to humanity's effort to serve that principle. Because of the low level of development of the productive forces the majority of the population must still be submerged in food production. Their participation in progress is thus indirect, and mediated through these liturgies which make God present to them in a way which She would not otherwise be simply on the basis of their labour, which *appears* reproductive rather than creative, and creates only through generation of a surplus. Innovation is largely the work of an elite of artisans and

The ambivalent social character of the Church was reflected in sharp internal ideological divisions, and especially in the struggle, which came to a head in the thirteenth century, between Augustinian and Aristotelian tendencies. The feudal element in the Church was represented ideologically by the Augustinian trend, which regarded order as something imposed from outside on recalcitrant matter – rather as a warlord imposes 'order' on 'his' peasants. We have already analysed the implications of this problematic in the epistemological field in Chapter 2. The more popular elements in the Church produced a variety of other ideological tendencies. Aristotelianism began to gain strength in the twelfth century with the emergence of towns and the rise of an urban petty bourgeoisie of skilled craftsmen and intellectuals, who not surprisingly stressed the self-organizing potential of matter under the attractive power of the Good, and the participation of the universe generally, and human beings in particular, in the creative life of God.

This Aristotelianism, under the influence of the Arab commentator Ibn Rushd, developed, as we have seen, in an increasingly materialistic and panentheistic direction. The result was a sharp controversy within the Church between traditional Augustinians like Henry of Ghent, who represented the older alliance between the hierarchy and the feudal landed elites, and progressive elements based in the urban guilds and above all in the faculty of arts in Paris. Thomism emerged as a kind of middle ground, which preserved the principal features of Aristotelian epistemology, cosmology, metaphysics and ethics, while making the adjustments which were necessary to conform to Catholic dogma. This meant rejecting not only the unity of the Agent Intellect, but also the eternity of the world and the radically immanent understanding of God which was current in Radical Aristotelian circles. These modifications were not enough for the Augustinians, however, and even before his death Thomas saw many of his propositions condemned as Averroistic. The result was a tendency for the Averroists to adopt an increasingly secular and anticlerical position, while the Church fell more and more under the sway of the Augustinians.

It was only after the Reformation that the Catholic hierarchy recognized the danger of Augustinianism, and turned to Dominican and Jesuit Thomists in order to shore up their position. Even so, there was a very real modification of Thomism in an Augustinian direction by many of the Baroque commentators, especially the Jesuit Suarez, and the complete liquidation of the semi-Averroist left from which Thomism had originally emerged, and which had helped to give it its vitality. It is true that Dominican Thomists (Cajetan and Poinsot) remained more strictly faithful to the teachings of their master than did the Jesuits, and the Dominican order produced some powerful advocates for social justice (Bartolomé de las Casas). But the Dominican voice was just one among many, and even it was relatively tame. One might say that it represented those intellectuals and associated popular elements who, having recognized the implicit nihilism of the marketplace, had made their peace with the hierarchy and were using the Church as a platform from which to criticize the ever mounting abuses which accompanied the European conquest of the Americas and the first stages in the primitive accumulation of capital. They did not, however, advance

---

intellectuals who, however, because their activity contributes to the human civilizational project, do not really constitute a distinct exploiting class, but rather an advanced sector of the emerging working classes.

an independent political-theological project during this period. The cutting edge of the popular movements had already been pushed outside the Church.

It must be pointed out, furthermore, that however much influence Thomism regained during the Baroque period, it largely lost this influence during the eighteenth and early nineteenth centuries when Descartes, Leibniz and Wolff replaced Aquinas in seminary textbooks and the real content of Thomism was almost entirely forgotten (McCool 1977).

This situation persisted up through the first three-quarters of the nineteenth century (allowing, of course, for occasional exceptions and alternative strategies in certain limited locales). It was only after the feudal forces were definitively defeated that the Church began to turn to the popular classes for support. And when it did this, it also turned back to Thomism to articulate a doctrine which would lay the groundwork for such an alliance. Indeed, Neo-Thomism must be understood in the context of the political-theological strategy of the Church after 1848 and especially after 1870, as it searched for new allies after a long series of defeats (McCool 1977).

The complex class character of the alliance the Church was attempting to build is visible in the structure of Dominican Neo-Thomism as we have analysed it. On the one hand, there is a fundamental revaluation of reason and thus of human creative potential, a potential which reaches all the way up to God. This is the popular and progressive (even proletarian) element in the system. It reflects not just a reaching out but an authentic appreciation of labour (manual and intellectual) as a real participation in the life of God. At the same time, the Dominicans 'leave room' for bourgeois science and bourgeois cosmological pessimism – and thus also for a doctrine of the supernatural which retains marked Augustinian tendencies. While the Dominican doctrine of natural knowledge stresses abstraction, even such progressive thinkers as Maritain revert to the Augustinian theory of illumination to explain revelation (Maritain 1937). At the political-economic level this is reflected in an (impossible) attempt to guarantee the priority of the common good (understood in terms no good Marxist could reject, as the full development of human excellence) with the persistence of market relations and de facto bourgeois private property. If the Social Christian and Christian Democratic parties which embodied this doctrine appeared a bit quixotic in their early days, as they pursued a 'third way' between capitalism and socialism, then it is only because they were founded on an impossible dream.

The political-economic reality of Christian Democracy is not really anything distinctively Christian or Catholic, but rather a reassertion of progressive bourgeois tendencies which had been eclipsed by imperialism and finance capital: an emphasis on creating opportunities for human development within the context of a market economy, on trying to treat individuals as ends while still respecting the 'rights' of the bourgeoisie. This is also the reality of Social Democracy, which no less than Christian Democracy seeks an accommodation between people and property, proletariat and bourgeois privilege. The difference is simply that Christian Democracy has defended the place of the Church in European society while Social Democracy has generally sought to restrict it. It is little wonder therefore, that Christian Democracy found its real ideology in the semi-Kantianism of the Transcendental Thomists, just as Social Democracy found its real ideology in the semi-Kantianism of Bernstein *et al.* As we have seen, where Dominican Thomism 'makes room' for the bourgeoisie in what it imagines will be a restored Christendom, Transcendental Thomism attempts to 'make room' for God and for Catholicism in the thoroughly bourgeois house of transcendental philosophy. Bourgeois science and epistemology, and the bourgeois rejection of any authentic metaphysics are all accepted – and along with them the bourgeoisie's whole worldview. It is just that the Transcendental Thomists insist on God as the 'condition of possibility' of this world, where orthodox Kantians do not.

Such a vision may have seemed plausible during the postwar period, especially in Europe, where Social Christian and Social Democratic governments really did build a society in which the wealth created by capitalist development was significantly redirected in a way which promoted the development of human potential, and where individuals really were, to an extent unique in the history of human civilization, treated as ends rather than as means. But this was never a global possibility for capitalism. The European welfare state was based on a high-end export-oriented capitalism which reaped unusually large profits and made it possible to reconcile bourgeois right and human development. But not everyone can capture the high end of the market. The far less complete North American version of the welfare state depended on extraction of surplus from the periphery (which was thus excluded from either strategy for generating surplus) and on extraordinarily high levels of deficit spending which has turned the USA into a country of debt-slaves and mobilized enormous resentment against taxation, which seems to do little to promote the development of ordinary people – because, in fact, so much of the tax revenue is going to make interest payments on the debt (and thus enrich the rentier elite) or to support an enormous military-industrial complex.

This said, we must point out that historical dialectics also has a rather more ambiguous social basis and political valence than is ordinarily recognized. And here the key factor is the bourgeoisie's polemic against prelate and peer, which mesmerized the intelligentsia during the entire period of the democratic revolutions, coupled with the alienating impact of the marketplace itself. We have already noted that Augustinian repression had already pushed many intellectuals working in the dialectical tradition, especially those who had been associated with Averroism, to take an increasingly secular and anticlerical stand. In the case of Hegel, anticlericalism takes the form of a Lutheran polemic against scholasticism, something which seems to have prevented him from ever really reading Thomas, or at least taking him seriously. The Catholic Church, rather than religion as such, takes the brunt of the anticlerical polemic and Rome the brunt of the anti-feudal polemic. The (Evangelical) Church and the German monarchy are not so much obstacles to progress as stages on the way. They are not to be abolished but rather 'transcended and conserved' (*Aufhebon*) by the new 'universal class', the intelligentsia, which – through the mediation of the philosopher – understands the Idea and can draw out its implications for the organization of human society, and then manage society rationally through a centralized rationalized bureaucratic system. Hegel, like the Neo-Thomists, still imagines that he can do this while leaving market relations intact, albeit strictly subordinate to the state, and even while saving a special place in the state for the monarchy and the landed aristocracy (Hegel [1820] 1942). Hegel's position reflects the naivety of a secular intelligentsia which has just acquired independence from the clergy (Collins 1994) and believes that it can, in effect, govern alone. The intelligentsia was soon disabused of any illusions on this point, and Hegelianism promptly dissolved into a reactionary right which sought alliance with the *junkers* and later with the imperialist bourgeoisie (Lukacs [1953] 1980) and a left which leaned towards alliance with the proletariat. The almost complete absence of a Hegelian 'centre' reflects the political impossibility of its position.

Marx and Engels imagine themselves to have transcended any illusions about accommodation with the bourgeoisie – *except in so far as that class still plays a progressive role.* But herein lies the problem. In the middle of the nineteenth century the progressive potential of the industrial bourgeoisie was still far from spent. The enormous dynamism of their organizing activity, their militance on behalf of democracy, and the power of their polemic against prelate and peer still set the pace for social development. And if Marx sometimes erred in attributing the progressive contributions of the bourgeoisie to the system under which they operated (the market system), the reality of these contributions cannot be denied. Thus the veritable hymn to the bourgeoisie which is to be found in such an unlikely document as the *Communist Manifesto* (Marx and Engels [1848] 1978). But it was precisely their openness to the progressivism of the bourgeoisie which made Marx and Engels vulnerable to the disorienting impact of the polemic against prelate and peer. They take for granted the critique of religion which the bourgeoisie began, and extend it in ways which are, to be sure, highly insightful. But they never ask themselves just how this critique and the critique of political economy are to be grounded. They never ask why the development of human productive capacity is a value – a question which, in the end, can be answered only when we have grasped that productivity, creativity, labour is, in the form of the infinite creativity of God, the ultimate ground and final cause of the entire universe. And this is why Engels, as he attempts to generalize dialectical materialism as a philosophical system, ends up 'making room' for bourgeois science, and thus bourgeois cosmological pessimism, every bit as surely as the Dominican or Transcendental Thomists.

This is not to say that any of these ideologies are organically 'bourgeois' in character.[6] On the contrary, as stages in the journey of the dialectic, they represent the struggle of the working classes to find a way forward, to achieve a sufficient understanding both of the organizing principle of the universe, and of the conditions of its own development, to realize its vocation as a real participant in the cosmo-historical evolutionary process. It is just that the task of extricating ourselves from the ideological

---

[6] The one exception we would make here is Transcendental Thomism, the underlying problematic of which we have shown to be Kantian rather than Thomistic and dialectical. Even here though the intention is not reactionary but rather progressive. We saw in Chapter 2 that Kant articulated the progressive, democratic aspirations of the bourgeoisie in its moment of ascent, aspirations which continue to exist among those (ever shrinking) elements of the bourgeoisie which are still innovating and creating new possibilities for humanity. We should say progressive, but also impossible. The impossibility of Kant (of treating human beings as ends while respecting bourgeois 'right') is just the impossibility of the progressive, industrial bourgeoisie itself. With the gradual 'perfection' of the capital markets the innovating entrepreneur, especially in high technology fields, becomes wholly dependent on rentier investors, and is either transformed into a rentier himself, as he transforms the 'equity position' he received in return for his technical or business expertise into a more diversified portfolio, or reduced to a de facto member of the intellectual proletariat with, perhaps, a few extra privileges. This is, in effect, the pattern of so many high tech start-up firms, which rapidly lose their entrepreneurial founders and reduce their technical leaders to the status of 'Chief Scientist'.

web spun by the bourgeoisie has turned out to be rather more difficult than anyone has expected, and it has taken us in a direction which would have been as surprising to Marx and Engels as to Leo XIII. This path would not, however, have been surprising to Socrates, Plato, or Aristotle, to Ibn Sina or Ibn Rushd, to Maimonides, Thomas or Dante. For it is the road mapped out by Plato centuries ago, the mind's one road to God, a road theoretical and practical, which begins with the senses and mounts through the various degrees of abstraction until at last it grasps the first principle – and then descends again, both in the deductive-explanatory activity of the sciences, and in practice, as it attempts to build a civilization which realizes ever more perfectly the incredible Beauty, Truth, Goodness and Integrity which it now knows is not only possible but necessary, and which exerts on it an irresistible attractive force.

Having identified the various degrees of abstraction, we need now to examine each in some depth. We will want, first of all, to specify what is actually involved at each level. Second, in so far as we have identified the Agent Intellect with human society itself, we will want to specify the social conditions for the development of each act of abstraction and show how definite social structures produce particular ideological configurations. Finally, we will want to show the limits of each form and how it passes over, naturally in the case of the first two degrees and 'supernaturally' in the case of the third, into a still higher form of knowledge.

Chapter 4

Totalization

What we have called totalization – the abstraction of a logical whole from its parts – is the most fundamental form of abstraction, on which all others depend. This is the sort of abstraction we use every day when we say that one object in front of us is mineral, is metallic, is a tool, and is, in fact, a hammer, while another is alive, is an animal, and is, in fact, a cat. Totalization also plays an important role in certain kinds of empirically oriented scientific activity. Before one can look for relationships between phenomena, whether these are understood as mere statistical correlations, or as stronger causal relationships, and whether the relationship is formalized mathematically, or integrated into a teleological explanation or both, one must first define the phenomena in question, and this requires totalization. Even when one is looking behind the phenomenon to some underlying structure, one must first have a well-defined phenomenon to look behind. Thus the chemist begins with the empirical chemical species – gold, for example, or common table salt, and only then develops, using quantum theory and other mathematical formalisms, a partial explanation for the properties which differentiate the species in question from other forms of matter. Similarly, the zoologist who studies the behaviour of cats must first know what a cat is, an activity which amounts to little more than a very sophisticated taxonomy, which locates cats in the animal kingdom, in phylum *chordatae*, subphylum *vertebratae*, class *mammalia*, subclass *placentae*, order *carnivoridae*, and then attempts a rigorous definition of the specific difference which characterizes the felines and sets them off from the canines, the ursines and all the other carnivore families. Only on the basis of this definition can we then even pose a question regarding feline behaviour – why, for example, cats hunt alone while dogs hunt in packs. Similarly, sociological debates regarding the relative merits of capitalism and socialism must begin with a rigorous definition of each which permits classification of empirical societies and thus the collection and presentation of evidence by each side.

One would think that the fundamental character of totalization would also make it the simplest to describe, explain and evaluate. This does not, however, turn out to be the case. The difficulty is that although this may not always be apparent to us, we *never* engage in an act of pure totalization. Even the most rudimentary acts of totalization are formed in some degree by the higher degrees of abstraction, formalization and transcendental abstraction. In order to see this, we need only remember that we have characterized totalization as, at base, a classifying activity. But all classification proceeds according to a principle or rule of some kind, and thus involves at least a rudimentary sort of formalization. Thus, for example, the division of things into hard and soft and light and dark sets up a two-dimensional cross-cutting or 'multiplicative' classification which presupposes the operations of multiplication and division and the rules governing these operations, even if this is never made explicit. Similarly, we possess an intuitive sense that some classifications are better than others, at least for certain purposes. A classification of things into hard and soft and light and dark might make sense for a field geologist or interior designer; it will hardly be useful to the biologist or musician. But in so far as our classifications are ordered to an end, they imply an act, however unconscious, of transcendental abstraction.

Because all acts of totalization are formed by higher degrees of abstraction, any effort to describe, explain and evaluate totalization is both difficult and dangerous. It is difficult because we will have to separate analytically acts which are never separate in fact. It is dangerous because to the extent that we succeed in separating out totalization analytically, we run the risk of giving the impression that the act of the intellect is something rather more rudimentary and mechanical than it actually is – that it is something of which rather simple machines might well be fully capable. We will see that in practice it is quite impossible to understand how human beings actually totalize without referring to the higher degrees of abstraction which always form the act of totalization. We will argue later in Chapter 6 that it is precisely a failure to consider the act of the intellect as a whole, and instead to look only at totalization and/ or formalization, which leads some to convince themselves that artificial intelligence is not only possible, but right around the corner, and that the human mind is, in fact, little different from some of our better supercomputers.

With these caveats in mind, then, we turn to our principal aim in this chapter: to analyse the act of totalization and its products in terms of the general account of the intellect which we have developed in the preceding chapters. This will require us to look at the respective contributions of the nervous system or 'Potential Intellect' and the social system or 'Agent Intellect', as well as their cooperation in the unitary act of knowledge. We will have an opportunity to test our account of totalization by seeing what light, if any, it can shed on the scientific discipline most concerned with classification – that is, taxonomy. We will also look at what, if anything, our theory implies about the product of totalization – something which will lead us to engage the old debate on universals. Finally, we will define the limits of totalization and show why it passes over necessarily into formalization and transcendental abstraction.

The Biological and Social Basis of Totalization

We begin, therefore, by assessing the role of the nervous system in the act of totalization. Given what we have already said in previous chapters, this role is limited but of fundamental importance. Data from the external senses (vision, hearing, smell, taste, touch and so on) is formed by the nervous system into topographic representations or images and stored as dispositional representations or memories, which can be recalled more or less at will. Now classification, at the neurological level, would seem to involve nothing more or less than the creation of links between groups of images or representations which are 'similar', or, to put the matter more formally, the creation of a system of mappings between representations, which defines 'similar differences' and 'different similarities'. There appears, furthermore, to be nothing exclusive about these systems of mappings. On the contrary there is no reason why things cannot be classified simultaneously based on colour, sound, smell, taste, texture and any of a variety of other sensible qualities or combinations of sensible qualities.

Once we have granted this, however, an important question arises. Can classification be explained exclusively in terms of neurological processes? There would appear to be a case for this. First of all, many other animals show evidence of a rudimentary form of classification. They can, for example, classify objects as potential food sources, potential mates, young who need to be cared for, and potential adversaries. Higher birds and mammals – especially psittaciforms (parrots), anthropoids (apes) and cetaceans (whales and dolphins) seem able to go further than this. Second, structural anthropologists such as Lévi-Strauss have marshalled extensive evidence that thought patterns, and especially classification strategies, do in fact remain fairly constant across cultures. Thus the predominance of what Lévi-Strauss calls 'dual organization', based on binary opposition, in kinship systems and mythic cycles, throughout the world (Lévi-Strauss [1958] 1963: 132–66 and passim). If forms of classification are universal, while human societies differ, it would seem to make sense to attribute the act of classification to something which is shared – the structure of the nervous system – rather than to something which differs radically from one society to the next.

Let us address each of these arguments in turn. We must begin by pointing out that what has been called classification by various subhuman animals is, in fact, a wide spectrum of behaviours. Some of these are clearly neurological driven or, in some cases, driven by simple chemical reactions. Thus, when an amoeba withdraws from a saline solution or moves towards a glucose solution, this hardly involves a classification of the chemicals involved as 'toxin' or 'foodstuff'. The same is true of more complex reactions, whereby certain animals always or almost always respond in exactly the same way to the same sensual stimulus – insects or birds for example, responding to a mating call. What seems rather more like authentic acts of classification are the behaviours of certain higher mammals, which have a wide repertoire of behaviours, each oriented towards a certain sort of object – especially to certain other animals of the same species. Thus dogs have their own hierarchy of dominance and submission, with which definite behaviours are associated. But there is more. Dogs seem able to classify non-dogs (specifically humans) within this hierarchy, so that their human 'masters' are treated with the deference due an Alpha-pup, while a small, frightened stranger is treated as a subordinate and harassed at every turn. And this despite the fact that at the sensual level the two humans seem more like each other than either is to a dog, dominant, submissive, or somewhere in between. What should be apparent here, of course, is that it is precisely among the higher, social animals that we see evidence of something which can really be called a rudimentary act of classification. And the basis for the classifying activity is not in the animal's nervous system (though this system is certainly involved) but rather in the social structure, however rudimentary that may be. It is, furthermore, when apes become enmeshed in our more complex social structure that they learn to use the more complex system of classification involved in language.

The purported universality of dual classification presents some more subtle problems. Let us begin by saying that, given our realist commitments, we should not be at all surprised to find similarities in the way different cultures classify the world around them. Of particular importance in this regard is the finding by taxonomists that people in many hunter-gatherer and horticultural societies recognize the same unit *taxa* (biological species) as do biologists from advanced industrial societies (Mayr 1982: 317). Dual classification, on the other hand, is something quite different. Anyone who reads Lévi-Strauss cannot help but marvel at the facility with which he has reduced the most diverse social structural and mythic content to the simplest and most universal formulae. Apparently, for example, both the Oedipus cycle and all known versions of the Zuni emergence myth – and indeed all other myths – can be reduced to the following formula:

$$f_x(a):f_y(b) \simeq f_x(b):f_{a-1}(y)$$

Lévi-Strauss arrives at this conclusion by dividing myths into what he calls their 'gross constituent units'. These units are not, furthermore, simply episodes, but rather relationships, or rather bundles of relationships, such as that between Oedipus and his mother, summed across all variants of the myth. Lévi-Strauss includes here not only different versions of an oral or literary tradition, but also modern reinterpretations such as that of Freud. And the 'relationships' are characterized in starkly simple terms as 'opposition' or 'negation'. In this way the opposition between autochthony and bisexual reproduction, which Lévi-Strauss sees as the heart of the Oedipus cycle, is identified with the opposition between agriculture and hunting in the Zuni emergence myth (Lévi-Strauss [1958] 1963: 206–31).

What is happening here is that Lévi-Strauss reduces the myths he analyses to such simple elements that they cannot help but appear identical. We have entered Hegel's 'night in which all cows are black' (Hegel [1807] 1967). What Lévi-Strauss discovers is nothing more than the logical limits on any possible system of classification: that it involves difference or distinction, and thus binary oppositions. While the more complex formalisms he develops to describe the myths may well hold, he does not show that these are the only possible way to formalize the myths nor even that they are the most economical. He merely shows that all classification, in so far as it depends on difference, involves binary opposition, and that this in turn imposes certain constraints on the form and pattern of classification. Any conclusion that this very thin universality of patterns of classification is based in universal structures of the human mind, neurological or otherwise, is entirely unwarranted.

The fact is that the evidence for diversity in systems of classification is every bit as strong as the evidence for similarity, if not stronger. And this evidence also points to a social basis not only for the act of classification generally, but also for a more specific determination of systems of classification by the structure of the society which produces them. We have already mentioned, for example, that the Inuit have far more names for snow than do Europeans, and appear to see these various forms of matter as distinctly as we might see rain and snow or sand and rock. The fact that languages like Inuit have far more names for snow than does English, for example, does not simply reflect environmental differences – that is, the fact that snow and its many varieties are far more important to the Inuit than they are to Europeans. It also reflects a fundamentally different linguistic strategy and thus a different way of thinking. 'Primitive' languages often have far richer nomenclatures than more 'advanced' languages, coupled with less sophisticated paradigmatic structures (hierarchies grouping similar classes into higher categories). Complex languages, rather than having a separate name for each genus or species, use category names and modifiers – wet, icy snow, dry, powdery snow and so on. We will see that this reflects a trend towards rationalization, or rather 'formalization' of the culture's categorical scheme, something which comes with increasing complexity of social organization.

The foundational research on systems of classification is Durkheim's study of aboriginal religion in Australia (Durkheim [1911] 1965). The indigenous peoples of Australia are organized in tribes composed of half-tribes or moieties and clans. Each clan has its own totem – a plant or animal which serves as its emblem or symbol. Clan solidarity is conserved and reproduced in communion feasts in which the totemic object, taboo during the rest of the year, is eaten in a great feast. There are also individual, moiety and tribal totems, though the clan, as the most important level of social organization, is also the focus of symbolic unity. But there is more. The system of totems functions as a kind of universal taxonomy. Members of a clan really *are* their totem. Thus some people are wallabies and others witchity grubs, as are certain kinds of rocks, rivers and so on. The existence of a scheme of social classification provides a basis in experience for the act of classification. To put the matter in Thomistic terminology, it creates a connatural knowledge of *taxis*,[1] and thus the capacity to produce a taxonomy. There is, furthermore, a kind of 'category of totality', the existence of which Durkheim attributes to the experience of inter-tribal relationships, which is represented in a kind of vague and remote 'Great Spirit' (Durkheim [1911] 1965).[2] This latter idea gains considerable strength with the establishment of settled inter-clan village communities, and the formation of a state uniting villages established by different tribes. Thus communitarian and archaic societies produce not only the vague idea of a Great Spirit or Great Mother but a complex mythology which represents the universe as a hierarchical system. Aspects of these mythologies, however – narratives of creation, judgement and redemption – reflect an incipient capacity for the higher transcendental abstraction, something we will discuss in a later chapter.

Now it should be clear that the sort of classification carried out by the Australian aborigines, while quite complex and sophisticated in its own way, is also quite different from any classification which people in an advanced industrial society – or for that matter most tributary societies – would be likely to produce. Even more striking evidence for the impact of social structure on forms of classification emerges from Luria's research in Uzbekistan, to which we have already referred. It should be remembered that Uzbekistan was the site of an advanced tributary civilization which, during the Middle Ages, produced the great cities of Samarkand, Bukhara and Khorezm, as well as the mathematician and astronomer Ulugh-bek, the philosophers Al-Biruni and Ibn Sina, and the poets Saadi and Nizami. Luria's team interviewed five groups of villagers in this region in the early 1930s, as the process of collectivization of agriculture was just beginning:

1   Ichkari women living in remote villages who were not involved in any modern social activities . . .

---

[1] *Taxis* is a Greek word for order. It connotes an arranging in accord with a principle or rule, much as a general might order his troops for battle – thus the word 'tactics' which is derived from the same root.

[2] Evidence for 'band societies' which lack a developed kinship system or other internal differentiation is very skimpy, but here one would still expect to find the concepts of part and whole, as well as the idea of different wholes, based on the experience of distinct individuals belonging to different bands – but not the highly developed system of classification we see in tribal societies.

2   Peasants in remote villages who continued to maintain an individualistic economy, to remain illiterate, and to involve themselves in no way with socialized labour.
3   Women who attended short-term courses in the teaching of kindergarteners . . .
4   Active *kolkhoz* (collective farm workers) . . .
5   Women students admitted to a teachers' school after two or three years of study. (Luria [1974] 1976: 15)

The interviews focused on a range of different cognitive activities. Here, however, we are concerned primarily with his questions on what he called 'perception' and 'generalization'. What is striking is that the majority of the villagers he interviewed showed little sign of being able to develop a complex taxonomy. Women presented with skeins of wool described their colours overwhelmingly by reference to other objects such as iris, liver, spoiled cotton, calf's dung, pig's dung, sky, air, decayed teeth, pistachio and so on. Only those who participated in collective farm organization showed any sign of using a 'hierarchical' nomenclature in which similar hues were grouped into basic colours (blue, yellow, red) and then coupled with modifiers (light, dark . . .) (Luria [1974] 1976: 25–6). Similarly, when presented with the kind of object series used in intelligence tests, and asked to identify which object doesn't belong to the series, the result was fascinating.

> Subject: Rakmat, age thirty-nine, illiterate peasant from an outlying district; has seldom been in Fergama, never in any other city. He was shown drawings of the following: hammer–saw–log–hatchet.
>
> 'They're all alike. I think all of them have to be here. See, if you're going to saw, you need a saw, and if you have to split something you need a hatchet. So they're all needed here . . .'
>
> We tried to explain the task by another, simpler example.
>
> 'Look, here you have three adults and one child. Now clearly the child doesn't belong in this group.'
>
> 'Oh, but the boy must stay with the others! All three of them are working, you see, and if they have to keep running out to fetch things, they'll never get the job done, but the boy can do the running for them . . . The boy will learn; that'll be better, then they'll all be able to work well together.' (Luria [1974] 1976: 55)

There are two sharp differences between the way these peasants classify and the way people in more complex societies would approach the same task. First, there is little or nothing in the way of a hierarchical nomenclature. Names are not grouped into higher *taxa*. Second, while there *is* a capacity to distinguish good and bad classifications, the principle used is not what things *are* but rather what they are *for*.

What are we to make of the sharp differences in the ways in which people in different societies classify? One possibility, of course, is that the increasing social complexity is *so* important to the development of rational taxonomies that people in tribal, communitarian, archaic and tributary societies simply don't think in a way which we can regard as recognizably human. Whether it is accompanied by a value judgement or not this approach would seem to undermine any possible realism and to undercut any attempt to define a universal human nature. It also fails to explain why so many of the products of pre-capitalist culture seem so attractive and meaningful to people in advanced industrial societies – and why members of surviving pre-capitalist societies are quick to adapt elements of advanced industrial civilization. Clearly we need to find a superior alternative to this approach.

Fortunately Luria's research gives us a hint at a better explanation, though he does not really develop it. The absence of any real hierarchical taxonomy may simply be a reflex of the fact that the Uzbeki peasant has little or no experience of participating in groups which are parts of other groups. Thus the rich nomenclature and the weak system of categorization. We will recall, furthermore, that Luria's peasants did indeed have a criterion by which they judged good and bad classifications. It is just that this criterion was teleological rather than formal. Things were grouped together based on use or function rather than their nature or some abstract quality. Far from indicating an inability to think complexly, teleological principles indicate the operation of the higher, transcendental abstraction. What is missing is simply the formal principle which people living in a market society, which lacks any global purpose, must use to classify objects, given the impossibility of making assumptions about the purposes of others.

We still have, of course, the troubling example of the Australian aborigines, whose taxonomy appears at first sight to be neither formally rigorous nor incipiently functional and teleological in character. Indeed, there is no obvious way in which one group of people, plants, minerals and so on are similar to wallabies and another closer to kangaroos. But let us look more closely. There is indeed one activity in which all of the things grouped together under a single totemic *taxon* are used, more or less at one time. This activity is ritual – arguably the most important function of aboriginal society. Indeed, it is ritual which creates the clan, the half-tribe and the tribe. Otherwise, given the dynamics of the hunter-gatherer economy alone, there would be no reason for anything but small, wandering bands. Ritual represents the reaching out of the hunter-gatherer band to a higher form of organization, which they have not yet discovered. The association of totems and clans and totems and 'member' minerals, plants and so on may originally have been the result of highly specific, contingent, historical events. The association, however, and the taxonomy which it generates, continues to make sense because the totem, the human members of the clan, and the auxiliary animal, plant and mineral members of the clan are all 'used' in the ritual in some way – or at least used in the life process which is ordered to the production of the ritual, which is the culminating moment in the life of the community.

The Act of Totalization

We are now in a position to describe the act of totalization in some detail. This act begins, like all acts of knowledge, with sensation. Data gathered by the external senses are formed into images and memories which can be recalled, divided, combined and so on. None of this, however, can properly be called totalization. Totalization depends on a pre-conceptual, connatural knowledge of *taxis* rooted in social structure, and more specifically in our participation in definite social categories. Being social means being part of a class, and as classified, we are naturally also classifiers. This pre-conceptual, connatural knowledge of *taxis* illuminates the images garnered from sensation and reveals the logical whole or universal of which the image is an example. The way in which we totalize will, however, be determined by the social structure of which we are a part. If we have a powerful experience of social categories which are ordered to an end, we will classify much as the Uzbek peasants do. If, on the other hand, we live in a market society in which there are no global purposes to which we can refer, such classifications will seem arbitrary. At the same time, we will bring to the act of knowledge a connatural knowledge of complex quantitative relationships – that is, relationships between supply, demand and price which govern the allocation of resources by the marketplace. Thus we will spontaneously tend towards the production of taxonomies which provide a basis for mathematical formalization – even if we ourselves have little or no formal mathematical training.

The actual process of classification thus involves nothing more than a systematic process of comparison, a search for similarities and differences. Looking at a meadow or forest, we notice things which are similar or different in colour, shape, texture and so on. We also make comparisons over time. We notice that some things seem to change little, while others seem to undergo a constant flux. But it is not enough to simply group together things which seem similar in some way. Consider, for example the following classification:

red things, loud things, soft things, pungent things, sweet things, living things . . .

Even a child could recognize that there is something wrong here. When we classify and define we are not looking for just any similarities and differences. We are looking for *similar differences* and *different similarities* (Bohm 1980) – that is, differences of colour, sound, smell, taste, texture and so on. As the process of classification proceeds, furthermore, we want differences of the same magnitude to define each taxonomic rank. 'Hunts alone' vs. 'hunts in packs' is not a difference of the same magnitude as 'eats meat' vs. 'eats vegetables', which in turn is not of the same magnitude as 'has a backbone' vs. 'lacks a backbone'. As we do this, however, we pass naturally over into formalization. When we say that the difference between felines and canines is, for example, somehow equivalent to the difference between bovines and caprines, we have defined a ratio and thus a measure. We may not know it, but we are doing maths. This statement, which certainly retains its qualitative content, can nonetheless be expressed in formal terms:

$$A:B::C:D$$

This ratio then gives us the notion of a unit, or the numerical one. As we build our taxonomy, unit *taxa* can be added together to arrive at higher *taxa*. Thus the felines, canines, ursines and so on all taken together make up the carnivores. Similarly, we can subtract *taxa*, moving down the ladder from the carnivores to one or two particular families, species, varieties or individuals. This means that additive classification is an 'operation' in Piaget's sense of the term: it is internalizable and reversible (Piaget 1968). We can also develop multiplicative taxonomies, by joining, for example, the taxonomic series: carnivore, omnivore, herbivore, and the taxonomic series: flying, terrestrial, marine. Multiplicative classification, like additive, appears to be reversible. Dividing *taxa* appears to be well defined. The only thing which prevents this sort of classifying activity from passing over into a fully formal abstraction is the absence of any reflection on the principles governing the taxonomy, and the definition of the idea of a unit or element, of sets and other categories, of operations and eventually of properties of operations (commutativity, associativity and so on).

Even so, it would be entirely possible to develop a taxonomy which seemed quite ridiculous. Finding similar differences and different similarities does not help us to distinguish the essential from the accidental. One might, for example, develop a universal, formal taxonomy in which humans were still classified as featherless bipeds. This is why mathematically-oriented sciences cannot tell us, for example, what an electron *is* but only how it behaves – and this only in the shape of a mathematical formalism. We also need to take into consideration just how important various differences are, not just quantitatively, but in terms of their place on a scale of values. We consider 'rational animal' a better definition of a human being than 'featherless biped' because we regard rationality and animality as more valuable than featherlessness or bipedal anatomy. Transcendental as well as formal abstraction thus enters into the actual act of totalization.

Concerns of this sort led the Dominican commentators to argue for a distinction between abstraction of a logical whole (*abstractio totalis*), which was characteristic of ordinary reasoning and which was also the first step in science, and *abstractio totius* which grasped the essential nature of things – which recognized, for example, that while humans may logically be classified as featherless bipeds, and that while such a classification might be useful for certain purposes, what we *are* is rational animals – with 'rational' here including the full range of functions of the intellect and which will make possible not only theoretical knowledge of intelligibles, but also art, prudence, love and so on, and ultimately our ordering to the Beatific Vision.

We rejected this approach in favour of the simpler threefold classification outlined in Chapter 3. We are now in a position to explain our reasoning in greater depth. The Dominican position fails to recognize the extent to which *all* abstraction is formed by formalization and transcendental abstraction. The *abstractio totalis* as they understand it is quite impossible. The Dominican distinction between the *abstractio totalis* and the *abstractio formalis*, furthermore, separates off scientific and philosophical reasoning from ordinary everyday abstraction. It follows that the latent potential for the higher *abstractio formalis* may or may not be present in all human beings, casting a shadow over the prospects for an authentic philosophical democracy. Our own approach, on the other hand, while acknowledging that the conditions for the full development of the higher degrees of abstraction are not always present, shows this abstraction to be immanent in the lower totalizing abstraction that we all use on a day-to-day basis, so that everyone has the experience of at least a rudimentary scientific and philosophical reasoning, even if they are not aware of it, creating a groundwork on which the teaching authority can build. People who imagine that these higher degrees of abstraction are beyond them – that they can never do sophisticated mathematical physics or philosophical theology – are missing the acts of formalization and transcendental abstraction which are implicit in their ordinary, everyday knowledge of the world around them. Becoming proficient at higher abstraction is not a matter of learning something entirely new, but rather of becoming excellent at an act we all perform countless times every day.

The approach which we are suggesting here at once finds confirmation, and helps to resolve current debates in, the one scientific discipline devoted explicitly to the problem of classification – taxonomy (Mayr 1982: 269–88). Taxonomy is focused, of course, on the classification of living organisms; larger questions with taxonomic import such as the line between living and non-living are left to one side. Even so, the scope of the enterprise is sufficient to generate some intriguing problems. At present there are three basic approaches to biological classification: numerical phenetics, cladistics and what has come to be called 'evolutionary classification'. Numerical phenetics is fundamentally an attempt to make quantitatively rigorous the systematic comparison of various observable characters.[3] Data on large numbers of characters is collected. In order to render the resulting classification 'theory free' all characters are given equal weight. The data is then manipulated using various algorithms in order to generate what is called a 'phenogram', which measures the relative distance between various specimens. This phenogram is then taken directly as a classification.

The difficulty with this approach is that different characters and types of characters yield different results. Organisms which are quite similar in their genetic structure or biochemistry may have vast morphological, physiological, or behavioural differences which make the claim that they are 'similar' seem ludicrous. At the same time, new information regarding biochemical differences among organisms which appear similar in morphology or behaviour cannot simply be ignored. Of particular interest in this regard is the case of the rabbits, hares and picas. Long classed on the basis of morphology and their gnawing behaviour as members of the order *Rodentia*, these animals are closer in biochemistry to the ungulates and have unique physiological characteristics, such as the capacity to extract proteins and vitamins from bacteria growing in a special form of excrement which they produce and then consume. What does one do with them? Simply placing them in a separate order (*Lagomorphidae*) does not resolve the problem. Is this order 'closer' to the ungulates or to the rodents?

On the whole numerical phenetics suffers from the problems we have already ascribed to totalization formed by mathematical formalization, which yields formalized but often entirely ludicrous classifications. While no practitioner of numerical phenetics would actually do so, there is little in the method to prevent classification of human beings as 'featherless bipeds', placed closer to the birds than to the mammalian line of insectivores and primates from which we probably descended. But the problems of the principal alternative strategy of classification – what is known as cladistics – are no less serious. Cladists classify exclusively on the basis of genealogy. Phylogeny, or the genesis of new *taxa*, is regarded as a completely dichotomous process. Parent species split into daughter species and then cease to exist. Sister species are always given an equal taxonomic rank. Ancestral species and their descendants are included in a single 'holophyletic' *taxon* – a *taxon* composed of descendants of a single ancestor. Cladistics has over phenetics the advantage that it is rooted in a real biological process which yields real biological relationships. Once again, however, the drive towards formalism yields results which are suspect at best. First of all, it is far from clear that evolution consists in a series of dichotomous splits in which parent species disappear. On the contrary, current research suggests that speciation occurs primarily through movement into new niches which 'form' behaviour differently and result in evolutionary pressure for the development of new characters. There is no

---

[3] 'Characters' is the technical term used by taxonomists for any observable quality or characteristic.

reason why this process should be dichotomous or why the parent species might not survive in its 'old' form in the older niche. The option for 'dichotomy and ancestral extinction' is driven by a desire for formalizability. Second, some new characters are simply of greater significance than others. Acquisition of organelles, the movement to land, or the development of tool-making are all changes of far greater significance than a shift from eating one kind of seed to another. All, however, came about through what at first was a simple process of speciation.

What this suggests is that in order to classify we need a principle which allows us to evaluate not just the magnitude but also the significance of differences, whether these differences are conceived phenetically (in terms of observable characters) or cladistically in terms of genealogical relationships. And this, of course, is an act of transcendental abstraction, because it involves placing value on a change, defining it as 'evolutionarily significant' or even 'progressive'. This is what practitioners of evolutionary classification are actually doing, even if they are reluctant to admit it. Classification is based primarily on genealogy, but it is not assumed that evolutionary changes are dichotomous or result in the extinction of ancestors. More important, both the magnitude and the importance of evolutionary leaps is taken into account in grouping species into higher *taxa*. Neo-Darwinists such as Ernst Mayr claim that it is possible to define non-teleological criteria for making these kinds of evaluations. Specifically, he suggests that a classification must not only allow us to store and retrieve information regarding organisms, but also 'establish groupings about which generalizations can be made' (Mayr 1982: 271). There is, therefore, no need to claim that the transition from prokaryotes to eukaryotes, from plants to animals, or the emergence of intelligence is progressive in order to demonstrate its significance. The difficulty with this position is that it fails to capture fully just why we actually treat these transitions as important. Saying that the emergence of intelligence, for example, is a useful adaptation or that it has survival value, does not really differentiate it from countless other adaptations. Bacteria and insects have found adaptations which are, if anything, far more 'useful' than our own in terms of survival value. Rather, we regard key transitions such as the emergence of sensation, intelligence and so on as important because they involve the emergence not only of new structures which serve an old purpose, but of new purposes which presuppose but go beyond the old. While it is certainly true that evolutionary biology cannot by itself establish the 'value' of these new purposes, such judgements of value are in fact implicit in its own more modest judgements regarding the relative importance of various evolutionary transitions, and thus the relative merits of various evolutionary classifications.

In other words, just as totalization is always subordinated to formalization and transcendental abstraction, classifying disciplines such as taxonomy are always subordinated not only to mathematical sciences which can help them to produce more formal classifications, but also to metaphysics which alone can ground the judgements of value implicit in its own classifying work.

The Product of Totalization

Let us suppose now that we have developed a classification – that we have defined a system of similar differences and different similarities and decided the relative importance of each degree of difference so that, for example, we are able to say that the relationship between dogs and cats is roughly the same as that between sheep and cattle. What is the status of the *taxa* which we have defined? More generally, what do we know when we abstract a logical whole from the individuals which compose it – that is, when we place the individual in a species and a species in a higher *taxon*? There are a number of dimensions to this problem. We must ask first about the ontological status of the *taxon*. Is it simply a name applied for good reason to a group of individuals which itself has no reality – the historic nominalist position? Or is the *taxon* itself something real, as realists have claimed for two and half millennia? Second, if it is real (and we will argue that it is), what is it? What does it mean to ascribe reality to something which is not a direct observable? And what is the relationship between the *taxon* and the individual? Is it a 'substantial form' in the Aristotelian sense which confers being? Or is it merely an essence distinct from the act of being? Or is it something else entirely?

In order to engage these questions we need to situate them properly in the context of two related philosophical controversies: the debate around universals (Stumpf 1994: 161–5) and the debate around substance. The first controversy goes back to Plato and Aristotle who, in their struggle against the relativism of the Sophists, were anxious to show that knowledge terminates in something more than a mere name – that we grasp the form or essence of a thing. Plato appeared in places to suggest that these forms actually exist apart from material things, which are reflections or copies of them – and rather poor ones at that. Aristotle was more modest, claiming that the form existed only in the thing, and later in the intellect of the knower, but not independent of both. The first position became known as radical or exaggerated realism, the second as moderate realism. Radical realism faced from the beginning a difficulty in explaining just how, where and in what sense these forms exist apart from matter. Is there a separate form for each shade of red? for each variety of sheep? If so, the resulting continuum infinity[4] of forms would seem to compromise the Platonic effort to explain the universe in terms of a single principle. Moderate realism, on the other hand, had difficulty explaining just what it meant to say that something (the universal) really exists if it is only present as the form of a multitude of other things. Isn't it simpler to just say that these things are similar, and are thus called by the same name?

The second controversy derives from a distinction made by Aristotle between substance and accident. A substantial form is something which can exist in itself, and which confers being on something. Thus 'rock', 'dog', and 'human' are substantial forms. An accident is something which can exist only in something else, such as 'white', or 'jagged', or 'wise'. This distinction helped to clarify the debate between the radical and moderate realist positions – much to the advantage of the latter. According to the radical realists the universal exists independent of the individuals, which merely participate in it, and independent of the knower, who enjoys a different kind of participation. It is thus a substance and not an accident. This implies that there is a continuum infinity of eternal separate substances – one, for example for each

---

[4] This is by distinction from an integer infinity. An integer infinity involves simply an unlimited application of the operation of addition (or subtraction). Thus the [. . . –3, –2, –1, 0, 1, 2, 3, . . .]. A continuum infinity, on the other hand, is one in which there is an infinity by subdivision as well as by addition. Thus the real numbers.

slight variation in the colour red – existing independently of both individual red things and minds which perceive them. This is hardly an attractive possibility. For the moderate realist, on the other hand, some universals exist as substantial forms which, joined with matter, confer being on individuals; others exist merely as accidents in individuals which derive their being from some other form. The universal, furthermore, whether it exists as substance or accident in the individual, is in the mind of the knower only as an accident – a perfection of the intellect.

The moderate realist position was restated for European philosophy by Boethius in his translation and commentary on Porphyry's *Isagoge* or *Introduction to Aristotle's 'Categories'*, and seemed to offer a sensible middle road between the extremes of radical realism and nominalism. Certain Augustinian theologians such as Odo of Tournai and Anselm of Canterbury, however, became convinced that moderate realism was not sufficient to support key Christian doctrines, such as original sin and the Trinity. If, Odo argued, the universal is not a real substance existing apart from the individual and the mind of the knower, then how can we share in Adam's sin? What Adam did would be his responsibility alone and the doctrine of original sin an absurdity. Anselm focused on the problems which moderate realism created for the doctrine of the Trinity. How, if the universal exists really and substantially only in the individual, can the three persons of the Trinity share in a common divinity in a way which makes them really and truly one? Doesn't moderate realism lead to tritheism?

Radical realism, however, was not without its own problems. It seemed, as Abelard pointed out, to imply that humanity as such was present in each individual. But since human beings differ from each other in at least accidental ways, this meant that contrary accidents could be predicated of the same substance, a claim which Aristotle had already shown to be untenable (Abelard, *Logica 'Ingredientibus'*, in Wippel and Wolter 1969). This led many to reject realism altogether, and to opt for a resurgent nominalism. Early nominalists such as Roscelin, accepted the heterodox implications of their doctrine. Later nominalists, such as William of Occam, avoided these implications by rejecting philosophical theology entirely in favour of what amounted to fideism. It is this latter approach which laid the groundwork for Luther's doctrines of *sola fides* and *sola scriptura*.

It was Thomas, finally, who produced at least a preliminary answer to Augustinian and nominalist objections. The Thomistic theory of knowledge, on which our own is largely based, disposes rather neatly with the nominalist position. In the act of sensation the internal senses actually take on the form of the thing known, the image. Totalization builds up relations between similar images, which themselves result in new, second order images or representations, with their own distinct forms. What is known, therefore, is not merely a name, but a real form which exists, albeit in different ways in the object (*in rem*) and in the knower (*post rem*). It is only in the individual that the universal can be a substantial form making a thing what it is; as for Aristotle in the mind it is an accident. Thomas adds that the universal also exists *ante rem* in the mind of God, where it is an exercise of divine power, not a substantial form (Aquinas, *Summa Theologiae* I, Q 15).

Thomas is also able to address Augustinian objections rather easily, by suggesting that the relationship between universal and individual is different at different levels of being. In material things, individuation is by matter. The universal, when it is a substantial form such as 'rock' or 'willow tree' or 'dog' or 'human', elevates matter from potency to act. Individuals within a species differ only 'accidentally', realizing the potential and achieving the perfections possible for their nature in different ways or to different degrees. Intellectual substances, such as angels, are differentiated by specific difference. Without any matter and thus with no possibility of realizing their natures in different ways or to different degrees, angels differ only at the level of their natures themselves. There is only one angel of each kind. The divine nature, on the other hand, is differentiated by 'procession', that is, by internal relationships which at once reflect the divine nature and which constitute distinct persons which are fully in possession of that nature and the faculties it confers. Tritheism is avoided for the simple reason that the divine nature, unlike the human, permits only relations of perfect knowledge, love, power and so on. There is no question of one or another person of the Trinity going off on his own and, say, having an affair or trying out his own unique strategy with humanity, as do the 'gods' of Olympus. There can be only one God; the multiplication of persons does not affect this (Aquinas, *Summa Theologiae* I, Q 27–31; Farrell 1945: 141–62). Thomas addresses Odo's objections regarding the implications of moderate realism for the doctrine of original sin by showing that it is human nature, and not our individuating matter, which is affected by Adam's sin. Once this nature has been changed, the change affects all individuals who share it – something that does not require that this nature exist as a separate substance apart from individual humans (Aquinas, *Summa Theologiae* I–II, Q 81–3).

There are, however, difficulties with Thomas's solution as well. First of all, the Aristotelian notion of substance on which it is predicated is not itself entirely coherent. While clearly there is a sense in which a burro or a human exists in itself, and 'red' only in something else, the fact is that both burros and human beings are themselves just aspects of far more complex systems, on the internal relations of which they are radically dependent. Burros and humans exist only 'in' certain sorts of ecological niches and social systems, which in turn depend on a complex biological and physical substratum, and on the global structure of the universe as a whole. The only true substance is necessary Being, or God – a point which Spinoza made to great effect in the seventeenth century (Spinoza, *Ethics* 1: 5, 14). Clearly we need a way of capturing the distinction which Aristotle made between different sorts of universals which does not imply an unwarranted ontological pluralism.

Second, the Thomistic doctrine does not really allow for the sort of internal differentiation within species which makes possible the emergence of new forms out of old – something which is essential if we are to take into account what the special sciences have discovered regarding the evolution of matter generally, the emergence of living from non-living matter, the evolution of increasingly complex forms of life, the emergence of intelligence from the matrix of biological matter generally, and the historical development of human societies towards ever higher levels of organization. This is the principal criticism raised by dialectical materialism (which otherwise also opts for moderate realism on the question of universals) against the Thomistic position, and it is an issue also raised by evolutionary biologists in particular, who point out that variation within 'species' is so great that classification is often nearly impossible, and who thus reject the 'typological' species concept which they associate with the Aristotelian tradition.

The solution to this problem is not difficult to find. Indeed, it is supplied by evolutionary biology and dialectical materialist sociology, though it involves a less dramatic rupture with Thomism than the practitioners of these disciplines imagine. Evolutionary biologists prefer to define biological species in terms of a specific sort of inter-relationship: inter-breeding. Organisms which inter-breed are part of the same species; speciation is differentiation which extends so far that inter-breeding becomes impossible. Dialectical sociology, similarly, classifies societies in terms of their relationship to the ecosystem (forces of production) and the character of their dominant economic relationships (relations of production). The boundaries of a society, furthermore, are the boundaries of its economic relationships – for example, the largest scale at which, for example, an effective taxing mechanism or unified market can really and truly be said to exist.

If we generalize this principle, then we arrive at the notion that the universal is, ultimately, a mode of organization – a structured system of relationships which is ordered to an end or purpose. This approach allows us, among other things, to extend Thomas's insight into the hierarchical differentiation of the relation between universal and individual at different levels of being. Simple forms of organization, such as electrons, cannot vary much among themselves and still be what they are. There are thus many individuals within the same species, which differ little if at all among themselves. As the degree of organization becomes more complex, so does the internal structure of the *taxon*. Chemical species may have many isotopes or isomers. Biological *taxa* are in principle capable of infinite subdivision, as one individual within one species, within one genus, family, order, phylum and kingdom, initiates a process of speciation which could in principle lead not only to a new species, but to higher order *taxa* at every level – even to something which is not only alive, say, but also intelligent. Sociological *taxa* present even more difficulties. Not only are the *taxa* infinitely divisible, but individuals are often impossible to classify properly. While 'proletarian' represents a definite way of being human, and thus a sociological species, with a well-defined structure and function, it is quite possible that there may, in any given society, be no one who belongs in this *taxon* and only this *taxon*.

Even so, at all levels of organization, not just the biological, *taxa* are defined by the ways in which individuals relate to other individuals of the same and different *taxa*. Electrons are defined by the way in which they relate to other electrons, to protons and so on. Chemical species are defined by the way in which their constituent elements (protons, neutrons, electrons) relate to each other, which in turn determines the way they relate to other members of the same chemical species as well as to individuals of others. Organisms are defined by the way their cells and organs relate to each other, which in turn determines the way in which they relate to other organisms of the same and different biological species. Societies are defined by the relations between their member organisms, and by the way in which they relate to other societies . . .

New ways of relating add new determinations to a system. To the extent that these new ways of relating do not simply represent the exercise of an existing power, but the acquisition of a new one, or of a qualitatively higher degree of the old power, we can speak of the emergence of a new species. We thus preserve the realism of the Thomistic solution, but overcome any implications that species are static and eternal. There is such a thing as the nature of gold, of wheat, of goats and of humans. These natures are defined by ways of relating which always allow for internal diversity – and change. When differentiation becomes so great that the new individuals can no longer relate in the same way as the old, we can speak of a new chemical, biological or sociological species.

This is actually more a clarification of than a break with Thomas. Matter, we must remember, is the potential for organization. It is, therefore, the possibility of relating in different ways. Material systems are those which have the possibility of relating in many different ways. In this sense individuation *is* by matter – that is, by being so little organized that it is still possible to develop in many different directions. As systems become more complex and more highly organized, the range of different possible courses of development, and thus their materiality, begins to contract. This is not because potential has been lost, but rather because it has been realized. An electron can become, or at least become part of, many different things: cosmic radiation, a star, a gold atom, a dog, a Communist society . . . A dog cannot, at least if it is still to remain a dog. But it has within it many, many electrons, whose potential it has ordered to its own higher purpose. Thomistic 'angels' represent a sort of limit case in this regard, at least for finite systems. Their potential is always and already realized; they thus have no matter, and can relate in only one way. There is only one individual angel of each kind – or to put it in another way, these angels are so unique that they take up an entire species by themselves. In the case of God as well there is only one possible way of relating – but this is the way of relating which includes all others, of which it is the single necessary and sufficient condition.

To put the matter somewhat differently, individuation is, at all levels of organization, by the same principle which Thomas recognized in the Trinity: that is, by relationship. It is just that this means different things at different levels of organization. In simple systems, it means that the species or type of system is defined broadly and can develop in many different directions. Thus Thomas's individuation by matter. In more complex systems differentiation is increasingly by speciation – by exploring new paths of development which exclude others, but still allow for some internal difference: that is, different ways of being human, feline, metallic and so on. At the limit case for finite systems relatedness becomes so rich and diverse that the system in question is fully determined. Anything else which shared in exactly the same relationships would, in effect, be the same thing. In the case of the infinite system, of which there can logically be only one, all relations are internal and of only one logically possible type, so that these diverse personalities share a common divine nature which makes them really and truly one.

Our approach also allows us to resolve the contradiction between the Aristotelian-Thomistic and the Spinozist doctrines of substance. As modes of organization, or ways of relating, universals exist only in the context of higher order systems on which they depend. In this sense, contrary to Thomas, there is only one substance, which is the whole or transcendental One. Finite systems share in this integrity, which gives them the appearance of substantiality – or one might say a participated substantiality. What Aristotle and Thomas would have called accidents – redness (that is, reflecting light of a certain range of wavelengths) or exercising intelligence – are simply aspects of finite systems, ways in which they relate to other finite systems; they lack even participated integrity or substantiality. We thus preserve the Aristotelian distinction without the unwarranted ontological pluralism.[5]

---

[5] One of the principal reasons why Thomists have been concerned to save the concepts of species and

Conclusion

What all this suggests, of course, is that totalization by itself gives us very little. Indeed, we can define the product of totalization only in terms of structure and function, and thus in terms which presuppose the two higher degrees of abstraction. It is, in part, the effort to make totalization stand on its own which leads to some of the errors which have been made in trying to understand the nature of universals. The universal is a mode of organization – a system of internal and external relations. At the level of totalization we know only the difference and similarity between this and other modes of organization, differences and similarities which are by no means univocally defined. In and of itself, totalization yields nothing but a series of bare, negative totalities, a series which terminates in the negative whole which is defined purely and simply by the lack of specifiers which would limit it. This is the whole as the merely general – the 'night in which all cows are black' – and the totality which the deconstructionists rightly abhor. Thus the appearance that classification is simply about naming, and ultimately arbitrary, and thus the 'truth' of the nominalist position. It is only as we advance to formalization that we grasp the real structure of the system, and leave naming behind. The structure, however, exists only in individual finite systems of a particular type and in our minds which have abstracted it. And it is only at the level of transcendental abstraction that we can show that this structure is a way of carrying out a definite purpose – and ultimately of participating in Being as such. It is only at the level of transcendental abstraction that we can show the universal to be real, not because it exists on its own, as the radical realists would have it, but precisely because it is (a way of Being) in God. It is because the structure is a way of Being that it is real, and not merely a product of the imagination, or of mathematical construction.

We thus need to move on to the two higher degrees of abstraction and see what further light a consideration of them can shed on the act of knowledge.

---

accident is that it forms the basis of the Thomistic theory of virtue and also of the Thomistic theory of grace. Both are understood as habits, the first as an operative habit or a perfection of a power of action, and the second as an entitative habit which inheres in the soul and creates a new capacity. Habits are regarded by Thomas as accidents. The approach which we are suggesting, however, can fully accommodate this doctrine. Virtues represent the full development of an existing power of interaction, grace an entirely new power of interaction which makes us something more than merely human. Indeed, the idea that grace is an accident would seem to compromise the notion that it actually elevates or divinizes our nature, something which is essential to the whole Catholic understanding of grace and which sets it apart from Protestant theories. This does also suggest that the boundary between nature and grace is not fixed, but relative – that the attractive power of God is always and only drawing forth from matter new capacities which in turn define new natures and are susceptible to being attracted by God in still new and more powerful ways. Grace, in other words, in so far as it confers a new, superhuman nature, is a sort of speciation.

Chapter 5

Formalization

The second degree of abstraction is the *abstractio formae* or, as we have called it, formal abstraction or formalization. This is the sort of abstraction which has historically been associated with the apprehension of mathematical objects, in terms of which it has generally been defined. Thus, despite their other differences, all of the various Thomistic schools associated formalization with the abstraction of the accidental form 'quantity'. Pure mathematics abstracts quantity as such and uses the rules of logic to derive all possible determinations of this accident; applied mathematics or mathematical physics describes material systems in quantitative terms, that is, in terms of their local motion or various state variables such as temperature, pressure, volume, density, entropy and so on.

There are three difficulties with this approach. First, it takes quantity as given, when in fact it may be reducible to a more fundamental category. Second, it is not at all clear that the form which formalization comprehends is best characterized as 'accidental'. On the contrary, while the formula for a parabola, for example, does not confer being on the parabola, it does define exhaustively what a parabola is, in a way that the determination 'red' does not define exhaustively the essence of the old Soviet flag. Indeed, what formalization aims at (but as we will see cannot always achieve) is precisely the apprehension of the essence of a thing, in such a way that all the properties of the thing can be derived rationally without any further recourse to observation. Third, defining formalization in terms of quantity fails to capture what is going on in a whole range of disciplines, especially but not exclusively in the social sciences, which have clearly made formalization their ideal but do this in a way which cannot, strictly speaking, be called quantitative. I am speaking most especially of the structuralist trend in psychology, linguistics and anthropology.

Because of this, we prefer to define formalization in terms of structure. When we abstract the form of a system we grasp the underlying structure of that system. From the resulting structural definition we can then derive deductively all of the properties of the system in question. This is easiest to see in the case of pure mathematical objects. Thus, for example, from the definition of a triangle, I can derive all of the properties of a triangle (for example, that the sum of its angles equals 180°), by means of logically necessary arguments, without observing or measuring particular triangles. The same is true for more abstract mathematical objects such as Hilbert spaces or discrete topologies. It is still, to be sure, necessary for there to be some primary observation, which serves as the basis for an image from which the form is abstracted and the definition achieved. This is true even for mathematical objects which we do not actually encounter in experience, or which are not possible objects of experience, such as infinite-dimensional spaces or unconnected topologies. Mathematicians arrive at such objects by abstracting a rigorous definition of the space-time which we experience, and then gradually removing elements of the structure which defines that space-time, achieving a higher degree of generality, or altering the structure in a way which does not violate the rules of logic.

But formalization is not confined to pure mathematics. Mathematical physics attempts to describe the structure of physical systems and to use this structure to provide a partial explanation for the observed properties or behaviour of these systems. Thus Kepler's laws described the structure of the solar system in precise terms; Newton's – and later Einstein's – field equations describe the still deeper structure of gravitational fields. Quantum mechanics allows us to describe the structure of matter at the atomic and molecular level in a way which, for example, explains why gold is yellow and shiny or why the various elements react with each other in the ways they do. Together quantum mechanical and thermodynamic laws permit an extremely rigorous description of complex chemical processes, including those involved in living matter. Other formalisms, such as the logistic equation, describe the way organisms relate to each other and to the ecosystem, or the way societies centralize and allocate resources for production.

All of the formalizations used in the foregoing examples are, however, transparently quantitative. Indeed, it remains to be shown that characterizing them as structural captures something more fundamental than characterizing them as quantitative. It is only when we come to the social sciences that we find attempts to formalize which are *not* obviously quantitative. Thus, for example, structural linguistics attempts to reduce languages to their syntagmatic and paradigmatic structures – that is, the rules which govern the way in which words are combined to form sentences, and the way in which the meanings of words relate to each other (Saussure [1915] 1973). Structural psychology in the manner of Piaget attempts to formalize, in so far as it is possible, the pattern of reasoning which characterizes each successive level of cognitive development (Piaget 1952, 1968). Structural anthropology formalizes the structure of kinship systems and, as we noted in the last chapter, mythologies as well (Lévi-Strauss [1958] 1963). In the case of each of these disciplines there is a reduction of the phenomenon to a formalism which permits the logical deduction of further properties, of the behaviour of the system and so on. In no case can the formalism really be called quantitative in any meaningful sense.

In order fully to establish our claim that what formalization grasps is first of all structure, and only secondarily quantity, we need to begin by describing the act of formalization in greater detail. This, in turn, will help us to identify its biological and sociological basis. We also need to look more closely at the product of formalization, something which will involve us in a discussion of the status of mathematical objects and other 'structures'. We will conclude with an assessment of the claim of formalization to disclose the essence of things and even to grasp the mind of God, something which will establish even more definitively than we have already the dependence of the lower on the higher degrees of abstraction – and of all on transcendental abstraction.

The Act of Formalization

We have already noted that formalization begins in an effort to render our systems of classification reasonable and rigorous. We look to classify on the basis of similar differences and different similarities. The result is a system of ratios. The relation between felines and canines is the same as (or similar to) the relationship between bovines and caprines – that is, both are 'families' within larger taxonomic orders. The ratio can, furthermore, be expressed in formal terms

$$A:B::C:D$$

This, or any other ratio, gives us two of the three building blocks of formal systems: a *relation* which defines *elements* in a system. Further development of the taxonomy gives us the other building block: *operations*. Thus we can add *taxa* and thus ascend the taxonomic hierarchy from family to order to class to phylum, or multiply this classificatory scheme by another: for example, the distinction between male and female, marine or terrestrial and so on. It is our contention that all formal abstraction arises out of such efforts to render classifications rigorous.

As Piaget points out (Piaget 1952, 1968), however, the operations involved in classification are still concrete, that is, operations on things rather than operations on propositions themselves. In order to advance to authentic formalization we must take one further step back and ask about the rules governing operations. The simplest examples of such rules are the laws of arithmetic. Are there, for example, additive and/or multiplicative identities or inverses for the operations we are using? Are the operations commutative? distributive? associative? We must also ask about the system itself. Is it closed under the operations in question? That is, if we perform the operation on one member of the system do we get another member of the system, in which case we say the system is closed, or do we get a result which is outside the system we were considering entirely? A system of elements, defined by their relationships with each other, in which defined operations have certain definite properties, is a *category* (Geroch 1985).

As we advance from totalization to formalization of any given system, we are, in effect, defining a category in which certain operations are possible and others are not, and in which these operations have certain properties. The more operations are defined within a category, and the more law-like the behaviour of those operations, the more *structure* exists within a given category. In the mathematics by which we half-unconsciously formalize our day-to-day experience, all of the arithmetic operations are commutative, associative and distributive, and all have identities and inverses. Thus we can add groups of objects to each other and subtract from them, multiply them and divide them, and expect all the rules of arithmetic to hold. More complex activities, however, such as the measurement of fields, the construction of buildings and the description of local motion, whether celestial or terrestrial, can be formalized only in terms of categories more complex than those we use to manipulate discrete groups of objects. Among other things, we must define distance, something which involves the notion of a *metric* and eventually such objects as *vectors*, which combine quantity with direction. This is sufficient structure to formalize most of the physics which developed up through the eighteenth century.

Certain kinds of physical systems, however, can be formalized only using categories with less or different structure than that used in the conscious or unconscious formalization of everyday experience. Thus, for example, formalization of gravity turns out to require the use of metrics or distance formulae different from the familiar

Pythagorean Theorem, with the counter-intuitive result that space is curved. Quantum systems can be described only using non-commutative operators, that is, operations which give different results depending on the order of the elements operated on, something which gives rise to such counter-intuitive results as the Heisenberg Uncertainty Principle. Other sorts of physical systems – for example, dynamic and thermodynamic systems such as weather patterns, heat engines and complex chemical interactions – can be represented formally only in 'abstract' spaces in which each dimension corresponds to a different property: temperature, density and so on.[1]

Efforts to formalize biological and social systems, furthermore, often yield categories with so little structure that we hesitate to think of them as mathematical. We have already seen an example of this in biological taxonomy. While both additive and multiplicative classifications of organisms are possible, biological taxonomies as they have actually developed are strictly additive systems. The operation of multiplication is undefined. Other aspects of biological systems, such as population dynamics, can be formalized easily using standard mathematics, and of course molecular biology and biochemistry depend on the same formalisms as the mathematical physics and chemistry of which they are applications.

The first dimension of social systems to be mathematized – the laws of the marketplace – turns out to be formalizable using categories similar to those developed in the service of the physical sciences, though here, of course, the 'spaces' in question are abstract and not real. The Infinitesimal Calculus, first developed by Leibniz and Newton to formalize the local motion of physical bodies, can also be used to formalise the 'motion' of commodities in the marketplace. And of course quantitatively oriented sociologists are forever identifying 'correlations' of various kinds between different social variables. More recently, however, there has been an attempt to formalize other aspects of social experience: language, kinship, myth and cultural 'texts' in general. It is this activity which has led to the emergence of the 'structuralist' trend which we noted above. It is rooted in the notion that social systems, as much as any other systems, are 'structures' and thus have the basic properties which make formalization possible. Piaget does a particularly good job of defining these properties. Structures are, first of all, characterized by wholeness. The elements can be defined – indeed, exist – only in relationship to each other. That this is true for the signs in a language, for positions in a kinship system, or for the elements in a myth should be fairly obvious. Words are defined in terms of other words. The position 'aunt' exists only in relation to the position 'nephew' or 'neice' and vice versa. The meaning of various elements in a myth depends on their relations to each other. Thus the cross has a different significance in the context of Christianity, where it represents redemption through suffering, than it does in Hopi culture, where it simply stands for the four directions of the universe. Second, structures are systems of transformation. They consist, that is, in operations which map one element in the system to another. Thus syntactic rules allow the mapping or association of one signifier with another, kinship rules the mapping or association of one individual with another, myths the mapping or association of one symbol with another. This claim is less obvious if it is intended as a unique way of understanding these phenomena, or if it is claimed that everything that happens in the systems in

---

[1] Readers interested in a more formal discussion of mathematical categories should consult Robert Geroch's *Mathematical Physics* (Geroch 1985).

question is formalizable in these terms. But there is little doubt that it is possible to discover formal rules of this kind. Finally, Piaget claims, authentic structures are 'closed' much as the set of real numbers is closed for addition, subtraction, division, multiplication and the taking of square roots or distances. This property he ascribes to sociological structures only in the looser sense that social systems are 'self-regulating' or have ways of maintaining their stability.

It follows from Piaget's formulation that to the extent that we are able to formalize social systems at all, the process involves defining categories with their own distinctive operations and properties. We begin, in the social as in the physical and biological sciences, by observing and classifying. But as we attempt to arrive at more rigorous classifications and to understand the relationships between various *taxa*, we inevitably pass over into formalization. What distinguishes the structuralist trend from other currents in the social sciences is simply the strength of the claims made on behalf of formalization, and especially the claim that it is in grasping the underlying structure of social systems that we best understand them. We will see later that there are good reasons to doubt this claim. For now it should suffice to point out that structure as we have defined it does not appear to be a strictly hierarchical principle. Clearly more complex systems are *not* always more highly structured. On the contrary, biological and social systems seem to require less structured categories for their formal description. At the same time, certain physical systems are also described in terms of low-structure categories – for example, quantum systems. All this suggests that formalization is missing something, something essential for understanding the universe. This is an issue to which we shall return.

One of the characteristics of formalization is that it permits us to move from forms to forms without reference to further experience. This movement of the intellect we call inference. Given a formalization, and given the rules of logic, we can manipulate a formalism to generate new formalisms which are logically consistent with the first. These inferences may, furthermore, themselves be more or less abstract. They may remain at the level of descriptions of some physical, biological or social system, in which case we call them *predictions* either of some past or future state of the system or of some property implied by the formalism itself. Thus Kepler's laws predict the motion of the heavenly bodies, the logistic equation predicts the change in the size of a population over time, and Marx's reproduction equations predict a declining rate of profit as an economy becomes more technologically sophisticated.

It is also possible, however, simply to consider the formal category itself, and to ask what kinds of systems are consistent with its structure, or to begin with a given category and ask what other categories might be *constructed* which are at least logically possible – that is, consistent with the rules of identity, contradiction and (for most mathematicians) the excluded middle. The role of the last rule is of particular importance. By showing that the contrary of a proposition is self-contradictory, and appealing to the law of the excluded middle, we can prove propositions which would otherwise resist demonstration. This makes possible the construction of categories which are not intuitively imaginable, such as actual infinities, certain kinds of topologies and so on. Some mathematicians – the so-called intuitionists – have rejected the use of the excluded middle for this reason, and argued that mathematics should be confined to the intuitively imaginable. This restriction, however, would render impossible many of the tools that are necessary for theoretical physics, which often formalizes physical systems using abstract spaces which are not themselves possible objects of experience.

We are now in a position to show that quantity, far from being an irreducible accident, is essentially derivative, a type of structure which appears only in systems which are, at the very least, partial orders by inclusion. In defining a ratio we define a unit, the numerical one, *in terms of its relations with the other elements of the formal category in question.* Just what operations can be made on the numerical one depend on what additional structure exists in the category under which it is considered. Thus as we move to increasingly complex categories, 'one' becomes the unit of increasingly 'complete' number systems. If we confine ourselves to the category of sets with simple relations such as an ordering by inclusion, all we can really do or need to do is list the various levels of inclusion. The set which does not include anything but itself – the null set – cannot be taken as zero, but only as the first level of inclusion, that is, as one. The result of this construction is thus the system of natural numbers $\{1, 2, 3, 4, \ldots\}$. This set, while ordered by inclusion, is not complete under even the simple operations of addition and subtraction. We cannot solve even a simple equation involving addition in the general case, within the system of natural numbers.

$$a = b + c$$

Like a young child, we can count but we cannot yet really do arithmetic. Higher order operations such as addition and subtraction yield results which are outside the natural numbers. Thus we need to expand the system we are using to include zero and the so-called negative numbers. The combined set is called the integers and the above equation can be solved in the general case within this system. But the integers are not closed under multiplication and division. Consider for example the equation

$$a = bc$$

which cannot be solved in the general case without yielding results which are not integral. Thus the need for the set of rational numbers – that is, a number system which includes ratios. The introduction of metrics, or distance formulas, defines an operation under which even the set of rational numbers is incomplete.

$$x^2 + y^2 = r^2$$

Thus the need for the real numbers, which constitute a complete field, ordered by inclusion. Even the real numbers, however, do not permit all logically possible algebraic operations on all numbers which we have already defined. The square roots of negative numbers remain undefined. We thus need to expand the system still further, to include the so-called 'complex numbers' formed by products of real numbers and the 'imaginary' component 'i', where $i^2 = -1$.

It is thus apparent that quantity, in all its diverse determinations, derives from the existence of certain kinds of structure, to which it is reducible, and from which it can be derived. This result is important because, among other things, it tells us why some systems are so resistant to quantitative description, even if they do permit a certain degree of formalization. Quantification depends on the presence of a partial order by inclusion. Only those elements of a system which are comparable, furthermore, can be quantified. Any attempt to quantify systems which are not ordered by inclusion, or in which not all elements are comparable, will run up against insuperable obstacles. Consider, for example, the ideas of evolutionary or social progress. Clearly there is a sense in which we will want to say that a human being is more highly evolved – more highly organized and therefore more valuable – than a goat, a goat than an peach tree, a peach tree than a slime mould, and the slime mould than a sapphire. But the sapphire has perfections which all the 'higher' systems lack. The order is not by inclusion. Indeed, such orders are rare in nature. The development of new capacities almost always entails the loss of old ones. Even the angels of Thomistic theology because they lack bodies also lack passions. Only God can really be said to exceed in a way which includes. When we say that a human is greater than a sapphire we are not making a quantitative judgement. The 'more' in 'more important' or 'more valuable' is not a quantitative 'more', or is so only analogically.

At issue here is not simply a limitation on our ability to hierarchize natural systems – though this is not without interest itself. The foregoing result helps us to understand better why quantitative science has difficulty theorizing cosmo-historical progress or cosmic teleology. From a quantitative standpoint we humans are *not* greater than the many natural systems which give no evidence of intelligence. Insects and microbes far outnumber us. Animal intelligence, even if it turns out to be widespread, is by nature confined to a very small region of the universe, most of which is inhospitable. The claims we make on behalf of progress are not quantitative or even formal, but rather judgements of value, and thus acts of transcendental rather than formal abstraction.

Before we proceed to our analysis of the biological and social conditions for formalization, it might be useful to point out that our way of deriving formal abstraction – and thus grounding mathematics – avoids the logical atomism which is characteristic of most existing approaches (Harris 1987). It is not the elements of a category but rather the relations between them which are primary. We thus respect the principle of internal relations – the idea that things are dependent on each other not just for their behaviour but also for their essence and existence – which is an important implication of relativistic and quantum physics.[2] At the same time, we should note, this is done only at the expense of reducing our formal definitions to definitions based on difference – precisely what we had hoped to escape by advancing to formalization in the first place. We wanted, in other words, to know not just how a circle and a parabola differ from each other – for example, as closed and open two dimensional curves, results we could get at the level of totalization – but what each actually *is*. We appear to have this in the equation for each curve. A circle is defined by the relation:

$$x^2 + y^2 = r^2$$

---

[2] The principal of internal relations is implied by the Einstein-Podolsky-Rosen nonlocality. Quantum theory predicts that if two particles interact and then are separated by a great distance there will, nonetheless, be a correlation between their behaviour greater than that predicted by their earlier interaction. The implication is that there is some kind of instantaneous signalling between the particles, but this is prohibited by special relativity. The most economic solution appears to be to regard the two particles as aspects of a single system – that is, as not really distinct, but 'internally related'.

where r is the radius; a parabola by the relation:

$$y = x^2$$

But these relations themselves are ultimately reducible to the relations of difference which define the elements of the sets or spaces across which they are articulated. In saving internal relations we necessarily lose the notion of a stable essence or definition of a thing, at least at the level of formalization. It is only at the level of transcendental abstraction that we will discover a way to theorize the radical interconnectedness of all things without becoming lost in the play of difference.

The Biological and Social Basis of Formalization

Formalization, like totalization, depends on definite biological and social conditions. The biological or neurological basis of formalization is, in principle, no different than that of totalization. Sensation produces images or topographical representations in the brain which are in turn stored as dispositional representations, which may be recalled, combined and so on. Formalisms are, neurologically, simply mappings between images or representations which are themselves stored and accessed as topographical and dispositional representations. The difference is, simply that here we are dealing with second, third and even higher-order mappings. Where totalization directly relates images to each other, placing them both, for example, in the category of dog, formalization relates the relationships between images, or the relationships between the relationships between images and so on, defining similar differences and different similarities. The result is a calculus of pure relationships which is at ever greater remove from the data of the senses, but which, at the same time, commands access to an ever greater range and diversity of actual and potential sensory data. As one moves up the ladder of formal abstraction, one establishes neural links between ever larger complexes of sensory data stored as first-order dispositional representations. When one moves down the ladder of formal abstraction, one can derive images which have not, and never could be, directly experienced, by using the faculty of the imagination to produce new first-order representations by transforming old ones in accord with well-defined 'similar differences and different similarities'. Clearly this sort of abstraction requires a more complex nervous system than totalization, and we would not be surprised to find animals which were capable of the one and not of the other. Formalization does not, however, require a different kind of nervous system. At the neurological level, at least, it differs in degree and not in kind from totalization.

Unlike totalization, however, which is universal among human beings, formalization seems to be much more highly developed in some societies than in others, and in some individuals than in others. While individual differences might be explained in terms of different neurological endowments or, more likely, in terms of different educational experiences, the marked differences between societies in terms of their cultivation of formal abstraction suggests that social structural factors are at work – precisely the conclusion which would be suggested anyway by our account of the act of the intellect. Our ability to apprehend intellectually second and higher-order relationships between images, and thus to formalize systems, is a product of lived experience. Living in complex societies the elements of which are related to each other in multiple and cross-cutting ways creates the basis in experience for thinking in terms of complex, higher-order relationships. Members of such societies have, in other words, a pre-conceptual, connatural knowledge of the formalism which illuminates their experience and their reflection on their first-order abstractions, which members of simpler societies do not. The member of a tribal or communitarian society knows herself only as a member of clan which is a member of a moiety and a tribe – a classification which is cross-cut a few times at most by band or village, gender and possibly religious society divisions. The result will be, at best, a multidimensional multiplicative classification. There is no experience of higher-order relationships which therefore remain invisible. The member of an advanced tributary, capitalist, or socialist society, on the other hand, is defined by a mind-boggling array of relationships to other individuals, in such a way that any classification seems ersatz and heuristic at best. The 'real' relationships between individuals can be described only in terms of the higher-order formalisms which govern the articulation of kinship and state/temple structures, the operation of the marketplace, or the complex articulation of enterprise, market, plan and party structures. The experience of higher-order relationships makes it possible to apprehend higher-order relationships.

We are, however, immediately confronted with a difficult problem. While there are many logically (and we would argue, sociologically) possible paths of social development, and thus many possible types of complex society, the principal pathway of development on our planet has been driven by the emergence, expansion and penetration of markets. The development of sophisticated formal thinking on our planet is thus intimately bound up with the progress of the marketplace generally and of capitalism in particular. Indeed, concern with formalization, as evidenced in the emergence of an abstract mathematics, is almost immediate with the emergence of a petty commodity economy in Ancient Greece – the first place such a system developed. The first pure mathematician, Thales of Miletus was, in fact, a merchant, and one who had a good grasp of the laws of supply and demand. The progress of mathematics generally, and its emergence as the 'ideal' of the sciences are, furthermore, closely associated with the development of generalized commodity production and the whole process of capitalist development.

The sort of formalization which is driven by capitalist development is, furthermore, of a very specific kind. It is mathematical and quantitative. This sort of formalization depends on the comparability of elements in the sets it considers, something for which we find a social basis only in a very specific type of relationship – the commodity relation which Marx analysed so brilliantly in the first chapter of *Capital* (Marx [1867] 1976), in which qualitatively very different things are treated as having equal or at least comparable (greater or lesser) value. Let us see how this works.

In communitarian societies, human beings experience themselves as members of larger wholes, such as clans, villages, which are in turn linked together by a common ordering to an end. In hypothetical archaic societies this ordering to an end is mediated by the emerging urban centre which becomes a focal point for surplus centralization and advanced research and development. On the one hand, the very existence and nature of the individual, the clan, the village and so on, is comprehensible only in terms of this ordering to an end. On the other hand, each part remains a discrete individual, comprehensible only in its qualitative specificity. The complexity of these societies, the potential for which was never fully realized on our planet, consists precisely in the capacity to relate many qualitatively different elements to a common purpose, and many qualitatively different purposes to each other, in a way which at once transcends and conserves individuality, the identity of particular subgroups such as clans, villages, religious societies and so on. Thus, for example, clans seeking admission to Hopi villages were judged in terms of what they could contribute to the Hopi ritual system, which is ordered to preserving the pure pattern of creation, and the ritual contributions of the clans were understood as responses to the activity of the Creator which alone made them possible. At the same time, it would have been inconceivable to the Hopi that incorporation into the system would have entirely redefined the nature of the clan in question, which is precisely why they were so careful about which clans they accepted.

In tributary societies this same dynamic persists, albeit in a distorted form, as the society is no longer ordered to the development of human capacities, but rather to warfare and luxury consumption. Thus conquered societies are expected to contribute what they have and what they produce, not to begin producing something entirely new and different. Their gods are subsumed into the larger pantheon as subaltern members, not simply obliterated or transformed.[3]

In a market society, on the other hand, people experience themselves as increasingly determined by their inter-relationships. These relationships are, furthermore, abstract differences which are more or less independent of the actual qualitative identity of the individuals related and, as marketization proceeds, actually begins to redefine those qualitative identities and ultimately to render them completely fluid so that all that is left is pure difference. Thus the worker who one year is producing steel in a factory in Hammond, Indiana may be studying criminology the next year in Whiting – and doing CAD two years later in Schaumburg, all as a result of market pressures. These changes in work situation, furthermore, require a basic change in identity, so that eventually the worker forgets who he is, and even begins to believe that he isn't anybody in particular, but simply a function of market relationships.

This flattening out of all particular identities by the marketplace is nothing other than the process of commodification. Commodities, in order to be exchanged, must be comparable. Value, which in communitarian, archaic and tributary societies is defined qualitatively in terms of the ordering of a particular thing to an end or purpose – that is, in terms of organization[4] – is reduced to quantitative terms: to the average socially necessary labour-time which the commodity contains. The reduction is not arbitrary. On the contrary, the degree of organization of a system is, generally speaking, reflected in the labour involved in ordering its elements to an end. A supercomputer is more highly organized, and takes more labour to produce, than a slide rule. What is lost, however, is the transcendental (and thus non-quantitative) judgement regarding the relative importance of ends. It takes more labour to produce a Porsche than it does to reproduce a teacher for a year, but yet the latter is more important from the standpoint of catalyzing the full development of human capacities. What happens in a market

---

[3] Where there is a move to impose or change the local religion, as in the case of the Seleucid monarchies of Hellenistic Syria, there is also already a significant degree of marketization present.

[4] Marx's term 'use-value', with its utilitarian overtones, captures this sense of value as organization only very imperfectly.

society is the emergence first of a partial and eventually of a total order by inclusion, as all systems are quantitatively rank-ordered based on the average socially necessary labour-time they contain. Things which are qualitatively different are rendered comparable and even equivalent. It should come as no surprise that when people's very lives are mathematized they should begin to think mathematically, and to regard the mathematical formalism as the ideal of knowledge. It is, after all, the formalism which describes the society in which they live, and thus what they are as members of that society: that is, factors of production with a definite value and so on.

This tendency develops only very gradually to be sure. In general, it is possible to identify four distinct stages in the process of marketization. During the first stage, that of petty commodity production, the real motive and directing force for the system is still something other than the marketplace – generally the demand for luxury goods on the part of tributary systems on the periphery of which the market system is emerging. Thus in Ancient Greece, which as we have noted was probably the first real petty commodity society, demand was largely driven by the extraction of surplus by tributary states in Egypt, Persia and Mesopotamia – a dynamic which continued even after these regions were conquered. Here the nature of the productive activity and thus the identity of the individual producer is still given by local ecological conditions, the level of technological development and local tradition. No one in such a society thinks of digging up olive orchards and planting vines just because there has been a drop in oil prices. And prices generally remain fairly stable. It is just that for the first time, everything has a price, an abstract equivalent including, sometimes, even labour-power itself. This creates a basis in experience for the definition of 'similar differences and different similarities'. The difference between three litres of wine and two litres of oil is the same as the difference between six litres of oil and seven yards of purple cloth.

The stability of prices and identities which characterizes this phase gives rise to the idea that each commodity has a 'natural price' – a concept which eventually became enshrined in various natural law doctrines. It is not surprising, therefore, that philosophers working in this sort of society, intrigued by the association of stable numbers (prices) with each thing, might develop the idea, which became popular among the Pythagoreans, that each thing has its own 'number' – a notion which seems entirely bizarre to those of us who live under generalized commodity production. Furthermore, it is the number which commands the commodity, not the commodity the number. Thus the idea that the world of mathematical objects constitutes something purer and truer than the world of the senses, and thus contains the key to the structure of the universe. At the same time, mathematics at this stage is still far from formalized. It still relies on observation, generalization and constructive proof – not on a series of purely analytic arguments using established rules of logic and a developed system of algebraic representation. It is only in the most advanced petty commodity societies, such as the great Arab empires of the Middle Ages, that we see the first steps towards this higher degree of formalization. And it is precisely in these societies, where rates of taxation were low and the scope of the market very large, that humanity first approached a system in which production was actually *driven* in some significant measure by market forces.

Such a system emerges in full flower, however, only in the *mercantilist* stage, which began with the European conquest of Asia, Africa and the Americas. Here commodities move and their prices change constantly in relationship to each other. Initially this relativistic motion is limited by the presence of significant nonmarket sectors: village communities, guilds, small private property, slavery, residual tributary structures and so on. Commodities affect each other, but not, for the most part, the larger social environment in which they are exchanged, and even as prices become more fluid – in fact sometimes wildly volatile – there remains the notion that wealth consists in some one good which is itself independent of the market: gold, land and so on. At this stage behaviour but not identity is subject to transformation by the market. The result is what is generally called a system of external relations. This in turn gives rise to the Newtonian view of the universe: that is, as a system of point particles with mass, each of which affects the behaviour of all others through gravity, in a law-like way which can be mathematically formalized, but which nonetheless does not affect the basic qualities of things themselves – extension, mass and so on – or of the fixed frame in which they move – three-dimensional space which constitutes the 'stage' on which motion is played out over time. The Newtonian universe is, of course, formalized in terms of the calculus. The fixed points of a fixed space are related by functions which can then be analysed for their rates of change and so on.

Gradually, however, market forces begin both to transform the larger social environment and to specify the characteristics of the commodities which are produced. The market can no longer be understood on the basis of more or less stable inputs which determine what is produced: land, labour, tools and a more or less traditional repertoire of basic and luxury goods which had been largely stable for millennia. Rather, the economic process as a whole, including the actual quantity of land, labour and tools, the nature of the production process, the shape of demand, what is finally produced, and the precise way in which it is distributed are all determined by the internal laws which govern the 'shape' of the marketplace itself. During this third, *industrial* stage of the development of the market system, we witness the development of theories which attempt to formalize the energy or labour which drives the system (electromagnetism, thermodynamics and also, in a somewhat different way, Marx's political economy). Interestingly enough, just as the market system is beginning to manifest the internal contradictions which lead to economic crisis and stagnation, physics recognizes for the first time the limits to the efficient utilization of energy and even proclaims, albeit a bit prematurely, the impending Heat Death of the Universe.

In the final stage of capitalist development – the stage of *imperialism and finance capitalism* – a large and diverse consumer market and an essentially infinite supply of all forms of labour and technology, even the most skilled and sophisticated, coupled with rising capital requirements for new ventures, mean that the capital markets begin to eclipse the consumer and labour markets as the main force shaping the organization of production. Living in a social space which is itself no longer fixed, people develop a connatural, preconceptual knowledge of the underlying interconnectedness and relativity of all things. This is reflected in the production of ever more general formalisms, which describe the universe in ever more relativistic form. Thus the discovery of special relativity, in which the relationship between objects shapes the basic properties of the objects in question: relative speed determines extension, mass and so on; and general relativity in which the very presence of physical objects with extension and mass and thus gravity is an artefact of the geometry of space-time – together with the pure mathematics which makes relativistic physics possible: differential geometry, topology and so on.

Gradually the idea arises of an instantaneous reallocation of all portfolios to the most profitable options, and capital is re-theorized as the sum total of all possible uses of a society's resources (Hayek's 1940 *Pure Theory of Capital*). People begin to experience themselves as an abstract bundle of possibilities the realization of which depends on the subjective decisions of others. This is, in turn, reflected in the emergence of quantum theory and more specifically the idea that the state of a system cannot be described in terms of a definite position, velocity, mass and so on, but rather in terms of a quantum wave function which reflects the relative probability of all possible states of the system. This idea, in turn has given rise to quantum cosmologies which make all of the basic characteristics of the universe – not just the gravitational metric and the nongravitational forces, but also the underlying topology (the basic shape of the universe) – dependent on a quantum wave function which, in effect, encodes all logically possible states. The leading question for mathematical physics then becomes how the actual state of the system is selected. Is the universal wave function just a rough description of the relative probability of different states – the realistic conclusion? Is it collapsed by observations made by individuals (the Copenhagen interpretation)? by intelligent beings in general (Wheeler's participatory interpretation)? or by some Ultimate Observer (the neo-Berkeley option)? Or do all possibilities exist mathematically, and those which contain observers exist physically, all converging on an Omega Point which knows (and owns?) all – Tipler's version of 'many worlds' (Tipler 1994)?[5]

However these questions are answered the result is a *forma mentis* in which knowledge gives way to 'information' or 'signification' – to pattern without referent. Meaning, such as it is, is constituted by *différance* – or at most the rules which govern the production of difference. This is the underlying basis for both of the two principal ideologies of finance capitalism, which taken together represent the triumph of formal abstraction: the information-theoretical neoliberalism which emerged out of a synthesis between Cold War theoretical physics and Austrian school economics, and postmodernism, which emerged out of the disintegration of functionalist sociology, structuralism and dialectical materialism on the Continent. While neoliberalism reflects a certain optimism about the possibilities of the market system – and indeed about the universe as a whole, at least in its radical Tiplerian form (Tipler 1994) and postmodernism a radical pessimism, both ideologies in fact share a common, underlying subjective idealist epistemology and metaphysics. Neoliberalism reflects the market resurgent; postmodernism legitimates the market to those sectors it has hopelessly left behind (Lukacs [1953] 1980; Mansueto 1998c, 1999).

The project of defining a universal formalism in terms of which the universe as a whole may be perfectly comprehended remains the ideal of mathematical physics. Pure mathematicians have, however, already recognized that this is quite impossible. Just as the market system depends on a nonmarket periphery for its stability and growth, so too does the formalism depend on an unproven assumption or intuition if

---

[5] Frank Tipler (Barrow and Tipler 1986, Tipler 1994) in fact notes that the original inspiration for his version of the many-worlds solution to quantum mechanics came while reading Hayek's *The Pure Theory of Capital* (Hayek 1940).

it is to be complete and consistent – a result Gödel established long ago. But in order to understand this we need to consider the product of formalization, the formalism itself, in more detail.

The Product of Formalization

The debate about the nature of the formalism[6] is closely related to the question we examined in Chapter 4, that of the status of the universal, of which it is, in a certain sense, a subset. The formalism is a sort of universal, but one which purports to go beyond the definition of a logical whole, to grasp the underlying structure of the objects described. Not surprisingly, the range of answers given to this question are essentially the same as those given to the problem of universals: from nominalism through moderate realism to radical or exaggerated realism. The only exception is that because of their enduring influence in the philosophy of mathematics, we need to address two positions of Kantian origin – what are known in the literature (rather confusingly for our purposes) as 'formalism' and 'intuitionism' – as well as a type of radical realism which is of objective idealist origin. We should note that most of the debate around the status of formalisms focuses on the specific mathematical formalism. This is because of the reduction of formalization to quantification which we criticized above. This reduction does not, however, affect the question at hand, for reasons which will become obvious in the course of the discussion.

What is interesting to note is that both nominalism and radical realism in the philosophy of mathematics, emerge out of a common approach to grounding mathematics, what has come to be called logicism. Logicism developed out of the work of rationalist and empiricist philosophers such as Leibniz and Hume who, despite their other differences, regarded mathematics as first and foremost an application of the principles of logic. According to this view mathematical statements are analytically self-evident and arise from the application of the rules of formal logic (identity/ contradiction, law of the excluded middle and law of sufficient reason) to the 'raw material' of set theory. Logicists differ among themselves over the question of whether or not this raw material is merely conventional – the position of mathematical nominalists such as Russell and Whitehead – or is, rather, a way of talking about real objects, which must therefore be shown to exist – the position of Frege. This debate tends, however to dissolve as information theoretical approaches to mathematics gain force. According to this view both real and conventional systems are reducible to systems of externally related bits of information, which are in turn convertible with the 'elements' of set theory, so that the two positions become equivalent, provided some criterion is defined for determining which systems exist only mathematically and which exist 'physically' as well. Radical empiricists such as Tipler suggest such a criterion: those systems exist physically which are sufficiently complex to contain observers (Tipler 1994).

Clearly the realist version of logicism corresponds roughly to the rationalist position in first philosophy: that we can use analytic methods to prove theorems about the

---

[6] Our discussion of the nature of the formalism is heavily indebted to Stephen Körner's *Philosophy of Mathematics* (Körner 1968).

existence and nature of real objects. The nominalist version of logicism corresponds to the empiricist position. It is important to note here that the claim is not that mathematical systems themselves are mere conventions, but only that the objects about which mathematics speaks are conventional. The system itself is, given the conventional objects, the only logically possible way to organize the set of objects. This view is thus convertible with the forms of liberal political economy which derive the market system from a given 'set' – that of self-interested individuals – and what they understand to be the rules of logic.

Like rationalist metaphysics, logicist mathematics has largely succumbed to the critique mounted by Gödel and his followers. If it is impossible, as Gödel has shown, to develop a system which is at once consistent and complete, and which contains even such simple rules as those of arithmetic, then it is not at all clear how the logicist project of grounding mathematics in the rules of logic can ever be realized. Like the market, purely formal systems are always parasitic on some external reality from which they ultimately derive their sustenance.

The mathematical doctrine now known as formalism was initially advanced by Kant to come to terms with the limitations of the rational project of Leibniz. According to this view, mathematical categories derive from the fundamental forms of intuition – space and time. Thinking in spatial terms is, for Kant, thinking geometrically; thinking in temporal terms, that is, in terms of succession, is thinking arithmetically. While Kant's formulation of the doctrine draws obviously on a Newtonian physics which regards space and time as distinct, it is certainly susceptible of reformulation in the light of special and general relativity – provided, of course, that we can develop a mathematics which fully unifies arithmetic and geometry.

The Kantian project has been pursued in two very different directions. Hilbert and other formalists have attempted to construct purely formal systems joining the basic forms of intuition to the rules of logic – and have run into many of the same problems as the logicists. Indeed, the internal structure of both types of mathematics are quite similar, the only real difference being the metaphysical status of the objects treated. Whereas for the logicists these objects are either real or purely conventional, for formalists they are forms of human intuition. The so-called intuitionists, on the other hand, have adhered much more rigidly to the original Kantian programme, insisting that all objects treated by mathematics be intuitively constructable. The idea of a possible infinity, for example, is intuitively constructable – indeed we do so whenever we say 'and so on and so on . . .' An actual infinity, however, cannot be imagined. The requirement of intuitive constructablity means avoiding the use of the law of the excluded middle in mathematical proofs, as this rule often leads to counter-intuitive results. Simply showing that the opposite of some proposition leads to contradictions does not mean that the object proposed by that proposition can be imagined, much less that it actually exists. Intuitivist mathematics avoids many of the self-reference problems encountered by the logicists and the more liberal interpretations of formalism, but it ends by excluding much of the mathematics on which contemporary physics is founded – something which calls into question the usefulness of formalization as such.

More broadly, however, both variants of Kantian mathematics are vulnerable to the criticisms levelled at critical philosophy generally. If mathematics is simply a function of the way in which human beings perceive the universe, then why is it that it proves so useful not only in organizing our experience but also in the development of technologies through which we interact with the real world? Formalism and intuitionism, in other words, do not explain the fact that at least one layer or level of organization of the universe does in fact seem actually to be mathematical, so that when we prove theorems or engage in mathematical constructions we are not merely organizing our experience in accord with certain innate mental structures but are, in fact, saying something about the real world.

Two ways out of this dilemma, little discussed in the mathematical literature, but at least worth mentioning, are the transcendental and objective idealist strategies. A transcendental idealist attempt to ground the practical usefulness of mathematics would, in effect, argue that the conditions of the possibility of human subjectivity include not only the forms of intuition which are the font of mathematical thinking, but also the mathematical organization of the universe – or even a specific mathematical organization of the universe. Here we are close to the cluster of issues discussed by the so-called anthropic cosmology. It turns out that certain basic physical constants are fixed at just precisely the levels which make life and intelligence possible. The question arises as to whether this is simply a selection factor affecting our observations: we are structured in such a way that we could not observe any region in which the constants were significantly different from what they are (the critical idealist position) or whether perhaps the existence of human beings actually requires that the universe be structured as it is, so that we can actually make anthropic arguments from the existence of intelligence, to various physical realities (more nearly a transcendental idealist position). There is no reason that a similar strategy cannot be used to impose mathematical requirements on the structure of the universe, something which, in most cosmologies, turns out to be the same thing as imposing physical requirements anyway. This doctrine is not too different from Tipler's neo-Berkeleyan solution to the question of which mathematical systems also exist physically – that is, those mathematical systems which permit the existence of physical observers are also physically real. The difficulty with this approach, as with transcendental strategies generally, is that it is not clear just how human subjectivity can 'require' anything of the universe, God and so on.

Objective idealist strategies are a bit more common in contemporary mathematics, and are sometimes invoked under the mistaken identity of 'Platonism', to provide a way out of the contradictions of logicist and formalist mathematics. This was, for example, Gödel's position. Here mathematical intuition provides a starting point outside the closed logical system, which is thus grounded in basic insights into the structure of the universe. Or, in the formalist or intuitionist case, the Kantian thing in itself is dispensed with and the phenomenon as it appears to human intuition is taken as the only reality. In either case, mathematical intuition is regarded as a means of accessing the real structure of the universe, and thus of resolving the contradictions posed by self-reference. Within this framework, differences are still possible regarding the nature and limits of further logical elaboration – for example, the status of the law of the excluded middle.

Where this approach differs from an authentic Platonism is in the more or less complete rejection of abstraction from sense-experience. Plato clearly regarded mathematical forms as in a sense more fundamental than the objects known in sense-perception, but he believed that we rose to these forms through the dialectic – not through an intuitive leap across a vast cognitive abyss. Indeed, for Plato mathematical objects were known through *dianoia*, that is, critical, discursive, analytical reasoning, not through *eikasis*, or imaginative intuition, a form of knowledge which ranks lower in the epistemological hierarchy than sense-perception, or through *noesis*, a kind of rational intuition of the Good itself. The possibility of a rational intuition into the underlying structure of the universe – mathematical or otherwise – is not to be excluded, but it must be grounded in experience and reason, and not constitute a solution *deus ex machina* to theoretical problems which do not seem otherwise susceptible to solution.

Our critique of the principal alternative theories has already suggested the superiority of the *via dialectica*, in this as in other matters. But here we need to distinguish between the idealist and materialist tendencies within the tradition. The dialectical tradition generally has historically been united around the doctrine known as mathematical realism, because of its conviction that mathematical objects are in fact real, and that we know them in much the same way we know everything else: through sensation and abstraction. It is only the more idealist tendency within the tradition, however, and more specifically that associated with Plato and his school, which has upheld the strong form of realism: the idea that mathematical forms exist quite apart from matter, and are even in a certain sense prior to matter. Plato, for example, argues in the *Republic*, that what mathematics does is to allow us to see beyond the changing impressions of the senses to grasp the eternal forms, the underlying structures of number, space, music and the heavenly bodies (music and astronomy, as well as arithmetic and geometry, being included among the mathematical sciences). In the *Timaeus* he seems to go further, suggesting that the material world itself is composed of basic geometric forms which combine in different ways to form bodies, as they are informed by the world soul and ultimately by the eternal forms themselves.

The difficulty with this doctrine is that once we abstract from everything except the mathematical structure of an object, we abstract from the very conditions of its existence – something which the Plato of the *Republic* understood implicitly when he taught that it is the Good (that is, ordering to an end or τελος) which brings things into being. Now mathematics itself cannot distinguish between forms which actually exist and those which are merely possible beings – a distinction which is, on the one hand, empirical, and on the other hand, depends for its comprehension on the completion of the philosophical cosmology which we are here only beginning. If Plato was, perhaps, unaware of this distinction, it is probably because the mathematics of his time was in fact still deeply rooted in experience. This was true even for the idealist Pythagoreans, who gained their insights from such activities as comparing the lengths of the strings on a harp which produce different notes, and not from formal-logical manipulations. But as the process of mathematical formalization has advanced, we have produced a rich diversity of mathematical forms which differ substantially from those which we can abstract directly from experience. It is possible, for example, to imagine a universe with a discrete topology and metric, even though we know that our universe is not structured in this way. From a Platonic standpoint such a universe exists, creating a whole complex of problems which turn out to be quite difficult to resolve.

Ultimately, Plato's claim that mathematical forms exist apart from matter must be ascribed to the alienating impact of petty commodity relations. In a society in which price is beginning to command production, and something purely quantitative (money) thus rules over the organization of matter, it is easy to believe that numbers are more real than the things which they enumerate. Even so, it is vitally important to maintain a sharp distinction between Plato's doctrine, in which mathematics is still grounded in abstraction from experience, and objective idealist mystifications.

The moderate realism of Aristotle, Aquinas and the dialectical materialist traditions avoids the problems of full-blown Platonism. For the moderate realist, mathematics describes a real level of the organization of matter – which, however, cannot exist apart from the matter which alone makes it possible. This permits a distinction between mathematical forms abstracted from experience, the existence of which may be inferred to be actual, and what Aquinas called possible beings of the intellect, constructed on the basis of forms abstracted from experience, using the tools of formal logic, which cannot be shown to exist in reality.

Here, too, however, there are difficulties. Specifically, we encounter here for the first time (it will not be the last) the ambiguity in the Aristotelian and dialectical materialist concept of matter. On the one hand, matter is regarded as the potential for organization. On the other hand, it is treated in this theorization of the nature of mathematics as if it were an actual principle of existence – as if by being 'joined' to matter a mathematical form could come into being. But the mere possibility of organization cannot confer actuality. This means that it must be something other than – or to be precise something 'more than' – matter which confers being on otherwise merely possible forms. This 'something more' is God, who alone can confer actual being on mere possibility and make organization emerge from the pure potency of matter.

What this suggests is that mathematical structures are indeed forms abstracted from experience, or constructions based on forms abstracted from experience, which cannot actually exist on their own, but what they are abstracted from is not lower but rather higher forms of organization, not naked matter, but rather actual physical, biological and social organization. More specifically, mathematics describes the most basic conditions for the possibility (not actuality) of any organization whatsoever: the underlying structure in which elements, relations and operations (and thus processes of transformation) alone are possible. This in turn involves describing a whole hierarchy of increasingly structured systems – sets, groups, various types of spaces and so on – in which ever more complex relations and operations are possible.

We should note here two distinct types of contact between mathematical abstraction and our experience of actual organization. On the one hand, there is an underlying real space – or rather space-time – which forms the simplest layer of physical organization. Mathematics attempts to describe the structure of this space-time in the theory of relativity and so on. This is the space described by the operation of gravity. But there are also a whole host of abstract spaces in which other, more complex processes unfold – the phase space in which a chemical reaction takes place or a population evolves, or the 'social space' in which one speaks of the ideological distance between two systems. Both uses of mathematics are legitimate, in so far as both help us to comprehend the organization of the universe. But in one case our use of mathematical description is univocal – as when we speak of the distance between two planets; in the other case it is analogical. Both are to be distinguished from 'pure' mathematics which considers possible forms without reference to their actual existence, and thus their usefulness in describing actual forms of organization.

Nothing need be changed in this formulation if we move beyond mathematics to a broader 'structural' understanding of the formalism. When we abstract the structure of a language, a psyche, a kinship system, an economy, a polity or a myth, what we abstract is an aspect of the way in which the system in question is organized. But as abstracted it is merely a possible being; there is nothing in the form itself which makes its existence necessary. As with quantitative systems, we can either use the structure we have abstracted in the context of a complete explanation, something which will require reference to a function or end and thus to transcendental abstraction, or we can move to higher degrees of generality. Thus, for example we might argue that a particular society has such and such a kinship system because that system helps it survive and develop under particular ecological, technological and economic conditions. Or, we might abstract from models of several different kinship systems to develop a general theory of the rules which govern kinship systems in general. This latter exercise is not so much scientific as it is purely formalizing, but it is not without its uses. On the basis of such a theory, one might, for example, deduce all logically possible kinship systems just as mathematicians abstract from the topology of our universe to consider the rules governing topologies in general and then derive other possible topologies. Or one might proceed further, considering the rules governing language, kinship, economy, myth and so on, and develop an analysis of the properties of social structures in general, which could then be joined with high-order analyses of other sorts of structure to produce an account of the rules which govern all logically possible types of structures. This is, in effect, what Piaget does in his book *Structuralism* (Piaget 1968), but the account needs to be elaborated further before mathematics and the structuralist enterprise are fully unified.

Why involve oneself in such an enterprise? Why not concern ourselves with the organization of what actually is, using formalization judiciously in the context of complete scientific explanations which terminate in a transcendental abstraction? Science is, to be sure, the higher calling and the one which leads most directly to metaphysics and thus to knowledge of God. But the task of pure formalization is not without its value. First of all, the sort of enterprise which I have outlined here might play a useful role in setting quantification in its proper context as the description of only a very limited class of structures. Second, in examining the rules governing all logically possible structures we are, in a sense, peering into the mind of God. To be more precise, we are charting out the limitations which God Herself faced in creating the universe – since even God cannot violate the rules of logic. This is an interesting activity in its own right; it may also help us to resolve some mysteries which resist scientific explanation – things which are the way they are not because they serve some ultimate purpose, but because it would involve a logical contradiction for them to be otherwise. This in turn may help resolve certain questions of theodicy and thus serve as a useful auxiliary to the more straightforward cosmological and teleological arguments for the existence of God.

We are now in a position to assess just what formalization can achieve – and just what it cannot. On the one hand, it should be apparent that formalization is a powerful tool. It liberates us from the fuzziness of the merely taxonomic definitions generated by totalization, and from the innumerable contradictions which exist within informal totalizing belief systems. With the kind of rigorous definition it makes possible, we can reason 'from forms to forms', without new sensory input, in a way that we couldn't at the level of totalization. We thus advance to real logical inference, as distinct from poetic or imaginative elaboration of totalizing abstractions. Formalization is capable of providing descriptions of physical, and within more stringent limits, biological and social systems which allow 'practical inference' or prediction. And without rigorous definitions and the sort of inference which it permits, the judgements of value which are characteristic of transcendental abstraction could never take place. Not only science but also philosophy and theology, all of which depend on rigorous definition and inference, would be impossible without formalization of some kind.

At the same time, it should already be apparent that formalization is also a highly problematic enterprise. Let us begin by considering the limitations of formalization as an instrument of scientific investigation. First of all, it turns out to be very difficult to obtain formal descriptions which actually permit a reliable inference to future states or properties of a system. It is one thing to claim, on the basis of the definition of a triangle, that the sum of the angles of each and every triangle will be 180°. It is quite another thing to claim, for example, that a formal description of some physical, biological or social system actually allows us to infer the past and future history of the system in question. This is because formalizations of actual systems are only approximations.

This problem is rapidly becoming apparent even at the physical level, where formalisms are most useful. Consider the example of physical cosmology. The current 'standard model' of 'Big Bang' theory is based largely on a 'solution' of Einstein's field equations, which constitute our best description *to date* of gravitational systems. Given certain not terribly unrealistic assumptions these equations seem to predict the expansion, and possible eventual contraction and collapse, of the universe. The Friedman models, as the equations which make these predictions are called, represent a triumph of formalization. And at first there seemed to be evidence to support the theory: the Hubble shift, the cosmic microwave background and so on. Increasingly however, the model has become difficult to sustain: stars which are older than the predicted age of the universe, structures which, given the very model of gravity on which the larger theory is based, would have required more time to develop than the theory allows, incorrect predictions regarding the basic ratios of such elements as Deuterium, Helium and Lithium, the prediction of magnetic monopoles and so on. Clearly something is wrong here (Lerner 1991). And the problem becomes even more serious when we attempt mathematical models of complex physical systems, organisms, or societies. It is not that these systems are not structured, or that their structures are not intelligible; it is just that the formal structure which we abstract cannot grasp perfectly the pattern of their development.

That formalizations of actual systems are always and only approximations, and that, even at the level of the simplest (for example, gravitational) systems, they tend to lead to incorrect predictions, suggests that the formalism does not govern actual systems at all, but is rather a rough sketch of the structure which has emerged in response to some higher governing principle which is invisible to formal abstraction.

The approximate character of formalisms is not, however, their only limitation. It also turns out to be very difficult to unify the formalisms which we use to describe the universe. Among the internal contradictions of mathematical physics the most important are:

1   an inability to unify relativity, which depends on the notion of a space-time continuum and a concept of signalling which imply strict causal relations, and quantum mechanics, which theorizes the universe as a discrete order and which calls into question certain aspects of strict causal relatedness (Bohm 1980);
2   an inability to unify dynamics (understood to include both relativistic and quantum theory), which treat reversible processes, and thermodynamics, which treats irreversible change (Prigogine *et al.* 1977, 1984); and
3   an inability to reconcile the results of thermodynamics, and especially such basic principles as the Second Law and the Boltzmann Order Principle (Prigogine *et al.* 1977, 1984) with the phenomena of self-organization, life and intelligence.

Far from being a seamless fabric of logically necessary inter-relations, mathematical physics is more like a patchwork of jerry-rigged formalisms, many of which work quite well but which cannot all be made compatible with each other – much less reduced to a unified deductive system. Even where authentically powerful explanations have been developed, these explanations depend on primary formalisms which ultimately contradict each other. Thus, one of the triumphs of mathematical physics is the explanation of chemical organization using quantum mechanics and thermodynamics – but these two theories have fundamentally different understandings of such basic concepts as 'time'. Quantum mechanical time is reversible; thermodynamic time is irreversible and describes a real process of change. When one extends the field of view to the biological and social sciences, this problem becomes overwhelming.

Closely related to the problem of unification is that of explanation. A complete explanation reduces the multitude of phenomena which we experience to a single explanatory principle from which they can all be derived. This is, in fact, what it would mean to unify science. But formalisms are, by nature, descriptive rather than explanatory and offer explanations only secondarily, in the sense that *given* a certain structure, certain things follow necessarily – including, perhaps, other structures. A complete explanation is possible at the level of formalization only under very rare circumstances – that is, where the existing state of affairs is the only logically possible one, and therefore once understood is analytically self-evident. Thus quantum mechanics explains the periodic table of elements, but the quantum nature of energy transfer itself goes unexplained. What this means is that the physical, biological and social sciences can never be wholly reduced to deductive systems by means of mathematical formalization. There always remains some fact or facts known empirically but which cannot be shown to be the logically necessary consequence of some unifying first principle.

The inability of formalization to offer a logically complete explanation of any actual system is intimately bound up with one of its principal characteristics – its exclusion a priori of teleological reasoning of any kind. It is not so much that formalism and teleology are logically incompatible. One can, for example, formalize the operation of a simple machine of some kind, and then also explain its structure in terms of the purpose for which it was designed. Similarly, there is no fundamental contradiction between a formal, mathematical description of some physical, biological, or even social system and an argument that the structure of that system serves some purpose, either internal to itself, in some larger system of which it is a part, or in the universe as a whole. Thus even those economists who are most attached to mathematical model building understand the economy as a structured system which serves a definite function. It is just that the teleological explanation itself cannot be formalized. One can, at least in principle, describe mathematically the changes involved in a teleological process, and it might even be possible to determine which classes of formalisms describe teleological processes, giving us a kind of 'quantitative indicator' of purposeful behaviour, but the τέλος itself is not formalizable. But the only complete explanations, as Aristotle demonstrated long ago, are teleological. This is because a complete explanation must terminate in a principle which (directly or indirectly) explains everything else while itself requiring no additional explanation. To use Aristotle's language it must be an 'unmoved mover', and it must be its own cause and thus a 'necessary being'. Now the only way in which something can move other things without itself being moved is by the attractive power of its own perfection (otherwise it would be in motion itself and would thus require some other explanatory principle, resulting in an infinite regress). And the only way in which something can be necessary is for it also to be infinite and perfect, so that there is nothing outside of it by which it might be affected (Aristotle, *Metaphysics* 1071b–1076b; Aquinas, *Summa Theologiae* I, Q 2).

The inability of formalization to comprehend teleological principles affects not only science, but also metaphysics. It is only a doctrine of cosmic teleology which can effectively ground the claim that the universe is ultimately meaningful and has as its first principle a God who *is* that ultimate meaning. The exclusion of teleology by a science which has formalization as its ideal and which is dominated by mathematical physics excludes a priori the possibility of ultimate meaning and the existence of God.[7]

Now it may be objected that there is in fact a way to rise to knowledge of God at the level of formal abstraction. At issue here is the so-called 'ontological argument' developed by St Anselm and elaborated by Descartes and by a number of contemporary thinkers. This is Anselm's form of the argument, restated in slightly more formal language:

> God is that than which nothing greater can be thought.
> Now everyone, upon hearing this definition, has in their mind the idea of such a being.
> But to exist in reality is greater than to exist in the mind.
> Therefore, in order to be 'that than which nothing greater can be thought' it is necessary to exist in reality as well as in the mind. Thus, God exists.
> (Anselm, *Proslogion*)

---

[7] One must, therefore, take the claim that 'modern science', which depends almost exclusively on formalization, has 'demonstrated' that the universe doesn't have a purpose with a grain of salt. This is rather like saying that a man blind from birth who has demonstrated his brilliance as a great composer, and justly won the respect of all, finding no evidence of light has 'demonstrated' that there is no such thing.

Descartes's version is even simpler:

> God is perfect.
> Perfection includes existence.
> Therefore God exists.
> (Descartes, *Meditations*)

This is a formal argument because it begins with a rigorous definition which is then analysed in order to discover its logical implications – which, in this case, appear to include existence.

Now most criticism of the ontological proof focuses, quite understandably, on the fact that it begs the question – that is, that it assumes what it attempts to prove, namely that there in fact is a being 'than which nothing greater can be thought' or a 'perfect being' (Aquinas, *Summa Theologiae* I Q 2, a1). Aquinas is willing to allow that the proof holds if we are able to first demonstrate the premise. Restated in this form, we get not a proof for the existence of God, but a proof that if there is perfect Being, such Being *is* necessarily. Kant's criticism is somewhat stronger. Being, he says, is not a true predicate, but rather a way of predicating. We cannot therefore derive the existence of something from an analysis of some other predicate. This renders the notion of a necessary being impossible (Kant, *Critique of Pure Reason*).

But the problems with the ontological proof run deeper than this – something which becomes apparent if we restate the argument in fully formal mathematical terms. The clue to this problem is in the quantitative language in terms of which both Anselm's and Descartes's versions of the proof are framed. Thus Anselm defines God in quantitative terms: God is 'that than which nothing greater can be thought.' Descartes's definition in terms of perfection might be understood in a non-quantitative sense, except that he then goes on to say that perfection 'includes' existence. Both Anselm and Descartes are defining a certain kind of relation – an order, and in the case of Descartes, an order by inclusion. Such orders can exist within even the simplest of mathematical categories – that is, sets. They then go on to conclude that the set on which the order in question has been defined (presumably the universe, or if one finds the pantheistic implications distasteful 'the universe plus God') has what mathematicians call a '*maximal element*', which is greater than, or includes, all of the others.

Now such a conclusion is not at all out of the question. It is, essentially, an application of Zorn's Lemma. According to Zorn's Lemma, if A is a partially-ordered set (a set in which at least some elements are comparable, that is greater than or equal to the others) and in which every totally-ordered subset (that is, every subset in which *all* elements are comparable) has an upper bound (an element than which all other elements are lesser or in which they are included) then A has a maximal element. We can restate the ontological argument in the following terms:

> Let U (the universe) be a set which is partially ordered, and in which every totally ordered subset is bounded above.

> Then (by Zorn's Lemma) U has a maximal element which we will call God.

Having restated the argument in this form, we are in a much better position to assess it. The first question which we must ask, of course, is whether or not (or in what sense) the hypothesis holds. And here we run into insuperable difficulties. There are many senses in which the universe *can* be described as a partial order. Consider, for example, an ordering of the universe in terms of space-time enclosures, across however many dimensions one believes the universe involves. In this case, barring the intrusion of truly exotic topologies, it should be easy to show that the universe is a partial order, that is, that

1   every region of space-time which is included in a larger region is also included in those still larger regions which include the first including region,
2   every region of space-time includes itself, and
3   any two mutually inclusive regions of space-time are equivalent,

together with the equally trivially true statement that all totally ordered regions of space-time have an upper bound, that is, that all regions of space-time in which all subspaces are included in, equivalent to, or include other subspaces are included in a single largest space. If all this is true, *and* Zorn's Lemma holds, then we have arrived at the truly momentous conclusion that the universe includes all its parts – hardly what is meant by the existence of God. This 'mathematical divine', however, is about the best we can do at the level of formalization. If we attempt to define the orders in terms of complexity, capacities and so on, we must have reference to a transcendental term in the light of which we make a judgement that a certain capacity is higher than another, something with which formal abstraction does not provide us.

All of these arguments, furthermore, have hanging over them the fact that Zorn's Lemma, on which they depend, has itself never been proven, though it seems to make intuitive sense and is probably a Kantian transcendental for formal operations – that is, a condition of their possibility, for which reason it is generally included in axiomatic systems (Geroch 1985: 42).[8]

Still other objections can be presented to the ontological proof. We have shown, for example, that formal definitions are still definitions in terms of difference. This means that 'God' can be defined only in relation to other terms in the system, so that even if God was shown to be the maximal element in the system, it would also be a radically dependent element, like all of the other others, and thus not God in any meaningful sense. Formal orders will not permit a definition of God; only a transcendental ordering makes this possible.

Another way of stating this problem is to say that any metaphysics developed at the level of formal abstraction, even if this abstraction is structural rather than purely

---

[8] It might be asked whether one might not rescue the ontological proof, or construct some other formal proof for the existence of God using the sort of non-quantitative structural formalism discussed earlier in this chapter. It is our view that a 'structural' version of the ontological proof is simply impossible, because of the irreducibly quantitative nature of the concepts on which the ontological proof depends. Whether or not a structural proof, using a strategy different from that of the ontological argument, might be possible is an open question, but it seems unlikely. This is because structural as well as quantitative formalism treats being as univocal, a problem we address in the following section.

quantitative, will be irrevocably committed to the doctrine of the 'univocity of being'. This is the claim, first put forward by John Duns Scotus, that 'Being' is predicated in the same way of all beings, including God. Being, from this point of view, is a vast field divided by *genera* which are defined not in relation to Being, which they all share in the same way, but only in relationship to each other. This is in distinction to the Thomistic tradition, which regards Being as an analogical predicate. Only God *is* in the fullest and most complete sense of the word; other things *participate* in being in accord with their nature. Thus the various *genera* and species are defined first and foremost as *different ways of being*, and thus ultimately in relationship to a transcendental term which can ground the stability of their natures.[9]

It is the inability of formalization to grasp the analogical character of Being which is at the root of its limitations as an instrument of both science and metaphysics. If Being is a univocal predicate and *genera* are defined only in relation to each other, there is an actual infinity of ways in which *genera* can be defined – an actual infinity of ways in which to formalize experience. Little wonder it turns out to be difficult to unify the sciences! Formalization terminates not in a unified theory of everything which derives the universe as a whole from a single, analytically self-evident formal principal, but rather in difference as such, which is the real first principle of formal reason, and which renders equally valid all logically consistent formalizations of human experience. Thus the passage from structuralism to postmodernism in the human sciences; thus the termination of information-theoretical systems theory in the radical subjectivism of thinkers like Frank Tipler.

But there is more. If Being is univocal then difference not only makes things *what* they are; it actually generates them, separating them off from the Infinite or mathematical divine. This means that God differs from particular beings only quantitatively, as the infinite and undifferentiated: that which is greater or more inclusive in the set-theoretical sense of being most general and least specific. Like the high-god of some ancient tributary empire (but only 'more' so) 'that than which nothing greater can be thought' transcends the universe of difference only in the sense that it remains undivided and thus purely potential, more like prime matter than pure form. The 'lesser' realms of actuality are ruled by the demigod of difference. Creation is always and only an act of division, division which also destroys, and which is, therefore, ultimately negation and violence.[10]

Nowhere is this ontology of violence more apparent than in the work of mathematical physicist Frank Tipler, which we have already discussed. Framed as an argument for the existence of God and personal immortality, Tipler's vision demonstrates the horrors of which formal reason is capable when it is unregulated by transcendental abstraction. The universe, for Tipler, is a vast information-processing system. Matter is the 'hardware' component of the system, the laws of nature the 'software'. Tipler argues that the organization of a system is its negative entropy, or the quantity of information encoded within it. 'Life' for Tipler is, as we have noted, simply information encoded in such a way that it is conserved by natural selection. A system is intelligent

---

[9] On the univocity of Being and its implications see Milbank 1990.

[10] High gods such as the Canaanite *'El* were remote and rather indifferent to human affairs. The real ruling deities, on the other hand, such as *ba'al*, were almost always warlord gods who governed the human realm by rape and pillage.

if it meets the 'Turing test', that is, if a human operator interrogating it cannot distinguish its responses from those of a human being. Tipler defines in rigorous physical terms what it would mean for intelligent life to continue forever (and thus for the universe to be ultimately meaningful), as well as the physical conditions for this happening – something which requires that intelligent life re-organize the entire universe to create sufficient gravitational shear to provide the energy necessary to process an infinite amount of information in the finite time permitted by the closed cosmology which he favours, so that the universe terminates in a omniscient, omnipotent and subjectively eternal Omega Point.

Tipler acknowledges that such a universe is only one of many possible worlds. The totality of possible worlds is described in terms of quantum cosmology. In quantum cosmology the universe is represented by a wave function $Y(h, F, S)$, which determines the values of h and F on S, where h is the gravitational and F the non-gravitational fields respectively, and S the underlying three-dimensional manifold (Tipler 1994: 174–5). Most formulations of quantum cosmology leave the selection of the underlying three-dimensional manifold S arbitrary. Hartle and Hawking extend the domain of Y to all possible values of S, but still require h to be space-like – something which contradicts general relativity. Tipler proposes instead to allow the domain of the wave function to include all four-dimensional manifolds which permit a Lorentz metric g. All possible universes exist mathematically; those which permit observers may also be said to exist physically. But the only universes which 'ultimately' contain an observer are those which contain an 'ultimate observer' – that is, those which terminate in an Omega Point. Thus only these universes are physically real. Given the unlikelihood of any given universe, including ours, matching the requirements, it will be necessary to re-engineer the universe. This re-engineering is to be carried out, or at least initiated by, a fleet of intelligent, self-reproducing automata which will, quite literally, devour the universe and, having transformed it into themselves, adopt the spatial distribution necessary to produce the required structure.

There are many scientific difficulties with Tipler's work which we have discussed elsewhere (Mansueto 1995). His understanding of organization is untenable (Bennett 1987), and he ignores the internal contradictions of mathematical physics, especially the contradictions between thermodynamics, with its commitment to the irreversibility of time, and dynamics, with its reversible processes, and the internal contradiction between relativity, with its concept of a space-time continuum, and quantum mechanics, with its commitment to discrete change. In the end one is forced to conclude that Tipler is trying to make mathematical physics say something it cannot, and ends up transforming the hope of a universe ordered to life and intelligence into a nightmarish vision of a universe consumed by self-reproducing automata and transformed into a gravitational supercomputer. Most important from the point of view of our argument, however, is the inability of formal reason to conceive of creativity and purposefulness except in terms of violence and consumption. Tipler claims, for example, that one can understand his theory either as an immanent requirement that the intelligent beings arise and re-engineer the universe – or, since causality is reversible under general relativity and quantum mechanics – as a claim that the Omega Point in fact creates the universe by exercising causality back through time. But the *most straightforward* way to understand it is as a claim that the intelligent robot probes, and we as their creators, are actually responsible for the creation of the universe, and that this 'creative' act consists first and foremost in the consumption of literally everything existing. The 'attractive power' exerted by his Omega Point is the prospect of immortality – little more than a Spinozist drive to persist in being. The universe is thus the product of our desire to persist in being through violent consumption of others. Predation is the first principle.

It is little wonder that postmodernist critics recoil in horror from this sort of vision, and attempt to use the arbitrariness of all formal schema against formalization as such, 'deconstructing' rationalist ontologies and exposing them as little more than an expression of a bare will to power. The difficulty, of course, is that 'deconstruction' itself presupposes the ontology of violence from which it emancipates us only in the limited sense of forcing us to acknowledge every act as violent, thus depriving would-be god-kings of legitimating metanarratives (Derrida [1967] 1978, Lyotard [1979] 1984). Nietzsche was more honest, embracing the will to power as a positive ethic, validating warfare and conquest and infinite consumption as not only permissible, but as, in fact, the only authentic expression of Being itself, realized as predation and difference, and driven by the *conatus* or the drive to become all things.

The tragedy here is not merely that formal abstraction seems to terminate in a nihilism which regards violence as at best inevitable and at worst something to be gloried in, but rather that a fundamentally creative drive, the drive to know all and become all – that is, the drive to be God – is cultivated in such a way as to become a powerful force for destruction. The result is a temptation to abandon the drive to become God altogether. Deconstructionism represents one way of doing this. Postmodernist Augustinianism represents another. At least two authors in recent years have argued that while deconstructionist postmodernism effectively rules out both Aristotelian and Enlightenment approaches to grounding ethics, certain forms of Augustinianism are not so vulnerable. Graham MacAleer (MacAleer 1996), for example, argues that Anselm offers just such an ethic. Anselm, like others in the Augustinian tradition, makes a distinction between two kinds of willing: the *affectio commodi* and the *affectio iusticiae*. The first is fundamentally a drive towards self-development and self-perfection, the latter a willing or loving of the other for his or her own sake. While not in itself evil, the *affectio commodi* is radically insufficient, and terminates ultimately in violence. Thus, according to Anselm, Lucifer sinned in wanting to be God, to annul the ontological difference which separates creature and creator. The *affectio iusticiae*, on the other hand, terminates in charity, which loves the other in the sense of affirming him in his difference. There is, MacAleer, argues, nothing in the currently fashionable ontologies of difference which make such an option impossible, or indeed any less consistent than the violent embrace of the will to power which characterizes Nietzsche and the postmodernists. John Milbank (Milbank 1990) makes a similar case regarding Augustine. Indeed, he argues, there is no reason why we cannot theorize creative difference as *caritas* rather than violence.

Two points are in order here. First, while MacAleer and Milbank are quite correct that difference may be theorized *either* as *caritas or* as violence, they do not provide any real ground for opting for the former, and thus fail to ground their moral claims adequately. Indeed, unless we can show that our moral demands are nothing more or less than an expression of the very structure of Being Itself, and thus implicitly of the person on whom we make the demand, those demands may be rightly denounced as themselves acts of violence. The best our postmodernist Augustinians can do is to opt out of the violence themselves, without so much as demanding that others do the same.

Or this would, at least, be the case were it not for our second objection. At least within the scope of formal reason, respecting difference inevitably means forgoing our own development. This is because growth can only be conceived quantitatively, and God as the Infinite. It is thus always better to have than not to have, and if one can find a way to 'have' the other fully and completely, so much the better. This issue becomes especially pressing if we take seriously the questions about our ultimate destiny raised by formalist science. If the 'standard model' or 'Big Bang' is the best possible description of the universe, then Tipler's vision, nightmarish as it may seem, represents our last, best hope for survival into infinity. But of course it is a strategy of survival through cosmic predation, a strategy which hardly respects, much less loves, the other in his or her otherness. Under such a cosmology, the only one with which it is really compatible, Anselm's ethic (and MacAleer's and Milbank's) implies abstaining from the struggle to survive or, what is the same thing, resigning ourselves to finitude and death. It is an ethics of suffering and ultimately a theology of death in light disguise. To use theological language, if Tipler proposes that we crucify the universe in order to resurrect it, MacAleer and Milbank are suggesting that we simply yield to crucifixion without hope of redemption.

However problematic their arguments may be, our engagement with MacAleer and Milbank does nonetheless suggest an interesting way to think about formalization unformed by transcendental abstraction – the mathematizing or structuralist intellect which sets itself up as the ideal of knowledge. While totalization without formalization is merely primitive and sloppy, formalization without transcendental abstraction – without reference to the τελος which alone can order and explain – is actually sinful. It is sinful in the strict sense of representing a turning away from the first principle – in this case, since it is a question of intellectual sin, of turning away from the first principle of explanation, which is God, and which is only accessible through transcendental abstraction. This is why, even as we respect our mathematical physicists for their intellectual prowess, we cannot help but have at least a faint sense that at least some of them are about something demonic or diabolical. Anyone who has spent time in one of the great centres of research in mathematical physics, and knows that these are nearly always also great centres of weapons research, realizes that this sentiment is not merely a prejudice. This same pall of the demonic hangs over 'emancipatory nihilists' such as our deconstructive postmodernists as well. They exchange the sin of violence for that of despair; both sins have the same intellectual root.

What may be less clear is that neo-Augustinians like MacAleer and Milbank commit the same sin. Turning away from transcendental abstraction[11] and thus

---

[11] The turn away from transcendental abstraction is always a product of immersion in market relations. As we have already suggested, and as we shall argue in greater depth in Chapter 6, in a society which itself is no longer ordered to some global end, people no longer have a basis in experience for seeking out the purpose of the universe as a whole, and thus no longer any basis in experience for the act of transcendental abstraction. There are, however, different ways of turning from transcendental abstraction. Where Tipler represents the resurgent 'information-age' finance capitalism of the 1980s and 1990s with its façade of

from an authentic philosophical knowledge of God, they despair of the ultimate meaningfulness of the universe and opt for a metaphysics and a cosmology in which the only alternative to violence is suffering. That they then turn to God in faith and submission changes nothing. They differ from the deconstructionists only in that their despair flows from faith and ends in humble resignation rather than flowing from intellectual arrogance and masquerading as intellectual sophistication. The solution to the internal contradictions of pure formalism is not to abandon reason, but rather to rise to a higher degree of abstraction, transcendental abstraction, which reveals the end to which structures are ordered, and on which they are ultimately grounded. From this new vantage point it becomes possible to respect and love the other in and through difference, without sacrificing the drive towards growth and development – even the drive to become God. The fact is that others, in and through their difference, contribute to our development. Sometimes this means growing together and annulling part of the difference, but not always. My theory, for example, benefits from interaction with MacAleer's, without becoming more like it. All this requires, of course, some way to show that the drive for development, of which the drive to become God is simply the logical extension, is something more than a drive to greater quantitative extension – that it is a real participation in a first principle which is also an attractive principle of value. It is to the search for such a principle of value that we now turn.

---

optimism about the future, postmodernism represents the resignation of the 'humanistic' intelligentsia in the face of this resurgence and the consequent defeat of socialism. It represents this resignation, but it also encourages it, by refusing to offer an epistemological and ontological ground to ethical claims which might challenge the market order. And for this service the postmodernists are well rewarded by their bourgeois masters. In 2001, the University of Illinois at Chicago, for example, offered postmodernist literary critic Stanley Fish $230,000 a year to serve as Dean of its School of Liberal Arts and Sciences. The social basis of postmodern Augustinianism is similar, except that the intellectuals in question are linked to religious institutions, which have themselves become increasingly rentierized. Here the refusal of violence renders the otherwise often quite vigorous critique of capitalism utterly innocuous. It is, after all, only the working classes which are being asked to disarm. The bourgeoisie keeps its imperialist military and its police. The only really serious philosophy and theology are those which join truth to arms – which are confident enough in humanity's ability both to know and do the Good that they are willing, when persuasion fails, to have recourse to measured and judicious violence.

Chapter 6

Transcendental Abstraction

We come at last to the form of knowledge, the possibility and necessity of which it has been our principal concern to establish throughout this work: knowledge of Being itself, and especially knowledge of its transcendental properties: the Beautiful, the True, the Good and the One. It is this knowledge alone which permits something like a complete explanation of the universe and which can provide us with a secure ground for ethical judgement.

We have already established that knowledge of the transcendentals is itself a form of abstraction. What transcendental abstraction does is to abstract not only from the individuality of particular systems to grasp their specific, defining differences, and not only to formalize these differences in a way which produces a preliminary definition of what the system is, but also to abstract from the underlying structure in question to the principle – Being Itself – which explains the existence of the system and the reason it is structured as it is and not in some other logically possible way. It 'separates' Being and the other transcendentals from the particular systems and structures to which they give rise – thus our term 'transcendental abstraction' and the traditional Thomistic term *'separatio'*. While the other forms of abstraction terminate in something which is still univocally a property of the object itself – for example, some universal which may be predicated of it, or some formalism which describes it – transcendental abstraction terminates in something other than the object, which can be predicated of the object only in an indirect and analogical way. The sun is a star. The gravitational field which it generates may be described with extraordinary (though not perfect) accuracy using Einstein's field equations. But the sun *is* only equivocally; it does not have in itself the power of Being which explains why it *is* rather than not being, and why *it is what it is* and *the way it is* rather than being some other thing in some other way. To put the matter differently, there is nothing which is more completely and fully a star than the sun; nor are there gravitational fields which are better described by Einstein's field equations than are those generated by old Sol. But if we are to account for the existence and structure of the universe and everything in it, we must have recourse to some principle which *is*, which has the power of Being and thus of creating in a way which is fundamentally more excellent than any of the particular things which we observe. This is the object of transcendental abstraction.

While clearly this sort of abstraction is most especially the province of metaphysics or the doctrine of first principles, it also plays a role in the sciences, in ethics and in the practical disciplines, that is, the arts and politics. In metaphysics it reveals the transcendental properties of Being and thus gives us a glimpse of the divine nature. In the sciences it appears in the form of a drive towards complete explanation which is never satisfied by or exhausted in taxonomies or formalizations, but which inevitably must have recourse to teleological reasoning. In ethics it is transcendental abstraction which provides the first principle (the Good) from which the principles of right and virtue and justice are derived. Practical knowledge is clearly possible apart from transcendental abstraction: we can understand how physical, biological or social systems work and then use that knowledge to affect the systems in question. It is only transcendental abstraction, however, which can provide the ends to which practical activity must be directed.

We begin our discussion of this topic with a detailed analysis of the act of transcendental abstraction. We then proceed to identify the biological and social basis of this act. From there we go on to show just what transcendental abstraction can achieve in the sciences, in metaphysics, in ethics and in the practical disciplines. Finally we identify the limits of transcendental abstraction and make a case for the necessity of a higher, revealed wisdom.

The Act of Transcendental Abstraction

The principal difference between totalization and formalization on the one hand, and transcendental abstraction on the other hand, is that while the former stop short at the apprehension of a universal (defined either in terms of a specific difference or in terms of a formalism), the latter proceeds to judgement. Where totalization and formalization conclude only to possible beings, transcendental abstraction concludes to actual Being and thus, we will show, to Beauty, Truth, Goodness and Integrity. At the same time, against Gilson and the Transcendental Thomists, and with Maritain, we maintain that the highest degree of abstraction involves not only judgement but also apprehension, and thus a real vision of being and its transcendental properties. How is this possible?

The process of transcendental abstraction takes place in a way which is at once remarkably simple and of such profound subtlety that we hardly notice it. Becoming good at it is less a matter of learning something new (as is the case with high level formalization) as it is of learning to notice what we are already doing. On the one hand, when we abstract from sensation, or more precisely, from the images we garner from sensation, we arrive at a *taxon* or a formalism – for example, 'circle' or '$x^2 + y^2 = r^2$'. It is in this moment of the cognitive process, and this moment only that totalization or formalization consists. From here, however, we inevitably turn back to the image, and through it to the object it represents, and conclude to a judgement.

'This is a circle'.

'This image, and the object it represents, is described by the above formalism'.

In this act of judgement we refer, usually without realizing it, to a property of the object other than the *taxon* to which we have assigned it or the structure which formalization has revealed: that is, the fact that it exists. We also, implicitly, make a claim regarding the truth value of the statement in question, and often, though not always, also make judgements regarding Beauty, Goodness and so on. Now ordinarily we simply pass over this second moment of cognition, and thus fail to complete the act of transcendental abstraction. But if, after predicating, we reflect on the act of predication, we find before us the verb 'to be', and the reality to which it refers, which is nothing other than Being itself, together with its transcendental properties of Beauty, Truth, Goodness and Integrity (though these may or may not be immediately visible depending on the character of the judgement made). We thus pass from judgement back to apprehension, but now to apprehension of something other than the object itself, in which the object participates, but by which it is far exceeded. And henceforth, when we apprehend the object, we see not only the object, and not only its membership in a definite *taxon* or its underlying structure, but also the transcendental principle, Being itself, in which it participates. In short, we see God reflected in the thing, much as God, in viewing the universe, sees Her own Being, Beauty, Truth, Goodness and Integrity reflected therein.

God saw all that He had made, and it was very good. (Genesis 1: 31)

There are certain thinkers, including Rahner (Rahner 1958), who argue that it is not properly the divine which we see in the finite existence of things, but that this is known only as a 'preapprehension' of *Esse* as such (Being Itself) which we know always and only in the limitation of finite systems. This is a mistake. It is certainly true that transcendental judgements imply a criterion which is infinitely 'in excess' of what we actually encounter in the particular system brought under that judgement, and that this criterion is known as infinite only by negation. This is, in effect, a variant of Thomas's fourth argument for the existence of God.[1]

Closely associated with Rahner's objection is that of devotees of the *via negativa*, who argue that representation or conceptualization of the transcendental principle discovered in the finite system might lead to an identification of that finite system itself with the divine, and thus to idolatry. This danger is real. This was, in a certain sense, Hegel's error, and it is the error which Judaism, in refusing to represent the first principle in image or concept, has struggled so vigorously to avoid (Fromm 1966).

Both objections are, however, easily answered. While it is true that the judgement of existence, beauty, truth, goodness and so on is prior to the apprehension of these transcendentals, and that we often fail to return to the image of this second apprehension, this does not, in any obvious way, imply that such an apprehension is impossible. It is true that the resulting vision is dim and indistinct (a problem we will have occasion to discuss later), but it is a vision nonetheless. It is, furthermore, this very vision, and not a negative pre-apprehension, which attracts us to God in the first place. We are drawn to God first of all as the Being of that which exists, the harmony, integrity and clarity of what we perceive, the explanatory power of the principles we discover, the attractive power of the ends we pursue, and the integrity of all things existing and seen and understood and desired. To deny this means to deny the validity of most religious experience. The day-to-day perception of the sacred by the vast majority of the people is a vision of God in the beauty, truth and goodness of physical, biological and social systems. And this is true not just of

---

[1] According to Aquinas, the fact that we make judgements of relative merit, implies the existence of some maximum in terms of which or by comparison to which we make such judgements. 'There is then, something which is truest, something which is best, something noblest and, consequently, something most being . . . And this we call God' (Aquinas, *Summa Theologiae* I Q 2 a3).

encounters with the sacred in the secular realm; much the same is true of the way most people meet God in liturgy and sacrament. To deny the possibility of a positive vision of the divine in finite systems means denying that the Australian totem, the Hopi katchina, the Egyptian Au Set and Keresian Sussistinako represent a real window on the divine, while privileging a critical negativity which, like that of Marx, can lead ultimately to theoretical atheism. We must not, in our efforts to avoid idolatry, fall into an equally disastrous iconoclasm.

The Biological and Social Basis of Transcendental Abstraction

It is one thing to describe a process, quite another to explain it. And the process of transcendental abstraction presents some peculiar problems. The biological basis, to be sure, is the same as for the other degrees of abstraction. The external senses provide a feed of data from the outside world, which is then formed by the internal senses into images which take the form of electrochemical patterns in the cerebral cortex. The complex cortex of the human brain and, quite possibly, the brains of certain other higher animals (primates, cetaceans, psittaciforms (parrots) . . .) are, furthermore, disposed to the establishment of complex links between these images. This is the 'potential' or organic intellect. As the organism becomes involved in increasingly complex social relationships, it becomes 'connatural' with increasingly complex ideal forms – taxonomies, formal systems and, eventually, the transcendentals. It thus 'sees' (or hears, feels, smells, tastes) the images garnered from the senses in the light of these forms, with the result that certain pathways are established linking images and, in the case of transcendental abstraction, also linking images to body states (passions) and actions.

Identifying the social basis of transcendental abstraction is more difficult. On the one hand, it is impossible to conceive of a human being or a human society which does not make judgements of existence, beauty, truth, goodness, integrity and so on.[2]

---

[2] This is the key to the otherwise difficult to answer question of what constitutes intelligence – and helps to explain why most of us are very suspicious regarding strong AI (artificial intelligence) arguments, and yet remain fascinated by science-fiction androids, and cheered on the Mars Rover 'Sojourner' as if 'she' were our little sister. It is difficult to argue that the current trajectory of information-processing technology will be unable to produce machines which can equal or best our ability to process data, producing complex taxonomies and manipulating mathematical formalisms. But these information-processing systems cannot, by their very nature, engage in transcendental abstraction. This is because their programs consist of mathematical formalisms and, as we have seen, the τελος cannot be formalized. Machines of this sort may be 'intelligent' in the sense of performing one of the acts of the intellect (formalization) but they are not 'sapient', that is, capable of the transcendental abstraction which concludes to first principles, and makes judgements of existence, value and so on. And sapience is an integral part of what most of us understand by intelligence. This does not mean that full artificial intelligence, including sapience, is impossible, just that it will consist in something very different from a really big Cray supercomputer. This is why so many people find a character like Data on *Star Trek* to be attractive and credible, while viewing the whole enterprise of AI as it is currently practised with suspicion and not a little fear. Data struggles towards transcendental abstraction – and towards its correlate, appetitive goal orientation (the development of passions and of the will) in a way that is simply not on the agenda for even our most powerful information-processing machines.

On the other hand, it is clear that thinking about the transcendentals develops over time. Communitarian societies have a more sophisticated discourse about principles of value than do tribal societies. The advent of the salvation religions, which corresponds roughly to the first crisis of tributary social formations at the end of the late Bronze Age and beginning of the Iron Age, represents a quantum leap in the sophistication of discourse about the transcendental. But it is not until the development of the Socratic dialectic in the petty commodity society of Hellenic Greece that we really see anything like a properly philosophical discourse.

What this suggests is that transcendental abstraction as such is available to us simply on the basis of our biology and the fact that we live in human society at all, even if the full development of this capacity depends on certain definite social developments. The fact that all societies – indeed all living systems – are structures ordered to an end creates a basis in experience for teleological reasoning in even the simplest societies, and thus for groping towards the transcendentals, to which any complete teleological argument must conclude. This is probably sufficient to explain the universality of judgements of existence and value.

We must, however, distinguish between this sort of implicit transcendental abstraction which accompanies each and every judgement we make, and an explicit discourse on the transcendentals. We must also distinguish between a discourse on the transcendentals which remains couched in the imaginative language of myth and ritual, and a fully philosophical discourse of the sort that first emerges in Greece with Socrates, Plato and Aristotle.

What is it that might make transcendental abstraction explicit? In order to make sense out of this problem we need only recall what we noted above: that unlike the other degrees of abstraction it involves not simply apprehension, but also judgement. Indeed, we first encounter the transcendental in the act of judgement – whether it is a judgement that something exists, that it is beautiful, true, good, one and so on. Only after the judgement can we turn to the principle implicit therein and find a vision, what Maritain calls an eidetic intuition, of Being itself. If we are to discover the social basis – or the social bases – for the differentiation of transcendental abstraction from the other forms in which it was implicit, then it will be in a moment of judgement or, to use a term which is synonymous and more usual in this context, it will be in a moment of crisis.

As it turns out this conjecture accords remarkably well with the evidence. We can, in fact, find four distinct historical junctures – all four real moments of crisis – during which humanity's capacity for transcendental abstraction makes a qualitative leap forward:

1   the crisis of the early tributary states and the emergence of the salvation religions beginning around 1000 BCE;[3]
2   the crisis of early petty commodity societies and the emergence of the philosophic tradition around 400 BCE;

---

[3] This is the approximate date of the crisis of 'late Bronze Age' tributary societies in Europe and Asia. A comparable crisis in the Americas came only much later, at roughly the time of the European conquest, which is why we see only the beginnings of salvation religion in the Americas – for example, the Hopi religion, the Aztec cults of Tonantzi, Quetzalcoatl and possibly Ipalneomani.

3   the crisis engendered by the political triumph of the bourgeoisie and the emergence of the communist movement around 1848; and
4   the comprehensive crisis of the present period, engendered by the global hegemony of the marketplace and the crisis of the socialist states.

Each of these conjunctures made a unique contribution to the differentiation of transcendental abstraction, and understanding each will help us to understand better the complex act of transcendental abstraction which is now possible for us.

Let us begin with the emergence of the salvation religions. Some time around 3000 BCE, societies inhabiting less favourable ecological niches, which could not support development along the communitarian-archaic pathway,[4] through scientific and technical innovation, discovered that they could use the metal technology developed by the communitarian societies to make powerful new weapons with which they could conquer their more favoured and more developed neighbours and put them under tribute. The result was a long period of stagnation, as surplus was redirected from research and development to warfare and luxury consumption. These new warlord states had a distinctly different perception of the universe. Partly, perhaps, because of the less favourable ecological niches they inhabited, but primarily because of their distinctly different social organization, they perceived the universe as a dangerous place, the locus of chaos and disintegration, where order could be imposed only by force, as the warrior shed his own blood and those of the enemy on the battlefield. Thus the emergence of a whole complex of new cults, which saw the high god 'creating' either by containing the flood tides of chaos (the Semitic myths), or, worse still, by means of self-sacrifice or self-immolation (the Vedas and the Aztec mythology) (Childe 1951, Lerner 1991, Mansueto 1995).

Always the people resisted these new states. Indeed the history of the warlord states is largely the history of peasant revolts. This ideological resistance was of two kinds. On the one hand, intellectuals tied to the village communities reasserted the matriarchal religion of the communitarian epoch – but with a difference. It was no longer obvious that the universe was an organized meaningful system – now a judgement was necessary, a judgement regarding the truth of two conflicting claims. Typical in this regard is the resurgent Mediterranean cult of the *Magna Mater*, in all its diverse forms. Consider, for example, the myth of Pluto and Persephone, central to one of the principal Mediterranean mystery cycles. This myth is usually told as a story explaining the origin of the seasons. Demeter, distraught by the abduction of her daughter by Hades, deprives the earth of her graces, and it becomes dry and barren. The people, threatened with famine, beseech Zeus for assistance. After the intervention

---

[4] The communitarian-archaic pathway, we recall from the discussion in Chapter 3, is a hypothetical pathway for social progress in which the rapid progress of scientific knowledge (especially astronomy, which permits development of a calendar and botany) leads to rapidly rising agricultural yields and thus an expanded surplus, which is centralized through noncoercive means and allocated to activities which promote the development of human social capacities. There is evidence that some advanced horticultural and early agrarian societies were in fact on such a pathway – for example, the matriarchal urban settlement at Catal Huyuk, the Anasazi and possibly the original civilizations of the great river basins – but most such communities were overrun by emerging warlord states and incorporated into their tributary systems shortly after 3000 BCE. All that remained outside these systems were communitarian villages in ecological niches incapable of generating the surplus necessary for an urban civilization.

of Hermes, sent by Zeus as an emissary, Hades agrees to release his prisoner, provided she has eaten nothing during her stay with him. Persephone, however, has swallowed six pomegranate seeds, and is thus condemned to pass six months of every year with Hades in the gloomy nether regions of Dis. It is during these six months that Demeter, ever distraught at the absence of her daughter, is mourning, and that the earth becomes dry and barren.

But this reading of the myth, like every naturalistic interpretation of the sacred, conceals another, more profound, and intensely political meaning. Demeter is the grain mother, and Parthenia/Persephone the new and the ripe, harvested grain. Hades, the god of the underworld, is so called because he is the god of the great underground storehouses where the grain was held. Thus the identification with Pluto, the God of wealth. The half year that Persephone spends with Hades is the half of the grain – the half-year's surplus labour – which customarily belonged to the landlord. The pomegranate seeds represent the loan of seed grain, the interest on which indebted the peasant to the landlord, a debt which was often used to justify the extraction of rents, taxes or forced labour.

This story should be read as a kind of 'myth of the fall'. For the peasant the rents, taxes and the corvée to which he is subject are somehow integrally bound up with the barrenness of the land. There is an important truth embodied in this 'mythological' notion. Historically, the destruction of mixed subsistence agriculture and the ensuing transformation of the uplands into pasture and wheat fields contributed in no small way to the deforestation and soil depletion which have been eroding the fertility of the Sicilian soil for millennia. The peasants of western Sicily hoped as late as the end of the nineteenth century that the expected revolution would bring about a transformation of the climate and a restoration of the soil as well as a new social order (Hobsbawm 1959: 60, 183).

The myth speaks to us as well of the integral relationship between economic exploitation and the oppression of women. At one level the story can be read as an account of an event all too familiar to the women of the countryside: rape and abduction by a member of the ruling classes, who held steadfastly to the 'right of the first night' well into the nineteenth century (Birnbaum 1980: 136) and who had few scruples about usurping the 'right' to any other night they might please. At a more profound level, the myth points towards the identification of sexuality and fertility with power and domination, which is the psychological basis of women's oppression (Rubin 1975), and which, in its turn, makes economic exploitation seem to be simply an integral, in fact a necessary, part of the natural order. Rape becomes identified with sexual prowess and fertilization; the forcible seizure of surplus, sanctioned by the cult of Pluto/Hades, is likewise the precondition for the fertility of the soil. The myth exposes this identification and tells us that confiscation of the surplus is, in fact, nothing more or less than the rape of the peasant and the rape of the land. The emergence of the warlord state and the development of commercial agriculture, far from being progressive forces, in fact hold back the development of human social capacities and even undermine the integrity of the ecosystem and the social fabric.

Similarly, the cult of the Egyptian Au Set, the Queen of the Universe and Cosmic Librarian, becomes the pan-Mediterranean cult of Isis, the goddess of wisdom. Typhon or Set, one of the new male deities of the warlord state, tears to pieces and scatters the sacred writings. Isis must find them and reassemble them. Clearly here we have a protest against the fragmented vision of the new tributary social formation, with its perpetual fear of cosmic chaos and its cult of death (Stone 1976). Analogous arguments can be made regarding the Hopi religion, and the cult of Tonantzi, as well as popular and philosophical Taoism in China (Mansueto 1995: 131–45).

What we see here is an advance to a kind of transcendental abstraction which is at once quite explicit but also prior to and without benefit of formalization. And the advance to transcendental abstraction is grounded in a judgement, a dual judgement in fact, on the one hand against the injustice of tributary exploitation and on the other hand against the falsehood of the warlord cults with their vision of cosmic fragmentation and disintegration. The resurgent cult of the *Magna Mater* upholds, against these cults, humanity's archaic vision of the universe as an organized system – as ordered to an end and thus ultimately meaningful.

At the same time, in certain regions a new form of socioreligious expression emerged on the basis of the religion of the warlord states. The clearest example is the cult of יהוה. Product of successful peasant resistance to the Canaan warlords and their Egyptian overlords during the late Bronze Age (Gottwald 1979), this cult took the Canaanite high god (*'El*, the father of *ba'al*, and a rather remote and insignificant figure in most Canaanite religious practice) and transformed him into *'El yahwi sabaoth yisrael* – El who brings into being the armies of Israel. We should note here that in many respects the cosmology and theology remain that of the warlord state. Israel retained the traditional Semitic creation story, the myth of the flood and so on, all of which suggest a sense of the universe as a system always on the edge of chaos. יהוה's interventions on behalf of his peasants are of a piece with his larger creative activity. Both are represented as containing a tide – be it that of the ocean with its great sea monsters or that of the Philistine flank on the west. And militant Yahwism was always hostile to the residual cult of the Great Mother, particularly the cult of Astarte, which it did not really distinguish (whether through patriarchal blindness or because the two were in fact intimately intertwined) from the cult of *ba'al*. This has given feminist theology reason to look at Yahwism with some caution. At the same time, Yahwism gave birth to a tradition which put the struggle for justice against overwhelming odds at the very centre of religious life.

This, in turn, opened up the possibility of a new kind of religious knowledge. Thus when the prophets speak of *da'ath elohim* (knowledge of God) they are not speaking of something theoretical, but rather an experiential knowledge which we gain in actually realizing the divine will.

> Hear the word of יהוה, O Israel;
> for יהוה has a charge to bring against the people of the land;
> There is no faith or mutual trust,
> no knowledge of God (*da'ath elohim*) in the land,
> oaths are imposed and broken, they kill and rob;
> there is nothing but adultery and licence,
> one deed of blood after another. (Hosea 4: 1–2 *NEB*)

> Let us humble ourselves, let us strive to know יהוה,
> whose justice dawns like morning light,
> and its dawning is as sure as the sunrise.

It will come to us like a shower,
like spring rains that water the earth. (Hosea 6: 3 *NEB*)

Now we have already discussed above the role of connaturality in the production of knowledge. We have argued that society itself is the Agent Intellect. Participation in definite social structures creates in us a direct experience of, for example, classification or certain mathematical formalisms. We experience ourselves as members of a definite class and are thus able to classify other objects. We experience ourselves as functions of complex variables and are thus able to formalize our experience in mathematical terms. The same is true at the level of transcendental abstraction. By *living* judgement we know experientially the principle of judgement and can thus apply it to any range of concrete circumstances. The difference, of course, is that here the principle known connaturally is nothing other than Divine Justice and thus God Himself, vindicating His people in the struggle against their oppressors. In the just act we have an immediate, if still radically imperfect, knowledge of the first principle.

This connatural knowledge of God in the just act is no more conceptual than the connatural knowledge which the Australian aborigine possesses of the principles of classification or the connatural knowledge which a shopkeeper has of the mathematical formalisms which govern the operation of the market system. But like these other, lesser forms of connatural knowledge, it illuminates the images which we garner from experience and allow us to see in the mirror of creatures the creative principle itself. Thus Israel soon began to understand that its revolutionary warrior God brought into being not only the armies of Israel, but in fact the cosmos as a whole, and did so in a single unified movement, so that creation and redemption were not radically distinguished. And in this insight Israel achieves an insight into the divine nature – that is, Being Itself. Thus the name 'יהוה' is the causative form of the Hebrew verb 'to be'. In this sense one could argue, using the language of later dialectics, that the judgement of justice and thus of the Good led ineluctably to the judgement of Being with which it is convertible. This is true in spite of the fact that Israel remained sceptical about elaborate cognitive claims regarding God, rejecting not only representations of the divine nature, but even pronunciation of the divine name outside of the most solemn context of the cult.

What this suggests is that knowledge of first principles is possible without an ascent through formalization, and is thus fully open to people who lack the training in the liberal arts which would make such an ascent possible. This is an important conclusion because it means that it is possible in principle at least for the whole people to participate in making judgements of meaning and value and thus in public life. We should note, however, that there is a certain discipline required for this. In the case of the cult of the *Magna Mater* it means conserving the ability to 'see' the cosmic order, and to see it through the chaos and disintegration of tributary and market societies, something which can be learned by habituation provided the communitarian structures which support it are still intact. In the case of the cult of יהוה there is the actual discipline of doing justice, something which presupposes either knowledge of what is just, or a habituation to just action which at the very least requires the disciple to believe a certain sort of action is just before he or she can really know this to be true. We thus encounter for the first time the role of faith, which is a kind of openness to being taught, a willingness to try the truth on before it is really fully understood. This is an issue we shall explore in greater depth later on.

It should be pointed out that up to this point we have not made any distinction between natural and supernatural knowledge – that is, between knowledge we have on the basis of purely human systems and knowledge which involves participation in some system which transcends humanity. It will turn out that at least part of the knowledge we have of God in the just act will be supernatural – that is, it is based on a participation in the life of God which transcends ordinary human capacities. The same may be said for the ability, cultivated by the other salvation religions, to actually *see* the cosmic order. But there is no reason to suppose that all of this knowledge is supernatural, and our interest at this point is still in the part which is natural, and might serve as a basis for philosophical knowledge of God, grounding ethics and so on.

Having shown the possibility of transcendental abstraction prior to any possible formalization, we must now point out that such abstraction has very serious limitations. Without benefit of formalization any concepts we develop are not sufficiently well defined to make possible rigorous inference from one concept to another, something which is always difficult in dealing with the transcendentals, but not altogether impossible. And apart from rigorous inference, there can be no argument and thus no proof. This has a number of implications. First of all, without argument there is no reasoned public discourse. While the whole people are in principle authentic participants in the acts of judgement which constitute public life, without the capacity to engage in argument they can only be passive participants, assenting to the judgements of leaders when they know connaturally that these are right, or else withholding assent, passing judgement 'in the village gates' in accord with a traditional law and so on, but never actually participating in the discovery and application of the principles of justice, and thus in the development of policy, strategy, tactics and so on. Second, the truth comprehended by the salvation religions is open only to those who share the experience out of which they arise: the resistance of village communities to the rise of the warlord state. To those cut off from the intact social fabric of the village community, or from the habitual pursuit of justice, the truth would be invisible. This becomes an increasingly important issue in market societies, which tend not only to exploit village communities, but actually to disintegrate them, undermining the social basis for perceiving the universe as an organized system, and thus for the teleological explanation which terminates in the first principle. From the standpoint of the market system, human society appears to be either a system of quantities (prices) or a system of only externally related individuals. Neither sort of system is ordered to an end. The result is the emergence of rationalist and empiricist doctrines which understand the universe on the model of the marketplace, and thus deny its ultimate meaningfulness. Similarly, the marketplace imposes a discipline of its own, which is hardly that of justice. Indeed, the market requires that we work in order to consume, rather than consuming only in order to develop our capacity to add something to the universe. The market, in effect, habituates us to injustice, and to the included vices of intemperance (in the form of excessive consumption) and cowardice (in virtue of its preference for 'team players' to those who go against the tide). The religious disciplines which make possible a rise to first principles thus disintegrate, and human society falls prey to unbelief and despair.

Here we see the importance of dialectics, which rises from totalization, through formalization, to transcendental abstraction. Dialectics begins with our existing ideas and then uses the tools of formalization to draw out their implications and internal contradictions, ever driving towards a higher synthesis, advancing step by step towards that Idea which alone constitutes an adequate principle of explanation and action – that is, the Idea of Being itself, with its transcendental properties (Beauty, Truth, Goodness and Integrity) or, what is the same thing, the Idea of God. Dialectics turns the sceptical attitude of formal reason against itself until at last it finds rest in knowledge of the transcendentals. Dialectics thus presupposes the market system, which at once poses the problem it must address – regrounding our knowledge of the transcendentals – and provides it with the tools it requires for this undertaking (formalization).

We have already seen, in Chapter 2, that the dialectical tradition in fact emerged in the planet's first real market society – the petty commodity society of Ancient Greece. Socrates, Plato and Aristotle all directed their efforts against the scepticism and despair, as well as the social disintegration, which accompanied the emergence of a market order in the Mediterranean basin. Here we need only stress certain points which may not have stood out clearly enough in our earlier presentation, because their significance could not yet be apparent at that point in the argument. First, the dialectical tradition has profound roots in the salvation religions and specifically in the resurgent cult of the *Magna Mater*. This is apparent for a number of reasons. First, there is considerable evidence (Stone 1976) that the early philosophers, including not only those of the Socratic school, journeyed to Egypt, where they would have been exposed not only to Egyptian wisdom generally, but more specifically to the cult of Isis. This cult, with its emphasis on recovery of lost wisdom, and a return to a golden age which we can only regard as communitarian-archaic, provides a general framework to which the dialectical tradition adheres even as it raises to a more formal level the cognition involved in recovering this lost wisdom. Plato, furthermore, sets two of his most important dialogues, the *Republic* and the *Timaeus*, at feasts of various goddesses, implying both that he participated in these feasts and that he regarded philosophical conversation as an appropriate way to honour the Goddess. Finally, as the dialectical tradition merged with Judaism and Christianity, there was a marked tendency to identify the Goddess, generally Isis, with the Divine Wisdom, and later with the Virgin Mother of God, in such a way that both philosophy and the popular religion of the Mediterranean peasantry found a place in a tradition which might otherwise have been hostile to them.

Second, dialectics was, from the very beginning, deeply rooted in a very specific social practice, that of justice. Socrates' principal concern, even when he addressed epistemological or metaphysical questions, was always moral and political, and both Plato and Aristotle were involved in political ventures which, however ultimately unsuccessful, were clearly directed at coming to terms with the corruption of Greek society as a result of the penetration of market relations in every sphere of social life.[5]

---

[5] Ellen Meiksins Wood and Neal Wood (Wood and Wood 1978) argue that Socrates and Plato collaborated closely with traditional landed elites which had been driven from power in Athens by the democratic

More importantly, Plato's own understanding of how one becomes a philosopher includes, as we have seen, not only intellectual but also political discipline, including both a period of military service and 15 years in subaltern political posts. Aristotle's suggestion that it is impossible to study ethics before one is 30 is an attempt to make much the same point. Just as much as for the devotees of יהוה or the *Magna Mater*, knowledge of God is grounded in practice, and thus in connaturality with the principle known.

Dialectics is, furthermore, ordered to practice – the practice of justice. We thus know God not only as the first principle of explanation, but also as the first principle for human action. Knowing the first principle, however imperfectly, and knowing that this first principle is also an end, we then return to the particular forms of matter not only to explain them but, through our labour, to cultivate them, releasing their latent potential and guiding them towards perfection. This in turn sets in motion a pattern of creative activity which deepens ever more profoundly our connaturality with God, and thus illuminates our apprehension and judgement ever more brilliantly, so that what previously seemed difficult and obscure now seems a bit more lucid and luminous. And this deepening knowledge kindles a deeper desire, a desire to know and love God in a way which, however, seems to transcend our abilities . . .

If the advent of the market system catalysed the emergence of dialectics, the triumph of capitalism resulted in both a deepening of the dialectical tradition and in the development of certain internal contradictions within it. We have spoken of both these matters in an earlier chapter, and here we need only recall what has been said in order to clarify further the social basis for transcendental abstraction. On the one hand, the experience of dramatic structural change in human society (from a tributary to a capitalist society, with initial movements towards socialism) and of social revolution directed at the conscious, rational, reorganization of human society, creates the basis in experience for understanding a new kind of teleology – historical teleology. This has implications at all levels of intellectual activity. It is the experience of historical progress which creates the basis for understanding cosmic evolution generally. Knowing ourselves as a drive towards ever higher degrees of organization, we simultaneously know the universe as a whole in the same way. This insight, furthermore, deepens fundamentally our understanding of the divine nature, and of our own participation in it. For Plato and more especially for Aristotle there was a tendency to finitize the Divine. The Unmoved Mover needed to be only great enough to account for a finite system of forms which, even if some underwent growth and

---

revolutions of the sixth century BCE, and that Aristotle eventually sold Athens out to the Macedonian Empire. They conclude that their philosphical position was fundamentally an attempt to legitimate the antidemocratic reaction. What they miss is the fact that Greek 'democracy' was fundamentally an instrument of nouveaux riches elements which had profited from the expanding market for oil and wine. The Socratic, Platonic and Aristotelian critique of democracy was fundamentally an argument against the dominance of 'moneymakers' in public life, and a call to restore to leadership those capable of making judgements on the basis of knowledge of the Good. That this now required formal training in dialectics, something which was not possible for the entire population because of the low level of development of the productive forces, led them to think in terms of a philosophical monarchy or aristocracy rather than a philosophical democracy. There is, however, nothing in their systems which would have ruled out wider particpation in principle, so long as the requisite training was available to all thus called to public life.

decay, itself remained static in all essentials. The Jewish, Islamic and Catholic commentators rejected this finitization of God only on dogmatic grounds; they as yet had no scientific basis for their insight into the qualitative infinity of God. But if the universe itself is infinite in space and time, always and everywhere giving birth to qualitatively new forms, the principal which explains it and brings it into being must itself be still greater. It must, indeed, be organization as such, a lure of such beauty that it can draw an infinity of forms out of nothing and, while itself perfect, leave nothing finite at rest, but always striving, always reaching beyond itself to become more. And the discovery of historical teleology creates a new and deeper grasp of humanity's connaturality with God: we understand ourselves not only as makers of artefacts and of relationships, but of entire social systems in which artefacts and relationships are produced. We come to understand ourselves as co-creators with God in a way that would have been impossible for Aristotle or Aquinas.[6] This, in turn implies a new type of ethical judgement. We make judgements regarding not only individual actions or the character of individuals, but also regarding the structure of human societies.

At the same time, the triumph of the market system created an ever deepening alienation which was felt even within the dialectical tradition itself – an alienation which has expressed itself, alternately, in over-reaching claims for human knowledge and human connaturality with God (something we see in Hegel especially) and also in a tendency towards atheism and eventually towards nihilism. The root of both errors is in the tendency of the marketplace to privilege formal over transcendental abstraction. Thus the tendency, on the part of thinkers like Hegel, to mistake the confused and imperfect knowledge of God which we gain in transcendental abstraction for the 'clear and distinct' knowledge we have of mathematical formalisms, and then to assume that knowing God we can deduce the rest.

The tyranny of formalism can, however, cut the other way. There are, in fact, two distinct and even opposing tendencies at work here which come together at a critical historical juncture to overdetermine the atheism of the socialist movement. These tendencies reflect different moments in the rise of capitalism and different political-ideological strategies on the part of the bourgeoisie. On the one hand, we have seen that formalism aspires above all things to be self-sufficient – to know all things by logical deduction from self-evident principles. While this impulse can be reflected in a claim to know God with the same precision with which we know an equilateral triangle, it can also lead to an attempt to explain the universe without reference to God. Thus Laplace's claim, when asked by Napoleon about the place of God in his system, that he had no need of that hypothesis.

This sort of optimistic and humanistic atheism was an artefact of the rising bourgeoisie. While it was still involved in its struggle against the old feudal nobility, the bourgeoisie needed allies among the intelligentsia, the industrial proletariat and the peasantry. It thus pressed for economic, political and cultural reforms which helped unleash the development of human social capacities. When progress is still

---

[6] It has been suggested to me by Maggie Mansueto that Aquinas might actually be a sort of transitional figure in this regard. While he lacked the experience of revolutionary social transformation, he did have the experience of membership in a mendicant order – an organization which, in a very real sense, was established and structured in order to change society.

taking place, even if this is in spite of rather than because of the market system, the bourgeoisie can present itself as a liberating and progressive force. In reality the Enlightenment, far from being a real 'age of reason', was in fact the first phase in a prolonged attack on the ability of human reason to grasp the ultimate meaning of the universe. This should be apparent to anyone who compares the powers allotted to reason by Ibn Rushd or Aquinas, with those allowed by Kant or Hume. But in the context of the other advances which were taking place at the time, it was possible to present the sceptical criticisms of the empiricists and the *philosophes* as a liberation from the authority of prelate and peer and a blow for freedom and progress. No one thought to ask just how the value of liberation or progress was to be grounded if reason cannot ascend to a principle which is infinite, necessary, perfect – and thus divine. One can still pick up the fading notes of this tune from neoliberals such as F.A. Hayek and Frank Tipler, so popular during the present period of relative stabilization, though the liberation they proclaim is no longer from prelate and peer but rather from commissar and community.

Around the middle of the nineteenth century, however, a new dynamic takes over. We have already seen that purpose cannot be formalized. A 'science' which idolizes formalism is a 'science' which rejects a priori the ultimate meaningfulness of the universe. And it was this conclusion precisely which bourgeois 'science' was beginning to reach in the middle of the nineteenth century, as the founders of thermodynamics began to make sombre prophecies regarding the impending heat death of the universe, and as Darwin proclaimed that what limited and local progress there was resulted from random variation and natural selection, and could thus be explained without reference to any teleological principles.

This line of reasoning reflects the new situation after mid-century. Its own triumph secure, the bourgeoisie now turns to combating the challenge from the rising socialist movement. Progress begins to grind to a halt, to be restarted only fitfully and only under pressure from the working classes (Lukacs [1953] 1980, Lerner 1991). Under such conditions, it becomes necessary to attack head on the idea of progress as such, lest capitalism be found wanting by its own criteria. The sombre visions of von Helmholtz and Darwin represent this trend in the sciences; Schopenauer (Schopenauer [1819] 1969) and Nietzsche (Nietzsche [1889] 1968) represent the same trend in philosophy.

Marx and Engels stand at the turning point between these two moments. Indeed the 'turn' itself is often dated to the uprisings of 1848, the first with a significant socialist element, and incidentally also the date of the *Communist Manifesto* (Lukacs [1953] 1980). And their own political position notwithstanding, they are at least partially hegemonized by both the earlier progressive and later reactionary bourgeois polemics. The progressive polemic is more apparent in Marx. To the extent that he thought about religion at all, Marx was concerned mostly that otherworldly religious expectation seemed to be substituting itself for effective action on behalf of social justice. Seen in the context of the Jewish tradition which located knowledge of God – *da'ath elohim* – in the just act, and which was sceptical about any attempt to 'capture' this knowledge, whether in representations or in concepts, this must be understood as a profoundly religious critique of religion. But this iconoclastic tendency also made Marx vulnerable to the 'progressive' bourgeois assault on religion as such. Failing to distinguish between religious alienation and religion generally, Marx unwittingly becomes an agent of the bourgeoisie's strategy for the intellectual and moral disarmament of the proletariat.

The second reactionary polemic is more apparent in Engels, who is much more clearly focused on the question of the ultimate meaningfulness of the universe and the existence of God. It is impossible to read the *Dialectics of Nature* (Engels [1880] 1940) without sensing the urgency of this question for Engels – and the tragedy of his inability to resolve it satisfactorily. Engels clearly understands that dialectical materialism implies a universe which evolves infinitely towards infinitely more complex forms of organization. He is less clear that this implies the existence of God. But Engels's road to God is blocked less by a failure to understand certain fine points of philosophical theology or by a secularizing iconoclasm than by what he sees to be the unavoidable results of the physical sciences and more specifically by the Second Law of Thermodynamics which, for him as for most of his contemporaries, appears to condemn the universe to a slow thermal death, and to predict a gradual degeneration and disintegration of intelligence, of life, indeed of all complex organization. Such a universe is clearly not ordered to an end, much less an end infinite, necessary and perfect and thus divine in character. It is the tyranny of formalism which made it impossible for nineteenth-century science to see past conclusions like the Second Law to the larger context in which they are embedded. The tyranny of formalism is, once again, a reflex of the marketplace. And so, ironically, it appears that the atheism of materialist dialectics, far from being revolutionary, is ultimately a residue of bourgeois ideology.

The current situation is characterized above all by the crisis of socialism and the resurgence of imperialism and finance capitalism. These two aspects of the situation are, of course, related. It was the internal contradictions of dialectical materialism, above all the failure to provide an adequate ontological ground for ethics, and thus for the critique of the marketplace, which made the socialist countries vulnerable to the bourgeois ideological assault. And it is the same internal contradictions of dialectical materialism which weakened it in the advanced capitalist countries and rendered the intelligentsia and proletariat intellectually impotent and thus unable to fend off the bourgeois counter-attack. The result has been a long period of technological stagnation and social disintegration. The much vaunted 'information age' in fact represents simply a fine-tuning of microelectronic technology which is already 50 years old, and which is based on science which is almost a century old. Families and communities are falling apart; people no longer have a sense of being part of something larger than themselves, something ordered to an end, on the basis of which they can think purposefulness in the first place. In a 'complete' or 'mature' market society global purposes have disappeared entirely. Individuals pursue their own ends – or increasingly simply respond to market pressures without even having a well-defined sense of their own self-interest. In the absence of structures which discipline the will to justice, 'there is no knowledge of God in the land' (Hosea 4: 1). Without connatural knowledge of God, theoretical knowledge is impossible.

What this situation has done, however, is to clarify for us the ways in which earlier dialecticians erred. We now see more clearly than Socrates, Plato and Aristotle, Ibn Sina, Ibn Rushd, Maimonides and Thomas, that for the full development of human capacities – and most especially the capacity for transcendental abstraction – we must transcend the market system. And we see in a way Marx and Engels could not that we can ground a critique of the market system – and indeed any sort of social criticism whatsoever – only on the basis of a cosmology and metaphysics committed to the ultimate meaningfulness of the universe and the existence of God.

The question, of course, is just how – if the social basis for transcendental abstraction has all but collapsed – we are able to know this at all. The answer is simple. Our own ordering to an end and that of the universe remains intact. Human beings are ordered to God, including rational philosophical knowledge of God, whether they know it or not. Living in a time of stagnation and social disintegration frustrates every authentic aspiration we have; our nature rebels against this situation. It is this frustration which suggests to us, sooner or later, that something is wrong, which puts us in touch with our deepest aspirations, and catalyses a return to the Truth. To put matters differently, having cast aside the discipline of a just social order, and the capacity for judgement which it makes possible, we have become subject to divine judgement and to the discipline of the cosmic order itself. This discipline is only just beginning to be felt, but in time (after a greater or lesser period of destruction) it will have its effect. In our discontent we will return to the path of the just act, the path of virtue, which leads to transcendental abstraction. And in this return we will comprehend and resolve the contradictions of the previous stage in the development of the dialectical tradition, conserving its powerful insight into historical teleology and cosmo-historical evolution, and its powerful critique of the marketplace, while at the same time recovering the historic dialectical commitment to knowledge of God. We know the dialectic (all at once and at the same time) as a call to revolution and to religion – a call to wake up, to struggle, to become, and thus to know God.

The Product of Transcendental Abstraction

At this point it might well be asked why we need theoretical knowledge, natural or revealed, at all? Transcendental abstraction and, as we shall see in Chapter 7, the very highest degrees of mystical contemplation are, after all, secondary to the connatural knowledge of God which we have in the just act. Why expose ourselves to the dangers of idolatry or expend energy on esoteric metaphysical speculations? This is a very important and a very difficult question, and answering it requires great subtlety. There are whole religious traditions – much of Judaism, for example – which shun difficult to solve 'metaphysical' puzzles about the divine nature in favour of the sure and simple path of *da'ath elohim*.[7] And we all know, or at least have heard of, people who not only reject revealed religion, but who claim to be convinced atheists, who nonetheless live lives of profound dedication to justice. Indeed, many of these professed atheists demonstrate virtues which qualify as supernatural – that is, implying an

---

[7] Typical of this position is the work of Erich Fromm (Fromm 1966), for whom it seems to provide a way to simultaneously affirm the dialectical materialist critiques of religion *and* the fact that religion has historically given expression to humanity's highest values and aspirations, values and aspirations which cannot be restated in purely secular terms without doing them irreparable violence. 'Radical monotheism', which refuses to predicate of God even existence, is for Fromm an extension of the historic iconoclasm of the Jewish tradition and defines a spirituality which is neither theistic nor negatively atheistic, but something more (Fromm 1966).

ordering to ends beyond those knowable by human reason alone. How great their sanctity – and how scandalous by comparison the 'practical atheism' of so many 'believers'! It is easy to understand how someone like Marx, coming out of a tradition which emphasized the priority of *da'ath elohim* over theoretical knowledge of God in the first place, and seeing the way in which the kind of Christianity hegemonic in the Germany of his time produced despair and passivity among the poor, and served as an alibi for the rich, might well have concluded that religion was an obstacle in the struggle for justice and ought to be rejected.

Matters are not, however, quite so simple. We have already, in our discussion of the lower degrees of abstraction, suggested why transcendental abstraction, and the real though limited knowledge of God in which it terminates, is so important. It is, first of all, quite impossible to construct scientific explanations (much less a complete cosmology) apart from teleological reasoning, something which we have associated with transcendental abstraction. Second, any concept of God which we achieve without transcendental abstraction is likely either to degenerate into idolatry or to wither under the critical scrutiny of formal reason. The most important argument for the necessity of transcendental abstraction, however, is ethical. It is one thing to entertain theoretical doubts regarding the existence of God, or even to profess atheism, in the context of a community or movement which disciplines the will and habituates it to the pursuit of justice, guiding it through the trials and tribulations which lead to authentic, connatural knowledge of the living God. It is quite another thing to do so in a larger social milieu – like our own – in which unbelief and despair are widespread, and where they serve as an excuse for lives of nihilistic hedonism and cynical consumerism. One can be awakened from such a life only by the conviction – or at least the reasonable hope – that there is a higher Truth and a higher Good. And apart from the transcendental principles (the Beautiful, the True, the Good and the One) which ground our judgements of value, we have no basis on which to judge a life of hedonism and consumerism to be wrong or unworthy. Even if a particular individual is drawn into a movement for justice on some basis other than rational conviction, *someone*, and in general very many people, must have such convictions if they are to found the movement in the first place. This is why atheism is so destructive – why it is, in fact, one of the principal reasons for the crisis of socialism both in the former Soviet bloc and in the capitalist countries. Unless one is taught from an early age that the universe is meaningful and that justice is, therefore, worth pursuing, the danger of falling into despair is overwhelming. And so in treating atheism it is necessary to divide the question, distinguishing between the demonstrated possibility of authentic sanctity on the basis of an entirely non-theoretical *da'ath elohim*, even for professed atheists, and the radical impossibility of a broad movement for social justice in the context of an atheistic culture – unless that movement itself breaks with the hegemonic atheism.

These claims regarding the importance of transcendental abstraction can, of course, stand only if transcendental abstraction can deliver what we are claiming it can – that is, only if it can actually demonstrate the ultimate meaningfulness of the universe, the existence of God, and the existence of transcendental principles of value. We need, therefore, to take a detour from the predominantly epistemological argument of this work, and illustrate in some detail just what transcendental abstraction contributes. We will begin with a consideration of the question of cosmic teleology, then turn to arguments for the existence of God and of transcendental principles of value. We will conclude with an illustration of just how these principles ground ethics and the practical disciplines which flow from ethics – the instrumental, fine and liberal arts and the 'practical art' of politics.

The Role of Transcendental Abstraction in the Sciences

It might be objected that, in attempting an argument for cosmic teleology, we are recommending a scientific strategy which has already been tried, and which has failed. Did not Aristotle attempt a complete explanation of the universe in teleological terms, an explanation which terminated in a First Unmoved Mover with the qualities which have been identified, and end up with serious internal contradictions? This is why so many contemporary theists – including, for example, the Transcendental Thomists – shun the ascent to God through cosmic teleology and opt for the sort of subjectivist, transcendental arguments we criticized in an earlier chapter. Such an approach, we have already noted, is fundamentally unsatisfying. Even if one *could* demonstrate that God is the condition of the possibility of human knowledge and subjectivity in general (and not, as Kant argued, merely a regulative, unifying ideal) such a God is utterly and completely removed from the actual conditions of our existence and does nothing to validate the cosmic significance of our productivity, nothing to vindicate our struggles for a social order which unleashes the full development of human creativity, nothing to answer our reaching towards a productivity and power and knowledge and love which is infinite and perfect, even if that perfection comes from something beyond ourselves. All really meaningful statements about the existence of God are also, equally, claims about the organization of the universe. Thus the element of truth in conservative suspicions that 'transcendental' and 'existential' Christians don't really believe in God. Clearly, therefore, it is necessary to answer the objection to cosmic teleology before we can proceed any further.

Let us begin by revisiting Aristotle. Aristotle argued that it was, indeed, possible to rise from sensory data to a single first principle – the First Unmoved Mover. Matter for Aristotle was the possibility of organization, form its actuality. Motion was the gradual realization, over the course of time, of the latent potential of matter as it moved towards the perfection of form. The explanation of particular forms of motion involved an understanding of the matter in question, of the form which was being perfected, and of the efficient cause – that by which the change took place, as well as the end towards which the change was ordered. Ultimately, however, the whole process of change was grounded in the attractive power of the First Unmoved Mover, the incredible Beauty, Truth, Goodness and Integrity of which drew all things to itself (Aristotle, *Physics*, *Metaphysics*; Lindberg 1992).

The Aristotelian synthesis collapsed for two reasons. First, it was unable to advance a unified theory of motion. How does one explain teleologically a decaying corpse or a thrown javelin? These processes do not seem in any sense ordered to the perfection of form. Thus the distinction between natural and violent motion. This in turn led to a distinction between the celestial realm, where all motion is natural, and the sublunar realm where both kinds of change occur. Second, Aristotelian science had considerable difficulty in coming to terms with the growing evidence that even the heavens were not ordered in the perfect manner required by theory. This was a problem long before Copernicus and Kepler. There are sharp differences between Aristotle's cosmology and the formal, mathematical models of his near contemporary, Eudoxus. Refinement of these models by Ptolemy and others involved a departure from the perfect spherical motion which was central to Aristotle's vision long before Copernicus opted for heliocentrism or Kepler displaced the circle with the ellipse (Murdoch and Sylla 1978, Grant 1978, Pedersen 1978, Lindberg 1992).

There were two ways to resolve this problem. One would have been to generalize the concept of teleology in such a way as to accommodate the reality of 'violent motion', and to abandon the particular cosmological models developed by Aristotle in order to save the principle of teleological ordering. There were powerful reasons to take just precisely this approach. Aristotle and his interpreters had, after all, already implicitly shown that the only complete explanation is a teleological explanation. This is because a complete explanation must terminate in a principle which (directly or indirectly) explains everything else while being self-explanatory. Such a principle must be necessary, infinite and perfect (and thus divine), and it must cause exclusively by the attractive power of its own perfection (otherwise it would be in motion itself and would thus require some other explanatory principle, resulting in an infinite regress) (Aristotle, *Metaphysics* 1071b–1076b; Aquinas, *Summa Theologiae* I, Q 2).

This was not, however, the road taken. The alienation generated by the advancing market order had already degraded humanity's underlying confidence in the ultimate meaningfulness of the universe. Teleology was abandoned altogether, and (though this was never acknowledged, or perhaps, even really recognized) the possibility of a complete explanation along with it. Instead, an attempt was made to develop increasingly general mathematical formalisms which *describe* motion (now conceived exclusively as change in place). Thus the whole history of mathematical physics, beginning with the special theories of Galileo and Kepler, up through the 'first unification' by Newton, and each of the successive generalizations and unifications: Hamiltonian dynamics, Maxwell's equations, relativity, quantum mechanics, and most recently quantum cosmology.

Mathematical physics has been remarkably successful at this enterprise of producing formal descriptions. And, perhaps because mathematics is ultimately the science of possible beings, it has provided an enormous impetus to the technological development which requires us to imagine new possible systems. Yet we also demonstrated convincingly in Chapter 5 that it has not been any more successful than was Aristotelian science at producing a unified theory of motion, nor is it able to describe – much less explain – anything like the full range of natural phenomena. Relativity is in contradiction with quantum mechanics, dynamics generally with thermodynamics, and thermodynamics with evolutionary biology and sociology. And these contradictions go to such fundamental questions as the discrete or continuous, commutative or noncommutative character of the formalisms which describe physical systems, the reversibility or irreversibility of time and thus of physical change, and the possibility of evolution towards higher degrees of organization.

What this suggests is that mathematical physics, while fruitful in many respects and certainly not to be abandoned wholesale, has not in fact been a successful scientific strategy. This is because, as we also suggested in Chapter 5, complete explanations are by nature necessarily teleological. What is required for the unification of the sciences is nothing more or less than a return to the 'road not taken', to an expansion of the concept of teleology to accommodate the reality of chaos, 'violent motion', and disintegration which were so difficult for Aristotle to theorize. While it is not, of course, possible to develop a complete theory in this context, we can suggest the outlines of such a theory and sketch out a case for cosmic teleology which is of sufficient rigour to meet the requirements of our larger argument.

It should, first of all, be noted that it is just precisely this kind of expanded understanding of teleology which characterizes the most advanced work in the physical, biological and social sciences. Ilya Prigogine, for example, attempts to resolve the contradiction between thermodynamics and theories of morphogenesis and evolution by arguing that complex organization in fact emerges out of instabilities in open, non-linear, non-equilibrium systems. His early work centred on showing that, provided there is sufficient exchange of matter and energy with the environment, fluctuations from equilibrium, far from being damped may in fact be amplified. This means that far from tending to a random and uniform distribution, matter can in fact become distributed in statistically unlikely ways which reveal intricate structures and which lead to large-scale organization in space and time (Prigogine 1977: 49–61; Prigogine and Stengers 1984: 140–41). This insight has profound importance for understanding how life could have emerged from inorganic matter, as well as for the description of a wide range of inorganic and organic processes which have hitherto seemed at variance with physical theory. It has also helped to clarify the distinction between order and organization – a point on which Aristotle was not entirely clear, and which led him into no small difficulties. An order is simply a system governed by a (formal) rule which allows us to predict both its overall state and the position of its various elements. It is, to use the currently fashionable language, low in entropy and high in information content. Ordered systems such as crystals can be fully described by the principles of linear, near-equilibrium thermodynamics and by the Boltzmann Order Principle in particular.[8] Organized systems, such as organisms and societies, cannot. Prigogine's approach has also inspired the first real break with the hegemonic Big-Bang cosmology. Hannes Alfvén and Eric Lerner (Lerner 1991) have argued that the facts of cosmic evolution are most economically explained by a universe infinite in space and time (so that any region, however large, has an environment with which it can exchange matter and energy) over the expanse of which fluctuations (initially electromagnetic, later gravitational) have produced departures from equilibrium, leading to the formation of large-scale structures, and eventually of galaxies and stars. From here nuclear reactions lead to the emergence of the heavy elements necessary for life. Whether or not their plasma cosmology is eventually born out by the evidence, the general direction of their work is clearly promising.

---

[8] The Boltzmann Order Principle states that closed, but not isolated systems (that is, systems which can exchange energy but not matter with their environment) tend towards minimum free energy

$$F = E - TS$$

where F is the free energy, E is the total energy, T is temperature and S is entropy. At low temperatures the entropy term becomes insignificant, permitting the formation of crystalline structures.

The role of teleological explanation in the biological sciences is even more well established – and this in spite of numerous attempts to expunge it by distinguishing, as Ernst Mayr (Mayr 1988) does, between teleomatic, teleonomic, adaptive and properly teleological processes. Teleomatic processes tend necessarily to some end because of the operation of physical law. Thus the tendency of two masses to be attracted to each other. Teleonomic processes are goal-oriented because of the presence of a 'program' which governs them – such as the genetic code, the 'open programs' which govern animal learning, or the program of an artificial information-processing system. Thus the construction of the digestive system or the complex reproductive behaviour of certain birds. Adaptive systems have programs which evolve by means of natural selection, making possible movement into new niches and resulting in a greater diversity of survival strategies. Thus the gradual transformation of the beak structure of a population of birds which has migrated into a different (and geographically isolated) niche. Mayr reserves the term teleological for explanations which have recourse to a non-empirical principle, such as a vital force or a final cause, something he rejects as contrary to his positivist epistemology, which deals only in observables.

Mayr's distinctions are useful, in so far as they identify different ways of being goal-oriented. His insistence that all explanatory principles be observable, is, however, highly problematic in the light of the argument we have already developed for the necessity of teleology to any complete explanation. And he himself has recourse to explanations which involve the use of a final cause. Later in the book, for example, he argues that new behaviours play a leading role in the evolutionary process. Members of a population often move into a new ecological niche for which they are at least partly pre-adapted – that is, they have anatomical and physiological characteristics which make it possible for them to obtain and eat a new food, and so on. This kind of pre-adaptation is precisely what an Aristotelian would call a 'latent potential'. The environment then selects for individuals who have characteristics which improve on this pre-adaptation and develop the latent potential. But this is precisely a teleological explanation in the strongest sense! There are, to be sure, biochemical mechanisms which are producing variation, and ecological mechanisms which are leading to the survival and reproductive success of some individuals and the death of others. But the whole chain of causation can be explained only in terms of the new behaviour, the new form, which mobilizes the chemical and biological forces and sets them into motion.[9]

This argument can, in turn, be extended into the realm of behaviour, physiology and morphogenesis. It is only in terms of certain ends that behaviour can be explained.

---

[9] We should, perhaps address more directly Mayr's rejection of final cause on the grounds that it is a non-empirical principle. This claim, which is common to all positivistic critics of teleological explanation, is neither well-defined nor consistent. If one means by empirical something which is directly observable, then Mayr and all evolutionary theorists use non-empirical principles every time they appeal to the 'survival value' of a particular physiological or behaviour structure. If, on the other hand, one means by empirical something which is reducible to physical interactions, then the criticism begs the question, assuming in advance what one is supposedly trying to demonstrate – that is, that physiology and behaviour, and their evolutionary transformation, can be explained without reference to a divine final cause. The whole point of teleological physics is, in any case, that the divine τελος itself is indirectly observable through the effects it has on the various forms of matter.

A turtle comes ashore in order to lay her eggs (yet another example which Mayr attempts to explain away). That this behaviour may be driven by a genetic program (in a way in which, however, we are as yet *very* far from understanding) does not change the fact that the genetic program itself can be explained only in terms of the τελος of reproduction and survival.

What modern biology *has* established and what sets it apart from earlier Aristotelian theories of morphogenesis is to show that organization is emergent and open-ended. On the one hand this means that instability, contradiction and struggle *do* play a role in biological processes, and especially in the evolutionary process. Just as life itself is possible only because the universe is, from a thermodynamic standpoint, imperfectly ordered, new life forms are possible only because ecosystems are never in perfect equilibrium. Climatic change, the impact of organisms themselves on the ecosystem, migration and so on, all present organisms with new challenges for which they are not fully prepared, and thus open up opportunity for emergent species which can transform stress and struggle into an opportunity. Similarly, competition and natural selection weed out organisms which fail to meet the challenge. On the other hand, it must be understood that neither ecological stress nor natural selection themselves explain evolutionary innovation. This requires (to use Aristotelian language) some disposition on the part of the matter in question. This might take the form of what Mayr calls pre-adaptation: existing structures which can be mobilized for new purposes. But there is growing evidence for the existence of a dynamic capacity to generate new form. Lynn Margulis (Margulis and Fester 1991) has stressed the role of symbiosis in early evolution. Others point to the existence of genetic algorithms which seem to search out promising variations far in excess of what would be expected from random mutation and recombination. In the final analysis, however, variation also presupposes the existence of a formal τελος – a new behaviour with survival value, for example, which sets in motion a process of selection in the manner noted above.

Indeed, it is very difficult to explain the whole process of evolution as it has actually taken place apart from some larger drive towards increased complexity and integration. Mayr is quite correct to point out that there is nothing in Darwin's theory which would validate the idea of evolutionary progress. What Mayr misses is the fact that this is actually a damning criticism of Darwin's theory. Selection for survival value alone fails to explain why we see any evolution at all beyond the level of virus and bacteria, which clearly outnumber higher organisms. And yet we see just precisely this sort of evolution. But a larger drive towards complexity and integration can be explained only in terms of a cosmic teleological principle.

In this sense, modern biology is more teleological than Aristotle. It at once accommodates and includes within itself instability and contradiction *and* demonstrates development at the level not just of the organism, but at the level of ecosystems generally, as life evolves from simpler to more complex forms.

In the social sciences, finally, the role of teleological explanation is hardly disputed. There are, to be sure, trends which stress formal description. Positivistic 'number crunchers' continue to look for statistical correlations between various social phenomena, without drawing conclusions regarding causality, teleological or otherwise. Structuralists attempt to describe language, the psyche, kinship systems and even myths as 'systems of transformations', without respect to the end to which these systems are ordered. But such descriptions are, by themselves, highly unsatisfying. Even most positivistic sociology is motivated by a desire to understand how various social institutions function, that is, carry out a purpose. One may attempt to formalize the process of cognitive and moral development, as Piaget does, but this does not eliminate the need to theorize the family and the school as institutions ordered to the cognitive and moral development of the child – that is, to the socialization process. The marketplace, similarly, whether formalized in terms of neoclassical equilibrium theory or dialectical materialist reproduction equations, is first and foremost a system structured *for* centralizing and allocating resources for production. Political and religious institutions can be theorized in various and sundry ways, but it is impossible to understand them apart from some function.

The real debate within the social sciences is over the precise level at which teleology operates. Bourgeois social science, with its subjective idealist foundations has, for the most part, attempted to confine purposefulness to the level of the individual organism – or even lower. Thus sociobiologists attempt to explain human behaviour as an attempt to reproduce the genetic material, an application of evolutionary theory which most biologists reject.[10] Neoliberal economics assumes that individuals seek to maximize their 'marginal utility', generally understood in terms of consumption interests. Interpretive sociology in the Weberian tradition recognizes that such motivation is far from universal, but still treats society as the product of meaningful action on the part of individuals. The task of sociology, according to theorists such as Weber, is to understand the meaning individuals give their actions, and to explain the patterns of action which arise on the basis of those meanings. For all these tendencies, higher-order systems are explained as the product of interacting human individuals (or their genes), to whose purposes they are ordered.

Individualistic approaches, however, whether they posit a universal aim shared by all individuals (as is the case with sociobiology and neoliberalism) or allow a diversity of different possible aims, leave these individual aims themselves unexplained, and thus fail to advance to a complete explanation. This is true both of the more mechanistic trends, such as sociobiology, which suffers from all of the ills of Neo-Darwinism generally, and of more voluntaristic approaches such as interpretive sociology, with its roots in Neo-Kantian agnosticism. They also fail to explain macrosociological trends, such as the long-term development of human productive capacities, revolutionary social transformations which alter fundamentally the way in which societies centralize and allocate resources for production, and global changes at the ideological level.

Objective idealist social science in the tradition of the French traditionalists and Talcott Parsons (Parsons 1957, 1964), recognizes human society as a globally teleological system. Parsons, we remember, regards the human 'action system' and the 'social system' it contains as structured to carry out certain definite functions: adaptation to the environment, goal attainment, integration and the maintenance of latent cultural patterns. The way in which these functions are carried out depends

---

[10] Most evolutionary biologists, even those who adhere more or less strictly to the Neo-Darwinian paradigm, regard the individual or the species, and not the gene or the genome, as the target of selection.

on the way in which a certain society perceives 'ultimate reality'. The result is an ability to explain macrosociological phenomena with far greater power than any of the strictly bourgeois trends. But just why a certain society perceives ultimate reality in a certain way remains unclear.

The great merit of dialectical sociology or 'historical materialism' is in its extraordinary explanatory power. According to dialectical sociology, human society is an advanced expression of the movement of matter towards ever higher degrees of organization. This movement is expressed, at the sociological level, in human labour, which adds to the level of organization of the universe by creating new forms in a way which biological reproduction never does. And of course technological innovation means new ways of creating new forms of organization.

What dialectical sociology, at least in its materialist form, has left incompletely explained is the process of production itself, something which makes the teleological character of the theory – and in fact its dependence on a cosmic teleology – less apparent. Largely as a result of their (understandable) frustration with German idealism, Marx and Engels failed to fully comprehend that production itself is an intellectual act – an exercise of the virtue which Aristotle called *techne* or 'art'. And art itself is dependent on theoretical knowledge – on a scientific understanding of how the 'raw material' works, and on philosophy to ground its judgements about what ought to be made and thus the proper ends of productive activity. Technological development – understood in the sense of a real advance in humanity's capacity to add something to the level of organization of the universe – is thus driven by developments in philosophy and science, that is by progress in our ability to know ever higher purposes or aims, and in our ability to know how to realize those aims. Soviet dialectical materialism admitted as much when, in the 1970s, it began to speak of science as a 'productive' force, and when, as far back as the 1920s, it placed the Institute of Philosophy in the leading position at the Academy of Sciences (Joravsky 1961).

Once we have made this move, however, the entire human civilizational project takes on a transparently teleological character. It does so, furthermore, not simply at the level of individual or collective purposes, in the sense of aims arrived at by human reasoning, but at the level of the larger cosmic purpose which this reasoning, as it develops within each cultural tradition, attempts however imperfectly to grasp. It is this cosmic τελος which is the real cause of human social development, a causation which is mediated through the human intellect and catalyses advances in human productive capacity.

This said, it must also be pointed out that the teleology in question is one which leaves ample room for instability and contradiction. As Marx pointed out, while human beings make their own history, they make it under circumstances not of their own choosing. Thus, we have already suggested that it was precisely the drive to develop, but to do so under conditions of scarcity, which led to the emergence of tributary states which, on a global scale, held back social progress for nearly four thousand years. The development of capitalism is a more complex phenomenon, but the reality is much the same. The drive to develop, far from creating social harmony, gives birth to contradictions which in turn require intense struggles – struggles between classes, nations and genders, to resolve.

The Role of Transcendental Abstraction in Metaphysics

The foregoing account demonstrates rather effectively, I think, the scientific power of teleological explanation. And much of it *points towards* the existence of a cosmic τελος. A real argument for cosmic teleology, however, is beyond the scope of the special sciences, even when 'formed' by transcendental abstraction. Such an argument, rather, at once completes science and passes over into metaphysics, which is so called precisely because it comes *after* physics. Once again, the primarily epistemological agenda of this work does not permit a complete treatment of the issues surrounding cosmic teleology, which will form the subject of a sequel. We can, however, pause briefly to illustrate what transcendental abstraction can accomplish in this field.

Before we proceed we need to make it clear just what is involved in demonstrating cosmic teleology, which we have thus far defined rather loosely as the claim that the universe is ultimately meaningful. Cosmic teleology requires a τελος to which the universe, and all elements thereof, are perfectly ordered and by which (and only by which) they can, in principle at least, be perfectly explained. Given a universe which is itself qualitatively infinite, such a principle must itself be infinite and perfect, containing within itself every perfection which it causes and which it is called on to explain. And while intermediate ends are not ruled out, the τελος in which we are interested is the ultimate τελος, which causes and explains without itself requiring cause or explanation outside itself. It must, in other words be not only infinite and perfect but also a necessary being. It must, in other words, be divine. A demonstration of cosmic teleology is thus a proof of the existence of God, but not just any such proof. It is a proof of the existence of God which also shows the ordering of the universe to God and thus the ultimate meaningfulness of the cosmo-historical evolutionary process.

Our argument turns on two facts which no special science can explain: the *existence* of the universe, and its *emergent organization*. This latter fact, in turn, has three dimensions, of which only two are really relevant to our argument. First, there appear to be many local systems which, as the foregoing argument suggests, are themselves teleological. Second, there appears to be a tendency of matter to develop towards increasingly complex levels of organization, suggesting a cosmo-historical teleology. Finally, there is significant evidence (as we shall see) that the universe is structured in just precisely the way necessary to make such cosmic evolution possible. The existence and the emergent organization of the universe each suggest what have historically been taken to be more or less independent routes to demonstrating cosmic teleology and the existence of God, but in the end these routes turn out to be one.

The argument from the existence of the universe to cosmic teleology is, in effect, a variant of what has historically been called the cosmological argument.[11] At base, what the cosmological argument claims is that, however we envision the causal chain leading up to the universe we now experience, whether we regard this chain

---

[11] For classical statements of the cosmological argument see Aristotle, *Metaphysics* XII: 6–10; Aquinas, *Summa Theologiae* I, Q 2 a3. For a summary of the contemporary debate around the argument, see Peterson *et al.* 1996: 145–230.

as finite and terminating in an origin of time such as the Big Bang, or as infinite in both space and time, unbounded in any direction, we still need some principle, which itself requires no further causal explanation, which can explain either that originating event or the existence of the infinite causal chain which is the universe. And a principle which itself requires no further cause or explanation is a 'necessary being'. By a necessary being we mean one which has its cause in itself, and thus logically *must* exist.[12] Now in order to be necessary, a principle must have no limits, otherwise it would, in a certain sense, depend for its very definition on what it was not, and thus not be truly self-caused. Necessary being is thus unlimited or infinite, and as infinite, it is also perfect, possessing all logically possible perfections. It is God.

In what sense does this argument imply cosmic teleology as well as the existence of God? In order to get at this point we must ask ourselves just how a principle which is infinite, necessary, and perfect brings the universe into being. If it does so through any action which might be described mechanically then the cause itself will undergo change – and is thus very far from being infinite, necessary and perfect. Final causes, on the other hand, move without themselves being moved. 'Survival' and 'digestion' do not themselves move; indeed they are, in a certain sense, wholly immaterial, but they cause the stomach, as well as other innovations in digestive physiology. Now 'survival' and 'digestion' are finite ends and thus can explain only certain finite systems. But God causes the universe in much the same way, with the single but all important difference that as infinite, She contains within herself sufficient attractive power to draw an infinity of finite systems into being.

The cosmological argument allows us to make a case for the ordering of the universe as a whole to God. It does a great deal less, if indeed anything at all, to show a detailed ordering of the fine structure of the universe to God. For this we must turn to the teleological argument. Broadly speaking, three variants of this argument can be made. The first, and oldest, begins with the fact that there are finite systems in the universe which appear to be ordered to an end or to show purposeful behaviour, but which are not themselves intelligent. But, the argument runs, it is impossible for something to act for an end without intelligent direction. Thus the need for a governing intelligence which orders all things to their appropriate ends.[13]

A few points are in order here. First, it should be noted that this is not, by itself, an argument for cosmic teleology as we have defined it. On the contrary, it *begins from* local and limited teleologies, such as the ordering of the stomach to digestion, and then concludes to God as an explanation for this ordering. Second, as Kant pointed out, even if this argument works, it does not require a truly divine (infinite, necessary and perfect) intelligence, but only a finite if highly advanced intellect.

---

[12] It is this recourse to the concept of necessary being (explicit or implicit, depending on the variant of the argument used) which led Kant to argue that the cosmological (and also the teleological) arguments ultimately 'reduce' to the ontological argument. What Kant missed was the tremendous difference between simply beginning with the notion of necessary being, which is essentially what Anselm and Descartes do, thereby 'begging the question', assuming what they are trying to prove, and showing that a necessary being is required if we are to account for our experience.

[13] This argument is often restated in terms which make no reference to purposefulness at all, but point rather to the fact of order. In these cases the argument is called 'eutaxiological'. See, for example, Barrow and Tipler 1986.

Third, it is no longer clear that the development of purposeful systems requires a designing or governing intellect. The limitations of Neo-Darwinism notwithstanding, the emergence of higher levels of organization from lower is well established. The traditional form of the teleological argument by itself, therefore, is of little use to us.

Our very critique of the argument, however, depends on a phenomenon which does, in fact, authentically point towards cosmic teleology. This is the phenomenon of emergent organization properly understood. We have already noted above that random variation and natural selection for variations which have survival value do not, by themselves, explain the emergence of life in the first place, or of the development of more complex living organisms. Simpler structures, which require less energy input to build and maintain, are far more probable. And if survival value is measured in terms of population size, simpler organisms would, in general, seem to be by far the better adapted. And yet matter manifests this powerful drive towards complex organization. This uphill struggle of the universe against the energy gradient and against the laws of probability can be explained only in terms of some attractive principle which draws matter from potency to act, from mere possibility into the rich diversity of increasingly improbable and complex, high energy forms of organization which we observe in the contemporary universe. And since it is the diversity and increasing complexity of different forms of organization, and not simply the fact of the universe in general, which we are attempting to explain here, we must conclude that each form is ordered to, in fact exists because of, the attractive principle which draws it from potency to act. Such a principle, furthermore, must itself require no further principle of explanation – it must, as we noted in our discussion of the cosmological proof, be infinite, necessary and perfect, that is, divine.

This second variant of the teleological argument is, we should note, actually convertible with the cosmological argument. This becomes apparent when we recognize that emergent organization in fact embraces not only the emergence of life and intelligence, and the drive to ever more complex forms of organic and social organization, but also the development of chemical systems from the merely physical, and the emergence of physical organization from the 'pure possibility' of prime matter. And in so far as 'pure possibility' is really nothing at all, emergent organization also embraces the very existence of the universe itself which we have, in any case, already explained in exactly the same way we explained the drive towards increasingly complex forms of organization. To exist is to be ordered to – to be organized. Being itself is the power to organize and thus to bring into Being.

The third form of the teleological proof argues from a growing body of evidence that the physical structure of the universe is 'fine-tuned' to permit the emergence of life and intelligence. At issue here are a variety of physical constants which are fixed at just precisely the levels necessary for the emergence of life and intelligence. Thus, for example, the relative strength of the various fundamental physical forces (the strong and weak nuclear forces, electromagnetism and gravity), the relative mass of the electron and proton, and a wide range of other, equally fundamentally if somewhat more obscure numbers must be within a very narrow range if stars are to evolve and complex chemistry is to be possible. Were gravity just a little bit stronger the universe would collapse on itself; were it just a little bit weaker gas would never condense to form stars. And stars make possible the formation of the heavy elements which are necessary for complex chemistry and thus for life. Similarly, given the existence of these complex elements, if electromagnetism were just a little stronger electrons would fall into their atomic nuclei; if it were just a little bit weaker they would never form part of atoms at all.[14]

There are, to be sure, attempts to answer the evidence for fine tuning in ways which do not imply cosmic teleology. The most popular of these involves positing the existence of 'many worlds' with different physical laws, from which our own world has been selected randomly by the purely coincidental fact that it is the only kind of universe we could perceive (Leslie 1989). This approach is driven by the 'many worlds' approach to quantum mechanics, which argues that all possible states of quantum systems actually exist, so that at each instant the universe in fact diverges into an infinite number of world lines each corresponding to a possible quantum state of a single elementary particle. But this approach violates a fundamental principle of scientific explanation – what is known as Occam's Razor. Such theories 'multiply beings unnecessarily', positing worlds for which there is otherwise no evidence, in order to explain (or rather explain away) evidence of fine tuning which can be explained far more economically in teleological terms.

The argument for such an interpretation is simple. We have already shown that there is only a universe in the first place because of a powerful teleological attractor which draws potency into act, the possible into the actual. This implies, furthermore, that matter can be drawn from the nothingness of pure possibility into actual being only by being ordered to an end which is infinite, necessary and perfect. 'To exist' *means* 'to be ordered to' or 'to be organized' and Being as such is nothing other than the organizing power of the τελος itself. Everything existing, therefore, in the degree to which it exists, is ordered to the τελος and thus manifests those properties which we associate with teleological organization: the differentiation of elements and their integration in relation to the end to which they are ordered. Now it is possible for us to imagine or to derive mathematically any number of possible universes, each with its own logically consistent topology, each with its own metric defining the relative strength of the fundamental physical forces. Only one such universe, however, actually exists, and it is the one which makes possible the emergence of life and intelligence. This means that to exist physically, and not merely mathematically – actually and not just possibly – is to make possible the emergence of biological and social organization. We are thus able to show that physical systems, which do not themselves give evidence of a direct ordering to God, are nonetheless indirectly so ordered. To be precise, they are ordered to life, which is ordered to intelligence, which is ordered to Truth (and its convertible transcendentals) and thus to God. Physical teleology is implicit; biological and social teleology increasingly explicit. All are real and must be comprehended if we are to develop a complete explanation of the systems in question.

If all of this seems a bit fuzzy, then it must be remembered that we are reasoning at the very outer limits of human capacity. One cannot expect the 'clarity and distinctness' which characterizes mathematical formalisms. But then mathematical

---

[14] For a complete discussion see Barrow and Tipler 1986. It is not necessary to accept the radical empiricist and neo-liberal philosophical perspective which drives their analysis to benefit from their detailed discussion of cosmological fine-tuning. For a more satisfying discussion of the philosophical implications, see Harris 1991, 1992.

formalisms merely tell us what is possible, not what actually is. Indeed, while the impulse to explain the universe in terms of a single principle is healthy and fundamental to science, one should be sceptical if the principle which is suggested is transparent and well-defined. It is hardly likely that something we can comprehend perfectly – that we can 'wrap our minds around' – could really explain something as beautiful and complex as this universe which includes us but which we, try as we might, can never completely include.

With these arguments we have, of course, already passed over from science to wisdom, or at least the pursuit of it, and specifically to metaphysics, or the doctrine of the first principle. Before we explore what transcendental abstraction can tell us about the first principle, it will be useful to note briefly what our passage implies about the relationship between science and philosophy and specifically between science and metaphysics. On the one hand, it is specifically through science, through the search for an adequate principle of explanation, that we rise to first principles. And our ascent depends, in a very real sense, on the results of the sciences – on the demonstration that the universe is an organized system. Indeed, thus far, our αρχη is little more than a means of accounting for what science – especially when it is freed from the idolatry of formalism – tells us about the organization of the universe. And it is only on the basis of science that we have any right whatsoever to conclude that there is a first principle.

Now it might be objected that our foundational argument in fact depends not on the details of cosmic organization, but simply on the fact that there is anything at all, rather than nothing. Would it not be possible to avoid this long detour and mount an argument for the existence of God from the simple fact of finite existence itself? To put the matter differently, doesn't Aquinas's third argument, from possible and necessary being (Aquinas, *Summa Theologiae* I, Q 2 a3), stand all by itself, quite independently of what the science of one or another epoch claims about cosmic organization? And isn't this route not only economical, but also much safer, in the sense that it does not risk being undermined, or requiring radical revision, every time the sciences make some new advance?

The difficulty with this claim, which at first sight seems so obvious, is that any argument from contingent to necessary being presupposes what has generally come to be called the principle of sufficient reason – the notion that everything has a principle or cause which can account for the fact that it is, and is the way that it is, rather than some other way. Now it is possible to derive this principle from the law of identity and contradiction, which in turn can be shown to be self-evident (Garrigou-Lagrange 1938). But such a proof remains vulnerable to the claim that it is not so much that everything *has* an adequate principle of explanation, but simply that we cannot *think* about things in any other way. What our journey through the sciences does is to bring the principle of sufficient reason (and the prior principles of identity and contradiction) under the protection of our earlier defence of objectivity against solipsism and critical idealism. The notion that everything has an explanation, while it may well be a function of the way the human nervous system and the social or Agent Intellect are structured, increases our ability to deal effectively with the world and therefore must say *something* about the way the world actually is. This is very important, because otherwise we become vulnerable to the possibility that the universe 'just happened' as the result of a random 'quantum fluctuation', or some other radically contingent event and is, therefore, ultimately meaningless.

Our ascent through the sciences has, furthermore, the advantage that it establishes clearly that the claim that there is a first principle is simultaneously a statement about the organization of the universe. While there are real limits to what can be expected from a philosophical doctrine of God, proceeding through the sciences assures us that we will not arrive at a principle which is simply a sort of odd consequence of the rules of logic, which has little or nothing to do with the way the world works, and therefore with what it is reasonable to believe and hope and desire. Indeed, proceeding in the manner in which we have will leave us in a far better position, in Chapter 7, to not only establish the possibility and reasonableness of revelation, but also to suggest just how it takes place.

At the same time, our ascent has also suggested that however much metaphysics emerges out of the sciences, as a consequence of the mind's search for an adequate principle of explanation, it is metaphysics in the end which rules science and not vice versa. This is a bold claim and one which is not likely to be received warmly in an age which glories in science and uses 'metaphysics' as a term of derision. But it follows necessarily from science's own conclusion to a teleological αρχη, which is infinite, perfect and necessary, as the condition of the validity of its own partial explanations. For if the universe as such has no explanation, the principle of sufficient cause is not valid and the whole edifice of the sciences crumbles like a castle made of sand swept away in the evening tide. But the study of this principle is the province not of the special sciences, but of metaphysics.

The conclusion that metaphysics rules the sciences has a very important consequence. From the standpoint of the sciences evidence of cosmological fine-tuning is certainly an intriguing mystery, but it cannot ever really become more than that. And it certainly isn't a principle of explanation. Attempts to make it one result in subjectivist nonsense of the Tiplerian variety, where human beings end up, in effect, creating the universe by building a race of intelligent robot probes, which in turn build a cosmic supercomputer, which then 'emulates' the universe back through time (Barrow and Tipler 1986, Tipler 1994). No, fine-tuning is something to be explained – and the special sciences cannot do this. From the standpoint of metaphysics, however, once it has been shown that the universe as such can be explained only in terms of teleological attraction, only in terms of ordering to a principle infinite, perfect and necessary, fine-tuning becomes simply the trace of divine necessity, a mark of the only kind of universe which can *actually* exist, in the light of the unique means by which something can be brought into being out of pure possibility – or, what is the same thing, out of nothing. Once we have made this move we are in a position to exclude scientific claims which would imply that the universe, or some particular system within it, is *not* ordered to God. This is a potent tool, and one which must never be wielded to curb authentic exploration or the search for the Truth, but which should be wielded ruthlessly against the pseudo-science which, as a result of some defect of the intellect or the will, betrays its calling, which is always and only to serve philosophy, and which pledges itself instead to the forces of darkness and despair.[15]

---

[15] The nature of such a dark science can be specified with precision: it is a science which relies exclusively on formalization, and which thus attempts to comprehend the universe deductively from what the human

Given the importance which we have attributed to metaphysics, it may be useful to illustrate at least briefly just what it can – and cannot – accomplish. Our emphasis here will be more on exposition and illustration than on rigorous argumentation, which will have to await another work.

A few words are in order, to begin with, regarding the method of this inquiry. While metaphysics is the product of transcendental abstraction, it cannot proceed by transcendental abstraction alone. This is because one cannot go any further in the process of transcendental abstraction than the idea of a τελος, infinite, perfect and necessary, with which metaphysics *begins*. Indeed, the very claim that the τελος, in order to exercise an attractive power sufficient to bring the universe into being, must be infinite, perfect and necessary, is itself an act not of transcendental but rather of formal thinking. To be more specific, it is the result of an analysis of the idea of a creative τελος possessing the power of being. Developed rigorously, it would involve formulating a definition of such a τελος, and then picking it apart intellectually to see what it implies, much as a mathematician might analyse an axiom in search of theorems or a theorem in search of a proof. And this will, in general, be the character of most arguments within metaphysics. That is why communitarian religion and salvation religions, prior to the advent of the marketplace and formalization, have profound insights into the first principle, but know no true metaphysics. And this is why the metaphysics of the Hindu Vedanta and the Confucian scholastics, which developed in societies where marketization and thus formalization were weak, seem to us to be at once full of powerful insights, and less concerned than their Western counterparts with formal inference and rigorous argument.[16]

---

mind recognizes as logically possible. That it may pause briefly to check its formalisms against observation means nothing. As we know from the experience of contemporary cosmology, observations which conflict with mathematically elegant theory can all too easily be explained away by postulating whole classes of matter (interestingly enough called 'dark matter') for which we otherwise have no evidence.

This approach to science is demonic in the strict sense of the word. According to Aquinas, Satan was among the very highest of the angels, drawn from the ranks of the cherubim, who mirror the divine wisdom. Now angels, for Aquinas, know through intuition of and deduction from their own essence and for a cherub this essence is of such a high order as to permit a great deal of knowledge indeed. Conclusion to a higher principle through transcendental abstraction is, however, impossible, since angels do not abstract. Satan's sin consisted in refusing to acknowledge his ordering to a higher principle, and thus in refusing to accept the divine revelation which would have permitted him to understand what his own nature was ordered to, and instead to attempt to know – and act – based on deduction from his own magnificent but still limited nature. And in refusing the principle to which his nature was ordered, Satan refused as well the source of his power, which withered and became deformed (Aquinas, *Summa Theologiae* I, Q 50–64; Fox and Sheldrake 1996).

Whatever one thinks about the existence and nature of angels, Thomas's account of their fall is a good description of the 'dark science' of mathematical physics and its offspring in other disciplines. In refusing transcendental abstraction, mathematical physics refuses the possibility of knowing anything higher than itself, and thus anything which could actually explain the structures it discovers in the physical universe. And like Satan it becomes cut off from the source of its power, which withers and becomes deformed. Little wonder that when we approach the great centres of research in mathematical physics – the universities but especially the national laboratories – we sense at once a great power and the shadow at least of a terrible beauty, but also an overwhelming evil. Little wonder that our mathematical physicists have so quickly sold out to the forces of imperialism and become a part of the war machine.

[16] This, we will argue in our work-in-progress, *The Journey of the Dialectic*, rather than any fundamental difference in content, is what sets 'Eastern' philosophy apart from 'Western'. Nearly all Hellenic, Islamic

The dependence of metaphysics on formal thinking and especially on analytic argument suggests a certain danger, and a need for caution. Here we have no empirical point of reference to which we can turn to check our claims against reality. This much, at least, we share with the mathematicians. The difference of course, is that mathematicians begin with clear and distinct ideas about things which may or may not exist; we begin with rather fuzzy and indistinct ideas about existence itself. The danger of drawing conclusions which are incorrect, and perhaps dangerously so, increases with each analytic deduction. And so, while we want to argue for both the possibility and the necessity of a doctrine of first principles, we need to caution against dogmatism of any kind. We also need to caution against absorption in metaphysical subtleties the degree of certainty of which is very, very low. The best safeguard against such dogmatism is to remember that our claims on behalf of metaphysics themselves depend on our demonstration of the possibility of transcendental abstraction. And this demonstration was based, at least in part, on a critique of formalization. Having shown the superiority of their discipline to that of the mathematicians and the mathematical physicists, philosophers do well not to imitate them. While metaphysics is the ruler of the sciences, her reign is that of a servant-queen. She secures the position of the sciences on the one hand, and ethics on the other hand, both of which she richly endows, while herself living as austerely as her office permits. Indeed, it will turn out that she is not really a queen in her own right at all, but holds her authority from another, higher and divine science, which she in turn serves by preparing the field, as it were, and crafting its tools.

These strictures notwithstanding we emerge from our ascent through the sciences with some very powerful insights regarding the nature of the first principle, and regarding being in general. It should be noted, first of all, that we have clearly established that Being is an analogical term, which has fundamentally different meaning when used of finite systems than it does when used of the first principle. To exist, in the sense in which finite beings exist, is always and only 'to be ordered to'. All finite systems are radically dependent for their existence on other finite systems with which they are interconnected in the most intimate way, and ultimately on the first principle, God, αρχη and τελος of all things. Being as such, the power of Being, is 'to Be the end to which all things are ordered'. Everything which we say about being can be said of both finite and infinite being, but only in a very different way – though finite systems, in so far as they become ends, participate in the divine power of Being in a secondary and derivative way. It is the fact that we are ordered to God – that we are in fact nothing more or less than this specific way of being ordered to God – which makes it possible for us to order things to ourselves as intermediate ends, and in general to participate in the creative organizing activity of the universe.

Some important conclusions follow from this analysis. First, it should be clear that it is not really possible, given our scheme, to conceive of being as substance – as

---

and European philosophical schools have close counterparts among the schools of Hindu philosophy, at least at the level of basic metaphysical doctrine. While Chinese philosophy is less diverse, it is possible to find counterparts for many European trends, including both a relativistic materialism and, in the Confucian-Taoist synthesis of Chu Hsi, a doctrine not unlike that of the great medieval commentators in Europe and the Mediterranean basin. It is just that marketization, and thus formalization, were less advanced in these regions. Apprehension thus continues to be valued more than inference or judgement.

something that exists in itself. Finite systems clearly derive their being from each other and from the infinite; the αρχη, on the other hand, while it clearly is the Power of Being, exists precisely in drawing others into being. Because of this both Aristotelian pluralism and Spinozist monism (while each grasping a part of the truth) are fundamentally inadequate. Neither really understands that Being is quite the opposite of self-possession.

Nor should we really think of Being as subject. Subjectivity, as a way of being ordered to others and to the infinite, is incipient and emerging in finite being, but it hardly makes sense to regard merely physical systems as subjective. But clearly such systems exist. Infinite being, on the other hand, while it can be shown to be an unlimited subjectivity and inwardness (a proof which will have to await a later work), does not exist in this subjectivity but rather precisely in its creative power, which is always and only directed outward, as the power of teleological attraction.

Rather preferable to either of these formulae is the idea of being as relationship. This way of understanding being has the merit, first of all, of grasping the interconnectedness of being without negating difference. Indeed, it makes it fully possible for us to meet the objection of existentialists and postmodernists who are concerned that any philosophical doctrine of God – or indeed any other totalizing metanarrative which attempts to describe or explain the universe as a whole – inevitably submerges difference into identity. And this is, indeed, a danger for both Spinozist and Hegelian monisms. When being is conceived as substance, and we assert (as we must, once we have taken this first step) that there is only one substance, one system which exists in and through itself, and that that system is the whole, we are, in effect, saying that particular systems don't exist and that the rich difference which makes life interesting is, in fact, a mere difference of location in a single system – in effect, an illusion. When being is conceived as subject, similarly, one ends up reducing individuals to mere vanishing moments of the One subject, Absolute Spirit, which develops itself and becomes conscious of itself through them – and then casts them aside. Aristotelian pluralism – and more especially Thomism – avoids this problem only at the price of a certain inconsistency, arguing on the one hand that there are many substances, and that difference is therefore real, while at the same time arguing their dependence on the teleological attraction of the Unmoved Mover (for Aristotle), and on the Single Pure Act of Being which is God (for Aquinas), an argument which is tantamount to admitting that they are not really substances at all. By conceiving being as relationship we unify in a way which not only conserves, but in fact presupposes difference. One cannot, after all, be meaningfully ordered to, in the sense we have defined it, without being different.

This character of being related, furthermore, also applies to God, even though (as Being is an analogical concept) God's mode of being related is different from ours. By defining the first principle in terms of teleological attraction we preserve divine self-sufficiency (God is attractive precisely because She *is* All Things) without making this out to be self-absorption. While one can certainly predicate of God an infinite self-knowledge and self-enjoyment, which are the correlates of our own limited self-knowledge and self-enjoyment (a proof which will, once again, have to await another context), it is not in this that God's act of existence consists, but rather in the creative attraction which draws the universe out of potency and into act. God's Beauty is the gift of Being to us and to all creatures who would otherwise be nothing more than possible beings, like mathematical objects and other hypotheticals, inhabiting possible worlds and never knowing the struggle and the joy of becoming.

At the same time, we avoid the fall into an infinite expanse of difference, without horizon or point of reference, which the 'postmodern' philosophy of difference celebrates but which in fact is nothing less than a wilful option for death and loss. The difference of being is always and only a difference of relationship, a difference of being ordered to, a difference of sensing and imagining, of knowing and judging, of desiring and hoping and willing, which are never possible for the same, but which nonetheless make difference a principle of unity rather than of division. And this series of differences, even if it is itself infinite in the sense of extending without limit through space and time (and we will argue there are good reasons, both scientific and philosophical to believe this) nonetheless terminates in a principle which unifies (because it is the common τελος) but does so precisely by creating 'infinite diversity in infinite combinations'.[17]

Our approach is also not without implications for the way in which we understand the problem of 'essence' or of 'what things are'. In a certain sense it was precisely this question which absorbed the lower degrees of abstraction, totalization and formalization, and which obscured the deeper question of Being as such altogether. Totalization attempted to abstract from the image a logical whole, only to find that there were countless ways of doing this, and that it was powerless to decide among them without reference to some higher principle which it could not itself supply. Formalization was able to do little better, working out definitions and descriptions of systems in terms of formal systems of similar differences and different similarities. Pursued just so far formalization was able to congratulate itself at having penetrated beneath and behind the 'appearance' of finite systems to grasp their essence or 'underlying structure'. But when it was pursued further, in search of its own foundations, it realized its own groundlessness and dissolved into a doctrine of pure difference.

Transcendental abstraction with its doctrine of Being as τελος can alone rescue the search for the essence of things, for the underlying structure of finite systems, from its post-structuralist oblivion. It does this through a return to formalization and totalization which, however, are now governed by a higher principle they themselves could not supply. This principle is the τελος itself, and it provides us with a criterion on the basis of which to judge between competing formalizations and the systems of classification which they imply, which otherwise might be equally possible from a logical point of view, equally economical, and perhaps even of equal explanatory power. The preferred formalization and scheme of classification is that which most clearly illuminates the system's *mode of being*, that is, the specific manner in which it is ordered to the τελος. Thus both neo-liberal and dialectical materialist economics produce logically coherent formalizations of the behaviour of the market system. Neo-liberalism, however, either fails to grasp the end of the market altogether, or understands it in terms of individual consumption interests. Dialectical materialism, on the other hand, grasps the real end to which the market system is ordered: the

---

[17] This phrase is put in quotations because it is a favourite slogan of *Star Trek* fandom. I am unsure of the origin. It does, however, speak of just what sort of popular ontology underlies this uniquely hopeful vision of humanity's future.

centralization and allocation of resources for investment in activities which promote the development of human social capacities, and allows us to understand just how the market enters into contradiction with itself, by failing to fulfil the function to which it is ordered, and thus necessarily passes away. Similarly, it is possible to classify organisms both on the basis of their functions and on the basis of the number of their limbs and their outer protective layer (skin, feathers, scales and so on). Both schemes allow us to specify humanity: as a rational animal and thus capable not only of conserving our form, but also of nutrition, growth, reproduction, sensation, locomotion and reason, or as a featherless biped. The first, however, is clearly to be preferred because it specifies in terms of the way in which various organisms are ordered to the τελος – by their intellect, by sensation, by sensitivity and so on, and it is this, precisely, which is their *mode of being*.

Finite systems, therefore, display not two but three layers to the intelligent observer. There is a distinction not only between outward appearance and underlying structure, but also between that structure and the end to which it is ordered, which is always also present in the finite system, as its act of existence. The essence of a system is indeed its underlying structure, but understood not simply as something formal, but rather as a way of being ordered to God.

This helps us to clarify the dispute between traditional Aristotelians and Thomists regarding the principle of Being – a dispute the more properly epistemological dimensions of which we have already touched on in an earlier chapter. For Aristotle it is the form of a thing which gives it its being. Nonbeing is, precisely, the formlessness of prime matter, the pure potency of what might be but is not. Thomas, on the other hand, argues that things are a composite not only of form and matter, but also of an act of existence which is derived from God. This is an important advance because, as we have seen, formal systems are purely possible. Structure does not explain existence. But Thomas's existential principle remains poorly integrated with the rest of his still fundamentally Aristotelian system. There is no clear, logically necessary relationship between form and existence. Our approach overcomes this difficulty, by showing how this relationship is, precisely, the analogical relation of Being itself. Form is the 'order' in 'to be ordered to'; Being as such is 'that to which things are ordered'. Neither can, in fact, be adequately understood apart from the other. It is the nature of ends to bring into being the means to their realization. These 'means' are nothing more or less than structures which attempt to realize the end of Being itself.

The result of the intellect's return from transcendental abstraction to formalization and totalization is a well defined ontological hierarchy of systems which, on the one hand, are more and more clearly 'ordered to' the τελος and, at the same time, increasingly approach the possibility of themselves becoming active participants in the creative activity of the τελος, both by acting as secondary and intermediate ends, and by organizing and reorganizing systems at lower grades of being. Thus physical systems are ordered to God only indirectly, in the sense that they appear to be structured in just the manner necessary to make life and intelligence and thus a direct relationship with the τελος possible. Living systems, on the other hand, display both a secondary intermediate teleology of their own, in their drive towards survival and reproduction which serves as a principle of organization for their organs and tissues, and in the act of reproduction itself which, while it creates nothing new is, nonetheless, an authentic bringing into being. Intelligent systems are ordered directly to the τελος, which they know, albeit imperfectly, in the act of transcendental abstraction, and in which they participate actively in the creative activity of Being by conceiving intermediate ends and bringing into being new forms of physical, biological and social organization which serve these ends. This creative activity is ultimately derivative from and is strengthened by conscious ordering to the Divine end which raises all things from potency to act. There is, of course, no reason to assume that there are not grades of finite being which are higher than our own, and of which we have only a vague and very imperfect understanding. This is the significance of the doctrine of angels and similar beings which play an important role in many theological systems.

At the end of this hierarchically ordered series we arrive, at long last, at the real aim of transcendental abstraction: the transcendentals themselves. Historically, the transcendentals – the Beautiful, the True, the Good and the One – have been regarded as terms 'convertible' with Being, meaning that they refer to the same thing as Being, but add some relation (Aquinas, *Summa Theologiae*, I, 5.1, 9.1, 16.3). What happens to this doctrine once we have recognized Being as *itself* relationship? Our approach to the problem of Being makes the transcendentals into windows on Being's own way of Being – that is, the 'essence' of Being, which is to be organization as such, the infinite end which draws all things out of potency and into act, out of their limitations and towards its own limitless perfection.

Consider, for example, the nature of Beauty. By the beauty of a system, we mean simply its level of organization, understood as the object of (sensory or intellectual) perception. The greater the diversity of the elements organized, and the more perfect the harmony in which they are united, the more beautiful the system. This is true throughout the natural world, from simple harmonies of the night sky, through the more complex forms of the crystalline structures and living organisms, to the rich, lush diversity of complex ecosystems and human societies. And it is true as well of great works of art, which are nothing if not a complex manifold of relations harmoniously arranged. Thus, we find a landscape, natural or painted, beautiful to the extent that it integrates a diversity of elements into a harmonious and purposeful whole. Not too many people are attracted by scenes of pure, undifferentiated grey. Things of great beauty, have, furthermore, the capacity to harmonize and integrate those that perceive them, and thus draw them closer to God. Thus the centrality of beauty in religious experience, in liturgy and so on. Beauty itself, as Albertus Magnus and Thomas Aquinas taught long ago, is the capacity to bring things into being, and is thus convertible with Being itself, or God (Eco 1988).

Now because Beauty integrates diverse elements into a harmonious whole it also possesses *claritas* – it constitutes a window on the Truth. When we are in the process of forming an idea, what we see first is a pattern, a harmonious integration of elements in our experience. The truth value of a statement, a concept or theory, is its capacity to organize large quantities of qualitatively diverse, and therefore highly complex experience. The concept or theory in question does this by explaining the experience in terms of a principle or principles. It is necessary in this connection to focus equal attention on the complexity of the experience organized and on the level of organization of the experience in question. Our experience is most highly organized when we identify highly compact 'organizing principles', knowledge of which permits us to derive logically all the rich particularity of the experience on which the principle was based. It is this organizing capacity of theories which leads us to speak analogously of their 'power'. The most powerful theories are those which comprehend the widest range of experience in unique compact statements which are themselves pregnant with rich experiential content. The Truth itself is, as we have seen, the infinite, necessary and perfect Being which alone completes our explanation of the universe and which grounds all other partial explanations.

The Good, finally, is an end desired or willed or pursued. It is at once the object of our desire or appetite, whether sensual or intellectual, and the actual capacity to organize, to draw things into being. While everything existing is good, in so far as it is capable both of being ordered to the End and of being an (intermediate) end itself, there is a clearly defined hierarchy of goods, measured by the degree to which the system in question is ordered to God and can itself therefore participate in the divine organizing activity. The Good itself is the infinite, necessary and perfect End which alone has the capacity to draw something out of nothing.

All three of these concepts – Beauty, Truth, Goodness – are ultimately determinations of the concept of Value. The more highly organized a system – the greater its 'ordering to' and its capacity to act as a secondary principle of order – the greater its value. That which has an unlimited capacity to order things to itself, and thus bring them out of potency and to act, is the principle and criterion of Value as such.

It is interesting to note the intrusion of quantitative language into our account of the transcendentals. This is unavoidable, but it is a bit deceptive. One may attempt to quantify value, by means of a return from transcendental abstraction to formalism, and this move is often quite useful. Marx's labour theory of value is, in effect, an attempt to quantify the degree of organization of products in terms of the quantity of organizing activity – the amount of average necessary labour-time – they contain. Charles Bennett's 'logical depth' approach to the organization of information systems, which quantifies organization in terms of the number of logical steps necessary to derive a system from its principle (Bennett 1987), is similar in many ways. Other approaches to quantifying organization (and thus value) which focus exclusively on the number of different elements (for example, information content) are more problematic for reasons we have already cited. But no quantification of value actually comprehends the fundamentally teleological character of the concept of value and thus the radical simplicity of the union effected among the complex elements of organized systems. And no quantification of value can comprehend the fact that the τελος, the End itself, far from negating difference when it unites, in fact multiplies it infinitely as it draws ever new and more diverse forms of organization into being.

This is the significance of the fourth and last transcendental: the transcendental One. While the numerical one derives *from* difference (as the 'ratio' of 'similar differences' and 'different similarities' which defines the unit of a formal system) and serves as a principle of identity, the transcendental One, in uniting all things to itself, in fact distinguishes them from the infinite sameness of mere possibility and draws them, in all their individual uniqueness, into the divine light of Being itself.

The Role of Transcendental Abstraction in Ethics

What this analysis of the transcendentals means is that transcendental abstraction provides us not only with a necessary first principle of explanation, but also with a principle of value which can serve as a first principle of action. Transcendental abstraction, in other words, grounds ethics and the practical disciplines which ethics regulates. It is obviously not possible, in this context, to develop fully the ethical implications of this approach, but a few remarks are in order.

We should begin by clarifying the nature of the moral question. A certain prejudice has developed in the field of ethics against what, following the analytic philosopher G.E. Moore, is called 'ethical naturalism', and 'metaphysical ethics', which attempt to reduce the good to some single property accessible either to the natural sciences or to metaphysics, or to both. The result is, devotees of this approach argue, a confusion of fact and value, 'is' and 'ought'. They argue instead that the predicate 'good' is simple and unanalysable, and in fact is applied to many different kinds of things. Clearly it is just precisely the kind of approach to ethics which we are proposing which is the intended object of this attack. The criticism, however, is self-contradictory, for it takes as its canon 'ordinary language,' the usage of which it claims merely to clarify. But what is this if not to confuse 'is' and 'ought'? The way people use a certain language, in this case English, is without any further justification made into the standard by which ethics is grounded, and so on.

At the same time, to say that 'good' is a simple and unanalysable predicate is to leave ethical judgement ungrounded and to transform it into nothing more than a peculiar use of language. What transcendental abstraction reveals is not a particular class of things or properties which are good, but rather a transcendental property of everything which *is*, to the extent to which it *is*. The moral imperative is nothing other than the imperative of Being itself understood as that which is desired and aimed for. The Good is what draws finite systems into being in the first place; finite goods are secondary, intermediate ends which possess a participating power to draw into being.

Our analysis of the transcendentals allows us, furthermore, to give this principle some very definite content. We have seen that being is organization. Infinite Being is the End which organizes, finite being is both that which is organized or 'ordered to' and that which, in varying degrees, acts as a secondary ordering end. To be good therefore, is at once to be organized and to participate in the divine creative power of organization. Concretely this means a drive upwards along the ontological hierarchy of being, a drive to grow and develop, to evolve, to bring into being ever more complex and integrated systems. It means the move from the pure potency of non-being to the act of existence, the move from physical to biological and from biological to social organization. It means social progress – the development of human creative powers and of humanity's capacity to participate in the self-organizing activity of the universe and thus to share in God's work of creation.

The moral imperative or principle of right can, therefore, be stated, in its most abstract and general form, in the following manner:

Act in such a manner as to promote the self-organizing activity of the universe, that is, to promote the development of ever more complex forms of organization.

By analysing the way in which self-organization actually takes place we can, in turn, derive more specific principles of right. In this sense ethics is indeed informed by science not only indirectly, through the mediation of the doctrine of first principles which completes scientific inquiry, but directly, by recourse to investigations which clarify the means to the End. Thus, for example, the fact that organization is indeed a kind of order, and is characterized by at least a relative and temporary stability, allows us to derive the *principle of public order*:

Act in such a way as to conserve the existing forms of organization unless acting otherwise can reasonably be expected to yield a higher level of organization.

The fact that organization emerges out of qualitative differentiation, symmetry breaking and instability, on the other hand, means that the structure of any given system ought not to be so rigid as to undermine these processes and the innovation they make possible. One way to insure this is to have multiple and diverse centres of power, each of which seeks the τελος in its own way and on its own terms. Thus the *principle of subsidiarity*:

Power and decision making should be as decentralized as is compatible with the ordering of the system generally to the common good.

Finally, we know that organization is an ordering to and is, therefore, fundamentally hierarchical in character. The *principle of hierarchy* states that:

Lower order activities must serve higher order activities and all must serve the τελος.

This is *not* an argument for unequal access to resources for consumption. On the contrary, it is precisely the ability to use resources productively, to order them to a higher end and thus bring into being new and more complex forms of organization which marks a system as 'higher order'. Unproductive consumption (luxury) is a mark of disorganization and disintegration.

Thus far, our consideration of the ethical implications of our doctrine of first principles has been very abstract and schematic. Understood as the first principle of *human* action, however, the moral imperative has much more definite and concrete implications, for it requires the ordering of both the *human psyche* and *human society* to the Good, so that they can function as secondary centres of creative activity and contribute effectively to the self-organizing activity of the cosmos. Our approach thus supplies doctrines of *virtue* and of *social justice*.

Here as well there is a turn to the sciences in order to give specificity to the general principle supplied by transcendental abstraction. The fundamental problem of virtue theory is just how human beings are ordered to the final end, which is God, and thus realize their latent potential to participate actively in the self-organizing activity of the universe. For the more fully a system is ordered to the End, the more organized it will be and the greater its secondary and derivative organizing power.

Now clearly human beings are ordered to their ends by both their cognitive powers (the senses and the intellect) and their appetites (the sensual appetites and the will or intellectual appetite). The cognitive powers sense ends or understand them in varying degrees; the appetites express the natural attraction of being towards its own principle which is the Good or Being itself. It is, however, clearly the cognitive powers, and especially the intellect, which play the leading role. This is because it is not possible to be drawn to a good which we do not know, or know in a way which does not reveal its intrinsic attractiveness. Development of the cognitive faculties we call cognitive or *intellectual virtue*. These virtues include not only understanding or clarity regarding the first principles of thought (the laws of identity and contradiction, the excluded middle and sufficient reason), and science, or the ability to develop explanations, but also wisdom, which is precisely excellence in the act of transcendental abstraction which reveals to us the τελος, the Good which draws all things to itself. And it involves excellence in reasoning regarding the means of reaching that τελος – that is, excellence in the practical disciplines. Apart from clarity regarding the end of human life and the means of achieving those ends, human beings cannot be fully ordered to the Good, and cannot participate in the self-organizing activity of the universe to the full extent permitted by their latent potential.

Development of the appetites we call *moral virtue*. The moral virtues include temperance, desiring the right things at the right time in the right degree; fortitude, the strength in battle which comes from balancing hope and fear and anger in such a way as to enable us to persist in the most difficult struggles without becoming rash or engaging in unwarranted violence; and justice, willing goods in proportion to their value as revealed by the intellect.

The appetites naturally seek the Good and so follow the intellect, aiming at the highest good of which they are informed. At the same time, the appetites can become habituated to seeking various ends, so that they either run ahead of the intellect – if we are habituated to pursue a higher Good which we do not yet fully understand – or else lag behind, remaining mired in the pursuit of lesser goods when we have already become aware of higher. This means that a kind of ordering to the Good is possible even without wisdom, by habituation to the pursuit of ends we do not yet comprehend. Indeed, such a prior ordering is in fact necessary to the development of wisdom since, as we have seen, it is the connatural knowledge of God in the just act which provides the basis in experience for the act of transcendental abstraction. The discipline of interaction with others, of participation in community, is a precondition for the development of virtue in the first place.

The problem of *social justice*, while distinguishable from that of virtue is, therefore, closely related. Ordering human society as a whole to the Good means, first of all centralizing and allocating resources for investment in activities which promote the development of complex organization (especially the development of human excellence) – and indeed assuring that resources are, at any given moment, allocated optimally, that is, to best promote this development. This excludes economic structures which, like the market system, have no access to information regarding the impact of various activities on the integrity of the ecosystem or the development of human social capacities (the two areas in which human activity most clearly affects the level of cosmic organization).

At the same time, particularly if we exclude impersonal organizers such as the marketplace, the decision regarding resource allocation remains a decision of some individual or group of individuals and is constrained by their level of moral and intellectual development. The problem of resource allocation is thus always also the problem of promoting virtue. Partly this can be done by means of external legal discipline which habituates people to just action. By requiring people to devote their labour and resources to activities which actually promote human development, they eventually become habituated to these activities and begin to will them prior to full understanding. This task of centralizing and allocating resources, including human labour, to various activities, and thus of ordering people to the Good through external discipline belongs properly to the *political authority*, which exercises the right of *dominion*.[18] Included in this is, of course, is the right to prohibit destructive activity.

There are, however, real limits to the effectiveness of external discipline. It is necessary to actually cultivate virtue by making the ends of human life present to people in a way which they can understand. Through participation in rituals which make the Good and the True present to the senses in Beauty, and which engage the worshipper in symbolic acts which order them to the first principle, people become habituated at a deeper level, embracing service to the cosmos not just as an obligation, but as something attractive. Active participation in a community dedicated to the τελος and led by people who can help others work through the obstacles to the development of virtue 'disciplines' them in a way which is at once less formal and more profound than the external force of the law. Thus the task of the *priestly* authority, which has the task of developing the appetites and of exercising the right of *sanctification*.[19]

Someone, finally, must know the End which is aimed at, and the more people participate in discerning this End, and the better prepared they are for that participation, the deeper and more profound a society's understanding of that End. Thus the centrality of the *philosophical authority* which exercises the right of *magisterium*, or the teaching authority. This is not primarily a right to regulate or censor teaching but rather a responsibility to seek the Truth, and to cultivate the ability to seek the Truth on the part of the people as a whole.

Operating together the political, priestly and philosophical authorities secure the ordering of human society to the Good, and thus our participation as a species in the self-organizing activity of the universe.

---

[18] This may seem like a rather quaint term to use, and hardly appropriate to an ethics which claims to be interested in liberation. We use it, however, by preference to the term more usually employed in this context: that is, sovereignty. As Jacques Maritain points out, this term implies a radical transcendence of the ruler *vis-à-vis* the ruled, as well as a lack of accountability to a higher principle or power. This is neither right nor possible. Political rulers are never sovereign in fact because they are part of the system that they govern. This is especially true of 'the people', in whom most democratic theory attempts to invest sovereignty. And they are always accountable, if only to history. Political rulers ought not to be 'sovereign' because, as we are in the process of demonstrating, political decisions must always be made in accord with cosmic law. Dominion, on the other hand, does not imply transcendence *vis-à-vis* the system governed, and is not unaccountable. It merely implies the authority to make final decisions regarding resource allocation.

[19] It should be noted that this right, like the others, is founded originally quite apart from revelation. When we address the question of revelation and revealed truth in Chapter 7 we will see that the philosophical authority is completed by the prophetic authority which grasps truths beyond demonstration, and that the priestly authority takes on a new importance, since revealed truth is something we know *primarily* by habituation, by living it, rather than by an act of discursive reason, though there is a place for this as well, in the discipline of theology. Similarly, the task of organizing resources to make possible the ordering of individuals and societies to the revealed Truth, and of exercising discipline with respect to the revealed Good in the external forum requires the constitution of a *pastoral authority* with its own specific rights and duties which grow out of but exceed those of the priestly office in general.

Conclusions

The extraordinary power of transcendental abstraction should by now be apparent. Transcendental abstraction makes possible:

1 the ascent of the intellect to a first principle of explanation, which can show the universe to be not only an order, but also an organization, a system ordered to an end, and thus ultimately meaningful;
2 proof of the existence of God, as well as a meaningful if limited reflection on the divine nature; and
3 an ethical theory which provides real guidance to human action, and which allows us to give some real content to the ideas of human excellence and social justice.

Given this extraordinary power, the question naturally arises whether or not transcendental abstraction is not perhaps sufficient to order us to the ends of human life – or if it is not, whether those ends are, tragically, ultimately unattainable, as the human mind, located as it were 'just a little bit lower than the angels' over-reaches itself, aspiring to goods which it cannot achieve. This impression may be particularly strong given what we have said about the relationship between the salvation religions and the philosophical tradition: that is, that philosophy, building as it does on formalization, in a sense offers *more* than the salvation religions, which are unable by themselves to offer arguments for their claims or to defend themselves against the scepticism generated by the market system.

A complete answer to this question will have to wait until Chapter 7, where we will attempt to demonstrate the possibility, necessity and reasonableness of revelation. For now we will confine ourselves to a determination of the limits of transcendental abstraction.

These limits are, essentially, three. The knowledge we have of God through transcendental abstraction is, first of all, indistinct. This means that although we *can* conclude with certainty to a first principle which at once grounds and completes scientific explanation, we cannot then turn around, and by analysis of the idea of God, derive the universe as a logical system. This is not because it isn't such a system. On the contrary, it is in this way precisely which God knows the universe, and patchwork deductions of this kind are possible even for us. But, as we noted above, such deductions are prone to grave error and the conclusions we arrive at on such a basis are gross approximations at best. The difficulty here is not just that, as in the case of formal abstraction, we may be making simplifying assumptions, so that our principle does not correspond exactly to the reality it claims to describe. With transcendental abstraction we must also contend with the fact that the principles in question are not 'clear and distinct' and thus do not permit of a univocal chain of deductions. This is why when one reads metaphysics and philosophical cosmology one is often confronted with two interpretations of essentially identical principles, which are both reasonable but which tend towards entirely opposing conclusions. Because of this we need to be very careful about what we claim for systems of the sort attempted by Hegel. Systematic philosophy grounded in transcendental abstraction can display in a synthetic manner, in a way studies in the special sciences cannot even if they make use of transcendental abstraction, the marvellous organization of the universe as it is drawn into Being by the incredible Beauty, Truth, Goodness and Integrity of God. They can never be complete or final and definitive.

The same thing must be said for ethical theory. Ethics understood as a deductive science drawing its principles from transcendental abstraction can provide answers to certain broad questions, but it must never become the sole or even the principle criterion of decision-making, which depends rather on the ability to grasp the latent potential in a given situation and discover the means to its realization – that is, on the virtue of prudence rather than wisdom.

Second, the knowledge of God that we have in transcendental abstraction is indistinct precisely because it is a finite take on the infinite. This means that no matter how profound our mastery of the philosophical disciplines, we barely begin to scratch the surface of what there is to know about God – and indeed about the universe which, even if it were itself to be finite in space and time, nonetheless exists in an infinity of relations to the divine Beauty, Truth and Goodness. Transcendental abstraction can only whet our appetite for a knowledge of God which it cannot provide.

The finiteness of transcendental abstraction is, third, intimately bound up with its character as an expression of our aspirations. Transcendental abstraction concludes to God as the Truth which answers our questions, and indeed which grounds our answers to our questions. It concludes to God as our Good, as the principle which alone can fulfil our aspirations and the desire for which in fact draws us out of the nothingness of mere possibility into Being. This indeed is philosophy's power and its grandeur, but it is also its gravest danger. 'Our Truth' and 'our Good' can be understood in two senses – as something final, an end in itself, or as a means to some still higher Truth and higher Good. To put the matter in concrete terms, it is the difference between developing our capacities in order to be able to produce more and therefore consume more, enjoying the fruits of our labour as an end in themselves, or consuming in order to be able to develop our capacities and thus add ever more to the organization of the universe. The human good – as the good of co-creators with God – is by its very nature ordered to a higher Good. The difficulty is that knowledge of this Good exceeds our natural cognitive capacities. There is thus a danger that, grounding ourselves only in philosophical knowledge of God, of God as 'our Good', we will fall into a kind of high-order consumerism. Similarly, at the cognitive level, knowledge of God as 'our Truth' may all too easily degenerate into an attempt to enclose God in concepts which are inadequate to Her, to make Her work for us as an auxiliary principle, rather than drawing us ever deeper into Her Truth which at once grounds and transcends our own.

From here the slope is slippery indeed. Inevitably we realize that our attempts at explanation, while not without merit, are incomplete and often wrong even when they are powerful. Inevitably we discover, through hard experience, that the realization of God as our Good does not mean that the universe is ordered to us, and we will gradually become bitter and lose even our natural knowledge of God, falling into cynicism and despair. A similar phenomenon occurs on the collective level, and is apparent in the tendency of purely secular, philosophical doctrines of justice to rapidly lose their emphasis on the full development of human social capacities and the service of humanity to the cosmo-historical evolutionary process – even when they affirm the existence of God and the ultimate meaningfulness of the universe. Thus the degeneration of Radical Aristotelianism into a secularizing liberalism; thus the crisis of socialism.

Because of its ordering to the first principle, human nature requires the completion which can come to its natural knowledge and love only through supernatural revelation and the pursuit of a supernatural justice. This is why, perhaps, the only place that one can find genuine philosophy being done – that is, an authentic attempt to rise to the first principle by rational means – is in contexts where the possibility and necessity of revealed truth is also acknowledged. It is to the question of such revealed Truth that we must now turn.

Chapter 7

Revelation and Faith, Mysticism, Prophecy and Theological Wisdom

The Act of Superabstraction

Up to now we have focused on that knowledge of God which is possible on the basis of human reason alone and have held to one side the question of revelation and faith, mysticism, prophecy and theological wisdom. Indeed our only mention of faith has been in the context of a general willingness to believe that the universe is in fact meaningful, as a precondition for the intellectual and moral disciplines which make speculative and connatural knowledge possible. This has been intentional. We live in an age which is suspicious of reason and my principal purpose has been to validate its powers and to demonstrate that even forms of religious knowledge which are primarily non-philosophical – such as the Jewish *da'ath elohim* – are still eminently rational and involve an authentic exercise of human cognitive capacities. Our account would be incomplete, however, without a consideration of those forms of religious knowledge which claim to transcend the capacities of finite human reason – and of their relationship to the ordinary exercise of transcendental abstraction.

There is a certain sense, of course, in which all knowledge is a product of divine revelation. What we know is, first and foremost, what is present – and thus presented to us – by a universe which we have now shown to be grounded in a principle which is infinitely Beautiful, True, Good and One, and which is thus (among other things) personal in a sense which radically transcends the finite and limited personality we encounter in ourselves and other finite intelligent systems.[1] And it is presented *first*, before we appropriate it through the senses and the intellect, so that the authentic creativity of these faculties in the production of knowledge does not in any way compromise the radical liberty of the divine act of self-presentation through the cosmos.

To point this out is not just to draw out a minor conclusion of the foregoing argument. It tells us something very important about what revealed knowledge is *not*. It is not knowledge in which the activity of the sense and intellect is wholly repressed and humanity adopts an attitude of radical passivity before the divine, for even in 'natural' knowledge the element of divine self-presentation always and only precedes the act

---

[1] The question of the personal character of the first principle, while a stumbling block for some philosophically inclined individuals who are put off by what they regard as 'story-book' images of God, is in fact quite easily resolved. That the first principle is a personal God follows necessarily from the conclusion that the first principle is infinite. To deny personality is to place a limit. It is, furthermore, difficult to see how a principle identified as Beauty, Truth, Goodness and the One *as such* could possibly be impersonal when even limited participations in these transcendentals such as ourselves show evidence of this perfection.

of human cognition. Nor does 'revealed' knowledge pertain to some object which is, in its nature, fundamentally different from the knowledge we have discussed in earlier chapters. On the contrary, we have already seen that transcendental abstraction has as its object the αρχη itself, as infinitely Beautiful, True, Good and One, as personal, that is, as God. Beyond this there is no higher object, though there is indeed a higher knowledge of this same object, as well as of the lesser finite objects which present themselves to sense and intellect.

We call knowledge 'revealed' or 'supernatural' rather, because it transcends the capacity of our natural human faculties of sensation and abstraction. It is a different and superior way of knowing the same objects we know on the basis of sense and human intellect, a way which supplies in measured degrees what we have already shown to be lacking in the knowledge conveyed by transcendental abstraction. The knowledge of God which we have in transcendental abstraction is indirect and by inference, and it does not present to us an authentic vision of the divine essence, in the way we 'see' intellectually the essence of a triangle or a tetrahedron. The knowledge which we have called revealed or supernatural is, on the other hand, in progressive degrees ever more direct and converges on the vision of the divine essence which we call the beatific vision because it alone renders us truly satisfied and truly blessed.

But is such a knowledge really possible? Can we see God? It would seem, at first glance, that the answer would be no. This is not because of any limitation on God's side. God already presents Herself to us in Her totality and in Her essence; this divine presence is nothing other than the αρχη and τελος which is visible in every object and which shines so clearly through our intellectual vision of the cosmos as an organized totality. And indeed, once we have shown that the αρχη is infinite, we can no longer predicate of it any limitation, including limitations on its capacity for self-presentation. The difficulty, rather, is on our side, the side of the human knower. For it is not clear how a finite system can comprehend one that is infinite. It would seem that God's infinite, free and generous self-revelation notwithstanding, our knowledge of God is limited to what philosophy can achieve. From this point of view, all purported 'revelation' is at best an imaginative figure of truths known more perfectly by philosophy and, at worst, mere charlatanism.

There is an important truth in this point of view. Much of what presents itself in religious texts as a higher revealed knowledge is, in fact, fully within the reach of ordinary human sense and intellect. And no finite system can ever validate a direct experience of the divine *as* divine. This is because it would take an infinite period of time to complete the experience and thus validate the claim that the object is in fact divine. The existence of God can be shown only indirectly, through the cosmological and teleological arguments that we validated in Chapter 6. Everything we have said and are going to say about the possibility and reasonableness of revelation depends on those arguments. In this sense *theology*, or reasoned discourse on revealed knowledge, is wholly dependent on philosophy, as is the prophet or mystic who takes seriously the responsibility to demonstrate that he is not merely mad. The content of revelation, furthermore, remains forever beyond rational demonstration – though one can, of course, show that it does not contradict reason and that it helps us to live more effectively.

This said, however, we want to suggest that it is possible for humans to rise to a knowledge which is, in fact, superhuman. In order to understand how this is possible, we need to remind ourselves that the problem of abstraction already presented us with what have seemed to many like insuperable difficulties. We had among other things to show how intellectual knowledge was possible for a material system such as an individual human being. We will recall that for Aristotle and his followers this was a difficult problem. Knowledge involves taking on the form of the thing known. It is not hard to see how the form of the body might be modified by data collected by the external senses, leading to the formation of images and the like. But it was hard to see how the form of the body could be modified by immaterial forms. Thus the emergence of the idea of a single Agent Intellect and, in the more radical forms of the doctrine, of a single passive intellect as well, which was wholly immaterial and was shared by all humans who remained, in effect, at the level of high-order data collectors for this collective intelligence. The difficulty is that this failed to explain why different individuals have not only different sensations, but also different ideas. We resolved the problem with the notion of the social intellect, which is at once collective and differentiated, both in the sense that the social structures in which individuals participate vary across geohistorical space and time, and in the sense that it is internalized differently in the course of the socialization process. We showed, in effect, that intellectual knowledge already depends on something which is supra-individual if not superhuman. Knowledge is an integral part of the cosmic dynamism which draws matter out of itself, calling it to become more than it is, to participate in and gradually to become the life of the spirit.

We propose to solve the problem of 'revealed' or superhuman knowledge in much the same way. Human society, after all, is not the only reality higher than ourselves in which we participate. On the contrary, human societies are embedded in a hierarchy of higher-order cosmo-historical evolutionary processes, a hierarchy which, in the light of the argument in Chapter 6, we know to be infinite and to terminate only in God. This hierarchy of processes and its terminus are also structured – the terminus, in fact, is the principle which defines all structure, and can thus also illuminate the images which we garner from experience in much the same way as the social intellect. This experience of participation in a trans-social, trans-historical reality gives rise, furthermore, to definite structures in society – religious institutions – which mediate that experience to the social systems in which they are embedded. 'Revelation' and other forms of supernatural religious knowledge, like all other knowledge of intelligibles, thus results from an abstraction – or what, for the sake of clarity, we will call superabstraction – from our sense experience. It is just that the abstracting agent is not merely human (the society) but rather superhuman and ultimately divine. Or, to put the matter differently, our participation in the structured totality of the cosmos, a totality which we have already shown to be ordered to God, provides the basis in experience for 'seeing' patterns which are not accessible on the basis of ordinary (total, formal and transcendental) abstraction grounded in ordinary social experience.

The question, of course, is just how this works. It is important to stress that revelation is no more a divine 'illumination' of the human intellect, in which the intellect is basically passive, than is ordinary intellectual knowledge. On the contrary, just like ordinary intellectual knowledge, revelation depends on connaturality and the sensation and abstraction it makes possible. By participating in certain definite social structures we become connatural with those structures and know them pre-conceptually. It is this pre-conceptual, connatural knowledge which then illuminates the images which we garner from experience. Similarly, by participating in certain 'supersocial' structures, we become connatural with *those* structures and know *them* pre-conceptually. It is *this* pre-conceptual, connatural knowledge which then illuminates the images which we garner from experience, resulting in what we call revealed knowledge.

What is somewhat more difficult is the task of specifying the precise nature of these 'supersocial' structures and of providing a method for distinguishing between them and the purely human social structures which make possible ordinary intellectual knowledge. In order to get at this question we need to recall that even our ordinary intellectual knowledge of God was grounded in a very specific social reality: the reality of the just act. It is in the just act that we have the pre-conceptual *da'ath elohim*, the connatural knowledge of God, which makes possible the rise to transcendental abstraction. The same is true at the 'supernatural' or 'supersocial' level, but now the justice in question is of a qualitatively higher degree. The ordinary knowledge we have of God through (transcendental) abstraction is only of God in relation to the universe, not of God in Herself. We know God in the mirror of natural beauty, not as Beauty itself, as a principle which helps us to explain the universe, not as the Truth itself, as our supreme good and not as the Good itself. And the divine *esse* and unity seem merely requirements of logic, themselves forever shrouded in darkness. Because of this our natural love of God is, in a certain sense, love of God as a means. We love God because She is our creator, the principle of our existence and the condition for the full development and exercise of our capacities. This kind of love is not to be disparaged. It is not sinful or even selfish. It is, on the contrary right and just – the part of justice which Thomas calls the virtue of religion. But it is not love of God for Her own sake, and it will not satisfy us. This is because, however noble the human condition, it is ordered to higher ends and those who love it as the highest good will inevitably be frustrated when they learn, as we all inevitably do, that the universe is not in fact structured to serve us. Only a love which loves the highest Good for its own sake will leave us at peace with a universe which is ordered to that Good and with our place therein. Revealed knowledge of God presupposes a love of God which is not merely a drive towards the realization of our own already comprehended dynamic of development (though it always also remains that) but a love of God which draws us into a dynamic of development which we do not yet understand, and which we do not yet, therefore, experience as our own. It presupposes a 'supernatural connaturality' with God.

Let us look at a couple of examples. *'El yahwi sabaoth yisrael*, God known through natural connaturality as the condition of the people's liberation, is recognized by the ordinary transcendental abstraction which arises on the basis of this connaturality as Being itself, the first principle of explanation and of action, the $\alpha\rho\chi\eta$ and $\tau\epsilon\lambda o\varsigma$ of the universe and of human life. But as the struggle for justice passes over into a pursuit of something which transcends any merely human development, we achieve a supernatural connaturality with God, and on the basis of this advance to the 'superabstraction' of revelation – to a wordless knowledge beyond all concepts, a knowledge of the great Unnameable-Bringing-Into-Being, which at once awakens and satisfies the deepest and most burning fires of love.

What happens here is that the will is formed by habituation, at first simply to the struggle for justice, as a means to the realization of one's own latent potential and that of the people to whom one is connected. But as one participates in this struggle, it becomes clear that often, from an individual standpoint, more is lost than is gained. And this experience is not just individual. It is collective as well. No sooner had the people of Israel recognized the hand of God in their amazing victories over enemies which far outmatched them in terms of military might, than that hand was withdrawn, or extended in ways that seemed directed to some end other than their own temporal well-being. It is at this point that one realizes that the struggle isn't about me, that it isn't even about us, if indeed it is about anything at all, and that any attempt to name what it is about, while necessary and even, within limits, satisfying, risks limiting its scope in a way which will inevitably lead to idolatry and disappointment. The struggle is about this Unnameable-Bringing-Into-Being which we experience in being called each and every day to become more than we are and which we learn to discover as much in the disappointments as in the successes, as these point us towards an ever deeper appreciation of divine nature. It is in this way that the divine name, יהוה, is revealed.

In this sense, it is quite correct to say that the movement from natural to revealed knowledge of God always involves a negative moment, that for growth towards the higher degrees of the spiritual life the *via negativa* is indispensable. In following the light we are always and only drawn into what at first seems like darkness. Gradually, to be sure, we become habituated to this new and more subtle light, and learn a free and easy love for the objects it reveals to us. But even so, if we are not to stagnate, we are always and only called to move on, to penetrate ever deeper into mysteries which are deeper and harder and which stretch us until we become, ever so gradually, something more than merely human. This is the significance of the 'dark nights' of which John of the Cross speaks and of which all authentic mystics are deeply and profoundly aware.

Similar dynamics can be found in other traditions. Thus the *Magna Mater*, symbolic expression of humanity's enduring faith in the ultimate meaningfulness of the universe, is not only the alluring maiden and nurturing mother, but also the Crone, who reminds us that in time we must let go of all finite goods – including our own life and even our personal identity – if we are to become what we are meant to be, and to know the principle which gave meaning to our lives and our identities in the first place. Thus the transition in Indian religion from the Vedic cults centred in inner-worldly goods to the later Buddhist and Hindu focus on transcending the ego. And in China the Tao appears both as a principle the partial comprehension of which can help us achieve finite, worldly aims, and as a Way which far transcends all such aims, which it ultimately washes over in pursuit of its own mysterious End, which is also our own.

One note of caution is in order. This higher love to which we are called and in which we are schooled by the trials and tribulations of living out our vocation to justice is not a self-sacrificial love and it is not pitted against the natural desire to realize our own potential. It merely exceeds it. It is a dedication to life which runs over the limits of our own finite living and finds rest only in the living God. Negativity is never an end in itself; there is no merit in continuing to follow in darkness when light and comprehension are within our reach.

This danger is greatest in Christianity, which has historically focused on the Cross as the principal locus for the revelation of a divine justice which transcends mere human fulfilment. Israel was seeking liberation from Rome; Jesus (the story goes) demanded that his disciples take up the Cross. But this focus on the Cross is very dangerous and can give rise to the gravest spiritual and political disorders. If we pit the Cross against our own struggle for liberation and development, we can be deceived into believing that loving God means hating ourselves and all of our finite gifts and aspirations, hating them even to the point of death – even, if we follow out the logic of this kind of Christianity, as Samuel Hopkins did, to the point of eternal damnation.[2] The result is that we end up hating everybody and everything and thus hating God as well. And hatred, as we know, has definite political consequences. It is precisely in those times and places where Christianity has become most focused on self-sacrificial love that its capacity for violence has been greatest. And the victims of this violence have, more often than not, been the Jews. Israel's own insights into the way in which divine justice at once includes and transcends our own are obscured and, in the Christian imagination, the Jews are transformed into those who uphold justice over love, human liberation and development over God's mysterious plan for humanity. The religion of *self*-sacrifice paves the way for a Holocaust of Christianity's Other.

The authentic meaning of the Cross can be understood only in the context of Israel's long history of struggle and long history of tribulations. It has meaning only for those who, like Mary, hoped that in this new human being which God was drawing forth from Her, He really did mean to 'cast down monarchs from their thrones and lift the humble high, fill the hungry with good things and send the rich away empty' (Luke 1: 52–3), and who like the disciples on the road to Emmaus really did 'hope that he [Jesus] would be the one to liberate Israel' (Luke 24: 21). And it has meaning only if we continue to believe that these are legitimate – no, Holy – aims. To those who shared these hopes, and who were close to Jesus of Nazareth, the Cross may indeed have seemed like the culmination of Israel's tribulations, and the Resurrection like the vindication of her millennium of struggle. But to suggest this after the horrors of the Jewish war, much less the Shoah, is nothing short of blasphemous. The Cross is legitimately central for Christians because and only because it is through Jesus of Nazareth that we came to share the light of the Law and the Prophets – and because the crucifixion of Jesus thus serves *for Christians* as a reminder of the same lesson which Israel has learned better and more often than others have: that God is calling us to a higher Justice than we can know except in doing it and which, therefore, we cannot name.

> And further, I tell you this in very truth: when you were young you fastened your belt about you and walked where you chose; but when you are old you will stretch out your arms and a stranger will bind you fast and carry you where you have no wish to go. (John 21: 18–19)

And the Cross has meaning, of course, only in the light of the Resurrection. However tortuous the path and difficult the journey on which God leads us – even if that journey leads through death, as it inevitably does – our love of life will carry us beyond the

---

[2] Samuel Hopkins, an important late eighteenth-century Reformed theologian, was a student of Jonathan Edwards and one of the founders of the abolitionist movement in the United States. He taught that only those who were willing to be damned for the greater glory of God had sufficient evidence of their salvation to be admitted to full communion in the Church. Needless to say he found himself pastoring a very small congregation.

term of our finite living into a future in which it will, somehow, in a way we cannot completely understand, be vindicated. And we know this in living out our vocation to justice, through all the pain and disappointment, so that living can never be a sacrifice but only a higher joy.

This, then, is at least a partial answer to the question of how we distinguish supersocial structures from merely social structures – how we tell if the structure with which we are becoming connatural makes possible just ordinary intellectual knowledge, or something deeper and more profound – something superhuman and 'revealed'. But it is only a partial answer – an answer that will, with some further elaboration later in this chapter, allow us to specify the nature of original revelation and its correlate, the prophetic office, as well as to outline the nature of infused contemplation and theological wisdom.

Everyone who travels the road of life has experiences which begin to stretch them beyond their merely human capacities, and to awaken within them their potential for the divine – though some do more with these experiences than others, and some, frankly, seem to be born further along on the road to begin with. And like our natural, human struggles, these experiences are reflected in the institutions we build, and especially in those institutions in and through which we come together to reflect on the ultimate meaningfulness of the universe: that is, religious institutions.

The religious institution presents to its members certain truths of such depth that no human understands them completely and that beginners may take only on faith, and then asks them to live these truths – that is, to love the objects they reveal and to act on that love – thus setting in motion a habituation to supernatural acts of justice which makes possible connaturality with the supersocial and ultimately divine structures of the universe. These truths may be presented directly through teaching or indirectly through the objects of the liturgy. The first way of presenting truth is an exercise of the *magisterium*, which we discussed in Chapter 6, but now at the level of supernatural, revealed Truth. The second way of presenting truth is an exercise of *sanctification*, again at the level of revealed truth. Third, the religious institution, through pastoral leadership which challenges and supports people in their private and public lives, helps them to interpret loss and tribulation in a way which makes it a real opening to higher Truth, rather than an occasion for falling into despair. This is an exercise of *dominion*[3] at the supernatural level, in that it claims people – including their talent and resources – for God's justice. In this sense the religious institution is the trace of the supersocial within the social, making participation in the supersocial more accessible, and concentrating in one place an important part, at least, of humanity's accumulated wisdom regarding it.

The Degrees of Superabstraction

With this basic account of how revelation occurs and is passed on, we are now in a position to analyse in some greater depth the various degrees and forms of supernatural knowledge. The foregoing analysis should already have made it clear that the beginning of revelation and of supernatural knowledge is always and only in faith. By faith we

---

[3] For a general discussion of the rights of magisterium, sanctification and dominion consult Chapter 6.

mean first and foremost a willingness to believe, in at least a tentative and preliminary way, truths which are being presented to the sense or the intellect, whether by experience or by the teaching or liturgical activity of some religious institution, but which are, at least initially, beyond demonstration or even understanding. Faith is that 'thinking with assent' (Aquinas, *Summa Theologiae* II, Q 2 a1) which alone makes it possible for us to love and act on love which is already more than human. For unless an object is 'known' in at least the rudimentary way that faith makes possible – unless we are at least aware of it, and believe it to be real, though at first without understanding – we cannot love it (Aquinas, *Summa Theologiae* II, Q 4 a7).

A few words of caution are in order here. First, we should reiterate that the necessity of faith in the journey towards knowledge is not peculiar to supernatural or revealed knowledge; on the contrary, we believe in the quantum theory long before we understand it well enough to be able to demonstrate that it actually does a half-way decent job of explaining the properties of the various chemical elements. It is just that because the revealed truths are so much more difficult the darkness of faith lasts longer and understanding does not penetrate to the point of comprehension and thus demonstration – at least not until we achieve the beatific vision. Second, as truths, the claims presented to faith can never contradict reason, though they may at times stretch our understanding of reason and display to us new and deeper dimensions of rationality. But on the road to supernatural knowledge we are never required to embrace propositions which violate the rules of logic or which contradict good science. If there appears to be a contradiction then we need to re-examine both the claims presented to faith and our logic and/or science. One or the other (or perhaps both) are clearly in error.

What faith does is to set us on the path of supernatural acts of justice which make it possible for us to actually begin to understand revealed truth – and to understand the universe generally, and human history in particular, in the light of that truth. These acts of supernatural justice make us connatural with the deepest and most profound supersocial structures of the universe and create the basis in experience for penetrating intellectually mysteries which, to begin with, we only believed. And the very act of remaining in faith, in so far as it is an act not only of the intellect, but also of the will (a willingness to believe) is already also an act of justice, and because it stretches us beyond the merely human, an act of supernatural justice. In this sense, Aquinas was wrong to argue that it is possible to have faith without charity, which is simply supernatural justice, but quite correct to point out that faith is never wholly without understanding. It is precisely the justice of faith that creates in us the connaturality with God which is necessary to begin to understand the divine mysteries. And as we are stretched to perform acts of supernatural justice, we develop the capacity to judge rightly regarding the first cause – what the Catholic tradition calls the gift of 'caritative wisdom' – and to judge worldly, and especially political matters, in the light of their larger spiritual significance – what the Catholic tradition historically called the gift of knowledge (Aquinas, *Summa Theologiae* II-II, Q 8, 9, 45; Maritain 1937; Garrigou-Lagrange 1938).

What has traditionally been called infused contemplation of the kind practised by the great mystics, as well as what has been called prophecy, is not really anything other than the exercise, with a particular degree of excellence and intensity – and, in the case of the prophet, of originality – of these capacities rooted in a supernatural connaturality with God. Indeed, the only difference between the ordinary person of understanding, knowledge and wisdom, and the mystic is that the latter has learned the lessons of the 'dark night' more fully, and thus been drawn more deeply into the revealed mysteries, whereas in their ordinary degree the exercise of these gifts is attenuated by a persistent tendency, in struggling to safeguard our humanity from the very real dangers to which we are exposed in the course of the dark night, to resist being stretched as well as to resist being broken. Where most enjoy only rare moments of deep understanding of and/or union with God, the mystic enjoys these fruits of the exercise of Her gifts with constancy and regularity (Garrigou-Lagrange 1938: 75).

The exercise of our supernatural intellectual capacities is 'prophetic' when it results in fundamentally new insights regarding the divine nature, or regarding the nature of the universe generally, and human history in particular. What the beginning believer takes on faith, and what the mystic understands, the prophet discovers for the first time. The prophet is, in other words, the site of original revelation, which takes place not through his or her power but rather through the power of the supersocial structures in which the prophet, like the mystic, has come to participate through supernaturally just action, and which illuminate his experience in a way which reveals for the first time fundamentally new truths about God and the universe, truths which are too profound to be proven by finite human reason, but which are not less but rather more certain than the truths of science and philosophy.

This original revelation may take place in either of two ways. It may be either imaginative or intellectual. Imaginative prophecy has the same relation to intellectual prophecy as the fine arts have to philosophy. Now we have already seen, in Chapter 6 that the fine arts, at least if they are actually fine, produce beauty; they are, in a certain sense, already posterior to the act of transcendental abstraction – to the transcendental judgement of Beauty, Truth, or Goodness and to the vision of Being that judgement makes possible. It is just that rather than forming, on the basis of that vision, a concept from which deductions and demonstrations can be made, the artist returns to the realm of the imagination, and forms an image (or more properly a complex of images) the inter-relations between which convey (if they are truly fine art) Beauty at the very least, and very often, in the case of literature and certain of the visual arts, a specific discursive content as well. Thus the images of human beings in Diego Rivera's *Lucha de las Clases* are not merely images of human beings, but an inter-related complex which is beautiful, and since beauty is a window on the truth, also conveys a certain truth – that is, a specific interpretation of the history of humanity. The characters of Dostoevsky's *Brothers Karamazov* are not merely imaginary humans; their inter-relations convey definite psychological and theological claims. Interpretation of the work of art releases this intellectual content, and would be quite impossible if the content were not already there, whether the artist was aware of it at a conceptual level or not.

What imaginative prophecy does is to return from a vision of the divine nature, or of human affairs in the light of the divine nature and, rather than attempting a conceptual formulation, to create a complex of images which attempts to convey the prophetic insight. These images are usually cast in the medium of language. Thus Isaiah's account of his vision of יהוה seated on a throne, surrounded by six-winged seraphim, thus John's vision of the beast, and of the woman clothed with the sun. The images may, however, be communicated in any medium. Joachim's figures of the three ages, for example, constitute a kind of 'painted prophecy' as does the image of *Nuestra Señora de Guadalupe* – however the image itself came about. The prophet may or may not be aware of the role of his own poetic activity in the way the vision is communicated. In other words, the prophet may or may not be aware that she is creating images in order to convey a truth known on the basis of supernatural intellectual capacities, and that the image is no more the Truth itself than are the images of a secular artist. This all depends on the prophet's grasp of the complex relations between intellect and imagination in artistic creativity. That the prophet may be unaware of this distinction, that he actually believes he saw a figure like a human on a throne surrounded by strange six-winged beasts, that indeed he may actually have seen such a vision, implies neither that this is what God actually is, nor that the prophet in question is no prophet at all but rather a superstitious fool. It merely implies a certain lack of theoretical sophistication, or perhaps a lack of concern with certain epistemological distinctions. It means that the prophet is not also a philosopher. And it means, of course, that the prophecy must be interpreted, that its intellectual content must be released as in the case of any poetic creation, all the while keeping in mind that if the prophecy is authentic, the truth in question will exceed any possible philosophical formulation just as it exceeds its own imaginative form.[4]

Intellectual prophecy, on the other hand, returns from the vision of the divine nature, or of human affairs in the light of the divine nature, and forms a concept, generally out of philosophical language which is already available at hand, though sometimes simply out of ordinary language, thereby also inaugurating a new philosophical vocabulary. The best examples of intellectual prophecy is the revelation of the divine name, יהוה. But much of Buddhist doctrine is also highly intellectual and would fall into this category.

We must not be deceived by the abstract, often extremely rigorously defined character of the concepts used in intellectual prophecy. This does not mean that in hearing the prophecy we comprehend the divine nature. On the contrary, already at the level of ordinary transcendental abstraction, we saw that the truth we were attempting to formulate so far exceeds the capacity of our language that deductions from such concepts as God, Being, the transcendentals and so on, were at best mere approximations and at worst highly dangerous. This is even more true at the level of intellectual prophecy, where the same limited language is being used to capture even more profound truths.

---

[4] This is an extremely important point. The imaginative character of most prophecy has led many philosophers – Ibn Rushd, for example, and Hegel – to regard religion generally as a kind of picture-language which states philosophic truths in imaginative language which is more accessible to the philosophically untutored. The implication is that philosophy is always superior to prophecy, because it understands what prophecy only imagines or represents. Now it must be acknowledged that *some* of the content of prophetic discourse falls into this category. This does not, however, mean that it all does; the fact that there are revealed truths which do not contradict logic or science, and which illuminate our lives and experience, but which cannot be proven is enough to validate this claim. A distinction must be made between a truth and its form. The intellectual or philosophical expression of a truth is always superior to its imaginative representation, because it opens the way to proof if this is possible, and allows us to penetrate closer to the essence of the truth even if it is not. This does not mean, however, that philosophy is always superior to imaginative prophecy. It is quite possible for a higher, supernatural truth, to be presented in a lower, imaginative form.

Sometimes prophecy integrates both intellectual and imaginative elements. This is often a result of inspired attempts to make sense out of imaginative prophecy. A good example of this is the doctrine of the Incarnation and the related doctrine of Mary as *Theotokos*, or God-bearer. The notion that God is born out of humanity, indeed out of woman, has profound supernatural intellectual content; the formulation in terms of one particular historical woman and one particular historical man reflects an imaginative residue. Most of the other Marian doctrines have a similar character.

We should note that prophecy may concern either the divine nature itself or the universe generally (and human affairs in particular), and may be either theoretical or practical in orientation – or both. The revelation of the divine name, יהוה, concerns the divine nature. The doctrine of creation and prophetic critiques of social injustice or prophetic announcements of a messianic age concern, respectively, the universe generally and human affairs in particular.

At times new prophetic insights and new errors arise simultaneously, and are almost inextricably bound up with each other in the prophetic text itself. This was especially true at the origin of Christianity. The foundation here remains the revelation of the divine name, something which we have said was grounded first of all in Israel's experience of struggle for its own liberation, and more specifically in the experience of struggle leading Israel into a deeper and more profound supernatural justice which included but also transcended the struggle for liberation and human development. Knowing יהוה experientially and connaturally, and understanding that this means that the entire universe is grounded in a great Unnameable-Bringing-Into-Being which includes but also washes over our own historical aspirations with an overwhelming tide of creative energy, we are also able to judge that Israel is the Chosen People and will not only be redeemed by God and live in peace in the land of Israel, in accord with the covenants, but will also become a light to nations, a centre from which the divine law is made effective throughout the earth, and will carry humanity forward to a future which it cannot even begin to comprehend. The action of the Jewish diaspora in making the light of the Law accessible to the nations opens up for the first time the possibility of a universal just state – what Philo of Alexandria called the 'cosmopolis'.

At the same time, the peoples of the Mediterranean basin to whom the Jewish diaspora brought knowledge of the Law had their own historic religion – the cult of the *Magna Mater*, which conserved humanity's archaic knowledge of the ultimate meaningfulness of the universe against the corrosive impact of the warlord state and the petty-commodity, slave-based economy of the Hellenistic-Roman era. And this cult, too, was grounded in justice – a justice which, if followed through to the end, through the tribulations which it inevitably required, eventually surpassed itself in a supernatural justice which made possible a supernatural knowledge of God – or, to be more precise, of the ultimate meaningfulness of the universe. And in what more profound way could the universe be ordered to God, than to actually bring God forth from itself? As these two traditions flowed together, something which was already beginning to happen before the time of Jesus, and which accelerated rapidly after the birth of Christianity, powerful new prophetic images were created. Thus the doctrine of the Incarnation, and the doctrine which was the historic occasion of the great debates around the Incarnation – the doctrine of Mary as *Theotokos* or God-bearer – as Mother of God.

Yet social disintegration also, inevitably, produces despair and alienation – even at the locus of a prophetic insight. Thus the assertion, which we see especially in Paul, that neither the Law nor Wisdom can save us, and that salvation is possible only through faith in the Crucified Christ. The emerging doctrine of the Incarnation, which is at base a recognition of humanity's extraordinary participation in the life of God, is turned upside down and becomes an instrument for teaching despair about humanity and human social capacities – a teaching which reaches its full form in Augustine, as the social injustice of the early empire becomes the global social disintegration of the late empire.

Problems of Interpretation and Theological Method

This approach to understanding revelation does, to be sure, place a heavy burden on the task of interpreting prophecy. Under no circumstances can the prophecy itself, especially in the case of imaginative prophecy but also in the case of intellectual prophecy, be purely and simply identified with the truth. This task of interpreting prophecy, and of trying to make some sense out of revealed truth, falls to the discipline of theology. Theology is the systematic, rational knowledge of God and of the universe which we gain by applying the methods of human science and philosophy to the revealed Truth, using these methods to help us better understand that Truth and, with the greatest care and caution, to draw out new conclusions which shed further light on the subjects in question. This means, first of all, interpreting imaginative prophecy in order to release its intellectual content, and then working on the intellectual content of both imaginative and intellectual prophecy in order to clarify and elaborate.

Our account of the nature of revelation has definite implications for theological method. Theology must begin where revelation does: with the complex social and supersocial structures which make possible human knowledge generally, and knowledge of God in particular. For this reason sociological methods are fundamental to the interpretation of the scriptures and other texts which contain prophetic insights. It is only by identifying the just act which makes transcendental abstraction possible, and the supernatural justice which makes superabstraction possible, that we are able to understand what a prophetic image, or even an intellectual prophecy means. At times this means recognizing the images or the philosophical language in which a prophetic insight is communicated as products of the very social structure which is being challenged or resisted by the prophet rather than as integral to the prophetic insight itself. Thus the depiction of יהוה as a warrior, and therefore as male, is clearly a reflection of the imaginative raw material out of which Jewish prophecy crafted the images which convey its prophetic insights. And this imaginative material was a product of the Canaanite, Egyptian and Mesopotamian warlord states which Israel was challenging in her struggle for liberation. What is new, and what is integral to the prophecy, is the mobilization of the warrior imagery on behalf of a struggle for liberation. Similarly, the images contained in the creation stories which depict the universe as a place of chaos and violence which is always and only contained by divine intervention, were found by Israel ready-made in the Semitic warlord states out of which she emerged, where they reflected an experience of social chaos and disintegration. The prophetic insight consists in displacing these images to the social field which originally produced them: thus the image of the Philistine tide which יהוה turns back when he liberates Israel from this new group of oppressors. That the prophets did not go back and completely clean up their borrowed Mesopotamian cosmology does not make that cosmology, either in its literal, imaginative form, or in its underlying intellectual content, normative for us.

Sociological criticism can, similarly, help us to discriminate between authentic prophecy and religious alienation which, as we have seen, are often bound up together in core religious doctrines, such as that of the Incarnation.

At the same time, our theory guarantees that such sociological criticism, properly practised, will not become reductive. The social structures which we live are a window on reality and the knowledge they produce is real if also limited and sometimes distorted. We have, furthermore, pointed out that human society itself participates in a larger supersocial reality which makes us capable of insights which authentically transcend our natural, human capacities. The divine name, יהוה, can be understood properly only when we realize that it emerged from Israel's struggle for liberation. But this struggle itself is always and already part of a larger cosmo-historical movement towards God which terminates well beyond our field of vision, and which illuminates our experience and reveals to us depths of justice which transcend national liberation and human development. We may reject doctrines of substitutionary atonement born of despair and still see in the crucifixion a reminder that while our struggles are a real participation in the life of God, the universe is not ordered to us but we to it. God does not exist for us; we exist to further the mysterious work of God – a work which sheds some of its mystery only to the extent that we persevere in justice beyond ends we can comprehend towards those we do not yet understand.

Sociological criticism has an especially important role to play with respect to political prophecy. Most political prophecy is extremely concrete, focused and empirical in its immediate import. A specific king is denounced for taking a specific vineyard (1 Kings 21) or, at best, we are presented with a general condemnation of those who 'join house to house and field to field' or who 'publish burdensome decrees' (Isaiah 5: 8, 10: 1). The difficulty is to ascertain what significance this has at a more general level, above and beyond a general admonition against injustice for which we hardly need prophetic advice. In order to make sense out of this very concrete sort of political prophecy we need, first of all, to analyse the systemic context in which it is made. This allows us to see, for example, that what is actually being criticized is an entire mode of production – generally, in the case of prophecy in the Hebrew scriptures, the tributary mode of production in which rents, taxes and forced labour are extracted from dependent peasant communities. We are then also able to see more clearly what is wrong with the cult of *ba'al*, whose name means lord, master, owner – and husband. It is a cult of the warlord and latifundialist, a cult of the rape of the people and the rape of the land. From here, of course, it is still necessary to ascertain *why* this mode of production is being condemned, and whether that ought to lead us to make a similar condemnation of other modes of production.

Generally political prophecy and its proper, sociological interpretation does not really lead us to any political conclusions which we could not have reached on the basis of a purely scientific sociology and a purely philosophical social ethics. Rather, it makes the critique of certain modes of production accessible to people who, for cultural reasons, may be incapable of or sceptical towards philosophy. More important, however, it reminds us that the place in which we are called to grow beyond our merely human preoccupations, beyond the struggle to advance the human civilizational project, the real locus of revelation, is always and only that struggle itself. If we don't meet *El yahwi sabaoth yisrael*, the God who brings into being the armies of Israel, who is the agent of her liberation, we will never meet the יהוה who is this but more, the great Unnameable-Bringing-Into-Being who vindicates our struggles only after calling us to grow beyond them, to realize our humanity in a superhuman destiny which remains forever beyond the horizon of comprehension, but only because it is infinite, and because our knowledge is ever and again rewarded with new questions, and our love with new struggles.

In the course of doing its work, sociological criticism inevitably extracts the intellectual content from prophetic images, and suggests alternative and perhaps more accurate ways to capture the conceptual content of intellectual prophecy. From here theology must turn to the tools of philosophy. Philosophy, like sociological criticism, makes both negative and positive contributions to the understanding of revelation. On the negative side philosophy excludes interpretations of prophecy which conflict with what we know on the basis of our natural, rational capacities. Revelation extends but never contradicts science and philosophy. Thus, for example, interpretations of the creation narratives which regard matter as dead and passive, rather than dynamic and self-organizing, as well as the pessimistic anthropology of someone like Paul, are excluded. The same is true of interpretations of the Incarnation which understand it to mean that one human, Jesus of Nazareth, was at once fully human (and therefore finite) and fully divine (and therefore infinite), something which contradicts the fundamental rules of logic and is thus impossible even for God. Philosophy must, to be sure, be cautious in exercising this negative office on behalf of theology. It must be open to discovering the profound truth which, due to the limitations of human thought and language or the alienating impact of an oppressive social structure, has been communicated under the form of an error, and must always search for ways in which prophetic insights can be interpreted so as not to conflict with reason. On the positive side philosophy makes two contributions. First, it attempts to explain revealed truths – to show how they make sense, and what they might mean, even though it cannot demonstrate them. Thus philosophy explains the positive content of a doctrine like the Incarnation in showing that it represents a supernatural affirmation of humanity's participation in the life of God. Second, philosophy may also attempt to draw conclusions from revealed principles, much as it does from the concepts it achieves through ordinary transcendental abstraction. Here, though, it must be even more careful than it is in metaphysics, since the revealed principles, while more certain than those we know through natural reason, are also less perfectly understood. The lack of clarity and distinctness which plagues metaphysics imposes even more stringent limits on speculative theology.

Theology is the highest of the sciences – that is, of those disciplines which produce knowledge by means of deduction from certain premises – because both its principles and its conclusions involve supernatural knowledge of the first principle which is God. It is not, however, the highest wisdom – that is, the highest discipline which makes judgements regarding the first principle. This honour belongs to prophecy, which is followed by infused contemplation, both of which enjoy preconceptual, experiential knowledge of the divine nature in the just act, prophecy producing original insights, infused contemplation arriving at insights already possessed by others. Authentic theology, furthermore, is not possible apart from both faith and real progress in the spiritual life. The theologian need not be a great mystic or a prophet, but must have the understanding, knowledge and wisdom which come from actually living the faith, that is, from engaging in the supernaturally just acts which make possible supernatural connaturality with God. Otherwise the act of interpretation will inevitably become reductive. Not only the imaginative form, but also the supernaturally intellectual content will be pared away, for the simple reason that this content is invisible to science and philosophy. Theology, rather than reigning as the Queen of the sciences, will be deformed into a peculiar discipline which disposes of vast erudition in order to inform us that the scriptures and the tradition tell us nothing more or less than what the theologian's favourite social scientists or philosopher said much more straightforwardly. As this is obviously false, lay people and clergy who are actually engaged in pastoral practice, and who have developed some modest understanding, knowledge and wisdom themselves, may perhaps be excused if they begin to believe that advanced theological study is a threat to a living spirituality – a much more serious threat than study in the sciences or philosophy themselves.

There has been much interest in recent years in the role of the magisterium as a safeguard against this kind of error, and it is true that this is one of the authentic functions of the pastoral teaching office of the Church. But some caution is required. First of all, the magisterium is no better able than the individual theologian to avoid error simply by applying some set of formal criteria. On the contrary, what the magisterium must make is a theological judgement which itself requires (the gifts of) understanding and knowledge and wisdom. And so the problem of cultivating theological wisdom enriched by both the sciences and philosophy on the one hand, and the gifts of the Holy Spirit on the other hand, remains. Those who exercise the magisterium, or advise those who exercise it, must be particularly excellent at this sort of theological judgement. Second, it is vitally important that caution about reductionism not be deployed against the interpretive task of releasing the intellectual content of imaginative prophecy or of extracting the implications of political prophecy for the present period. The imagination can be no less reductive than the secular sciences or philosophy; holding fast to images is not the same thing as holding fast to the deposit of the faith. And refusing to abstract from the particularity of the prophetic critique to its broader structural content is nothing more or less than a refusal to hear the Word and a refusal to take our place in the struggle for the human civilizational project where alone we are called to become something more than merely human.

The surest way to cultivate theological wisdom is by living the virtues, by struggling for justice and seeking truth, making full use of the tools of the sciences and of philosophy and applying them rigorously to the interpretation of the scriptures and of the tradition, while also allowing life itself, which is the presence of the Living God, to stretch us, to make us more than human, and thus to create in us a preconceptual, connatural knowledge of truths which transcend the merely human, and which can illuminate both our own experience and our reading of the scriptures and of the tradition. And nothing is more dangerous for the theologian (especially one who exercises the pastoral magisterium) than to separate theory and practice, to imagine that theology is just a university discipline, and thus to close oneself off to the rich diversity of experiences, of struggles, achievements and disappointments, which are the real font of the spiritual life. The best thing that religious people can do to combat reductionism and defend the deposit of faith is to challenge the people (and the theologians) to grow in the supernatural justice in the light alone of which revealed Truth makes sense.

It would be possible at this point to speak in more depth of theological method, but this would begin to take us beyond the bounds of this primarily philosophical treatise, the purpose of which, in any case, has been to chart a path from nihilism to knowledge, from despair to hope – and not to provide direction for practitioners of particular intellectual disciplines. It may, however, be useful to summarize what we have said, and restate it in the form of a guide to those who want to follow the path we have charted here, in the hope of finding deeper and more certain knowledge in the sciences, of discovering in the midst of the sciences a road to God, and of following that road through philosophy and beyond, towards theological wisdom and even to the borderlands of mystical contemplation and prophetic innovation. It is to this task which we turn in our next and final chapter.

Chapter 8

The Path of Knowledge

We have seen over the course of the preceding chapters that, the critical and postmodern assault not withstanding, it is in fact possible to rise from sensation, by means of abstraction, to a first principle which is infinite, necessary, perfect and thus divine. We have also seen that it is possible, on the basis of the superabstraction of revealed knowledge, to begin to penetrate the very nature of that principle and thus come to know God. Science, philosophy and revelation each in turn give reason for hope, so that knowing the Good, and believing in the possibility of its realization, people will work for it.

Arriving at this point has required a complex and often circuitous argument and there is a danger that in the process the *path* of knowledge has not been made clear. And so, by way of summary I want to spell out for my readers the intellectual (and moral) disciplines which are demanded of those who would know – and do – the divine Good. This chapter provides both a brief and informal account of human intellectual development and, in so far as the two turn out to be inextricably bound up together, moral development as well.[1] It also attempts, at the same time, to serve as a 'guide for the perplexed', explaining just what one must do if one hopes to overcome nihilism and despair and grow in science and wisdom.

The Process of Intellectual and Moral Development Underlying Dynamics

The starting point for human development, as for the development of all animals, is sensuality. By sensuality we mean the pursuit of the finite good which we know on the basis of the senses. It may be useful to recall briefly here what we said earlier about the nature of sensory knowledge. Data received by the external sense organs is transmitted to the brain where it forms 'topographical' and 'dispositional representations'. These representations actually encode information received from the outside world and thus, while limited and reflecting a particular perspective, nonetheless also convey, even in this raw state, real knowledge of the world. These representations may, furthermore, be stored, recalled and even transformed by the

---

[1] The account is informal in the sense that it is not documented by new empirical research. The various stages of development which we identify are given by our account of the act of knowledge, and readers who are familiar with the literature on intellectual and moral development will recognize that while grounded in a fundamentally different psychology and metaphysics, they recognizably point to the same empirical phenomena as those identified by Piaget, Kohlberg and so on, with the exception of the fact that neither of these researchers (due to the structuralist orientation of their studies) really comprehends what we have called transcendental abstraction (Piaget 1952; Kohlberg 1963).

imagination, either unconsciously, in dreams, or consciously – as when a dog imagines a really juicy bone or a child a very big pile of candy.

As these examples already suggest, these dispositional representations are connected not only to the outside world, but also to body states, some of which are instinctive (these are few or non-existent in human beings) and others of which are learned. We thus associate some images, in general those which are good for us at the organic level, with pleasure, and others, generally those which are bad for us at the organic level, with pain – though as evolutionary biologists are wont to point out, there may well be some lag in our adaptation to changed ecological circumstances, something which would explain why we take such pleasure in fats and sugars, once scarce and to be consumed in large quantities when available, and now all too available.

This, in effect, is the condition of all higher animals – those which possess the full range of internal as well as external senses. It is also the condition of the infant, in whom the intellect has not yet been awakened, and who, in the earliest stages of its development, is concerned primarily with the development of the senses and the appetites, as well as with the animal task of locomotion (what Piaget called sensorimotor tasks), rather than with intellectual development as such.[2] This condition of sensuality is no more evil or sinful in a child than it is in a dog or a horse which we praise for its fine nose or powerful legs, and which is motivated in its exercise of those organs largely if not exclusively by the pursuit of pleasure. Sensuality is the foundation of all development in animals, for the simple reason that sensation is the basis for knowledge of the universe, and without it we will find ourselves unable to grow. This is why, if we want to cultivate the development of the child, we should cultivate its sensuality, encouraging its explorations and rewarding its movements towards the good, so that its life remains rooted in the profound pleasure of being. And this is why, in the course of our own development, we must never lose touch with our sensuality, for this would be to lose touch with the most basic form of our ordering to the good. No one who has lost touch with what it means to be drawn to a warm bowl of pasta dressed with olive oil, garlic, tomatoes and a good pecorino cheese, or who has forgotten the movement which is awakened in their loins by the form of an attractive human being, can ever *really* know what it means to love God.

This said, it must be acknowledged that sensuality is limited because the senses are limited. Our full capacity for joy can be realized only as the intellect is awakened and begins its journey towards the Truth. There is, however, in the development of the individual human being, a kind of intermediate stage between sense and intellect, a stage which plays a crucial role in the development of the child, and which remains in the adult as a vital substratum for further development, but which also presents to us a real danger of stagnation and/or disillusionment if we do not navigate it properly. In order to understand the nature of this stage it is important to recall the central role of the internal senses – imagination, memory and the estimative faculty. Now these are still essentially animal faculties, but they also play a critical role in intellectual knowledge. It is the image which is illuminated by the social intellect to reveal the intelligible nature of the object, and it is the estimative faculty which habituates us to making judgements of good and evil, even if these are always, to begin with, simple

---

[2] To the extent that the development of language has begun, of course, properly intellectual developments are also at work.

judgements regarding finite, sensual goods. The estimative faculty makes possible both discipline and cunning. And memory, of course, makes it possible to store and recall our images and the body states to which they are linked.

Now we humans live in a world of images and, in a way which is not true for the cat or the dog, or even the chimpanzee, dolphin, or parrot, many of these images are of our own making. They are images which are posterior to society, on which they depend, and thus to the social intellect. This means that they bear an intelligible content in excess of that attributable to the natural objects to which they refer. This complex web of second order images is constituted, first of all, by language, which is simply a structured system of images which refer to other images both inside and outside the language system. Thus the word 'tree' is not merely a complex of sounds at definite wavelengths; it refers to something in the real world. Out of the fabric of language we weave complexes of images which in turn refer not only to objects in the real world but also to higher, often transcendental principles. Thus the image of the stars in a story – in Dante's *Commedia* for example – refers to something more than simply the points of light we see in the sky at night. It refers to a high-order theological abstraction, and would do so even if those who produced the story and those who retell it never themselves interpret the image to release its intelligible content. The same is true of the image of an attractive woman posing next to an expensive automobile, which embodies a definite (and perverse) understanding of the good life.

What this suggests is that it is vitally important both that the child be surrounded by an environment rich in images, and that it makes an enormous difference just which images are used. Now this may seem like a commonplace, simply a restatement in terms of our theory of knowledge of something which is already widely acknowledged by students of child development and which forms so much a part of public discourse that parents have begun to talk to their children in the womb and have become quite conscious about what kind of television their children watch, what they encounter on the internet and so on. But most of our concern is negative. We protect our children from dangerous images; but we do not present to them images which mediate the Beautiful, the True, the Good and the One. Look at our places of worship and our religious education programmes. The walls are bare and the stories are gone. And it is precisely the visual and verbal images which attract children and which enable them to enter into a story and into the tradition and the Truth which that story mediates. The sanctuary should be a place which is interesting and enticing for children, rich with colours and sounds and smells which convey a sense of Beauty and thus indirectly of Truths which are now only mysteries but which, with effort, they may some day begin to penetrate. Religious education programmes should immerse children in stories which point towards the reality of God and the ultimate meaningfulness of the universe. Images and stories give children something to ask questions about, something to become engrossed in . . . something to criticize and from which to distil pure Truth. This is especially important at a time when the television and the computer and internet offer such a rich diversity of images, so many of them luring people away from higher Goods and towards lesser, and mediating a deformed understanding of the Good life. For the most part, however, our concern for the images to which our children are exposed, when not merely negative and protective, focuses only on exposing them to 'good role models' which will help them to become good employees. We give no thought to exposing them, through the medium of images, to the Truth which relativizes all roles and always challenges us to become something more than we are – to the Truth which, once they have glimpsed it, will make them forever unemployable, friends of God and enemies of the bourgeoisie. It is little wonder that our high school and college students seem so radically secular, in a way that even radical secularists never have been – not rejecting religion or the sacred, but utterly and completely unconcerned with it.[3]

What is true for children remains true for adults. Just as sensuality continues, even among the most advanced, to provide the original basis in experience for ordering to the Good, so too it makes a difference in our continuing development if we are surrounded by images with a high intelligible content, images which mediate to us knowledge of the higher Truth which we already know with the power of our intellect. Only if we are surrounded by Beauty will we find ourselves drawn to the Truth. Only if we surround ourselves with images which are constructed so that the ultimate meaningfulness of the universe shines through the sensible particulars will we learn to see the intelligible truth behind the play of sensations. Only if we find ourselves in stories which are meaningful will we be able to cultivate the ability to see in the complex history of the universe and of human society the meaning which shines through the complex twists and turns of evolution and social development. Just what this means depends on your starting point. For some the beauty of the natural world is the best starting point. For others it may be the beauty of the liturgy. Still others, who feel a deep-seated alienation from religious institutions, may find it best to begin by surrounding themselves with paintings and music, and to immerse themselves in great poetry and great novels. Study the frescos of Rafaello Sanzio and the murals of Diego Rivera; listen to the symphonies and sonatas of Beethoven or songs of struggle from people who have fought to make a difference, immerse yourself in the narratives of Dante and Dostoevsky.

---

[3] The following incident may illustrate this point. My wife taught religion several years ago at an inner city Catholic high school in Chicago. At the beginning of the term, in order to get a handle on where her students were coming from, she asked them to write a brief essay identifying their religious tradition and explaining a little bit about it – core beliefs and practices and so on – and also to explain where they stood in relation to that tradition. The results were truly frightening. The Mexican and Puerto Rican students, who together make up roughly two-thirds of the student body, did identify themselves as overwhelmingly Catholic. But *none* of the Catholics showed even a rudimentary grasp of the Catholic tradition, much less any evidence of interest in or commitment to the Church. Understanding of core beliefs was limited to listing 'God, Jesus, Mary and the saints'. Many said that their religion was practised by 'going to listen to the priest each week' (a practice which many did not even know had a name). Most said they avoid mass whenever possible because it is deathly boring. None associated their religion with struggling for excellence or service to the community. Among the African Americans (very few of whom are Catholic), on the other hand, and especially among the very significant number of Mexicans and Puerto Ricans who had been recruited by various evangelical churches, religious knowledge, interest and participation ran high. Many said that they practise their religion first and foremost in struggling to be the best they can be and by serving the community – this in spite of the fact that it is Catholicism, with its virtue ethics and tradition of strong social teachings, which better supports this understanding of what it means to be religious. Many of those who had left Catholic parishes for evangelical congregations said they did so because they learn more at their new churches. And this is the situation among students from families with sufficient commitment to the Church to spend over $3000 annually to send their children to a Catholic school!

What this involves, of course, is a disciplining of the senses – and thus an habituation of the estimative faculty. Even before our intellects are awakened enough to be able to interpret the image and release the intelligible content, there is more complexity, and therefore more beauty, in an image with high intelligible content than in one with little or none. And even the young child begins the work of interpretation, adding the joy of understanding to that of sensation. And so by exposing ourselves and our children to images rich in Truth, we will gradually begin to find those images which would order us to a life of consumption less seductive. This habituation will, however, be easier and more complete if we also avoid those images which are structured in such a way as to seduce us to such a life. Of particular danger in this regard is the emergence of a whole industry dedicated to marketing consumerism to those who fancy themselves 'socially responsible' or 'spiritually evolved'. This is the world of 'knowledge workers' and 'socially responsible investment funds', of rabidly anti-union natural foods stores and chic boutiques selling merchandise which may as well have been stolen from third-world villages – the world into which an entire generation of our intelligentsia has been socialized, so that the revolutionary ferment and spiritual searching of the 1960s and 1970s, always overestimated to begin with, has been lost forever.

Images which mediate higher Truth inspire us to do, to give, to create, and to become more than we are; images which mediate lower truths make us want.

Images and imagination can, to be sure, only take us so far along the road to God. Full development of the human capacity for knowledge of God depends on the cultivation of the intellect. We have seen that the human intellect results from the confluence of two distinct factors: on the one hand the relatively high level of development of the human nervous system, and on the other hand the emergence of the individual human organism into the complex organization of human society. Society functions as an Agent Intellect, illuminating the images we garner from experience and revealing their intelligible content. The degree of abstraction from sensation depends on the complexity of the social structure into which the individual is inserted. Totalization, or abstraction from the individual to the logical whole of which it is a part, depends only on participation in very simple structures, such as the band or tribe, which provide a basis in experience for the ideas of part and whole or, at a slightly more complex level, for the elaboration of complex classificatory systems which parallel the system of social classification (tribe, phratry, clan and so on). Formalization, on the other hand, abstraction of the intelligible structure of the thing known, emerges only in complex societies. Transcendental abstraction, we have seen, presents a more difficult problem. Here the abstraction is to the function or purpose of the system in question, which is its final cause, and ultimately to the τελος as such, or God. On the one hand, this form of abstraction appears in rudimentary form in all human societies, which are, after all, ordered to an end (the survival of the community) and thus provide a basis in experience for the necessary act of abstraction. This sort of transcendental abstraction generally results in production of an image rather than a concept. Thus the image of the *Magna Mater*, Goddess of fertility and also of wisdom, or the Keres *Sussistinako*, who thinks outward, and in so doing creates the universe. At the same time, fully developed transcendental abstraction is posterior to marketization, and arises as a form of resistance to marketization, as the working classes attempt to reground ethics in the face of rationalist, empiricist and sceptical critiques. Here it is the resistance itself, or the institutional forms which carry it, and not the hegemonic social structure, which provides the basis in experience.

Now the question arises why, in a complex society like our own, which provides the basis in experience for all three degrees of abstraction, some individuals in fact master all three degrees, while others enjoy only a very truncated and limited exercise of formalization and/or transcendental abstraction? The answer cannot lie exclusively in differences at the level of the potential (organic) intellect. Studies of cognitive development suggest that progress towards higher degrees of abstraction is at least partly independent of level of intelligence (Piaget 1952; Luria [1974] 1976). It is, rather, the complexity of the social structure itself which accounts for differences in intellectual development. While everyone in a market society is subject to the pressure of market forces, not everyone is involved in making decisions in reference to those forces or, in general, in having to take and defend positions in open public debate. This is because most of the working class lacks sufficient resources to have options between which they must decide, and even where there are decisions to be made, they are generally individual or familial. Skilled workers, and especially members of the intelligentsia on the other hand, as well as the petty bourgeoisie and bourgeoisie, bring sufficient assets to the marketplace, or are entrusted with sufficient assets by others, to require and create an experience of calculated decision-making. The ability to consider a number of hypothetical situations and decide rationally among them involves doing algebra even if the decision maker is not aware that that is what she is doing. And this is something which is required of even the small shopkeeper, in a way it is not required of the unskilled labourer.

Much the same is true with respect to transcendental abstraction. Here, however, what is required is not simply calculated decision-making, but an experience of resistance to the dominant paradigm be it scientific, philosophical, theological or political. This, in turn, requires participation in a community or an organization which supports such resistance and makes it meaningful in terms of its own ordering to a higher end. Ordinarily this will mean participation in a local religious community which is engaged in resistance of some kind, but the same function may be fulfilled directly by the village or neighbourhood community, by a trade union or community organization, or by a political organization of some kind, provided the community or organization in question is *objectively* ordered to transcendental ends. It must, in other words, be structured in such a manner as to promote the development of human social capacities and, in general, the emergence of ever higher degrees of organization. Resistance ordered to lesser ends will produce only an attenuated transcendental abstraction, regardless of the explicit ideology of the community or organization in question.

The individual's first encounter with the social structure is not direct and immediate, but is rather mediated by the family and later by the school, which serve as agents of the social system. Families socialize their children for the world they expect them to inhabit. Thus children of the lower strata of the working classes are generally trained to hard work and submission, because these are the qualities which are thought to have survival value;[4] children of the skilled workers and the intelligentsia are trained

---

[4] My wife reports the following incident from her days teaching at a grammar school in Fort Worth, Texas. During the run-up to the 1988 presidential election she asked her fourth-grade class to stage a mock

to show greater initiative. A family history of participation in resistance to oppression will also be mediated to the children, who will be encouraged to ask questions, to stand up for themselves and others, and in general to hope and even expect their efforts to pay off.[5]

None of this is intended, to be sure, to minimize the importance of formal study. To actually learn algebra or dialectics one must engage in disciplined and focused study of the disciplines in question. What we are attempting to explain, rather, is why some students seem to have an almost intuitive sense of what a certain discipline involves even if they are a bit 'slow' intellectually, while others, to all appearances bright and hard-working, just can't seem to see the point. The path of knowledge (even the path of formalization) is a path of practice as well as of theory. If you want algebra to make sense to you, then it is necessary not only to study, but also to put yourself in a situation which exercises your ability to think hypothetically and counter-intuitively in ways which make a real difference in your life and the lives of others. If you want to cultivate transcendental abstraction then you must participate, in one way or another, in a community which is ordered to a higher end than is the existing social order, and above all participate in the struggle for justice. This is what Luria's research in Soviet Asia in the 1920s and 1930s suggested (Luria [1974] 1976), and it is something Plato himself already knew when he argued that the Guardians, in addition to formation in mathematics and dialectics, should spend 15 years in subaltern political posts before they could truly be considered philosophers.

It is, of course, possible to find oneself in precisely these circumstances and still make no progress in intellectual development. If this is the case, then in all probability the problem is psychological. One may be dealing with the traces of a socialization process which did not prepare one for calculated decision-making or resistance to injustice. Authoritarian child-rearing which represses sensuality, imagination, and/or the child's awakening critical capacities serves precisely this function. Increasingly common is a kind of child-rearing which cultivates flexibility and the capacity to think quickly in diverse situations, without the ability to think about the *aims* of one's activity. What else is the computer game if not a tool for training people to think hypothetically *within* a structure, without criticizing the 'rules of the game'? Obstacles of this kind are best confronted through psychotherapy. The work of Alice Miller is especially important in this regard (Miller [1981] 1984).

---

election, complete with campaigns, voter registration, balloting and so on. One day she received a visit from an irate mother who did not want her child to participate. My wife thought surely the mother had misunderstood, and assumed she was upset because of some imagined partisan bias in the proceedings. But reassurances to the contrary were to no avail. 'I don't want my child getting the idea that he can make a difference in the world,' she said, 'and this sort of exercise puts those kind of ideas in his head. He needs to learn to accept things the way they are.'

5 One of the most striking patterns which I have noticed over years of teaching ethics and related disciplines to working-class students is that working-class women who are raising or have raised children often show more capacity for transcendental abstraction than working-class men or women who have not raised children. Does the day-to-day experience of making and changing rules create a basis in experience for this sort of thinking?

The Problem of Sin

Up to now we have considered the process of intellectual and moral development as if it were constrained and facilitated only as a result of the prevailing social structure and the specific social location and socialization of the individual in question. But what about sin? Don't we sometimes fail to make full use of the possibilities for development which are presented to us? Is it possible that we sometimes refuse development entirely? And how is it that oppressive social structures come about in the first place? Does human choice and human failure play a role here?

The problem of sin has become difficult to discuss intelligently, in large part because a corrupt form of the doctrine of original sin has become so widespread that it is taken for granted, even by those who reject the rest of the Christian tradition – indeed even by those who reject the existence of God. The idea has its origin in Paul who spoke of 'another law' in his members which was contrary to the law of his mind, and which made him the 'purchased slave of sin', unable to do what is right – even if he willed it (Romans 7). There can be little doubt that this doctrine resonated with Paul's largely urban constituency, among whom the experience of the petty market order was already making it seem difficult indeed to do the right thing – and all too easy to believe that everyone is out for himself. Even so, the doctrine formed merely one current in early Christian thinking on sin. Among thinkers from the periphery of the Empire, Pelagian tendencies dominated. It was only the intense experience of social disintegration by the ruling classes of the centre which eventually allowed Paul's doctrine to triumph – and in the still more radical form proposed by Augustine. According to Augustine we are so crippled by sin that we cannot even will God apart from the assistance of divine grace.

The revival of social progress in the twelfth century meant a revival of Pelagian optimism about humanity, an optimism which is reflected in the rebirth of Aristotelian psychology. Whatever the theologians may have said in order to maintain the appearance of conformity to Church teaching, sin was treated in practice, by the high Middle Ages, simply as habituation to pursuit of a lesser Good, and grace as the attractive power of God mediated by the institution of the Church. Even Augustinians had to acknowledge the presence in humanity of drives which were not purely evil. This concession is reconciled with Augustinian pessimism by such thinkers as Anselm and Scotus by means of a distinction between our natural drive to develop physically, biologically and socially (what Scotus, following Anselm, calls the *affectio commodi*) and an authentic love of the other, and ultimately of God, for his own sake (*affectio justitiae*). Only the latter is salvific. Indeed, it was Satan's over-reaching *affectio commodi* – his desire to become God – which introduced sin into the world in the first place.

Even so, for medieval Augustinianism the *affectio commodi* was not regarded as wrong or evil in itself. This innovation was left to the Reformers who, once again, are responding to resurgent market forces and the growing alienation which they engender. As petty commodity production gives way to generalized commodity production, historic Augustinian pessimism gives way to a full-blown doctrine of radical depravity, according to which human beings are, as a result of the fall, fundamentally incapable of right action. Freud merely takes away from the Reformed doctrine the possibility of divine redemption, which is regarded as wish-fulfilment, leaving us with only the possibility of repression and sublimation. Indeed, it is only a small step from this doctrine of original sin to the 'ontology of violence' advanced by modern nihilism (Nietzsche, Heidegger, Derrida), which alone can make it fully consistent. Only if there is no God and the universe is first and foremost a place of conflict and violence can the claim that all finite systems are evil make any real sense. And yet this is, in effect, the 'common sense' of our time. To the extent that a universal human nature is acknowledged at all, it is reduced to a rapacious desire to consume limited only by the presence of still more powerful destructive and self-destructive tendencies.

It should be apparent that our own system is incompatible with such a doctrine. If all things are ordered to God, then all strivings are fundamentally good, though some of course may be better than others, and many of us may fall short of our End. But if this is so, then how is it possible for there to be evil at all? More especially, how is it possible for an intelligent animal which knows the incredible beauty of God to turn away and plunge into darkness and despair instead? A systematic response to the ontological and anthropological issues involved in this problem must await another context. For here it will suffice to suggest an alternative more consistent with the argument we have been developing.

Our starting point must be to affirm that in a certain sense we never turn wholly from the Good. If we did, we would cease to exist. As we have shown, existence is, precisely, an ordering to God. Rather, we pursue the Good in ways that end up being dead ends – or even being destructive for us and for others. At certain times and places the conditions for human development are unfavourable. Resources are scarce. A road forward is possible only on the basis of violence – by taking what the other has produced, by making the other into merely a means of our own aggrandizement. There is good evidence that the first warlord states emerged when societies occupying relatively unfavourable ecological niches, in which production of a sufficient surplus to support the development of an advanced civilization was all but impossible, gained access to metal tools which allowed them to conquer their more developed neighbours and force them to pay tribute (Childe 1951; Lenski 1982). And what is done at the level of society as a whole is repeated at the individual level. Warlord states require warriors and submissive peasants. And families always socialize their children to survive in the world as it is. Thus children are denied the nurture they require – or rather forced to purchase it by learning warlike behaviour or submission or both. In either case the authentic vocation of the human being, which is to know and develop towards the Good, by adding to the degree of organization of the universe as a whole, is to a greater or lesser degree forgotten. Because the welfare, and even the existence of their society (as well as their place in that society) depends on warfare and exploitation, people begin to imagine that the universe itself is a place of radical violence (Lerner 1991) and, to a greater or lesser degree, lose sight of the Good which even now they seek, however corruptly.

It is worth noting here that even those who resist unjust social structures are affected by those structures. The prophet draws his images of God from the same warlord cult as does the priest or sacral king; the revolutionary warrior is every bit as much a warrior, with all of the spiritual dangers that entails, as the oppressor against whom he struggles.

In market societies the dynamic looks a bit different. Here it is not conquest but rather exchange which has become the dominant survival strategy. Individuals and societies prosper to the extent that they produce things other people want – especially those with money, who often, though by no means always, are the descendants of those who first acquired their resources through an act of violence. Those who are extremely rich simply attempt to conserve what they have so that they can avoid the necessity of labour; others seek to sell themselves so that they can become rich, or at least survive and prosper. It is not surprising that people begin to believe that there is no Good in itself, that value is simply a matter of personal preference, and that the universe itself is not ordered to a single τελος, but rather to many competing ends. And here we are, back again at the ontology of violence.[6]

The deformation of the individual which accompanies the emergence of tributary and capitalist societies and the exploitative and marketing character orientations which they encourage is, we should note, prior to any individual act of will. While the individual is not born deformed, he is socialized in a way which reproduces the deformity, so that every act of the intellect and the will is tainted by the corruption. In this sense, what we have outlined here, while avoiding any suggestion of radical depravity, is nonetheless an authentic doctrine of original sin.

We should note that in each of these cases the corruption of human nature which takes place has both an intellectual and moral component. This is, indeed, what we would expect from our account of the role of the social intellect in the production of knowledge. Deformations of the social structure produce intellectual deformations even as (being *directly* distortions in the reality people are living) they also produce moral evil. And the deformation which is produced, while it has infinite variations, is really quite specific in its general character. To the extent that we become enmeshed in exploitative or marketing structures, we lose sight of the universe as an organized system and of the τελος to which it is ordered, and begin the slide towards atheism and nihilism.

As already noted in Chapter 7, this does not mean that it is impossible for the theoretical atheist to be virtuous – provided the conditions exist for habituation to virtuous acts without knowledge of the End to which they are ultimately ordered. And we must distinguish between the atheism of a Marx or an Engels, or even of a Sartre, and that of a Nietzsche, a Heidegger, or a Derrida. For Marx and Engels and Sartre atheism is fundamentally a misfortune. A universe ordered to God, a universe in which there is ultimate meaning and value and which continues to develop infinitely towards the realization of that meaning and value, would be a superior universe. If there is any rejoicing here in the triumph of secularity it is only because so much religion is about promoting passivity rather than about catalysing growth towards the Good. Atheists of this sort *will* God even if they do not believe in God, and thus the extent of the corruption is limited. The radical nihilist, on the other hand, rejoices in the discovery of a meaninglessness which makes him the highest principle (at least potentially) in the universe. He wills atheism even before he ceases fully to believe in God – a belief the trace of which is still present in Nietzsche's constant invocation of pagan mythologies and in the highly ambiguous use of theological language by Heidegger

---

[6] This discussion is deeply indebted to Erich Fromm's account of non-productive character orientations in *Man For Himself* (Fromm 1947).

and Derrida. Similarly it must be noted that there are certain types, which those of us who work in ecclesiastical circles encounter all too frequently, who profess belief in God but whose whole *modus operandi* speaks of a radical lack of confidence that the universe is ordered to this God they profess, but rather depends on their own efforts, which are generally centred on rooting out heresy and suppressing dissent. These too are nihilists, practical if not (though who can read their souls?) theoretical atheists.

The question must be posed here – even if we do not answer it in full – whether it is possible for someone to make a radical decision against God, and whether (for this is a separate question) such a decision is ever actually made. We are required by the logic of our argument to affirm the possibility at least of such a decision. Once someone has become a convinced atheist and has embraced the implications of his unbelief – or, while still believing in God, wills God's non-existence and thus cosmic chaos and destruction – he has, in fact, set himself against God in a fundamental way. The question, of course, is the extent of the wilful embrace of these consequences. The adolescent atheist who rejects God because God has become bound up in his mind with psychological or political repression may well be in danger, but he is also, probably, embracing the possibility of liberation and development for himself and for humanity. The ecclesiastical bureaucrat for whom God is wholly confined by doctrine and for whom doctrine is an instrument in a personal war against social and cosmic chaos (Dostoevsky's Grand Inquisitor) may well have decided long ago against God and for the forces of darkness and destruction.

We should point out that a radical decision against God (what the Catholic tradition calls mortal sin) is *not* the same thing as radical depravity. The very will to power which is at the heart of the radical nihilist's rejection is itself (though he does not know this) a response to the attractive power of the Good, and the nihilist's persistence in being is also a persistence in goodness and in the possibility to turning back towards the Good. Clearly this must be even more true where the option for nihilism is less complete and the sin 'venial' rather than mortal.

It is interesting to note that the intellectual effects of sin are not distributed evenly across our cognitive faculties, but rather affect one faculty in particular: the capacity for transcendental abstraction. This is because the lower cognitive faculties – the external and internal senses and total and formal abstraction – depend only on the existence of a certain degree of organic and social complexity, whereas transcendental abstraction is rooted in the experience of being ordered to – an experience the character of which is radically altered by the effects of sin. To the extent to which we cease actually to be ordered to the Good, we lose the basis in experience for the transcendental judgement – the judgement of existence and value in which Being, Beauty, True, Good and One are convertible with each other. We become cut off from the teleological directionality of the social and transcendental intellects which illuminate the images we garner from experience, and become, to a greater or lesser degree, incapable of perceiving meaning and value.[7]

---

[7] This is, of course, the reason why it is possible to be a great scientist – or at least a great mathematical physicist – and still be profoundly evil. The darkening of the intellect by sin does not affect our capacity for formalization, and thus our capacity to describe how the world works and to use this knowledge to create ever more powerful instruments of destruction.

The extent of the damage to our capacity for transcendental abstraction depends on whether there is a radical decision against God or only a failure to actually believe, hope and love as fully as we might. Insertion into a tributary or market society habituates us to a life of predation or submission to predation, or of constantly selling ourselves in order to be able to consume. And we cultivate those intellectual faculties which serve our survival in the society in which we live. As creativity in relation to physical, biological and social matter is subordinated to the imperatives of predatory warlords or of the market system, the search for the latent potential and purpose of things yields to mere estimative calculation, which is served rather than governed by the higher cognitive faculties. Totalization and formalization become instruments of greed. If we are able to rise to the idea of God at all, it is only in the distorted form of a heavenly warlord, or an inscrutable cosmic sovereign, reflex of the marketplace, whose purposes remain forever concealed from human reason – images which are rightly subjected to scorn by critical reason, armed with the tools for formal abstraction, as soon as it is able to secure its emancipation from the forces of darkness. Religion becomes confused with submission to authority and enlightenment with urbane detachment and scepticism regarding the ultimate meaningfulness of the universe. In neither case is there a real engagement with the transcendental question.

A radical decision against God, on the other hand, entails not so much a slow atrophy of our capacity for transcendental judgement, but an exercise of this capacity in the negative. It involves a wilful blindness to our own act of existence and that of everything around us which, even in the times of deepest despair over the ultimate meaningfulness of the universe and of human history, serves as a sign of the immediate presence of the divine, which *is* this act of existence. Where someone who is spiritually alive, no matter how damaged, cradles each object in his or her hands, wondering at the very fact of its presence, the nihilist rejects presence as something unwarranted and unasked for, as if to refuse the divine gift of Being itself. A radical decision against God is a decision against Beauty – a wilful blindness to the integrity and harmony of all things and a refusal of the clarity which makes every image a window on the truth. Where the spiritually healthy person is quite literally seduced by the universe and everything in it into a gradual engagement with the True and the Good,[8] the nihilist rapes and destroys, seeing Beauty as a threat to his 'right' to remake the world as he pleases. A radical decision against God is a decision against Truth – a wilful refusal of the already comprehended truth that God alone is a sufficient principle of explanation. Where someone who is spiritually alive searches for God and, if unable to find God mourns, the nihilist rejects the principles of identity, contradiction and sufficient reason on which science itself is based in order to prevent science from ever arriving at the Truth which alone can satisfy it. A radical decision against God is a decision against the Good – a wilful refusal to be drawn out of potency and into act. Where the spiritually healthy person yearns to be and to become what he or she is, the nihilist rejects such yearning as merely the projection of a will to power in conflict with all other such wills, and without any ultimate meaning or validity. A radical

---

[8] Dostoevsky, remember, said that it is Beauty which will save the world. This is because it is Beauty which is always and only our first approach to the True and Good. Appealing to the sensuality which we can never escape, it secretly orders us to God without us even knowing it, so that we find ourselves believing and hoping and loving before we can help it.

decision against God is a decision against the transcendental unity which comes only from being ordered to. For someone who is spiritually alive contradiction between aims is either a healthy dialectic which expands our possibilities or – when it becomes antagonistic – a tragedy which entails the loss of potential which might otherwise have been realized. The nihilist on the other hand glories in a universe in which the first and last words are words of war and the end, like the beginning, is really nothing at all. Where the sceptic, having become habituated to using his mind only in service of finite ends, rejects 'metaphysics' as mere nonsense, the nihilist is the supreme metaphysician. He knows the mind's road to God and lies in wait along the way to ambush the unwary traveller, with no aim other than to claim another soul for the darkness.

Once again, we must remind ourselves that the nihilist, unlike the sceptic, does not always use the language of atheism. On the contrary, 'theologies' which, however much they claim to glorify God, do so at the expense of the ultimate meaningfulness of the universe, which is seen as something separate from and opposed to God, thereby make God into a finite albeit very powerful system and ultimately opt for an ontology of violence. The difference between the atheistic nihilist and the theistic is that the first sets out to become the greatest power in the universe, knowing full well that his quest is doomed; the latter allies himself with a great but finite power, which imposes its will on the universe by fiat and force, bringing death and damnation in its wake. The 'theistic' nihilist is above all a person of the lie.

The Dynamics of Supernatural Development

We need, finally, to consider briefly the dynamics which govern development in excess of natural human capacities: that is, the cultivation of caritative wisdom and progress along the illuminative and unitative ways. Here, as we suggested in Chapter 7, the underlying motor of development remains the attractive power of God, which draws us into a struggle for Goods which transcend anything which is capable of realization within the sphere of human history and human society. Lured by the incredible Beauty of God, we find ourselves involved in a struggle for justice which transcends our own interests, or even the interests of our own people or civilization. And by involvement in this process we are stretched and gradually become more than merely human.

While this process is always and only one of growth and development, we experience it, at least at first – and then repeatedly as we advance to still higher stages of development – as painful and negative. This is because we are not really able at first to understand the Good we seek and thus to enjoy it, and because we are being forced to let go, by slow degrees, our attachment to lesser goods which stand in the way of our service to and enjoyment of God. Having carefully built up our ego and identity in the earlier stages of development we are now called on not so much to dismantle the ego as to set it – or allow it to be set by the painful experience of reality itself – in a much larger context in which it no longer looks so brilliant or magnificent.

Sociologically it is always historical contradictions which make this growth and development possible. Even social structures which have clearly promoted the development of human capacities run up against their limits and require fundamental reorganization. And reorganization requires sacrifice. It requires those who are most developed to recognize that they are not nearly developed enough, to let go a way of life which has nurtured and sustained them, to make way for new forms of organization which will make possible still higher levels of development. Those higher levels will, to be sure, subsume the old. But until the development in question has taken place, it is quite impossible for the old to see itself in the new, and thus resistance and struggle are inevitable.

This dynamic is further complicated by the fact that historical development has rarely taken the form of a simple exhaustion of the potential of one structure followed by the construction of new, more complex forms of organization. Civilizational progress has almost always been marred by oppression and exploitation for the simple reason that, as we noted above, exploitation has often seemed like the only road forward. Thus the leader of an impoverished tribe on the arid steppes who becomes a warlord and eventually a sacral king. Thus the humble inventor who becomes a captain of industry living off the labour of millions. Development does not necessarily stop for those who follow the path of exploitation, but it will be distorted and the possibility for stagnation and regression is increased.

The same is true, unfortunately, for those who resist oppression, for the simple reason that they too must travel the road of warfare and sacrifice. While the prophet or revolutionary commander stands in the right against the warlord or capitalist he opposes, he is not thereby liberated from the dangers of stagnation and distortion due to inflation of the ego. On the contrary, the knowledge of being in the right if anything increases the danger of such inflation and makes this path all the more difficult and dangerous. And the danger is not diminished by choosing the road of non-violent resistance. Here the revolutionary leader simply plays the role of priest, offering up the oppressed as victims for sacrifice, rather than the role of sacral king. The danger remains. *Corruptio optimi pessimi est.* (Corruption of the best is the worst.)

The key is to transform the ambiguity of one's position into a spiritual asset. Once we understand that it is possible to be both in the right and morally compromised, to be highly developed intellectually and morally, spiritually and politically and still be in mortal danger of sin, we no longer look on ourselves as little gods, but rather as finite human beings struggling towards God, more advanced than others perhaps, entitled and even called upon to lead, but still very, very far from our goal. And when we do this the goal becomes much, much closer.

These same strictures apply to those whose callings are less obviously political. Personal contradictions are a reflex of social contradictions and the counsellor or spiritual director whose focus is on the individual rather than on the institution or the civilization is presented with both opportunities and challenges by the contradictions which drive the historical process. And if the temptation toward grandiosity is perhaps less, the temptation of seeing oneself as 'above the fray' is much greater. Like the revolutionary warrior or public prophet, the counsellor or spiritual director brings particular skills and personal characteristics which humanity requires for its development. And as with the revolutionary warrior or public prophet these skills and personal characteristics carry their own dangers: for example, an excessive concern for peace and harmony when only struggle can carry us forward. The key, once again, is to transform the ambiguity of one's position into a spiritual asset, recognizing the partial character of one's contribution and one's dependence on people very different from oneself if humanity, individually and collectively, is to move forward.

The Stages of the Spiritual Life

As a result of the complex and contradictory character of human social development generally, the process of human spiritual development does not follow any one, single path. Thus, while it is possible, and indeed useful, to identify rough stages of development, we must also note some characteristic byways and culs-de-sac. And even here we cannot be exhaustive. What follows is intended as a rough guide and not as a definitive statement.

The first stage of development is pure and simple sensuality. Here the good known and the good sought remain purely sensual. There is nothing inherently wrong or sinful in this condition. Indeed, as we noted above, we praise sensuality in animals and ought to value it in ourselves. There are, furthermore, no human beings born with a normal potential or organic intellect who remain at this stage. Human sensuality is, after the advent of language and other cognitive functions, always formed in some degree by those functions.

The second stage of development is that of imagination. Here the internal senses have come into their own and authentic interiority becomes possible. We no longer simply respond to external stimuli, but rather long for things which we remember or imagine. Once again, no human beings born with a normal potential or organic intellect will remain at this stage. The operation of the internal senses is, like that of the external senses, formed by at least rudimentary intellectual capabilities. The cultivation of the imagination is, however, essential to further intellectual development, for all of the reasons we noted above.

The third stage of development is marked by the advent of totalization. Here images and the objects they represent are recognized as examples of more general classes of things which have definitions and characteristic properties. The full development of ordinary linguistic capacities makes possible the formation of complex interpersonal relationships and thus the capacity to seek specifically intelligible ends: a good marriage, friendship and so on. People at this level are able to generalize from particular images, experiences and so on, in a way that our iconic dogmatist and our instrumental hedonist could not. If they are Christian, for example, they know that Moslems believe in a God not *entirely* unlike their own. God here is a function defined by analogy to ordinary social roles, not a thing associated with an image. They have grasped the fact that moral rules exist in order to maintain harmonious relationships between people. They easily take lessons learned in one context and apply them in other contexts which are similar. The *results* of formal and transcendental arguments are, furthermore, accessible to them as facts and rules, even if the arguments tend to escape them. What they cannot do is to penetrate behind the facts and rules to the structures and arguments behind them; indeed it is not generally clear to them why one would even need to do this. Individuals at this level of development generally score at Stage Three on Kohlberg's Moral Development Scale, and function (even if they score higher) at the level of 'concrete operations' on Piaget's Cognitive Development scale. We will refer to them as conventionals.

This conventional level of development is, generally speaking, accessible to nearly everyone in most human societies. There are, however, two characteristic byways in which people often become trapped, so that they develop only a truncated version of the capacities which characterize people at a conventional level of development. There are, on the one hand, those who seem never to have developed an appreciation for such higher goods as friendship, and remain focused on gratifying purely sensual desires, even at the expense of others. They become little more than sophisticated machines who are manipulated by monetary rewards and punishments into producing whatever the ruling class requires. If they cannot produce they are discarded and turn to a life of addiction or crime. These are people who test as preconventional (Stage One or Stage Two) on Kohlberg's Moral Development Scale. We will call them instrumental hedonists. They make up a larger part of the population than one would expect. Second, there are those who, while they often show an intense interest in things religious, seem only marginally capable of even the rudimentary degree of abstraction represented by totalization. They use language in what seems like a normal fashion but identify the image with the truth it conveys, so that there is not even an ability to see that very slightly different images or names refer to the same reality, or are of the same type. A person of this sort believes that Moslems don't believe in God – that they believe in Allah instead. With respect to moral reasoning they are apt to regard moral rules as simple facts and when asked why the rule should be followed, to simply restate how they learned it. 'That's how I was brought up' or, at best, 'If you do that you will be punished.' There is no understanding of the reason why the rule exists. People like this also test at the preconventional level on Kohlberg's Moral Development scale, and are not unlike the purely secular instrumental hedonists which we described above. We will call them iconic dogmatists.

Both of these problems arise when people have unusually truncated social relationships, which serve merely as a means to realizing lesser goods and are not treated as ends in themselves. Most often this occurs when people are subjected to brutal oppression and are treated themselves as means to the enrichment of another. They then raise their children to fill this role as well and in the process never cultivate their love of intelligible goods. The difference between instrumental hedonists and iconic dogmatists is that the latter have generally been exposed at some point to images rich with intelligible content which, however, they cannot abstract. Questions about meaning and apparent contradictions, about why the images in a friend's house are different or why some people don't believe in God, were repressed or given pat answers which stop thought. And so they were left to believe that it is the image itself which is important, rather than the Truth to which it points. Of the Truth itself they remain wholly unaware.

The fourth stage of development is characterized by the advent of formalization. There is an increasing ability to grasp the underlying structure of things and to reason hypothetically. Algebra and even higher mathematics become transparent. Thinking about God becomes increasingly abstract, as it is realized that any function God serves is cosmic and not merely social and, given the increasing focus on formal description, it is not clear just what that function would be. God is an hypothesis for which they, like Laplace (Laplace 1799–1825), have no need. Moral norms are regarded as mechanisms for maintaining social order (a subtle but important difference from the previous level – the concern here is for the structure of a general system and not for interpersonal relationships). As empirical knowledge of the diversity of social structures increases, the problematic character of the concept of social structure becomes increasingly apparent, leading to the emergence of increasingly relativistic tendencies. People at this level of development test at Stages Four, Five, or Six of Kohlberg's Moral Development Scale, and actually function at the level of Piaget's formal operations.

Ordinarily formal abstraction, like the lower degrees of cognitive development, is formed by at least a rudimentary capacity for transcendental abstraction. Here, however, the conclusions of transcendental abstraction are not simply taken as givens, to be implemented flexibly in the context of concrete social responsibilities. They become, rather, the object of analysis – an analysis to which, because of the limitations of the purely formal intellect, they cannot generally stand up. Because the capacity for formalization is more developed than the capacity for transcendental abstraction, it is supposed that the former faculty is in fact the higher of the two, and transcendental judgements are treated as little more than folk wisdom or mores.

In some cases this sort of orientation can result in a rationalistic theism or pantheism of the sort we see in Anselm or Descartes. More often, though, the result is a movement in the direction of increasing scepticism, something which can lead those who reach this stage off the main course of spiritual development and on to some dangerous byways. Here it is important to distinguish, however, between rationalistic scepticism and a wilful nihilism. Scepticism arises from an inability to rise rationally to the first principle. While it may be accompanied by considerable inflation of the ego and, because it leaves moral principles ungrounded, it may lead to some significant degeneration, it is far from demonic. On the contrary, sceptics are in danger spiritually in significant measure because they do in fact perform an important service in challenging prejudice and superstition and may thus come to believe that they are more advanced than they really are.

A much smaller group, finally, make the breakthrough to transcendental abstraction. Here it is necessary to distinguish between those who make this breakthrough prior to or without formalization, and those who do so after achieving formalization. Without formalization, or with only attenuated formalization which does not actually shape day-to-day operations, transcendental abstraction is most likely to express itself in a return to imagination – though the difference between the image and the reality it expresses is now clearly recognized and in fact understood as the mark of the transcendental character of the reality known. Elements of religious and other ideological traditions become tools for envisioning a better world and for organizing people to create such a world, whether through technological or artistic innovation or through organizing for social justice. It is possible to distinguish people at this level of development from iconic dogmatists or conventionals who simply happen to embrace a tradition critical of the existing social order by their intuitive sense that the Beauty, Truth and Goodness they know radically exceeds the form of their knowledge, and their sophisticated aesthetic or prudential judgement. Even if they have had limited exposure to other traditions, and no formalization, someone who has advanced to transcendental abstraction will understand him/herself as devoted to the τελος behind the images and not to the images themselves. This results in an openness to other approaches to the Truth, coupled with an ability to judge correctly traditions which do not approach Truth. Similarly, where the iconic dogmatist knows only rules, the preformal transcendental is actually able to see the latent potential in a given situation, and judge how to cultivate that potential, even if the capacity to justify the judgement in a formal argument is not present. The result is an approach to decision-making marked by flexibility and innovation. This is a type which we see less frequently in highly marketized societies than we might have in times past, partly because social disintegration undermines traditional communities of resistance, and partly because preformal transcendentals at best go utterly unrecognized by the marketplace and by corporate and state bureaucracies, and at worst are viciously repressed. But anyone who has worked for a long time in working-class communities or the parishes which serve them knows that even in the midst of the information revolution and market-driven globalization it is the 'village elders' who make authentic community possible and among whom, in varying degrees, this sort of transcendental abstraction still very often develops.

With formalization, transcendental abstraction makes possible a dialectical ascent to the transcendental principles of value, coupled with an ability to apply those values to particular situations. What formalization supplies is the capacity to grasp the underlying structure of physical, biological and social systems, and thus determine just how to reorganize them in order to release their latent potential and promote the development of complex organization. It also supplies the ability to demonstrate the possibility and necessity of an ascent to the first principle. This is the level of the philosopher, or of the political or pastoral leader informed by philosophy.

Like those at lower levels of development, transcendentals face their own dangers. There is, on the one hand, a danger of stagnation as a result of overestimating the power of philosophy and denying the possibility of supernatural knowledge simply because such knowledge is most often presented in imaginative form. In its more extreme forms this can lead to an overarching egoism in which the philosopher imagines he has comprehended the divine and thus has full access to the 'secrets of nature' (Eamon 1994) and 'the riddle of history' (Marx [1844] 1978). Here authentic intellectual and moral virtue becomes the basis for a pride which eventually eclipses knowledge of God and leads to a wilful nihilism which is far more malevolent than anything the sceptic is capable of mounting. Preformal variants of this deformation are rarely seen in our own society, but we must imagine that those regarded as sorcerers and sacral kings were especially prone to it.

Whether or not we suffer a serious fall and travel along one of the byways of the spiritual life, we are all affected by the deformed social structures in which we live, and we all at some point falter and stagnate. This means that the path to knowledge is always also a path of conversion, of a turning or a returning towards God. This is especially true as we approach the supernatural levels of development which require what always seems like a break even from healthy manifestations of the natural levels of human spiritual development.

This said, some words of caution are in order. The word 'conversion' is frequently used carelessly and its meaning has, to a certain extent, become hegemonized by evangelical Christians for whom it is intimately bound up with the doctrines of radical depravity and substitutionary atonement. According to this view human beings are naturally evil and incapable of good, and can be 'saved' only because Jesus bore the pains of sin on our behalf, and his merit is imputed to those who believe. Conversion is fundamentally a matter of submission and a negation of a human intellect which is regarded as the cutting edge of humanity's prideful rebellion against God. Needless to say nothing could be more foreign to our perspective. Even the nihilist who makes a radical decision against God is not radically depraved but, on the contrary, naturally ordered to God (though denying it) and eminently worthy of salvation, if for no other reason than to put his faculties to work adding to, rather than taking away from, the universe.

What we understand by conversion is, rather, first and foremost a turning towards God in an act of transcendental judgement, a judgement which is followed both by an imaginative and/or intellectual vision of God and by acts of hope and love. Conversion is first and foremost a *metanoia*, a change of mind driven by a qualitatively new act of the intellect.

It is certainly true that, given what we have said about knowledge in general, and the corruption of the intellect by sin, this act is not, strictly speaking, something which we are capable of on our own. It depends immediately on an act of the social intellect, and indirectly on the reordering of the social intellect to the αρχη and τελος of all things. In this sense it is radically dependent on divine action. At the same time, this divine action is nothing other than the single, perfectly simple and unique divine action of Being itself, which shines through the Beauty of all things, illuminating their authentic meaning, purpose and value, and drawing them to Itself so that all things are, while authentically different also, ultimately One. The divine action on which conversion depends is free in the sense of being a free expression of the divine nature. But to act in some other way would not be divine.

If conversion takes place in some and not in others, and proceeds further in some than in others, the explanation is not on the side of God but on the side of humanity. The social conditions for conversion must, first of all, exist. There must be some region of human society which, however imperfectly, has nonetheless authentically become turned towards God. This turning may, and eventually will, express itself in the development of an imaginative and intellectual discourse on God, and God's plan for the universe and human society. But it may initially – and at some point must, if it is to be authentic – express itself in a turning towards humanity's practical and theoretical vocation in the universe, towards participation in the creative work of God, organizing and reorganizing physical, biological and social forms of matter, advancing the human civilizational project and thus the cosmo-historical evolutionary process. And in reality, because everything that persists in being persists in some degree in its cosmic function, this social reality always exists. It is just stronger in some places and times than in others. This social subspace, with all of the rich and diverse relationships, organizations and institutions which develop within it, is what Catholic theology has called the invisible Church.

There is a practical lesson here for those who seek conversion, but are having difficulty accomplishing it. Put yourself in this social subspace, where people are advancing the cause of human civilization, and where they are advancing a discourse which understands this work as a real participation in the life of God. Avoid the corrupt regions where people seek only to consume. Live out the specific creativity which is your calling. Avoid the naysayers who would keep you chained to market imperatives. Then you will find yourself on the road back to God.

Second, of course, conversion requires a free response from the person to whom it is offered. Just being in the social space of grace does not by itself mean that we have made a decision in favour of meaning and in favour of God. There are many who sit on the fence for a very long time and many who never, ever decide. Our decision for God, like God's offer of grace, is simply a free expression of our nature. To do anything else is to be less than fully human. Unlike God, however, we are not fully and perfectly, but only potentially and incompletely, what we are. We can become stunted or deformed. We can refuse.

It may be helpful at this point to analyse in greater depth the specific decision that is involved in conversion, something which leads us into a clarification of the whole process and an explanation of the different stages or degrees of conversion, something at which we have already hinted. The decision for conversion is a decision in favour of the ultimate meaningfulness of the universe: a decision to believe in it (and thus in God), to serve it, and to hope that our specific contributions and thus we ourselves make a difference and thus are, in some way which we cannot yet understand, preserved eternally. This is what the Catholic tradition has historically called the 'first conversion' (Garrigou-Lagrange 1938), and its tentative and limited character should already be apparent. There is, first of all, as yet only a willingness to believe, based on a decision that the weight of the available evidence is on the side of meaning, and not yet authentic understanding, either natural or supernatural. Second, the hoping and loving of which we become capable as a result of this conversion are still, very largely, a hoping *for ourselves* – for the ultimate meaningfulness of our lives and work – and a loving of God as *our* Good. This does not mean that the faith, hope and love which are involved here are somehow false or inauthentic. On the contrary, God is our Good and there is hope and there is reason to believe. It is just that the act of the appetites is always and only constrained by the act of the intellect, and until believing advances to seeing and understanding, it is still impossible to hope in and love God for Her own sake.

This conversion can take place at any level of intellectual development. One can make the decision to believe at any of the different levels of development we have identified, including those which indicate some stagnation or deformation. If conversion takes place at a preconventional level (during childhood or from the standpoint of instrumental hedonism or iconic dogmatism) it is apt to be articulated in terms of visions or of powerful affective experiences. This is because these are the only means open to the individual in question to articulate a fundamental shift in direction. We should remember, however, that imaginative visions and affective intensity can also accompany conversion at higher levels of development as well. If conversion takes place at a conventional level of development, it is apt to express itself primarily in the lightly intellectualized language of the religious tradition in which it occurs, and in a fundamental shift in relationships – that is, joining or becoming active in a local congregation and so on. In neither case does the first conversion require an advance to a higher level of abstraction.

Matters are quite different at the levels of formalization and transcendental abstraction. Here, the question of God will almost always have been considered, and a tentative conclusion reached in favour of atheism or agnosticism. If the existence of God has already been affirmed it will have been in a form which still negates the ultimate meaningfulness of the universe – for example, Spinozism. A decision to believe represents a decision for transcendental judgement. For the convert from the level of formalization this means recognizing in the transcendental judgement the ground for the existence of what he has hitherto analysed, in effect, as only a possible being. It means confronting the act of existence in a universe which has hitherto been apprehended only as intelligible form. For the convert from the level of a truncated transcendental judgement – for example, someone, such as a dialectical materialist, who has found meaning in history, but not in the universe as such – it means finding new and deeper meaning and thus the completion of what was hitherto an interrupted course of development. For the convert from nihilism it means reversing the negative transcendental judgement and affirming what had previously been rejected in a radical and decisive way.

Conversion need not be sudden and dramatic – though for someone engaged with questions of fundamental meaning and value there will inevitably come a well-defined moment of decision. This moment is, however, generally preceded by a slow accumulation of evidence which already affects the appetites even before an explicit judgement has been rendered.

It should be noted that the first conversion is only to what amounts to philosophical wisdom, though theological truths may also be formally affirmed. Indeed, the possibility of such revealed truths is, as we saw in Chapter 7, already included implicitly in the affirmation of infinite, perfect and necessary Being, of which no limitation of any kind can be predicated. At the same time the option for philosophical knowledge of God, from within a society deformed by tributary or market structures (the only societies in which philosophy arises in the first place) itself requires an authentic conversion, and a decision against the fashionable options of scepticism and nihilism.

This does not mean that an option for God as an answer to our questions and as our own Good necessarily opens the way to continued spiritual development. On the contrary, spiritual stagnation is a persistent danger at all levels of development. For those who experience the first conversion at the lower levels of development, the danger is likely to come from a tendency to cling to images or simple dogmatic formulae[9] on the one hand, or to certain relationships which developed at the point of conversion on the other hand.

For those operating at higher levels of abstraction, the dangers are rather different. It is possible, first of all to choose to believe *against* what is regarded as compelling evidence to the contrary, or from the standpoint of a considered rejection of the possibility of any rational metaphysics. This is the standpoint of a Pascal or a Kant respectively. The danger here is that one remains perpetually at the level of faith even though it would be possible, were it not for serious intellectual errors, to rise to understanding, first of what philosophy can teach us about God and eventually of the supernatural truths revealed by prophecy. This error is especially pernicious because it tends to regard faith as actually superior to understanding, and is generally quite public about this conviction. The result is that many are led down the wrong path.

---

9 'Images' here does not refer only to religious artefacts, but also to verbal images such as 'Jesus is my friend' or 'Jesus is my personal Lord and saviour'. Indeed, such verbal formulae, because they have the appearance of a higher degree of abstraction and universality, may prove more difficult to transcend than icons, for example, which all but the most simple-minded know fall short of capturing the sacred reality they represent.

It is possible as well for spiritual stagnation to occur because the intellectually advanced believer confuses theological wisdom, which he comprehends using the tools of the dialectic and of philosophy, with supernatural understanding. Mastering various theories of the Trinity, the way one might for a licentiate exam, is not the same thing as penetrating the mystery through the gift of understanding (on which, however, authentic theological innovation depends). If one misses this distinction, one may stagnate for no reason other than the fact that, advancing rapidly along one dimension, other, more fruitful dimensions are ignored.

If the dangers of stagnation are avoided, the way is open to the second conversion. This is a passage from knowledge and love of God as *our* Truth and *our* Good, to a knowledge and love of God *in Herself*. This results in a deepening of the gifts of the Holy Spirit, so that the revealed mysteries gradually begin to make sense, we feel authentic hope not only for ourselves, but for the universe quite apart from ourselves, and the contemplation of God's incredible Beauty, Truth and Goodness becomes our principal delight.

The passage to this second conversion is not, however, any easy matter. It involves what has traditionally been called the 'dark night of the soul' or, more specifically, the first of these nights, that of the senses. Most of the treatises on this subject treat it from the standpoint of the contemplative religious life, so that even active religious (much less the great body of the laity) are left without real guidance. Even the Dominican Garrigou-Lagrange (1938) gives only a broad indication of the specific forms this dark night takes among those who lead an active or active/contemplative life. The result is an excessive emphasis on trials experienced *in contemplation*: an inability to see God in the universe as we once did, and a loss of appetite for prayer and contemplation. Now it is not that these things will not be experienced by those who lead a more active life, on the contrary. But they are apt to be both linked to and overshadowed by trials of a quite different kind, which tend to preoccupy us and which seem to explain our difficulties in contemplation, so that we may never realize that we are in the midst of the dark night, but may simply think we have become lazy or even that we are experiencing a fundamental crisis of faith. For the active person, the dark night involves, first and foremost, difficult struggles and setbacks which bring home the reality of our own finitude, and the fact that the universe is not ordered to us, but rather we to the universe and ultimately to a divine plan or teleology which, however rational, is beyond the comprehension of any finite mind. The result is that God seems to have abandoned us. The beautiful and nurturing power which we thought we had found in the moment of our conversion is no longer there. We are left to fail miserably at what we are doing, to get sick, and eventually to die.

That this kind of crisis can be hard on our contemplative life should come as no surprise. A universe which before seemed full of brilliant colours suddenly becomes dark and grey. God, who just a minute ago, it seems, was everywhere – in the brilliant leaves of autumn, in a kitten's play, in the beauty and power of our work – is suddenly gone. And when God is gone, so is that easy affection with which we loved the God of the autumn leaves and of our own success.

At this point several options are open to us. Some, in fact, actually despair and turn back to nihilism and darkness. For these the dark night is an authentic crisis of faith. Others – the majority, probably, of those whose first conversion was complete and secure – forge ahead in the darkness, but never really learn, except in brief moments of insight and vision, the truth it was meant to teach. One crisis passes and is followed by a time of renewed joy which provides strength for the next trial. And so it continues until death. Spiritual life becomes a matter of keeping the faith, of perseverance and fortitude, rather than of growing joy. Life is lived out in the dark night.

A few, however, make the passage to what is known as the illuminative way (Garrigou-Lagrange 1938). They learn to see God not only in what is obviously good for them, but also in their trials and tribulations. They begin to find meaning even in events which would seem to question the ultimate meaningfulness of the universe. And they find themselves loving this strange God who constantly surprises us with Her elegant strategy and wily tactics. They feel honoured to have been called to play some small role in *Her* plan and begin not to mind so much that they are no longer being nurtured like little ones. It is as if, having learned to love God as nurturing Mother, they now must learn to love Her as a brilliant and challenging teacher, and eventually as a leader in a struggle which they are gradually beginning to understand is about far, far more than ourselves. It is experiences of this kind which make it possible to understand the revealed mysteries – especially the dark ones, such as the tribulations of Israel or the crucifixion.

Once again we must point out the dangers which face us at this level. The dark night is not about learning self-sacrifice or self-sacrificial love. On the contrary, an obsession with self-sacrifice and martyrdom is one of the ways in which the transition to the dark night can be short-circuited. It is a way of refusing to live through the darkness we have entered, either by actually dying, or by providing too easy an answer to the question of meaning which is re-posed at this point in our spiritual development. For if God is about self-sacrifice, then all the suffering makes perfect sense. The mystery, and the contact with the infinite and incomprehensible, is dissolved every bit as completely as it is for the arrogant rationalist. Carried through to its logical conclusions, furthermore, an emphasis on divine self-sacrificial love transforms the God of life into a God of death and thus into something other than God entirely. And martyrdom is, after all, still about us. No, navigating the dark night means learning the discipline of doing what God requires of us even after it has become apparent that the struggle is not only or primarily about us. It means staying in the darkness and becoming accustomed to it. Only then will the skies clear, so that we can 'once again see the stars' (Dante, *Commedia*, III.33).

It is also possible to complete the second conversion successfully, but then to stagnate. As in the case of the first conversion, this results from absolutizing the form of knowledge which has already been achieved, and forgetting the higher tasks which still lie ahead for us as participants in an infinite Universe. Most commonly this means taking excessive pride in our status as servants of God, and in the intellectual and moral sophistication we have acquired as a result, and assuming that this is the very pinnacle of spiritual development. Especially for those who are conscious of having successfully traversed a difficult road, of having persevered through a long dark night, which has not so much ended as cleared to reveal the beauty of the stars, there can also be a kind of second-order cynicism, and a contempt for those who find in God an easy joy, and in service to God a straightforward realization of their talents. Gradually this shades into a kind of spiritual aristocratism, fed by the notion that it is only the hardened few who can really undertake the business of the universe in a serious or significant way, and who can handle the knowledge that this business isn't always pretty. At the end of this road lies an arrogant claim of responsibility for the universe which is ultimately very difficult to distinguish from theistic or god-building nihilism. It is sometimes difficult to discern this spiritual deformation because, in Christian contexts, at least, it is often bound up with an ideology of self-sacrificial love, so that one cannot tell if the individual in question is liquidating the dark night in advance by rendering suffering transparently meaningful, if they are suffering from the spiritual deformity we have been discussing, or if they are authentically saintly and wholly devoted to the service of God (even if their theology is a bit confused).

The second conversion is not, in any case, the end of the road. Indeed, the 'end' is nothing other than God Herself. Our calling as human beings, as matter, is nothing less than to actually *become* God. Being loyal and effective servants of God, even servants who take more pleasure in God than in ourselves, is only a stage along the way. But here we seem to confront a barrier of insuperable proportions. To become God means to be infinite, and the whole journey of spiritual development has thus far been nothing if not a lesson in our own finitude. And the more proficient we are in our service, the sooner we rediscover this finitude and find ourselves in the midst of a second 'dark night' – what the tradition has historically referred to as the dark night of the spirit. For it appears that what God does with Her servants after their long lives of usefulness is to discard them.

At issue here is not so much a questioning of the promise of eternal life, as a probing of the meaning of this promise, a probing which ends up in questioning its value from a human standpoint. Neither the beatific vision of God outside of space and time or nirvanic release sound much like a guarantee of permanence for the identities we have so carefully built up. Indeed, both sound suspiciously like ways of putting a positive spin on what amounts to effective annihilation of the self we have become so attached to, and to which we continue to cling even after we have learned the hard way that it is not the end to which the universe is ordered.

These are questions that trouble all believers, but they are especially difficult for the proficient servant of God, who has learned deeply and profoundly that God's work is about so much more than any one individual that it may as well disregard the individual entirely. We have no claim on God. There is no good reason why a finite system ought to experience eternity. But if this is so, then of what significance is our modest service? Doesn't this make our lives ultimately meaningless after all? Once again the world seems drained of colour. The stars do not simply become clouded over; they seem to disappear entirely.

There are, to be sure, ways to avoid this second dark night. The easiest is simply to plunge ourselves back into our work, to keep focused on our service and not face questions about its ultimate meaning and value at the court of an infinite God. And for some, this works, though it also closes them off to achieving a higher wisdom. Others, however, will find that this path leads them into the spiritual arrogance we spoke of above, or that the opportunity for usefulness is closed off to them entirely. For it is one thing to find that our efforts and our projects seem to be in vain; it is quite another thing to have no possibility to contribute.

The exit from this second dark night comes only in the realization that becoming God – which is our deepest desire and our true calling – involves ceasing to be simply human. We cannot continue to be our finite selves and still grow beyond finitude towards God. With this knowledge we pass to the unitative way.

Of course God always already *Is*. And as infinite, She excludes nothing. In reality we have always been in God and always will be. What we lose in death is our finite knowledge of a limited region of space–time, our selves developing across that region and, if we rise to first principles, of God as the first principle. But God's knowing includes and contains that knowing, and includes it as a real knowing, known better than we ever have or ever could know it. What remains is a knowledge of the world and of ourselves through God – a knowledge which is joyful or painful in whatever degree our use of our talents has made us a cause of joy or pain to our God.

There can be no doubt that the passage to this higher knowledge is painful. All growing is also a parting, and even those who were anxious to grow up soon learn to look back on childhood with nostalgia. There is a freshness and an openness to what seems like an infinite future with infinite possibilities which has been lost. But almost no one – certainly no one who has lived a good life – would actually choose to go back, to forfeit the gains we have made, which are far greater than the mere possibility which has been lost. Rather we take joy in the freshness and potential of our own children and students, guiding them as best we can into a future in which that freshness will become ripe and the possibility actual. Through the second dark night and the third conversion we learn to look on death in the same way.

But more is at issue here than a theological reflection on individual eschatology. When the servant of God lets go of his or her finitude and begins to see with God's eyes, the result is an authentic union with God – a real foretaste of the beatific vision. Knowing God in Her essence, we see the whole universe, all of human history, and our own lives, in the light of that essence. The supernatural act of the will, a perfect charity, follows with iron-clad necessity. We become perfectly free, but are still in our freedom because we know the Good with such clarity that our will cleaves to it and remains there, caught in joy, having no reason to stir.

From this state we can bring no discursive knowledge. And we may, at first, experience it with terror, as an obliteration of the intellect and an overwhelming of the senses. This is because our capacity for knowledge and love and sensation and pleasure has been exceeded. Were we able to remain in this ecstatic state long enough, perhaps our minds would clear and, still transfixed in joy, we would once again become capable of real discourse. Such, at least, is our hope for the beatific vision itself, which we will experience not only on the basis of our own finite bodies, with their limited internal and external senses and potential intellects, but in God Herself, whose infinite capacities we will engage to the full extent of our own particular development.

It should be noted that all three conversions involve judgements and a consequent act of the will, on the basis of which an immediate, connatural and pre-conceptual knowledge of God becomes possible. In the case of the first conversion, the judgement in question is an affirmation of the basic meaningfulness of the universe and thus of the reality of God. In the case of the second conversion, it is a judgement of the value of God in Her own right, and not simply as *our* principle of explanation, *our* good, the object of *our* contemplation. In both cases the judgements are judgements of ascent – ascending from the universe to God, in the first case by affirmation (God is our Good), in the second case by negation (God is *not merely* our Good). In the case of the third conversion, the judgement in question is one of descent. It is a judgement of our own existence, and that of the universe, in God, and thus marks a higher degree of connaturality. But as at all degrees of knowledge, the foundation remains our connaturality with the object known, and ultimately with God, who is the αρχη and τελος of all things.

A Guide for the Perplexed

It is here, at least, that our journey ends. There will, no doubt, be those who will read what we have written with derision – who confuse intellectual maturity with scepticism and power with negation. But for those who are open to the Truth, who want to see but simply cannot, I think we have offered a modest path forward. Perhaps this advice can be stated in the form of a few simple rules:

1   Relish the senses and the good they reveal. Eat and drink and explore your sexuality. Glory over spring and over the autumn leaves and mourn their passing each and every year. And never believe for a moment that any of this is bad – or else you blaspheme.
2   Immerse yourself in beauty, both natural and artistic. Seek out especially images which claim to convey something of the divine, and see what, if anything they stir in you. Expose yourself to a diversity of traditions, but immerse yourself especially in your own. And read great religious poetry and literature: not only the scriptures but also Dante, Shakespeare and Dostoevsky, and the great revolutionary and post-revolutionary novels of the twentieth century (Gorky and Malraux, Silone and Lessing). And begin to cultivate the ability to discover the universal and intelligible contained in these images.
3   Submit to the discipline of ordinary good works and become part of a community dedicated to helping you be effective. This may be a trade union, a community organization, or a political party. If (or rather when, because the capacity *will* develop) you feel able to do so honestly (though still not without questions and trepidation), place yourself in the social space of those who believe: in a parish or synagogue or other local congregation.
4   Always seek patterns, analyse relations, and look for complete explanations. Train yourself in the liberal arts, especially in mathematics and dialectics and in the sciences. Remember that science is not just what scientists say they do, or even what they actually do (though that is a far better guide) but rather a search for a complete rational explanation of the universe. Avoid intellectual fads and be willing to go against the tide. Apply these tools in your practical work, looking behind appearances and analysing underlying structures. The world will gradually become intelligible and you will become more effective.
5   Master at the very least the principal works of the philosophical tradition, beginning with Plato's *Republic*, and determine for yourself whether the argument for meaning isn't stronger than the argument against. This will be easier to see if you have persisted in good works, and developed to the point that you are able to act not only for good within the existing social order, but also and more especially for a social order which is truly good.
6   Learn that for the universe to be meaningful does not mean it is ordered to you personally, or even to some end you can fully understand – that would be boring. Hold fast to your love of and struggle for things human, but allow yourself to be

stretched beyond the merely human, towards the divine. As you do this some theology, at least, will begin to make sense. (Some of it, after all, is simply nonsense).

7   Allow your knowledge of your own finitude to become God's knowledge of that finitude, so that you begin to actually see from a divine perspective and thus, in a small way at least, to actually become God. And know that God's infinite power does not make your doing irrelevant; your doing *is* God's doing, and through God's own power, is vindicated and sustained for ever.

This is, to be sure, a modest guide, and it is not intended for the advanced, but rather for those who, under the pressure of our difficult times, have forgotten how to believe and hope and love – but not so much that they no longer want to. Those who follow this path will find that they do not lose themselves, that they do not need to abandon their sensuality or their critical rationality or anything else that is properly human. Rather, they will find these things affirmed and extended in a higher knowledge which gives meaning to their lives and direction to their efforts and hope in a dark time from which they will, at long last, emerge first into the light of the sun, which shows things as they are, and then into the clear and cold light of the stars, which shows why and for what they are, and at long last into the light of the Empyrean heaven where knowing and loving and being are indistinguishable in the One in whom and through whom all things are.

Bibliography

Abelard (1969), *Logica 'Ingredientibus'*, in John Wippel and A. Wolter (eds), *Medieval Philosophy From St Augustine to Nicholas of Cusa*. New York: Free Press

Alighieri, Dante ([1300–18] 1969), *Commedia*. trans. as *The Divine Comedy* and with commentary by John D. Sinclair. New York: Oxford

Allman, J.M., McLaughlin, T., and Hakeem, A. (1993a), 'Brain weight and life-span in primate species', *Proceedings of the National Academy of Science* 90: 118–22

——— (1993b), 'Brain Structures and life-span in primate species', *Proceedings of the National Academy of Science* 90: 3559–63

Amin, Samir ([1979] 1980), *Class and Nation, Historically and in the Current Crisis*. New York: Monthly Review

Anderson, Perry (1974), *Passages from Antiquity to Feudalism*. London: New Left Review

Anselm ([1077–8] 1970), *Proslogion*, in Eugene Fairweather, *A Scholastic Miscellany*. New York: Macmillan

Aquinas, Thomas ([c. 1256–59] 1994), *Truth Questions*, trans. Robert Mulligan. New York: Hackett

——— ([c. 1260] 1963) *In Boethius De Trinitate*, in Armand Maurer, trans. *The Division and Methods of the Sciences*. Toronto: Pontifical Institute of Medieval Studies

——— ([1260] 1955–57), *Summa Contra Gentiles*, published as *On the Truth of the Catholic Faith*, trans. A.C. Pegis *et al.*, 5 volumes, *Summa Contra Gentiles*. Garden City, New York: Hanover House

——— ([1272] 1952), *Summa Theologiae*. Chicago: Encyclopaedia Britannica

Aristotle ([c. 350 BCE] 1949), *Prior Analytics*, in W.D. Ross, *Aristotle's Prior and Posterior Analytics*. Oxford: Oxford University Press

——— [(c. 350 BCE] 1952), *Metaphysics*, trans. Richard Hope. New York: Columbia University Press

——— ([c. 350 BCE] 1973), *Ethics*, in *Introduction to Aristotle*, trans. Richard McKeon. Chicago: University of Chicago Press

——— ([c. 350 BCE] 1973), *De Anima*, in *Introduction to Aristotle*, trans. Richard McKeon. Chicago: University of Chicago Press

Augustine ([c. 386] 1969), *Contra Academicos*, in John Wippel and Alan Wolter, *Medieval Philosophy*. New York: Free Press

——— ([c. 395] 1969), *De libero arbitrio*, in John Wippel and Alan Wolter, *Medieval Philosophy*. New York: Free Press

——— ([426] 1972), *The City of God*, trans. Henry Bettenson. New York: Penguin

Avenarius, Richard ([1876] 1888–90), *Philosophy as a Conception of the World According to the Principle of the Minimum Expenditure of Effort: Prolegomena to a Critique of Pure Experience*. Leipzig

Averroes (*c.* [1175] 1978), *The Incoherence of the Incoherence*, trans. Van Den Greg. David Brown Book Company

Avicenna ([*c.* 1025] 1973), *The Metaphysica*, trans. Morewedge Parvis. London: Routledge and Kegan Paul

———— ([*c.* 1025] 1981), *Psychology*, trans. F. Rahmah. Westport, CT: Hyperion

Avineri, Shlomo (1985), *Moses Hess: Prophet of Communism and Zionism*. New York: New York University Press

Ayer, Alfred (1936), *Language, Truth and Logic*. London: Victor Gollancz

Barrow, John, and Frank Tipler (1986), *The Anthropic Cosmological Principle*. Oxford: Oxford University Press

Bashkar, Roy (1989), *Reclaiming Reality*. London: Verso

Bellah, Robert (1973), 'Introduction', in Emile Durkheim, *On Morality and Society*. Chicago: University of Chicago Press

Bellah, Robert, Richard Masden, William M. Sullivan, Ann Swindler and Steven M. Tipton (1985), *Habits of the Heart*. New York: Knopf and (1991) *The Good Society*. New York: Knopf

Bennett, Charles (1987), 'Dissipation, Information, Complexity, and Organization', in *Emerging Syntheses in Science*, (ed.) D. Pines. New York: Addison-Wesley

Berkeley, George (1710), *Three Dialogues Between Hylas and Philonous*. London: Henry Clements

Birnbaum, Lucia Chiavola (1980), 'Earthmothers, Godmothers, and Radicals', *Marxist Perspectives* 1

———— (1983), 'Religious and Political Beliefs of Sicilian and Sicilian American Women', presentation to the Conference of the American Italian Historical Association, San Francisco, California, 30 December

———— (1985), *Liberazione della Donna*. Middletown, CT: Wesleyan University Press

Bogdanov, Alexander ([1928] 1980), *Tektology*. Intersystems Publishers

Bohm, David (1980), *Wholeness and the Implicate Order*. London: RKP

Bonaventura ([*c.* 1274] 1970), *Quaestiones disputate de Scientia Christi*, in Eugene Fairweather. *A Scholastic Miscellany*. New York: Macmillan

Budiansky, Stephen (1992), *The Covenant of the Wild*. New York: Morrow

Cahoone, Lawrence (1988), *The Dilemma of Modernity*. Albany: State University of New York Press

Cajetan (*c.* 1520), *In De Ente et Essentia, Prooemium*

———— (*c.* 1520), *De Nominum Analogia*. http://www.fordham.edu/gsas/phil/klima/ANALOGIA.html

Childe, V. Gordon (1951), *Man Makes Himself*. New York: Mentor

Collins, Randall (1994), *Four Sociological Traditions*. Oxford: Oxford University Press

Dahm, Helmut (1988), *Philosophical Sovietology: The Pursuit of A Science*. Dordrecht: Reidel

Daly, Mary ([1978] 1990), *Gyn/Ecology: The Metaethics of Radical Feminism*. Boston: Beacon

———— (1984), *Pure Lust: Elemental Feminist Philosophy*. Boston: Beacon

Damasio, Antonio (1994), *Descartes' Error*. New York: Grosset/Putnam

de Ste. Croix, C.E.M. (1981), *The Class Struggle in the Ancient Greek World: From the Archaic Age to the Arab Conquests*. London: Duckworth

Deborin, A.M. (1916), *Introduction to the Philosophy of Dialectical Materialism.* Petrograd

———— (1930), *Dialectics and Natural Science.* Moscow

Deleuze, Giles (1988), *Spinoza: Practical Philosophy.* San Francisco: City Lights

Derrida, Jacques ([1967]1978), 'Violence and Metaphysics', and 'From a Restricted to a General Economy: For an Hegelianism Without Reserve', in *Writing and Difference.* Chicago: University of Chicago Press

Descartes, René ([1637]1975), *Discourse on Method*, trans. Laurence J. Lafleur. Cambridge, UK: Cambridge University Press

———— ([1641]1975), *Meditations*, trans. Laurence J. Lafleur. Cambridge, UK: Cambridge University Press

Durkheim, Emile ([1893]1964), *The Division of Labor in Society.* New York: Free Press

———— ([1897]1951), *Suicide.* New York: Free Press

———— ([1911]1965), *Elementary Forms of Religious Life.* New York: Free Press

Eamon, William (1994), *Science and the Secrets of Nature: Books of Secrets in Medieval and Early Modern Europe.* Princeton: Princeton University Press

Eco, Umberto (1976), *A Theory of Semiotics.* Bloomington, IN: Indiana University Press

———— (1988), *The Aesthetics of Thomas Aquinas.* Cambridge, MA: Harvard University Press

Engels, Frederick ([1880]1940), *The Dialectics of Nature.* New York: International

Farrell, Walter (1945), *Companion to the Summa.* New York: Sheed and Ward

Feuerbach, Ludwig ([1841]1957), *The Essence of Christianity.* New York: Harper

Fichte, Johann ([1845]1982), *Science of Knowledge.* New York: Cambridge University Press

Foucault, Michel ([1966]1970), *Les mots et les choses.* Paris: Editions Gallimard

Fox, Matthew and Rupert Sheldrake (1996), *The Physics of Angels.* New York: HarperCollins

Frend, W. (1957), *The Donatist Church.* Oxford: Clarendon

Fromm, Erich (1941), *Escape from Freedom.* New York: Holt Reinhart Winston

———— (1947), *Man For Himself.* New York: Holt Reinhart Winston

———— (1966), *You Shall Be As Gods.* New York: Holt Reinhart Winston

Gal-Or, Benjamin (1987), *Cosmology: Physics and Philosophy.* New York: Springer Verlag

Gamwell, Franklin (1990), *The Divine Good.* New York: HarperCollins

———— (1999), *Democracy on Purpose.* Washington, DC: Georgetown University Press

Garrigou-Lagrange, Reginald (1938), *Three Ways of the Spiritual Life.* Rockford, IL: Tan

Geroch, Robert (1985), *Mathematical Physics.* Chicago: University of Chicago Press

Gilson, Etienne (1968), *Dante and Philosophy.* Glouster, MA: Peter Smith

Goerner, E.A. (1965), *Peter and Caesar.* New York: Herder & Herder

Gottwald, Norman (1979), *The Tribes of Yahweh.* Maryknoll: Orbis

Gramsci, Antonio (1948), *Il materialismo storico e la filosofia di Benedetto Croce.* Torino: Einaudi

———— (1949a), *Il Risorgimento.* Torino: Einaudi

—— (1949b), *Note sul Macchiavelli, sulla politica, e sullo Stato Moderno*. Torino: Einaudi

—— (1949c), *Gli intelletualli e l'organizzazione di cultura*. Torino: Einaudi

—— (1950), *Letteratura e vita nazionale*. Torino: Einaudi

—— (1951), *Passato e presente*. Torino: Einaudi

—— (1954), *L'Ordine Nuovo*. Torino: Einaudi

—— (1966), *La questione meridionale*. Roma: Riuniti

Grant, Edward (1978), 'Cosmology', in David Lindberg (ed.), *Science in the Middle Ages*. Chicago: University of Chicago Press

Harris, Errol (1965), *Foundations of Metaphysics in Science*. London: Allen & Unwin

—— (1987), *Formal, Transcendental, and Dialectical Thinking*. Albany: SUNY Press

—— (1991), *Cosmos and Anthropos*. Atlantic Highlands, NJ: Humanities International

—— (1992), *Cosmos and Theos*. Atlantic Highlands, NJ: Humanities International

Hartshorne, Charles (1967), *A Natural Theology for Our Time*. LaSalle, IL: Open Court

Hawking, Stephen (1988), *A Brief History of Time*. New York: Bantam

Hayek, Frederick (1940), *The Pure Theory of Capital*. London: Routledge and Kegan Paul

—— (1973), *Law, Liberty, and Legislation, Volume One: Rules and Order*. Chicago: University of Chicago Press

—— (1988), *The Fatal Conceit*. Chicago: University of Chicago Press

Hegel, G.W.F. ([1807] 1967b), *Phenomenology of Mind*, trans. J.B. Baillie. New York: Harper

—— ([1812] 1969), *Science of Logic*, trans. A.V. Miller. Atlantic Highlands, New Jersey: Humanities Press International

—— ([1817] 1990), *Encyclopaedia of the Philosophical Sciences (Outline)*, trans. Steven Taubeneck. New York: Continuum

—— ([1820] 1942), *Philosophy of Right*, trans. T.M. Knox. Oxford: Oxford University Press

—— ([1830] 1971), *Encyclopaedia of the Philosophical Sciences,* trans. William Wallace. Oxford: Oxford University Press

—— ([1831] 1956), *Philosophy of History*, trans. J. Sibree. New York: Dover

Heidegger, Martin ([1928] 1968), *Being and Time*. New York: Harper & Row

Hobsbawm, Eric (1959), *Primitive Rebels*. New York: Norton

Hume, David ([1777] 1888), *An Enquiry Concerning Human Understanding*. London

—— (1779), *Dialogues Concerning Natural Religion*. London: Longmans, Green

Husserl, Edmund ([1929] 1977), *The Crisis of the European Sciences*, trans. David Darr. Evanston, IL: Northwestern University Press

John of St Thomas ([1632] 1962), *Outline of Formal Logic*, trans. F. Wade. Milwaukee: Marquette University Press

Joravsky, David (1961), *Soviet Marxism and Natural Science*. New York: Columbia

Kant, Immanuel ([1781] 1969), *Critique of Pure Reason*, trans. Lewis White Beck. Indianapolis: Bobbs-Merrill

—— ([1781] 1969), *Foundations of the Metaphysics of Morals*, trans. Lewis White Beck. Indianapolis: Bobbs-Merrill

Kierkegaard, Soren ([*c.* 1840]1941), *A Concluding Unscientific Postscript*, trans. Walter Lowrie. Princeton: Princeton University Press

Kohlberg, Lawrence, C. Levine and A. Hewer (1963), 'The Development of Children's Orientation Toward a Moral Order', in *Vita Humana* 6: 11–33

—— (1983), *Moral Stages: A Current Formulation and A Response to Critics.* Basel: Karger

Körner, Stephen (1968), *Philosophy of Mathematics*. New York: Dover

Laplace, Pierre Simon (1799–1825), *Treatise on Celestial Mechanics*. Paris

Leibniz, Gottfried von ([1713] 1992), *Monadology*. Amherst, NY: Prometheus

Lenin, V.I. ([1908] 1970), *Materialism and Empiriocriticism*. Moscow: Progress

—— ([1916] 1976), *Philosophical Notebooks* (Volume 38 of the *Collected Works*). Moscow: Progress

Lenski, Gerhard and Jean (1982), *Human Societies*. New York: McGraw Hill

Lerner, Eric (1991), *The Big Bang Didn't Happen*. New York: Vintage

Leslie, John (1989), *Universes*. London: Blackwell

Lessing, Doris (1979), *Shikasta*. New York: Knopf

—— (1980), *The Marriages Between Zones Three, Four, and Five*. New York: Knopf

—— (1980), *The Sirian Experiments*. New York: Knopf

—— (1982), *The Making of the Representative for Planet 8*. New York: Knopf

—— (1983), *The Sentimental Agents in the Volyen Empire*. New York: Knopf

Lévi-Strauss, Claude ([1949]1969), *The Elementary Forms of Kinship*. Boston: Beacon

—— ([1958]1963), *Structural Anthropology*. New York: Basic

Lindberg, David (ed.) (1978), *Science in the Middle Ages*. Chicago: University of Chicago Press

—— (1992), *The Beginnings of Western Science*. Chicago: University of Chicago Press

Locke, John ([1690]1967), *Two Treatises on Government*. London: Cambridge University Press

Lonergan, Bernard (1957), *Insight: A Study of Human Understanding*. London: Longmans, Green

Lukacs, Georg ([1922]1971), *History and Class Consciousness*. Cambridge, MA: MIT Press

—— ([1953]1980), *The Destruction of Reason*. London: Merlin Press

Luria, Aleksandr (1973), *The Working Brain*. New York: Basic

—— ([1974]1976), *Cognitive Development*. Cambridge MA: Harvard University Press

Lyotard, Jean François ([1979]1984), *The Postmodern Condition*. Minneapolis: University of Minnesota Press

MacAleer, Graham (1996), 'Saint Anselm: An Ethics of *Caritas* for a Relativist Agent', in *American Catholic Philosophical Quarterly* LXX

Mach, Ernst (1900–14), *The Analysis of Sensations and the Relation of the Physical to the Psychical*, trans. C.M. Williams. Chicago: Open Court Publishing Co.

MacIntyre, Alisdair (1981), *After Virtue*. Notre Dame, IN: University of Notre Dame Press

—— (1984), *Whose Justice? Whose Rationality?* Notre Dame, IN: University of Notre Dame Press

Mandel, Ernest (1968), *Introduction to Marxist Economic Theory*. New York: Monthly Review

Mannheim, Karl (1936), *Ideology and Utopia*. New York: Harcourt, Brace, and World

Mansueto, Anthony (1995), *Towards Synergism: The Cosmic Significance of the Human Civilizational Project*. Lanham, MD: University Press of America

—— (1996), 'From Dialectic to Organization', in *Studies in East European Thought* 48: 1

—— (1997a), 'Organizing for Synergism', in *Dialectic, Cosmos, and Society* 10

—— (1997b), 'Organization, Teleology, and Value', in *Journal of Religion* Volume 77, Number 1

—— (1998a), 'Journey of the Dialectic', paper presented to the XX World Congress of Philosophy, Boston

—— (1998b), 'Cosmic Teleology and the Crisis of the Sciences', paper presented to the XX World Congress of Philosophy, Boston

—— (1999), 'In Defense of Metaphysics', in *Dialectic, Cosmos, and Society* 12

Mansueto, Anthony and Maggie (1998c), 'Against Philosophical Appeasement', in *Dialectic, Cosmos, and Society* 11

Mao Zedong ([1937a] 1971), 'On Contradiction', in *Selected Works*. Peking: Foreign Languages Press

—— ([1963] 1971), 'Where Do Correct Ideas Come From?', in *Selected Works*. Peking: Foreign Languages Press

Marechal, Joseph (1964), *Le point de depart de la métaphysique: Leçons sur le développement historique et théorique du problème de la connaissance. Vol. 3: La critique de Kant*, 4th edn. Paris: Desclee de Brouwer

Margulis, Lynn and Rene Fester (1991), *Symbiosis as a Source of Evolutionary Innovation*. Cambridge, MA: MIT Press

Maritain, Jacques (1937), *Degrees of Knowledge*. London: Bles

Marx, Karl ([1843] 1978), 'Contribution to the Critique of Hegel's Philosophy of Right: Introduction', in *Marx-Engels Reader*. New York: Norton

—— ([1844] 1978), *Economic and Philosophical Manuscripts* in *The Marx-Engels Reader*. New York: Norton, and [1846] 1978, *The German Ideology* in *The Marx-Engels Reader*, New York: Norton

—— ([1859] 1966), 'Contribution to the Critique of Political Economy: Preface', in Erich Fromm, *Marx's Concept of Man*. New York: Continuum

—— ([1867] 1977), *Capital*, Volume One. New York: Vintage

—— ([1905–10] 1969), *Theories of Surplus Value*. London: Lawrence and Wishart

Marx, Karl and Frederich Engels ([1848] 1978), *The Communist Manifesto* in *The Marx-Engels Reader*. New York: Norton

Maurer, Armand (1963), 'Introduction', Aquinas, Thomas. *In Boethius De Trinitate*, in Armand Maurer (trans.), *The Division and Methods of the Sciences*. Toronto: Pontifical Institute of Medieval Studies

—— (1993), 'Thomists and Thomas Aquinas on the Foundation of Mathematics', in *Review of Metaphysics* 47

Mayr, Ernst (1982), *The Growth of Biological Thought*. Cambridge, MA: Harvard University Press

—— (1988), *Toward a New Philosophy of Biology*. Cambridge, MA: Harvard University Press

McCool, Gerald (1977), *Catholic Theology in the Nineteenth Century*. New York: Seabury

———— (1994), *The Neo-Thomists*. Milwaukee: Marquette University Press

Meikle, Scott (1985), *Essentialism in the Thought of Karl Marx*. London: Duckworth

Milbank, John (1990), *Theology and Social Theory*. Oxford: Blackwell

Miller, Alice ([1981] 1984), *Thou Shalt Not Be Aware*. New York: Meridian

Moore, G.E. ([1903] 1988), *Principia Ethica*. Amherst, New York: Prometheus

Murdoch, John and Edith Sylla (1978), 'The Science of Motion', in David Lindberg (ed.), *Science in the Middle Ages*. Chicago: University of Chicago Press

Nietzsche, Friedreich ([1889] 1968), *The Will to Power*. New York: Random House

Ogden, Schubert (1966), *The Reality of God*. New York: Harper & Row

Parsons, Talcott (1957), *The Social System*. New York: Free Press

———— (1964), *The Structure of Social Action*. New York: Free Press

Pedersen, Olaf (1978), 'Astronomy', in David Lindberg (ed.), *Science in the Middle Ages*. Chicago: University of Chicago Press

Peifer, John (1964), *The Mystery of Knowledge*. New York: Magi

Peterson, Michael, William Hasker, Bruce Reichenbach and Peterson Hasker (1996), *Reason and Religious Belief: An Introduction to the Philosophy of Religion*. Oxford: Oxford University Press

Piaget, Jean (1952), *Logic and Psychology*. New York: Basic

———— (1968), *Structuralism*. New York: Basic

Plato ([c. 385 BCE] 1968), *Republic*, trans. Alan Bloom. New York: Basic

———— ([c. 385 BCE] 1960), *Timaeus*. New York: Penguin

Prigogine, Ilya (1979), *From Being to Becoming: Time and Complexity in the Physical Sciences*. New York: Freeman

Prigogine, Ilya and G. Nicolis (1977), *Self-Organization in Non-Equilibrium Systems*. New York: Wiley

Prigogine, Ilya and I. Stengers (1984), *Order Out of Chaos*. New York: Basic

Prigogine, Ilya and Tomio Petrosky (1989), 'An Alternative to Quantum Theory', in *Physica* 147A: 461–86

Pugh, Matthew (1997), 'Maritain, the Intuition of Being, and the Proper Starting Point for Thomistic Metaphysics', in *The Thomist* 61: 3

Rahner, Karl ([1957] 1968), *Spirit in the World*. New York: Herder & Herder

Reith, Herman (1958), *The Metaphysics of St Thomas Aquinas*. Milwaukee: Bruce

Resnik, Stephen and Richard Wolff (1987), *Knowledge and Class: A Marxian Critique of Political Economy*. Chicago: University of Chicago Press

Rubin, Gayle (1975), 'The Traffic in Women', in Rayna Reiter, *Toward an Anthropology of Women*. New York: Monthly Review Press

Rubin, Lillian ([1974] 1992), *Worlds of Pain*. New York: Basic Books

Russell, Bertrand (1957), *Why I Am Not a Christian*. New York: Simon & Schuster

Russell, Mary Doria (1996), *The Sparrow*. New York: Villard

———— (1997), *Children of God*. New York: Villard

Sacks, Oliver (1985), *The Man Who Mistook His Wife for a Hat*. New York: HarperCollins

Salvini-Plawen, Luitfred von and Ernst Mayr (1977), 'On the Evolution of Photoreceptors and Eyes', in *Evolutionary Biology* 10

Sartre, Jean-Paul (1943), *L'être et le néant*. Paris: Gallimard

———— (1960), *Critique de la raison dialectique*. Paris: Gallimard

Saussure, Ferdinand de ([1915] 1973), *Cours de linguistique générale*. Paris: Payot

Scheler, Max ([c. 1928] 1961), *Man's Place in Nature*. Boston: Beacon

Schelling, Friedrich ([1810] 1994), *Stuttgart Seminars*, in Thomas Pfau, *Idealism and the Endgame of Theory*. Albany, New York: SUNY Press

Schopenauer, Arthur ([1819] 1969), *The World as Will and Representation*, trans. E.F. Payne. New York: Basic Books

Segundo, Juan Luis (1985), *Theology and the Church*. New York: Harper

Shannon, Claude and Warren Weaver (1949), *The Mathematical Theory of Communication*. Urbana: University of Illinois Press

Sheldrake, Rupert (1981), *The New Science of Life*. Los Angeles, CA: Tarcher

——— (1989), *The Presence of the Past*. London: Fontana

Simmons, Edward Dwyer (1952), *The Thomistic Doctrine of Intellectual Abstraction for the Three Levels of Science: Exposition and Defense*. Notre Dame, IN: University of Notre Dame

Soloviev, Vladimir ([1878] 1995), *Lectures on Divine Humanity*, ed. by Boris Jakim. Lindisfarne Press

Spinoza, Baruch ([1675] 1955), *Ethics*. New York: Dover

Stone, Merlin (1976), *When God Was A Woman*. London: Dorset

Stumpf, Samuel (1994), *Philosophy: History and Problems*. New York: McGraw-Hill

Tillich, Paul (1967), *Systematic Theology*. Chicago: University of Chicago Press

Tipler, Frank (1989), 'The Omega Point as Eschaton: Answers to Pannenberg's Questions for Scientists', in *Zygon* 24: 2

——— (1994), *The Physics of Immortality*. New York: Doubleday

Tyler, Hamilton (1964), *Pueblo Gods and Myths*. Norman, OK: University of Oklahoma

Vatican I ([1870] 1990), *Dei Filius*, in Norman P. Tanner (ed.), *Decrees of the Ecumenical Councils*. Washington, DC: Georgetown University Press

Vatican II (1966), *Gaudium et Spes*, in *The Documents of Vatican II*. New York: Guild Press

von Balthasar, Hans Urs (1968), *Love Alone*. London: Allen & Unwin

von Neumann, J. (1966), *Theory of Self-Reproducing Automata*. Urbana: University of Illinois

von Steenberghen, Fernand (1980), *Thomas Aquinas and Radical Aristotelianism*. Washington, DC: Catholic University of America Press

Waters, Frank (1963), *The Book of the Hopi*. New York: Viking Penguin

Weber, Max ([1920] 1958), *The Protestant Ethic and the Spirit of Capitalism*. New York: Scribners

——— ([1921] 1968), *Economy and Society*. New York: Bedminster

Wetter, Gustav (1958), *Dialectical Materialism*. New York: Praeger

Wood, Ellen Meiksins and Neal Wood (1978), *Class Ideology and Ancient Political Theory: Socrates, Plato, and Aristotle in Social Context*. Oxford: Basil Blackwell

Woods, Richard (1986), *Eckhart's Way*. Wilmington, DE: Michael Glazier

Index